www.wadsworth.com

wadsworth.com is the World Wide Web site for Wadsworth and is your direct source to dozens of online resources.

At *wadsworth.com* you can find out about supplements, demonstration software, and student resources. You can also send e-mail to many of our authors and preview new publications and exciting new technologies.

wadsworth.com

Changing the way the world learns®

The Writer's Response
A Reading-Based Approach to College Writing

Wadsworth Developmental English

New for 2000

Writing
Rogers/Rogers, *Patterns and Themes: A Basic English Reader*, 4th Ed.

Robinson/Tucker, *Texts and Contexts: A Contemporary Approach to College Writing*, 4th Ed.

Tyner, *College Writing Basics: A Student-Writing Approach*, 5th Ed.

McDonald/Salomone, *In Brief: A Handbook for Writers*

Reading
Maker/Lenier, *College Reading with the Active Critical Thinking Method, Book 1*, 5th Ed.

Maker/Lenier, *College Reading with the Active Critical Thinking Method, Book 2*, 6th Ed.

Sotiriou/Phillips, *Steps to Reading Proficiency*, 5th Ed.

Study Skills
Van Blerkom, *College Study Skills: Becoming a Strategic Learner*, 3rd Ed.

Other Developmental English Titles

Writing
Richard-Amato, *World Views: Multicultural Literature for Critical Writers, Readers, and Thinkers* (1998)

Salomone/McDonald, *Inside Writing: A Writer's Workbook, Form A*, 4th Ed. (1999)

Wingersky/Boerner/Holguin-Balogh, *Writing Paragraphs and Essays: Integrating Reading, Writing, and Grammar Skills*, 3rd Ed. (1999)

Reading
Atkinson/Longman, *Reading Enhancement and Development*, 6th Ed. (1999)

Maker/Lenier, *Academic Reading with Active Critical Thinking* (1996)

Study Skills
Longman/Atkinson, *College Learning and Study Skills*, 5th Ed. (1999)

Longman/Atkinson, *Study Methods and Reading Techniques*, 2nd Ed. (1999)

Sotiriou, *Integrating College Study Skills: Reasoning in Reading, Listening, and Writing*, 5th Ed. (1999)

Smith/Knudsvig/Walter, *Critical Thinking: Building the Basics* (1998)

College Success

Gardner/Jewler, *Your College Experience: Strategies for Success*, 4th Ed. (2000)

Gardner/Jewler, *Your College Experience: Strategies for Success*, Concise 3rd Ed. (1998)

Holkeboer/Walker, *Right from the Start: Taking Charge of Your College Success*, 3rd Ed. (1999)

Petrie/Denson, *A Student Athlete's Guide to College Success: Peak Performance in Class and Life* (1999)

Santrock/Halonen, *Your Guide to College Success: Strategies for Achieving Your Goals* (1999)

Wahlstrom/Williams, *Learning Success: Three Paths to Being Your Best at College and Life*, 2nd Ed. (1999)

The Writer's Response
A Reading-Based Approach to College Writing

Second Edition

Stephen McDonald
Palomar College

William Salomone
Palomar College

Wadsworth
Thomson Learning™

Australia • Canada • Mexico • Singapore • Spain • United Kingdom • United States

Production: Johnstone Associates

Interior and Cover Designer: Rob Hugel/
 Little Hill Design
Cover Image: Corbis Images
Cover Printer: Phoenix Color Corp.
Compositor: TBH Typecast, Inc.
Printer: R. R. Donnelley, Crawfordsville

For more information, contact

Wadsworth/Thomson Learning
10 Davis Drive
Belmont, CA 94002-3098
USA
http://www.wadsworth.com

International Headquarters
Thomson Learning
290 Harbor Drive, 2nd Floor
Stamford, CT 06902-7477
USA

UK/Europe/Middle East/South Africa
Thomson Learning
Berkshire House
168–173 High Holborn
London WC1V 7AA
United Kingdom

Asia
Thomson Learning
60 Albert Street #15-01
Albert Complex
Singapore 189969

Canada
Nelson/Thomson Learning
1120 Birchmount Road
Scarborough, Ontario M1K 5G4
Canada

For permission to use material from this text,
contact us by
 Web: http://www.thomsonrights.com
 Fax: 1-800-730-2215
 Phone: 1-800-730-2214

Library of Congress Cataloging-in-Publication Data
McDonald, Stephen.
  The writer's response : a reading-based approach
 to college writing / Stephen McDonald, William
 Salomone—2nd ed.
   p. cm.
 Rev. ed. of: Reading-based writing. c1996.
  Includes indexes.
  ISBN 0-534-57303-7
   1. English language—Rhetoric. 2. English language—
 Grammar. 3. College readers. 4. Report writing.
 I. Salomone, William. II. McDonald, Stephen. Reading-
 based writing. III. Title
 PN1408.M267 2000
 808'.0427—dc21   99-048122

This book is printed on acid-free recycled paper.

Dedication

With love to

George and Joan McDonald

and to

Kathryn and Michelle Salomone

Contents

Readings Listed by Rhetorical Mode

Articles that illustrate several modes may appear more than once.

Illustration

Cause-Effect

Argument and Persuasion

Preface

The premise of *The Writer's Response* is that it is nearly impossible to write well without also reading well, that college courses today demand not only that students write clearly and read accurately but also that they write effectively *about* what they have read. *The Writer's Response* is designed as an introductory text to academic writing, the type of writing based on the careful, deliberate reading and the clear, critical thinking demanded of students throughout their college careers.

The Reason for This Text

Writing in Response to Reading.   College courses outside of our English departments rarely ask students to write personal experience essays, nor do they ask students to write papers on topics *similar* to those they have read in some textbook. Rather, such classes more often ask that students write papers and essays in direct response to ideas they have encountered in assigned reading. Such writing assignments demand careful reading and clear summary. They demand that students be able to recognize and respond to specific points in the material they have read, to synthesize ideas from several reading selections, and to evaluate and to argue about the ideas they have found in their reading material. *The Writer's Response* introduces students to these and other skills they will need to write successful college-level papers.

Using Personal Experience.   Although *The Writer's Response* introduces students to academic writing, it does not at all ignore the importance of their personal experiences, nor does it fail to recognize that writing about themselves is often the best way for writers to find their own voices and to discover that they do indeed have something to say. For this reason, the assignments throughout *The Writer's Response* ask students to use personal experience to respond to the material they have read in the text when it is appropriate to do so. Chapters 1–4 in particular emphasize personal responses. Then, when the students are writing more directly *about* what they have read in Chapters 5–8, optional assignments allow instructors to assign personal experience responses when they want to do so.

About the Text

The Writer's Response integrates reading, writing, sentence combining, and editing. Its writing instruction is kept simple and clear, and its reading selections consist of over sixty short articles, most of which are both recent and timely in their subject matter.

Organization

Part 1: The Reading-Writing Conversation.   Part 1, consisting of the first four chapters, introduces students to the reading and writing processes and to the concepts of unity, coherence, and development. Each of these chapters contains a variety of reading selections to illustrate the points being made and to provide material that students can respond to using their own personal experience. In these first four chapters we want students to become comfortable with the writing process and familiar with the elements of well-written paragraphs and essays. At the same time, we want students to become careful readers and to recognize that accurate reading is an integral part of clear thinking and good writing.

Part 2: Writing about Reading.   Part 2 consists of four chapters that introduce students to ways of writing *about* what they have read. We start Part 2 with a chapter on how to write brief summaries, extended summaries, and summary-response essays because so often students have trouble doing much more than identifying the central idea of what they have read. Writing the summary gives them practice in recognizing and expressing both the central idea and the supporting points of a reading selection. We then move to a chapter on evaluating the effectiveness of material they read. In this chapter students must read accurately as well as explain why they have or have not found a selection convincing, persuasive, or effective. In the next chapter, students synthesize the issues involved in several reading selections. Here, students must not only summarize what they have read but also recognize connections among reading selections and explain those connections in their papers. The final chapter of Part 2 asks students to argue from several reading selections, using material from a number of brief articles to support their positions.

Part 3: Editing Skills.   Part 3 of *The Writer's Response* is meant to act as a supplement to the primary instruction provided in Parts 1 and 2. It serves as a brief handbook for those students who need help with grammar, punctuation, or usage problems, and it allows the instructor to cover such material as needed. We have arranged it as a separate part of the text rather than spreading its material throughout each chapter so that the student can quickly and conveniently use it as an aid in the editing process.

Part 4: Additional Readings for Writing.   Part 4 includes twenty-six reading selections for the instructor to use in addition to those in the body of the text. The first sixteen selections cover a variety of topics appropriate for the writing assignments in the first six chapters. The remaining ten selections are then grouped into three specific topic areas so that they can be used as synthesis and argument topics in Chapters 7 and 8. All of the reading selections reflect the criteria discussed below.

Features

The Reading Selections. In choosing the reading selections for *The Writer's Response*, we have kept several criteria in mind. First, we wanted most of the selections to be relatively brief since this text is, after all, an introduction to academic writing. For that reason, the majority of the selections are only a few pages in length. However, we also wanted our students to have to "stretch" their mental muscles at times, so we have included some longer, more complex articles for instructors to use as they see fit. Second, we wanted the reading selections to be both timely and interesting, appealing to as wide a range of students as possible. To achieve this end, we have chosen articles that challenge the students to think about who they are as well as about how they fit into our increasingly multicultural world. Titles ranging from "Are You Living Mindlessly?" to "A Generation of Bigots Comes of Age" to "The Changing Face of America" reflect the variety of topics to be found in this text. Finally, to allow for the kind of synthesis and argument that *The Writer's Response* is meant to encourage, we have included several articles grouped around common topics, such as "Should Drugs Be Legalized?" "Flag Burning and Free Speech," "English as the 'Official' Language of the United States," and "Animal Experimentation."

Evaluating Student Models. In addition to writing instruction and brief reading selections, each of the chapters in Parts 1 and 2 includes a section on evaluating sample student papers. This section has two purposes. First, it is designed to provide students with "models" of successful papers that can be used to discuss what is expected of well-written paragraphs or essays. Second, it is meant to teach students to distinguish between successful and less successful papers so that they can better evaluate the effectiveness of their own writing.

Sentence Combining. Each chapter in Parts 1 and 2 includes a section on sentence combining. Since so many student writers rely primarily upon compound and relatively brief complex sentences, the sentence combining sections are designed to give students practice in writing sentences that move beyond the patterns they are most comfortable with. Beginning with simple exercises in recognizing when modifiers in one sentence can easily be "embedded" within another sentence, these sections gradually introduce more difficult sentence structures involving the use of coordination, parallelism, subordination, participial phrases, appositives, and sentence variety.

Group Work. Throughout the text, exercises and writing assignments encourage students to work together, discussing the reading selections, comparing their responses to those selections, and helping each other develop their papers. While individual instructors will, of course, use such group work as they see fit, we have found it to be an invaluable teaching device, helping students to clarify their own thinking as they work with those around them.

New to This Edition

If you used the first edition of this text, you have already noticed that its title has changed from *Reading-Based Writing* to *The Writer's Response: A Reading-Based Approach to Writing.* We were convinced to make this change by many instructors who said they were confused by the original title, unsure whether this text was primarily directed toward a reading class or a writing class. It is, of course, directed toward writing classes. In particular, it is designed for writing classes that emphasize responding to, summarizing, synthesizing, evaluating, or arguing from reading selections. We hope this new title will help to convey the purpose of the text more accurately.

Of a more substantive nature, we have made the following improvements to the text.

- A new editing chapter entitled "Clear and Concise Sentences" provides instruction on avoiding wordiness and on using forceful subjects and verbs.

- Cultural diversity and reactions to it are emphasized in many articles throughout the text and in a separate section in Part 4 entitled "Culture and Country."

- Chapter 1 has been thoroughly revised to improve the instruction on writing topic sentences and thesis statements, organizing ideas, and producing the first drafts of paragraphs and essays. This important chapter is now much clearer and easier to use.

- A section entitled "Explaining the Significance of the Support" has been added to Chapter 3.

- A discussion of how to improve coherence through a clear thesis/topic sentence relationship has been added to Chapter 4.

- A new two-color design highlights key pedagogy.

- Many new exercises have been added and others have been revised throughout the first eight chapters of the text.

- Over twenty new reading selections as well as many new student essays have been added to the text. More than 35% of the readings are new.

- More thematically related reading selections are now in the text, including ones on behavior, education, physician-assisted suicide, and animal experimentation.

- Article groupings that worked well already have been retained, such as *The Effects of Television; Schools, Teenagers, and Part-Time Jobs; Should Drugs Be Legalized?; Flag Burning and Freedom of Speech;* and *English as the "Official" Language of the United States.*

- Several of the reading selections removed from Chapters 1–8 have been placed into Part 4 so that instructors who still wish to use them may do so.

Teaching Aids

Print Supplements

Instructor's Manual (0-534-57304-5)   The Instructor's Manual for *The Writer's Response* provides suggestions for teaching the course on a chapter-by-chapter basis and offers comments about the reading selections. It also includes answers to all exercises in the text.

Newbury House Dictionary (08384-5613-8)   Make this developmental-level dictionary available to your students at a reduced cost by bundling it with this text. Contact your sales representative for information on this option.

Electronic and Online Supplements for Developmental English

Web Site   Visit Wadsworth's Developmental English web site at *www.devenglish. wadsworth.com*.

InfoTrac® College Edition   A fully searchable, online database with access to full-text articles from over 600 periodicals, provides a great resource for additional readings and/or research. Now available for cost-effective bundling with this text, InfoTrac College Edition offers authoritative sources, updated daily and going back as far as four years. Both you and your students can receive unlimited online use for one academic term. (Please contact your Thomson Learning representative for policy, pricing, and availability; international and school distribution is restricted.)

Wadsworth Developmental English Internet at a Glance Trifold (0-534-54744-3)   This handy guide shows your students where to find online reading and writing resources. Package this trifold card with any Wadsworth Developmental English text for a very small cost. Contact your local Wadsworth representative for more information.

Custom Publishing   You can combine your choice of chapters from specific Wadsworth titles with your own materials in a custom-bound book. To place your order, call the Thomson Learning Custom Order Center at 1-800-355-9983.

Videos   Wadsworth has many videos available to qualifying adopters on topics such as improving your grades, notetaking practice, diversity, and many more. Contact your local Wadsworth representative for more information.

AT&T World Net   Get your students on the Internet with AT&T—one of the fastest growing Internet access service providers.

Acknowledgments

We want to thank our friends and colleagues at Palomar College for the invaluable advice they have given us while using the first edition of this text. In particular, we thank Jack Quintero, who has encouraged and supported us from the start. His thoughtful suggestions have helped to shape the text in many ways. We also thank Brent Gowen, who is always ready with another potential reading selection for us to try. And to the many other English instructors at Palomar who have taken the time to suggest ideas or to respond to our questions about the text, thank you.

We also extend our thanks to the many professionals at Wadsworth who have worked with us on this text. Our special thanks go to Kim Johnson, Senior Developmental Editor; Karen Allanson, Publisher; Christal Niederer, Project Editor; Godwin Chu, Editorial Assistant; Kelli Goslin, Marketing Assistant; and Judy Johnstone, who managed production from manuscript to bound book.

We are especially grateful to the following students, who graciously allowed us to use their work as models for evaluation: Nancy Kwan, Elizabeth Santos, Rosemarie Tejidor, Amy Duran, Sherrie Kolb, Jason Pauley, Brian Schmitz, Jessica Thompson, Alicia Sanchez, Saori Kurosawa, Tami Jacobs, Desiree Gharakanian, Scott Tyler, Jung Yun Park, Rosa Contreras, Elizabeth Harding, Chaz Knurck, Tracy Thornton, Alison Martin, Christina Silva, Louise Homola, Justin John, Junior Monta.

Finally, we are grateful to the following professors who took their time to provide valuable input for this text.

First Edition Reviewers

William Bernhardt, College of Staten Island

Linda J. Daigle, Houston Community College

Dianne Gregory, Cape Cod Community College

Kathleen M. Krager, Walsh University

Milla McConnell-Tuite, College of San Mateo

Second Edition Reviewers

Nancy Anter, Wayne State University

Debra Bailin, Lyndon State College

Kathleen Beauchene, Community College of Rhode Island

Dianne Gregory, Cape Cod Community College

Joyce Malek, Anoka Ramsey Community College

Linda Ranucci, Kent State University

The Writer's Response

A Reading-Based Approach to College Writing

Part 1

The Reading-Writing Conversation

Have you ever talked to someone who wouldn't listen or listened to someone who just rambled on and on without making a clear point? Probably you tried not to have many more conversations with that person. After all, in a conversation, both listening well and speaking clearly are important, and a poor listener or a confusing speaker is not a very enjoyable person to talk to.

Writing and reading are very much like speaking and listening. When you read, you listen to what someone else has to say; when you write, you speak your own ideas. Together, reading and writing make up a conversation between the reader and the writer, and either a poor reader or a poor writer can pretty much spoil that conversation.

As students in college classes, you will be asked to participate in this reading-writing conversation by writing in response to what you read. Depending on the instructor or the class, you might be asked to summarize the ideas you have found in textbooks, to analyze topics after reading about them, to evaluate opinions expressed by a writer, to define concepts discussed in several articles, or to respond in any number of other ways to what you have read.

Obviously, to write clearly and accurately in response to what you have read, you need to read clearly and accurately too. Part One of this text will help you work on both activities at the same time—clear and accurate reading and writing.

Chapter 1

Writing with a Central Idea

The curse of "artist's block"

The Writing Process

Writing is a messy business. It is full of stops and starts and sudden turns and reversals. In fact, sometimes writing an essay can be one of the most confusing, frustrating experiences a college student will encounter. Fortunately, writing does not have to be a horrible experience. Like almost anything in life, writing becomes much easier as you become familiar with the "process" that makes up the act of writing.

Writing is often called a *recursive process*. This means that the many steps to writing an effective paper do not necessarily follow neatly one after the other. In fact, often you will find yourself repeating the same step a number of different times, in a number of different places, as you write a paper. For example, you might jot down notes on scratch paper before you start writing your first draft, but at any time while you write, you might stop to jot down more notes or to rethink what you are writing. To help yourself understand this writing process, think of it as divided roughly into three stages: **prewriting, writing,** and **rewriting.**

Prewriting involves anything you do to help yourself decide what your central idea is or what details, examples, reasons, or content you will include. Freewriting, brainstorming, and clustering (discussed below) are types of prewriting. Thinking, talking to other people, reading related material, outlining or organizing ideas—all are forms of prewriting. Obviously, you can prewrite at *any* time in the writing process. Whenever you want to think up new material, simply stop what you are doing and start using one of the techniques you will study in this chapter.

The **writing** stage of the process involves the actual writing out of a draft. Unfortunately, many people try to start their writing here, without sufficient prewriting. As you may know from firsthand experience, trying to start out this way usually leads directly to a good case of writer's block. During this stage of the writing process, you should be ready to do more prewriting whenever you hit a snag or cannot think of what to write next.

Rewriting consists of revising and editing. You should plan to revise every paper you write. When you *revise,* you examine the entire draft to change what needs to be changed and to add what needs to be added. Perhaps parts of your paper will need to be reorganized, reworded, or thoroughly rewritten to express your ideas clearly. Perhaps your paper will need more examples or clearer explanations. Unfortunately, people pressed for time often skip this stage, and the result is a very poorly written paper. Finally, after you have revised your work, you must edit it. When you *edit*, you correct spelling, grammar, and punctuation errors. A word of warning: Do not confuse editing with revising. Merely correcting the spelling, grammar, or punctuation of a poorly written paper will not make much difference in the overall quality of the paper.

Prewriting: From Writer's Block to Writing

Have you ever had a writing assignment that absolutely stumped you? Have you ever found yourself *stuck,* staring at a blank sheet of paper for fifteen minutes (or thirty? or sixty?), wondering what in the world you could write to meet the assignment?

If you have not had this experience, you are a lucky person. Certainly almost everyone knows the frustrated, sinking feeling that comes as minute after minute passes and nothing seems to get written. In fact, for many writers, *getting started* is the most agonizing part of the entire writing process.

What we're talking about here is **writer's block,** a problem as common to professional writers as it is to student writers. Because it is so common, you need to learn how to get past it quickly and painlessly so that you can get on with your assignment. Here are a few prewriting techniques to help you.

Freewriting

Since writer's block means that you aren't writing, one of the quickest ways to get around it is to write anything at all. You can write whatever you are thinking, feeling, wondering about, or trying to get out of your mind—just start writing. The only rule here is that you must not stop to correct spelling, grammar, punctuation, or other parts of your writing. Set a time limit for yourself—five or ten minutes— and just keep writing.

Let's say you were asked to write a paragraph or an essay explaining your reaction to the Gary Larson cartoon on page 2. To help yourself get started, you might try freewriting first. Here is how some freewriting might look:

> Okay—time to start writing—but what to write?? The cartoon is funny, but so what? What could I possibly write about this? I really don't know. What a frustrating assignment! I thought it was funny, but I don't really know why. And I'll bet some people think it's stupid. What could I write? Maybe I could—no. Why do I think it's funny? Well, partly because I've been stuck just like the guy in the picture. I guess I kind of relate to him. But it's also funny because of the cow. I mean, anyone knows what a cow's head looks like, so why is this guy confused? Maybe that's why it's funny. He really shouldn't be confused. And he doesn't have a clue! He hasn't even thought of a cow's head yet. It would really be funny if he ended up thinking of a different head. Also, I think the guy's appearance looks pretty strange. He's really freaking out—bug-eyes—and he's just an overall strange-looking guy.

As you can see, freewriting is very informal. Notice that the above freewriting moves from questions that express general frustration ("What could I write?") to answers that the writer might be able to use in a paper ("I've been stuck just like the guy in the picture." "But it's also funny because of the cow." "He's really freaking out—bug-eyes"). This movement—from searching for ideas that you might use to focusing on specific details—is very common in freewriting.

Brainstorming

Brainstorming is like freewriting in that you write down whatever comes to mind without stopping, but it is different because it looks more like a list of ideas than a string of sentences. Here's an example, again about the Gary Larson cartoon:

How I reacted—laughed—why?

Funny—what's funny here?

—cow with no head

—man stuck—can't think of cow's head

—bug-eyes

—look of panic

—frustration—hands by head

—even his body

—fat stomach—scraggly beard

Maybe he'll use wrong head!

Funny because I've felt same way (Why is that funny?)

This writer has a number of specific observations about the cartoon that she could use in a paper, but she did not waste time staring at a blank page. Instead, she just started making a list.

Clustering

A third technique to help you generate ideas is called clustering. It differs from brainstorming and freewriting in that what you write is almost like an informal map. To *cluster* your ideas, start out with a topic or question and draw a circle around it. Then connect related ideas to that circle and continue in that way. Look at the following example of how the brainstorming material might look if it were clustered.

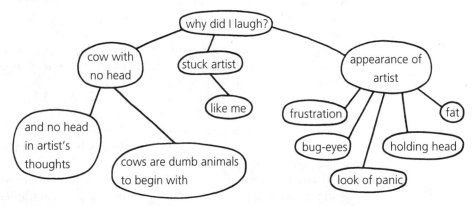

As you can see, clustering provides a mental picture of the ideas you generate. As a result, it can help you to organize your material as you think of it.

Freewriting, brainstorming, and clustering are only three of many techniques to help you get past writer's block. When you use them, you should feel free to move from one to the other at any time. And, of course, your instructor may suggest other ways to help you get started. Whatever technique you use, the point is to **start writing.** Do your thinking on paper (or at a computer), not while you are staring out the window. Here's something to remember whenever you have a writing assignment due: **Think in ink.**

Readings

Read the following articles. Then practice your prewriting techniques by responding to the questions at the end of each article.

Before You Read

1. Look up the words *carpe diem* in a dictionary. What do they mean? What do you think about them as an approach to life?

2. Where would you like to go, what would you like to do, or who would you like to see if you had the time or were not as busy as you are? What prevents you from going to those places, doing those things, or seeing those people?

Live Each Moment for What It's Worth

Erma Bombeck

I have a friend who lives by a three-word philosophy, "Seize the moment." Just possibly, she might be the wisest woman on this planet. Too many people put off something that brings them joy just because they haven't thought about it, don't have it on their schedule, didn't know it was coming, or are too rigid to depart from the routine.   1

I got to thinking one day about all those women on the *Titanic* who passed up dessert at dinner that fateful night in an effort to "cut back." From then on, I've tried to be a little more flexible.   2

How many women out there will eat at home because their husband suggested they go out to dinner AFTER something had been thawed? Does the word *refrigerator* have no meaning for you?   3

How often have your kids dropped in to talk and sat there in silence while you watched *Jeopardy*?   4

I cannot count the times I called my sister and said, "How about going to lunch in half an hour?" She would gasp and stammer, "I can't." Check one: "I have clothes on the line." "My hair is dirty." "I wish I had known yesterday." "I had a late breakfast." "It looks like rain." And my personal favorite, "It's Monday." She died a few years ago. We never did have lunch.   5

Because Americans cram so much into our lives, we tend to schedule our headaches. We live on a sparse diet of promises we make to ourselves   6 when all the conditions are perfect. We'll go back and visit the grandparents . . . when we get Stevie toilet-trained. We'll entertain . . . when we replace the carpet in the living room. We'll go on a second honeymoon . . . when we get two more kids out of college.

Life has a way of accelerating as we get older. The days get shorter 7 and the list of promises to ourselves gets longer. One morning we awaken and all we have to show for our lives is a litany of "I'm going to," "I plan on," and "Someday when things are settled down a bit."

When anyone calls my "seize the moment" friend, she is open to 8 adventure, available for trips and keeps an open mind on new ideas. Her enthusiasm for life is contagious. You can talk to her for five minutes and you're ready to trade your bad feet for a pair of roller blades and skip an elevator for a bungi cord.

My lips have not touched ice cream in 10 years. I love ice cream. It's 9 just that I might as well apply it directly to my hips with a spatula and eliminate the digestive process.

The other day I stopped the car and bought a triple-decker. If my car 10 hit an iceberg on the way home, I'd have died happy.

Copyright 1991. Reprinted by permission.

Prewriting Practice

1. Freewrite for five minutes (or for a time specified by your instructor) to react to Bombeck's article in any way that you want. Write whatever comes to our mind.

2. Discuss your freewriting with other members of your class. Did they have similar responses?

3. Respond to one of the following questions by using the prewriting techniques of freewriting, brainstorming, and/or clustering:

   a. What does Erma Bombeck mean by "seize the moment"? Do you live by that philosophy, or do you avoid doing things that are spontaneous or unscheduled? Give some examples to illustrate your response.

   b. Think about your friends, relatives, and acquaintances. Do any of them "seize the moment"? Do any carefully avoid living in a spontaneous way? Describe any people you know who do or do not "seize the moment."

4. Discuss your responses to the above questions with other members of your class. Explain to them why you or people you know do or do not "seize the moment."

Before You Read

1. What do you make of the title "Without Emotion"? What does it make you expect to find in the reading selection?

2. Who is G. Gordon Liddy? If you don't know, ask other members of your class or your instructor. Does his background affect how you read this selection?

G. Gordon Liddy

Squirrel hunting was a popular sport in West Caldwell in the 1940s. I   1
loaded my homemade rifle, cocked the spring, and waited on the steps of
the porch. A squirrel was in the top of the pear tree. I raised the rifle. The
movement startled the squirrel and he jumped to the oak tree and froze as
I stepped off the porch. I sighted along the side of the barrel, aimed for the
squirrel's head, and fired.

I missed the squirrel's head and gut-shot him. Bravely, he clung to   2
the tree as long as he could, then started to come down, clutching
piteously at branches as he fell, wounded mortally.

I didn't know it, but the shot alerted my mother. She watched the   3
furry creature's descent until it fell to the ground and I shot it again, this
time through the head at point-blank range, to put it out of its suffering,
then cut off its tail to tie to the handlebars of my bicycle as an ornament.

When I came into the house my mother told me reproachfully that   4
she had seen from the kitchen window the suffering I had caused. I went
off and wept. The dying squirrel haunted me. I kept seeing it fall, clutching and clawing from what must have been a terribly painful wound.
I was furious with myself—not because I'd caused the pain, though I
regretted that, but because I hadn't been able to kill without emotion.
How could I expect to be a soldier in the war? I had to do something to
free myself from this disabling emotionalism.

I cast about for an idea and found it across the street. Bill Jacobus's   5
father, to help combat the wartime food shortage and to supplement
rationing, had built a chicken coop in his backyard. He and his son used
to butcher the chickens, then drain, scald, pluck, and clean them for sale.

I asked young Bill if I could help kill the chickens. He was glad to   6
have the help. He showed me how to grasp the bird in such a way as to
have control of both wings and feet, lay its neck on an upended stump,
and then decapitate it with one chop of an ax held in the other hand. Bill
explained that the shock made the corpse convulse and, if I let go, the
body would run about, wings flapping, and bruise the meat. I'd need to
control the corpse until the shock wore off and the limp body could be
hung up by the feet to drain the remaining blood. I should wear my old
clothes.

Using the ax tentatively rather than making a bold stroke, I made a   7
mess of my first chicken kill; it took me a number of chops to get the head
off. The bird slipped out of my grasp and half flew, half jumped about,
blood spurting from its neck all over me and everything else in range. Bill
was good about it and gave me another chance.

I got better at it, and over a period of time I killed and killed and   8
killed, getting less and less bloody, swifter and swifter, surer with my ax

stroke until, finally, I could kill efficiently and without emotion or thought. I was satisfied: when it came my turn to go to war, I would be ready. I could kill as I could run—like a machine.

Prewriting Practice

1. Freewrite for five minutes (or for a time specified by your instructor) to react to Liddy's article in any way that you want. Write whatever comes to mind.

2. Discuss your freewriting with other members of your class. Did they have similar responses?

3. Now respond to one of the following questions by using the prewriting techniques of freewriting, brainstorming, and/or clustering:

    a. Did your feelings or thoughts change as you moved from the start of this article to the end of it? If so, what parts of the article caused them to change?

    b. Have you ever had to act "without emotion"? Describe any times you can remember when you had to repress or ignore your emotions.

4. Discuss your responses with other members of your class. Did they develop ideas that had not occurred to you?

Before You Read

1. As you read this selection, watch for the "view" to which the writer refers. What does he see from Mount Ritter?

2. Has any experience with nature ever changed your attitude toward life? In what way?

A View from Mount Ritter

Joseph T. O'Connor

"I hate this," I thought. We were on our way to the top of Mount Ritter in   1
northeastern California. You would think everyone, near one of the tallest ridges in the Sierra Nevadas, would be in high spirits. But on this particular day the rain fell in torrents. Quarter-size hailstones pelted our protective helmets as thunder echoed through the canyons.

It was the second week of my mountain expedition in California. The   2
first week there had not been a cloud in the sky, but on Tuesday of week two, a dark cover crept in from the west, painting the sunlit, blue sky black. The storm came in so fast we didn't even notice it until our shadows suddenly disappeared.

"Here it comes," our guide warned. As if God himself had given the order, the heavens opened, just a crack. Huge drops began falling but abruptly stopped, as if to say, "You know what's coming; here's a taste." As we began searching for shelter, a bolt of lightning ripped open the blackish clouds overhead and in unison thunder cracked, leaving everyone's ears ringing. We were in the midst of a huge July thunderstorm. Ethan, our guide, had said that during the summer in the high Sierras it might rain twice, but when it does, it's best not to be there. Suddenly lightning struck a tree not 20 feet from where I was standing. **3**

"Lightning positions!" Ethan yelled frantically. A little too frantically for my taste. I thought he was used to this kind of thing. As scared as I was, squatting in a giant puddle of water and hailstones, with forks of lightning bouncing off the canyon walls around me, I couldn't help chuckling to myself at the sight of Ethan's dinner-plate-size eyeballs as he panicked like an amateur. Soon after the lightning died down some, we hiked to the shelter of nearby redwoods to put on rain gear. While we prayed for the rain to subside, I watched the stream we stood beside grow into a raging, whitewater river. Another expeditioner, Mike, and I were under a full redwood donning our not-so-waterproof equipment when I realized we were standing on a small island. **4**

"Mike! Let's go!" I yelled, my exclamation nearly drowned out by the roar of water surrounding us and another roll of thunder. **5**

"I'm way ahead o' ya!" he screamed in his thick New York accent, and his goofy smile broke through the torrents. "Ya ready?" **6**

"Yeah!" I yelled back, and jumped from our island into the knee-deep water. He followed as we slopped through the storm, losing our footing every few feet. **7**

The unforgiving downpour lasted all day and into the night as we stumbled down the rocky cliffs seeking the driest place to set up camp. It was dusk before we found a small clearing in a pine forest and began what was to be the worst night of my life. We constructed our tents in the dark, fumbling with the ropes with our frozen hands and finishing just as a stiffness like rigor mortis set in. We lay awake all night, shivering in our wet sleeping begs while rain poured down and a small stream made its way through our tent. **8**

It's funny how these memories keep coming back to me as if it were just yesterday. All this happened last summer, after my junior year in high school. I had decided to attend a mountaineering program in the Sierras. Two weeks in the back country with no sign of civilization. It sounded exciting and slightly dangerous, and I've always been up for a good adventure. I found out on that trip that nature is underestimated. The experience was the most invigorating, fulfilling, stimulating two weeks of my life. For the first time since I could remember, my head was crystal clear. I felt born again, only two weeks old. On top of Mount Ritter, 13,000 feet above sea level, I was entranced at the sight of the orange-red sun as it peeked over the glistening peaks far off in the east. Cumulous clouds appeared transparent as they glowed bright red in the morning glory. **9**

The wonder of all I'd experienced made me think seriously about 10 what comes next. "Life after high school," I said to myself. "Uh-oh." What had I been doing for the last three years? I was so caught up in defying the advice of my parents and teachers to study and play by the rules that I hadn't considered the effects my actions would have on me.

"Youth is wholly experimental," Robert Louis Stevenson wrote. Sure, 11 there will be mistakes, but there will also be successes. I was a confused kid. Everyone—my parents, teachers and coaches—offered suggestions, but I chose to ignore them. I had "potential," they told me. As a typical teen, I thought I could make it on my own. I didn't want any help, and the more people tried to give it the more distant I grew. I was the kid who thought he could be perfect at anything without any preparation. I was lost in the daydream that I didn't need to study; I was going to play professional soccer. My game was good and I thought that practice, or getting good grades, for that matter, was unnecessary. Stubbornness and rebellion can be terrible things if they get out of control.

"To get back one's youth one has merely to repeat one's follies." A 12 day before my awakening on that fateful July sunrise, I would have disagreed with this quotation from Oscar Wilde. But after recognizing the results of my own follies for the first time, I thoroughly agree.

This year, my final year in high school, I've at last cleared my head 13 and buckled down. Judging by the past semester, I'm on the right track. My D average has U-turned into this report card's three B's and one A, landing me on my first Honor Roll. I intend to he on the Principal's List after this semester: then I hope to graduate and attend a community college in northern California, near the mountains, before transferring to a four-year school.

Thanks to that morning's conversion, I am a new person. Now, I 14 know I'll have to work hard. The sun streaming over the eastern Sierras wiped out the dark clouds that blurred my vision. Jonathan Harker in Bram Stoker's "Dracula" must have felt exactly the same way when he wrote in his journal: "No man knows 'till he has suffered from the night how sweet and how dear to his heart and eye the morning can be."

From Newsweek, *May 25, 1998. © Newsweek, Inc. All rights reserved. Reprinted by permission.*

Prewriting Practice

1. Freewrite for five minutes (or for a time specified by your instructor) to react to O'Connor's article in any way that you want. Write whatever comes to your mind.

2. Discuss your freewriting with other members of your class. Did they have similar responses?

3. Respond to one of the following questions by using the prewriting techniques of freewriting, brainstorming, and/or clustering:

    a. Halfway through his article, Joseph O'Connor writes, "I found out on that trip that nature is underestimated." Have you ever had an encounter with nature that affected you deeply? Briefly describe any such encounters that you can remember.

b. O'Connor goes on to write, "The experience was the most invigorating, fulfilling, stimulating two weeks of my life." Have you ever experienced something that affected you in such a way? Briefly describe any such experiences.

c. Consider the final quotation from the article: "No man knows 'till he has suffered from the night how sweet and how dear to his heart and eye the morning can be." What do you make of this statement? Do you think it expresses a truth about life? Describe any instances from your own life or from the lives of people you know that might illustrate its truth.

4. Discuss your responses to the above questions with other members of your class. Explain to them why you reacted to any specific experiences the way that you did.

Prewriting: Choosing a Preliminary Topic Sentence or Thesis Statement

Once you have developed some ideas by using the prewriting techniques discussed so far, you are ready to decide on the topic and central idea of your paper and to focus those two elements into a **topic sentence** (for a single paragraph) or a **thesis statement** (for an entire essay). Your ability to write clear topic sentences or thesis statements can determine whether or not your readers will understand and be able to follow the points you want to make in the papers you write. In college classes, that ability can make the difference between a successful paper and one that is barely passing (or not passing at all).

Finding the Topic

In academic writing, deciding upon the topic of your paper is often not very difficult because it is assigned by your instructor. You may be asked to write about child abuse or a piece of literature or a particular political issue—but rarely (if ever) will your assignment simply be to "write about something." Of course, many times you may be asked to choose your own topics, but even then you will know what topics are appropriate and what are not. (For example, in a class studying the history of the Arab-Jewish tension in the Middle East, you probably would not choose state lotteries as the topic of your paper, right?)

Finding the Central Idea

This is where many student writers get stuck. The problem is not "What is my topic?" but "What should I be *saying* about my topic?" For example, if you were asked to write a paragraph explaining why the Gary Larson cartoon on page 2 causes many people to laugh, you would know what your topic is (the cartoon), but you might not have *any* idea why people laugh. To put it another way, you wouldn't know what your *central idea* is, so how could you possibly write a topic sentence or a thesis statement? How do you decide what your central idea is? Here are two suggestions.

Look at your prewriting to find a central idea.   As you examine your prewriting, watch for recurring ideas or for any idea that sparks your interest. For example, in the prewriting on pages 4 and 5 about the Gary Larson cartoon, you might notice that there seem to be several different reasons that people may laugh at the cartoon. Your preliminary central idea might be expressed this way:

> *central idea*
> People might find the Gary Larson cartoon funny <u>for several different reasons</u>.

Start writing your first draft to find a central idea.   You may have been taught in the past that you should not even *start* writing until you have focused your central idea into a topic sentence or thesis statement—and you might have found that such advice led you right back to a good case of writer's block. Certainly, it would be convenient if you could simply sit down, think up a perfect topic sentence or thesis statement, and start writing, but the process of writing is just not that neat and orderly. So if you are not sure what your central idea is, but you do have details or ideas you know you want to write about, just start writing about them. Many times your precise central idea will develop while you write.

Forming the Preliminary Topic Sentence or Thesis Statement

Once you are somewhat sure what your topic and central idea will be, write them as a single sentence. If your assignment is to write one paragraph, this sentence will serve as its **topic sentence.** If you are writing an essay, this sentence will serve as its **thesis statement.** In either case, it will state the topic and central idea of the assignment. As you prepare this sentence, keep these points in mind:

Make a statement that demands explanation. Do not merely state a fact.   Because a central idea demands some explanation, argument, or development, a simple statement of fact will not work as a topic sentence or thesis statement. Note the difference between the following two statements:

Fact

> The Gary Larson cartoon shows an artist trying to paint a cow.

Demands Explanation

> The Gary Larson cartoon elicited some very strange reactions from my family.

Make a limited statement that can be reasonably supported with facts or examples. Do not be too general, vague, or broad.   Very general topic sentences and thesis statements result in very general papers. When you choose a topic and a central idea, **limit** your choice to something that can be covered in detail.

Ineffective

> broad topic   vague central idea
> Gary Larson's cartoons are funny.

The sentence above commits the writer to discussing *all* of Gary Larson's cartoons (a very broad topic), and its central idea focuses on a vague term (*funny*) that will mean something different to every reader.

Ineffective

> limited topic   vague central idea
> Gary Larson's cartoon about "artist's block" is interesting.

In the above sentence the topic "Gary Larson's cartoon about 'artist's block'" is limited well enough, but the central idea—that the cartoon is "interesting"—is much too vague and noncommittal.

Effective

> limited topic
> Several characteristics of Gary Larson's cartoon about "artist's block"
> limited central idea
> reflect how I feel whenever I have to write a paper.

The statement above would work as a topic sentence or thesis statement because it is focused on a limited topic (several characteristics of one cartoon) and because its limited central idea (how they reflect the writer's feelings when he is writing a paper) could be fully explained in one assignment.

Exercise 1.1

Examine each of the following sentences. If the sentence would be an effective topic sentence or thesis statement, underline its topic once and its central idea twice. If the sentence would not be an effective topic sentence or thesis statement, explain why not.

Examples

> Two weeks ago, the Beach Boys gave a concert at the stadium.
> (Not effective because it merely states a fact.)
>
> Current movies are very enjoyable to watch.
> (Not effective because its topic and central idea are too general.)
>
> <u>Attending Marine Corps boot camp</u> was <u>the most challenging experience of my life.</u>
> (Effective because the topic is quite limited and the central idea demands explanation and support.)

1. I have played on our college basketball team for two years.
2. My first job taught me how rude some customers can really be.

3. My family consists of some of the most obnoxious people you will ever meet.

4. Last January, a friend and I skipped work and went to the mountains.

5. This paper will be about affirmative action.

6. If people listened to all the warnings about eating sugar, fat, caffeine, or cholesterol, they would never have any fun at all.

7. Many food labels today are both confusing and misleading.

8. I love watching the seagulls and listening to the waves at the beach.

9. Although I don't approve of lying, sometimes a lie is both necessary and ethical.

10. If we are going to advance as a democracy, we need to improve our society. ■

Placing the Topic Sentence or Thesis Statement

As we mentioned above, the primary difference between a topic sentence and a thesis statement is that the topic sentence identifies the central idea of a paragraph and the thesis statement does the same for an essay. As you will see in Chapter 2, topic sentences and thesis statements can appear many places, depending on the purpose of a particular piece of writing. However, in college classes you will be writing academic papers, and in almost all academic writing the topic sentences and thesis statements must be placed very carefully.

Place the topic sentence at the start of the paragraph.   Although there are exceptions, the first sentence of most academic paragraphs should be the topic sentence. The body of the paragraph should explain and support that topic sentence. (See Chapter 3 for a discussion of support within a paragraph.)

topic sentence   **One serious problem for many newly arrived immigrants is that they do not speak English well, if they speak it at all.** For example, when my parents left Hong Kong in 1972 and came to America, they couldn't understand what people were saying, so they didn't know how to respond to them. Not knowing how to speak English was a horrible experience for them. Because everything was in English, they couldn't even watch TV, go to the store, or read the newspaper. The only thing they could do at that time was to stay home. One of the most terrible experiences that my mom had happened when she got lost while trying to pick me up at school. Because she didn't speak English, she couldn't even ask for directions, so she just drove around in circles for hours. Although people in the neighborhood tried to help her, my mom just couldn't understand what they were saying. One group of people just pointed and laughed as my mom drove by. After that experience she said, "If I don't learn to speak English soon, people will take advantage of me all the time."

Nancy Kwan, student writer

Place the thesis statement at the end of the introductory paragraph.   Again, there are many exceptions, as you will see in Chapter 2, but the thesis statement in most academic essays appears as the last sentence of the introductory paragraph. (See Chapter 3 for a discussion of writing introductory paragraphs.)

thesis statement

> Doesn't almost everyone want a good education? That is why most people, after graduating from high school, go on to college. Whether it is at a community college or a four-year university, people young and old spend their mornings, afternoons, or evenings in class studying and getting closer to a college diploma. Currently, I am completing my second year at Palomar College, and my attitude today about my education has drastically changed from when I started my first semester. **I believe that if I had known how important education is when I first enrolled in college, I probably would have done things quite differently during my freshman year.**
>
> *Elizabeth Santos, student writer*

Exercise 1.2

Reread the prewriting you did in response to the prewriting questions at the end of "Live Each Moment for What It's Worth," "Without Emotion," or "A View from Mount Ritter." Using that material, write a sentence that you could use either as a preliminary topic sentence for a paragraph or as a preliminary thesis statement for an essay.

Compare your results with those of other members of your class to determine which sentences contain specific topics and clear central ideas. ■

Prewriting: Preparing a Rough Outline

If you have ever been required to turn in a complete outline of a paper before the final paper was due, you know how difficult—even impossible, sometimes—it is to predict exactly what you will include in a paper, much less what *order* it will follow. So rest easy—although preparing a *rough outline* is part of the prewriting process, it is not at all the same as writing a complete, perfect, formal outline. Instead, it involves looking at what you have written so far in your prewriting, deciding what ideas you *may* use, and listing those ideas in the order in which you will *probably* use them. Essentially, you are trying to give yourself some direction before you start writing the first draft.

Grouping Related Points

Let's use the Gary Larson cartoon again as an example of how to write the rough outline. The first step is to look at the prewriting on pages 4 and 5 and group any details that seem related. (You might notice, by the way, that the clustering example has already grouped some of them.) They could be organized this way:

A	B	C
appearance of artist	cow with no head	artist is like me
bug-eyes	no cow head in artist's thought	artist's block = writer's block
look of panic		I've felt same way
fat stomach	cows seem dumb anyway	
scraggly beard		
holding head		

Choosing a Tentative Organization

Once you've grouped the details that you want to include, you need to decide in what order you will discuss them. Here are three common ways to organize your material.

Emphatic Order

If you think some of your details should receive more emphasis than others because they are more important, complex, colorful, or memorable, arrange them so that they move from the least important to the most important. This type of organization will leave your readers with a strong impression of your most effective details.

For example, when organizing the above material from the Gary Larson cartoon, you might decide to use category *A* last because the appearance of the artist seemed to be the funniest part of the cartoon to you, and you want the reader to focus on it. On the other hand, another writer might choose to save category *C* until last because she wants to emphasize how strongly she identified with the artist in the cartoon.

Chronological Order

Chronological order presents details in the order they actually occurred. Whatever occurred first is discussed first, whatever occurred second is discussed second, and so on. This type of organization is very effective when you want to describe an event or explain how something happened. If your first reaction to the Gary Larson cartoon was that you have felt exactly the same way as the frustrated artist, then you would present category *C* first in your paper.

Spatial Order

Spatial order consists of describing a place or an object in such a way that a reader can clearly picture the various details and their relationship to each other. One way to do so is to describe the larger elements of a scene first, identifying where they are in relation to other elements, and then moving to a description of the smaller details. For example, to describe the Gary Larson cartoon, a writer might decide to completely reorganize the three categories listed above, placing all larger details in one category and then moving to smaller, more subtle, details as the paper progresses.

Exercise 1.3

Using the prewriting you did for "Live Each Moment for What It's Worth," "Without Emotion," or " A View from Mount Ritter," group the ideas or examples that you have developed so far into a rough outline and decide on a tentative organization. If you need to, do more prewriting to develop more details. ■

Writing: The First Draft

If you have a preliminary topic sentence or thesis statement and have prepared a rough outline, you have everything you need to write your paper. So now is the time to sit and write. However, now is still *not* the time to worry about whether everything is spelled exactly right or worded perfectly. If you try to write your first draft and avoid all errors at the same time, you will end up right back where you probably started—stuck. Of course, you can correct some errors as they occur, but don't make revising or editing your primary concern at this point. What you want to do *now* is to write out your ideas. You can "fix" them later.

The Single Paragraph: A First Draft

If your assignment is to write one paragraph, open the paragraph with your *preliminary topic sentence.* Then use your details from your rough outline to explain and support the central idea of your topic sentence. Here is the first draft of a paragraph about the Gary Larson cartoon.

preliminary topic sentence

I found the Gary Larson cartoon funny for a number of reasons when I first read it. First, the artist was feeling just like me when I have writer's block. I guess I just related to him—but I was laughing at myself as well as at him. As I did some freewriting about it, I realized there were other reasons the cartoon is funny. The overall appearance of the artist is ridiculous. There he sits. He has his head in his hands. His eyes are bugging out in panic, and his fat stomach is hanging over his belt. The whole thing is just really funny. The funniest part of the whole thing is that he hasn't even thought of a cow's head yet. (I think someone else showed me this.) I can just imagine him putting a crocodile's head on the cow. The cartoon really sums up how I feel when I'm stuck with writer's block. The whole situation is ridiculous and absurd.

Exercise 1.4

Respond to the following questions.

1. What is the central idea of the paragraph? Where is it stated?
2. Which of the organizational patterns from page 17 is the writer using?
3. What details that appear in the rough outline on page 17 has the writer left out?
4. What idea in the final sentence could be used to improve the central idea of the preliminary topic sentence? ▪

The Brief Essay: A First Draft

If you are writing an essay, open your draft with an introductory paragraph that ends with a *preliminary thesis statement*. Then start each body paragraph with a *preliminary topic sentence* that supports or explains the central idea of the thesis statement.

In the following first draft, notice how the previous sample paragraph has been restructured to serve as the start of a brief essay. Each body paragraph is quite short, needing more details and explanation, but a clear topic sentence opens each one.

preliminary thesis statement

Gary Larson's cartoons always make me laugh, but I have never really thought about why. **However, as I considered his cartoon about "artist's block," I finally decided that it is funny for a number of different reasons.**

preliminary topic sentence

First, the artist was feeling just like me when I have writer's block. I guess I just related to him—but I was laughing at myself as well as at him.

preliminary topic sentence

As I did some freewriting about it, I realized there were other reasons it is funny. The overall appearance of the artist is ridiculous. There he sits. He has his head in his hands. His eyes are bugging out in panic, and his fat stomach is hanging over his belt. The whole thing is just really funny.

preliminary topic sentence

The funniest part of the whole thing is that he hasn't even thought of a cow's head yet. (I think someone else showed me this.) I can just imagine him putting a crocodile's head on the cow.

The cartoon really sums up how I feel when I'm stuck with writer's block. The whole situation is ridiculous and absurd.

Exercise 1.5

Respond to the following questions.

1. What is the central idea of the essay? Where is it stated?
2. What is the central idea of each preliminary topic sentence?
3. What would you add to each body paragraph to expand and develop it? ■

Rewriting: Revising and Editing

Revising

As we mentioned at the start of the chapter, rewriting consists of two stages: revising and editing. Unfortunately, many people—especially if they are pressed for time—omit the revising stage and move directly to editing, often with disastrous results.

The problem is that editing will correct grammar, spelling, and punctuation errors *without* improving either the content or the organization of your paper—and these larger areas do need to be addressed before you submit your work. Now is the time to *read* what you have written, *think* about it, and *decide* what changes you should make. Here are some suggestions.

Refine your topic sentence or thesis statement.   Usually, writing the first draft of a paper will help you become more specific about what your central idea really is. In fact, if you look at the concluding sentences of your first draft, you will often find a statement that sums up your central idea better than your preliminary topic sentence or thesis statement did.

When the writer of the first draft about the Gary Larson cartoon (above) read the last sentence of her draft, she realized that the key to the humor in the cartoon is its absurdity. When you read the revised draft (below), note how she refined her central idea.

Reorganize your material.   The writer of the above first draft reorganized the groups of details (*A, B, C*) listed on page 17 so that they appear in the order *C, A, B*. This reorganization allowed her to follow a chronological pattern, ending with what she sees as the funniest element of the cartoon.

Add details.   The first draft has left out several details from the lists on page 17. Note how the writer has restored them in the revised draft below.

Reword sentences.   Many times you will find that your original wording of sentences can be improved. Note the changes made in the middle of the revised draft below.

The Single Paragraph: Revised Draft

Here is a revised version of the paragraph on page 18. Changes are shown in boldface.

Refined topic sentence

I found Gary Larson's cartoon about the painter with "artist's block" very funny because the situation it describes is so familiar yet so absurd. The first thing I noticed was that the artist was feeling exactly what I feel when I have "writer's block." **His frustration and look of panic reminded me of myself, and I had to laugh because the situation really is ridiculous.** I guess I just related to him—but I was laughing at myself as well as at him. As I did some freewriting about it, I realized that **the overall appearance of the artist is ridiculous. He's just sitting there, with his head in his hands, his eyes bugging out in panic, and his fat stomach hanging over his belt.** The whole thing is just really funny. **He's even dropped his paintbrush on the floor, as if he can't hold it any more—or maybe he's thrown it down.** Finally, the **most absurd** part of the whole thing is that he hasn't even thought of a cow's head yet. **He's thought of a bird, a duck, a donkey, a rhino, a hippo, even a crocodile—but no cow!** I can just imagine him putting a crocodile's head on the cow. The cartoon really sums up how I feel when I'm stuck with writer's block. The whole situation is **just absurd.**

added details

reworded sentence

added details

added details

reworded sentence

Exercise 1.6

Identify the central idea in the topic sentence. Then point out words that emphasize that central idea throughout the paragraph. ■

The Brief Essay: Revised Draft

Here is a revised version of the brief essay on page 19. Changes are shown in boldface.

expanded introduction

refined thesis statement

Gary Larson's cartoons always make me laugh, but I have never really thought about why. **As I examined his cartoon about the painter with "artist's block," I began to realize that his humor comes from at** least two sources. **The cartoon is funny because the situation it describes is so familiar yet so absurd.**

refined topic sentence

The first thing I noticed was **how familiar the situation was. That poor artist, sitting there completely stuck, was feeling exactly like me when I have "writer's block."** His frustration and look of panic reminded me so much of myself that I had to laugh. The situation really is ridiculous. I guess I just related to him—but I was laughing at myself as well as at him.

added details

refined topic sentence

As I did some freewriting about it, I realized that **the overall appearance of the artist is ridiculous. He's just sitting there, with his head in his hands, his eyes bugging out in panic, and his fat stomach hanging over his belt.** The whole thing is just really funny. **He's even dropped his paint brush on the floor, as if he can't hold it anymore—or maybe he's thrown it down.**

added details

added details

refined topic sentence

Finally, the **most absurd** part of the whole thing is that he hasn't even thought of a cow's head yet. **He's thought of a bird, a duck, a donkey, a rhino, a hippo, even a crocodile—but no cow! And, to make matters worse, two of the heads that he is considering are facing in the wrong direction.** I can just imagine him putting a backwards crocodile's head on the cow.

added details

added details

expanded conclusion

The cartoon really sums up how I feel when I'm stuck with writer's block. **I'm frustrated, angry at the situation, and starting to panic.** The whole situation is **just absurd.**

Exercise 1.7

Identify the central idea in the thesis statement. Then point out words in the topic sentences of the body paragraphs and in the details of each paragraph that emphasize the central idea. ■

Editing

Now for the final step. You need to **edit** your draft before typing the final copy. Read your draft over carefully, looking for spelling, grammar, or punctuation errors as you do. If you are using a computer, be sure to proofread a printed copy of your paper, not just what appears on the screen. Once you have corrected any errors and are satisfied with the final product, prepare a clean copy (double-spaced) and submit it to your instructor.

Assignments
Writing with a Central Idea

Write a paragraph or a short essay, whichever your instructor assigns, in response to one of the following assignments. If you write a paragraph, be sure to include a topic sentence. If you write an essay, include a thesis statement.

1. After reading "Live Each Moment for What It's Worth," write a paper in response to one of the following suggestions.

   a. Explain whether you do or do not live by the "seize the moment" philosophy. As you give examples to illustrate the type of person you are, be sure to make clear what you think about your approach to life.

   b. What do you think about Bombeck's idea that we should "seize the moment" more often? Give examples from your own life or from the lives of friends, relatives, and acquaintances to illustrate and explain your reaction.

   c. Discuss this article with your classmates or with people you know outside of class. Have any of them "seized the moment" in ways that you particularly admire? Describe one or more of those people, making it clear how they have lived by Bombeck's philosophy.

2. After reading "Without Emotion," write a paper in response to one of the following suggestions.

   a. If your reactions to G. Gordon Liddy or to the events in the article changed as you read it, explain which parts of the article caused your reactions to change.

   b. If you have found that at times you have had to repress or ignore your emotions, write a paper in which you describe specific situations that have caused you to do so.

   c. Interview other members of your class about this article. How did they react to it? Write a paper in which you explain the different types of reactions you discovered.

3. After reading "A View from Mount Ritter," write a paper in response to one of the following suggestions.

   a. Has nature been an important part of your life? Do you camp in the mountains, walk in the woods, listen to the waves at the beach? If you do, choose one particular event that you remember vividly. Briefly describe it, and then explain how or why the event affected you. Give examples to illustrate your points.

   b. Choose any event that affected you deeply, that somehow changed how you think or feel, that helped you to become a different person. Briefly describe the event and then explain in what ways you were changed by it. Give examples to illustrate your points.

c. Choose a quotation from the article that seems to express a truth about life. Explain what the quotation means to you, and then illustrate its truth with examples from your own life or the lives of people you know.

4. Write a paper in response to one of the articles in Part Four, as assigned by your instructor.

Evaluating Sample Papers

At one time or another, most students have had the experience of turning in a paper they were *sure* they had done a good job on, only to have it returned a few class meetings later with a grade much lower than they expected. Even professional writers have the disappointing experience of having their manuscripts returned by editors with less-than-favorable responses. Perhaps you can *never* be 100% sure that your writing is perfect, but you can *greatly* improve the odds of submitting a successful paper if you learn how to judge the quality of what you have written.

One way to become a good judge of your own writing is to practice judging what others have written. You can get such practice by evaluating sample papers. In this text, each chapter will provide you with several student paragraphs and essays. Practice your judging skills by using the following checklist (or a format provided by your instructor) to determine which paper is the most effective one. If your instructor asks you to, use the same checklist to evaluate the papers of some of your fellow students.

Student Model Checklist

1. Thesis statement or topic sentence:
   a. If you are reading an essay, underline the thesis statement and circle its central idea. If you are reading a single paragraph, underline the topic sentence and circle its central idea.
   b. Can the thesis statement or topic sentence be more exact or specific? Is it too broad? Should the thesis or topic sentence be revised to incorporate a term used in the last few sentences of the paper?
   c. Rank the overall effectiveness of the thesis statement or topic sentence:

   1   2   3   4   5   6
   (ineffective)   (excellent)

2. Support:

   Look at the examples used. Do they refer to specific personal experiences and exact details, or are they general and vague? Rank the overall effectiveness of the examples:

   1   2   3   4   5   6
   (general and vague)   (specific and detailed)

3. Organization:

Can you tell where one idea or example ends and another begins? Rank the clarity of the organization:

1   2   3   4   5   6

(unclear, confusing)   (clear)

4. Spelling, punctuation, grammar:

Underline or circle any spelling, punctuation, or grammar errors that you find. Rank the effectiveness of the spelling, punctuation, and grammar:

1   2   3   4   5   6

(ineffective)   (excellent)

5. Rank the overall effectiveness of the paper:

1   2   3   4   5   6

(ineffective)   (excellent)

Sample Student Papers

The following paragraphs and essays were submitted as first drafts that would later be revised. To evaluate these papers, follow these steps:

1. Read the *entire* paper through before making any judgments about it.
2. Reread the paper to identify its topic sentence or thesis statement.
3. Identify the major sections of the paper.
4. Respond to the items on the checklist on pages 24 and 25 or to questions provided by your instructor.

Paragraphs

The students who wrote the following papers were asked to write a 250- to 300-word paragraph responding to one of the writing assignments on pages 23 and 24.

Student Paragraph 1

My interpretation of Erma Bombeck's "seize the moment" is that one should live his or her life to the fullest. If some opportunity crosses your pathway you need to jump on it. A "just go for it" type of attitude is necessary. In my own life, I see this being needed in three areas. The first area is being able to have the "just go for it" attitude no matter what the cost. Who knows if I will have the chance to ever go to that place or do that something ever again. I tend to have too much to do to be able to drop every thing and seize the moment. Also, now everything tends to cost so much money and I don't have the resources to pay the expenses. The second problem I have is the lack of ability to stand up for and tell people what I believe in. That is the perfect time to seize the moment, express your feelings and tell people your personal views. You might help other people to understand, learn, and grow. So, it's important to stand up strong and speak out. When ever you are given the opportunity. For me, I struggle when I tell people about how God has changed my life. The last problem I have deals with grabbing job opportunities to move up in the working world. My employer demands a lot from me, and I should be able to stand up for my rights and demand things as well. I also need to jump on any opportunity to move up or to take on different responsibilities. So, these are the three problems I have with the quote "seize the moment." However, I do believe people need to seize the moment whenever given the opportunity. Never let it slip by, because once its gone who knows if you will ever have the opportunity again.

Student Paragraph 2

The article "Without Emotion" stirred up a few unpleasant feelings inside of me that I certainly was not expecting. When I first started this article and read about how the author went outside, lifted his rifle, and shot a small defenseless squirrel, I felt very horrified and sad. Still, I was able to make it okay in my head because he was only a boy and all kids do mean things. Then he went on and wrote, that after his mother had told him it was wrong to kill things it made him cry. This made me feel very relieved to know that he didn't really enjoy causing pain to another creature. It was certainly a shock to me when I read that he wasn't crying because of the pain he had inflicted, but because he couldn't shoot the squirrel without feelings. I felt sick to my stomach at this point and I actually did not want to continue reading. My curiousity lead me to the next surprise which was him wanting to kill chickens so that he wouldn't feel anything. By this time the author could have said just about anything and it still wouldn't have shocked me. However, I did become a little scared and I was even more frightened when I read that he was able to kill and not feel bad. I wasn't only afraid of him doing the killing, but mainly of him wanting to do the killing. At the end of this horrible article I felt shivers inside of me and kept thinking of this person being out in the world with me. This article certainly did arouse quite a few negative feelings inside of me. It amazes me that such a short article could bother me so much.

Student Paragraph 3

After reading "A View from Mount Ritter," I was reminded of a humbling experience that I also had with nature. The summer after my freshman year in high school, my family and I decided to raft down the Grand Canyon on a six day, seven night adventure. The first day was uneventful as we floated through several class one rapids, but day two was exciting as soon as we got back on the raft in the morning. Immediately our raft was bombarded by a class three rapid, followed by a class four rapid named Triple Threat. The sheer force of the water was unbelievable, we were completely at the mercy of the river. I knew that if I fell overboard, I would have to fight for my life. For the first time in my life I was faced with my own mortality. By day four we had already floated through about one hundred seventy-five miles of the Grand Canyon. By this time the walls of the canyon beside us were so tall that I could only see a tiny strip of blue sky when I looked up. In the middle of day five we hit the bottom of the canyon. We were told that the jagged rock walls beside us were over ten million years old. As we floated past canyon walls which had been here since before prehistoric times, I suddenly realized how small I really was and just how wrapped up in my little life I had become. The force of nature is truly awe inspiring. I realized how insignificant my life and contributions are and will be in comparison to the mighty canyon walls and the incredible force of the river that caused them. Before my trip river rafting down the Grand Canyon, I took the wonders of nature for granted. I always thought of man, myself included, as superior. This trip changed my thinking and made me realize that the force of nature is far superior to anything man could ever invent.

Brief Essays

The students who wrote the following papers were asked to write a brief essay responding to one of the writing assignments on pages 23 and 24.

Student Essay 1

I have always been the kind of person who likes to take all opportunities. Erma Bombeck's "Live Each Moment for What It's Worth" could have been written about me. From an adventurous trip to a tropical country to hang gliding, mountain climbing, and bungee jumping. I've done them all.

I try to do everything possible to enjoy my life, and seize all moments, making the best out of them. My friend Alan is also like me. Last summer we went to Rio de Janeiro, and all we did was meet women and play volleyball. I'm happy for being a spontaneous person, it makes life less boring.

However, nothing beats the fear and adrenalin rush of a high altitude sport. I remember as if it was yesterday when my cousin asked me if I wanted to go hang gliding. I didn't think twice and I said yes. Hang gliding was alot of fun and I'll never regret that day.

My cousin also took me mountain climbing. Although I didn't quite like being two thousand feet up on a mountain with a little rope tied around my waist and a heavy bag on my back. It was an experience I'll never forget.

The last of my crazy high altitude adventures was bungee jumping. Until last year I was eager to feel the wind going against my face and the adrenaline rush on a hundred mile per hour vertical dive. However, on November 25, about 3:30 p.m., I bungee jumped and turned into a human yo-yo.

As I finished reading the article "Live Each Moment for What It's Worth," I realized how important it is to take chances and seize the moment. There are opportunities that only come up once in a lifetime. People should take their chances because they might not get another one.

Student Essay 2

When I first read Liddy's "Without Emotion," I was horrified by his desire to kill without feeling anything. However, the more I thought about it, the more I realized that there have been times in my own life when I needed to act without feeling too. In fact, many times I have had to repress my personal feelings just to make it through an unpleasant experience.

For instance, in 1984 I had to face the realization that a divorce was in order. I had no emotional or financial support, and I had an eleven-month-old son to take care of. It was a time when emotions had to be shelved, temporarily, and all of my attention directed toward how I would handle the more pressing issues. Those issues being: food, shelter, clothing, and a job. I struggled through the transition from marriage to solo living by remaining unemotional and methodical. There would be time enough to process feelings once the necessary tasks were taken care of.

A few years later, after the divorce was final and I was well settled into the daily living as a single parent, I was laid off from a typesetting position with a local newspaper. This time, also, I did not allow myself the luxury of feeling frightened, not even for a minute. I immediately busied myself with the task of finding a job. I didn't take time to feel sad or to feel sorry for myself; I just proceeded with what needed to be done, never once allowing myself to give in to everyone's barrage of "What if's?"

I think Liddy was trying to get to a point where he could kill without feeling emotion if he had to. He was aware of the "kill or be killed" probability that faced him as a soldier. For me, it was either conquer the challenges that had befallen me or be conquered by them.

Student Essay 3

When my parents separated, it was a very difficult and tough time for not only myself but my whole family. It changed my life forever. Everything was going great, and then my parents began to fight. It seemed to be no big deal, but after weeks and weeks of fighting, I started to get scared. One morning my mom told my brother and me that she was going to move into our other house so my dad and her could have some time apart. Since that time about two years ago, my parents are still not the best of friends, and I still cry at night when I think about the situation. This whole event caused me a lot of pain, but I have learned to bring a lot of positive things out of the whole situation.

I've learned to not take things for granted and to cherish every single day and everyone I love. This event has made me realize that one day I may have everything I need but the next day it all could be lost. That was how I felt when my parents separated. The whole time I was growing up I thought I had the perfect family and I was the luckiest kid. The family trips together to Utah and Canada were the greatest, and I thought it would always be that way. This event made me change the way I felt. I felt I had lost everything I had loved. Now everyday I live that day as if the next may take some bad turn. I don't want to look back and wonder, "What if?"

Now if I have a problem or I see that someone else needs some help, I'm always the first to ask for help and the first to give. Two weeks ago one of my good friends was having some girl trouble, so I decided to ask him what was wrong. He told me that they had got into a fight , so I sat down and had a nice talk with him. I helped them solve their differences. Before this event happened, I felt afraid to talk about my problems or others' problems. Today, I am more open as a person. I really enjoy helping others during their troubled times.

This event made me feel like I can do more things on my own and not be dependent on everyone else all the time. I used to go places with others and have them help me with stuff I could have done on my own. Last week I went to a movie by myself where before this event I would have been afraid to go by myself. This event made me realize that everyone else won't always be there for me but that I should always be there for myself as well as for others.

At the beginning this was a very tough time for me, and it is still very hard to handle. It is a tough subject, but it has taught me a lot of great lessons that would have been hard for me to figure out. Don't get me wrong, I would give anything to have my family back the way it used to be, but I know that's never going to happen. So I'm really glad I was able to learn such a valuable lesson at an early age and take something out of my parents separation other than anger and pain. Some people never have a chance to learn these valuable lessons. They can change the way you look at life.

Sentence Combining
Embedding Adjectives, Adverbs, and Prepositional Phrases

As you have worked through the writing process presented in Chapter 1, we hope you have discovered that good writing develops as you write. Many times, for instance, you will not know exactly what your central idea is until you have done a substantial amount of prewriting, and sometimes you may not know exactly how your ideas or paragraphs should be organized until you have tried one or two different organizations to see which works best. This willingness to make changes and to rethink material as you discover new ideas is at the heart of all good writing—

and it works at the level of individual sentences as well as at the larger levels related to the central idea or the organization of a paper.

As you write the initial drafts of your papers, you will express your ideas in sentence structures that are comfortable to you because they reflect your personal style of writing. (You *do* have a personal style, even if you write very rarely.) However, as you become more and more proficient in using the writing process, you will find that you can improve your personal style. At the level of sentence structure, this improvement can include, among other things, recognizing when separate sentences contain related ideas that should be expressed in one sentence and learning how to use different types of sentence structures to express different types of ideas.

Exercise 1.8

To illustrate what we mean, let's compare the following versions of a passage drawn from an article by Lois Sweet entitled "What's in a Name? Quite a Lot." One passage is just as Lois Sweet wrote it. The other is written as a beginning writer might have written it. Which is which? How can you tell?

> 1 Over the years, a lot of my friends have changed their names. 2 A number of them began to take an interest in their cultural backgrounds. 3 Their parents had wanted to deny cultural differences. 4 As a result, their parents had anglicized their names. 5 My friends were horrified. 6 They had been pushed into the great bland melting pot. 7 They felt more like they were being drowned than saved. 8 For them, their culture was a source of pride. 9 They demanded recognition for their "ethnic" names.

> 1 Over the years, a lot of my friends have changed their names. 2 A number of them began to take an interest in their cultural backgrounds and became horrified that their parents had anglicized their names in an effort to deny cultural differences. 3 To my friends, being pushed into the great bland melting pot felt more like being drowned than saved. 4 Their culture was a source of pride and they demanded recognition for their "ethnic" names. ■

As you can see, these two versions are quite different from each other, although they both express the same ideas. The first version uses nine sentences and eighty-two words. The second version uses nearly the same number of words (seventy-five) but only four sentences.

The second version is Lois Sweet's original. In it, you can see the ability of a professional writer to combine related ideas into sentences that are longer and more varied than those written by an inexperienced writer. In her version, Sweet has written in a single sentence (sentence 2) what it took three sentences (sentences 2, 3, and 4) for the first writer to express. And Sweet has written in two sentences (sentences 3 and 4) what the first writer expressed in four sentences (sentences 6, 7, 8, and 9).

Of course, combining related ideas is a skill all writers have to some degree, no matter how experienced or inexperienced they may be. For example, when you see that two or more ideas are related, you probably combine them without thinking much about it. Would you write this?

> My brother is an auto mechanic. I asked my brother to fix my car. My car had not run properly for weeks.

Probably not. But you might express yourself any one of these ways:

> My brother is an auto mechanic, so I asked him to fix my car because it had not run properly for weeks.
>
> I asked my brother, who is an auto mechanic, to fix my car because it had not run properly for weeks.
>
> Because my car had not run properly for weeks, I asked my brother, an auto mechanic, to fix it.
>
> I asked my brother to fix my car, which had not run properly for weeks, because he is an auto mechanic.
>
> My car had not run properly for weeks, so I asked my brother to fix it because he is an auto mechanic.

Which sounds better to you? Each of the above sentences might work in your speech or in your writing, depending on the situation. The point is that you already can and do combine related ideas in many different ways. And with practice, you will become even better at what you already do.

Exercise 1.9

To see what we mean when we say you already know how to combine related ideas, rewrite the sentences below. Join those ideas that seem obviously related into sentences that make sense to you. Don't worry about getting the "right" answer—just combine the ideas that seem as if they should go together.

> The woman held a book. It was in her left hand. She was tired. The book was thick. She waited for her ride. She was in the parking lot. Finally a car stopped. It was small and blue. It stopped next to her. She opened the door to the car. A poodle jumped out. It was white. It ran into the parking lot. It ran quickly. It disappeared between the parked cars. ■

The Embedding Process

One of the most common ways to combine ideas is to use **adjectives** and **adverbs** to modify other words. For instance, in the exercise above, if you described the book the woman was holding as a "thick" book, you used *thick* as an adjective. If you wrote that the poodle ran "quickly" into the parking lot, you used *quickly* as an adverb.

What's the difference? It is that adjectives modify nouns and pronouns while adverbs modify verbs, adjectives, and other adverbs. However, knowing these definitions is not as important here as recognizing when a word in one sentence is related to a word in another sentence.

In sentence combining, the act of placing words or phrases from one sentence into another is called **embedding.** Look at the following examples. Note how the underlined adjective or adverb in the second sentence can be embedded within the first sentence.

Examples

The movie was about a tomato.
The tomato was <u>enormous</u>.   (adjective)

The movie was about an <u>enormous</u> tomato.

The lamp fell to the floor.
It fell <u>suddenly</u>.   (adverb)

The lamp <u>suddenly</u> fell to the floor.

Prepositional phrases also modify words, so in a sense they are adjectives and adverbs too. You use them all of the time in your speech and in your writing. You use prepositional phrases when you write that you are <u>in the house</u> or <u>on the step</u> or <u>at the store</u> or <u>from Indiana</u>.

Each prepositional phrase starts with a preposition and ends with a noun (or a pronoun), called the *object* of the preposition. Between the preposition and its object you may find modifiers. For example, in the prepositional phrase "from the tired old man," *from* is the preposition, *man* is the object, and the words between the two are modifiers.

preposition	modifiers	object of the preposition
from	the tired old	man

Here is a list of common prepositions:

above	before	for	on	under
across	behind	from	onto	until
after	below	in	over	up
among	beside	into	past	upon
around	between	in spite of	till	with
as	by	like	through	without
at	during	near	to	
because of	except	of	toward	

Prepositional phrases should be embedded in sentences they are related to just as adjectives and adverbs should be. Look at the following examples:

Examples

The lawnmower was old and rusty.
The lawnmower was in the garage.   (prep. phrase)

The lawnmower in the garage was old and rusty.

Wild Bill Hickok was killed when he was shot.
He was killed during a poker game.   (prep. phrase)
He was shot in the back.   (prep. phrase)

Wild Bill Hickok was killed during a poker game when he was shot in the back.

Exercise 1.10

Rewrite each of the following groups of sentences into one sentence by embedding the underlined adjective, adverb, or prepositional phrase in the first sentence of the group.

Example

We washed the dishes.
We washed them after dinner.
We washed them carefully.
The dishes were expensive.

After dinner, we carefully washed the expensive dishes.

1. The horse stood.
    The horse was in the pasture.
    The horse was old.
    The horse was swaybacked.
    The pasture was deserted.

2. It switched its tail at the flies.
    The flies were on its back.
    The flies were irritating.
    It switched its tail slowly.

3. A boy climbed into the pasture.
    He climbed over the fence.
    He climbed carefully.

4. He approached the horse and called its name.
    He approached it slowly.
    The horse was tired.
    He called it softly.

5. The horse turned and reared.
    It turned toward the boy.
    It reared suddenly.
    It reared on its hind legs. ■

Exercise 1.11

Combine each of the following sets of sentences into one sentence by embedding adjectives, adverbs, and prepositional phrases.

1. The novel was about a murder.
   It was a mystery novel.
   It was new.
   The murder was violent.
   The murder was in St. Patrick's Cathedral.
   St. Patrick's Cathedral is in New York City.

2. The newspapers carried the story.
   The story was on the front pages.
   These newspapers were in almost every city.
   They carried the story prominently.
   The story was of the murder.

3. The basketball game was held in the gym.
   It was for the state championship.
   It was in a small town.
   The town was on the banks of a river.
   The river was wide and muddy.

4. The game was held in the afternoon.
   The game was sold out.
   It was on a Saturday.
   It was held between one team and another team.
   One team was from a small town.
   The other team was from a large city.

5. When the team won, the town held a parade.
   The team from the small town won.
   The town was surprised.
   The parade was big.
   It was held in celebration of the players. ■

Exercise 1.12

The exercise below is substantially more difficult than the previous ones. In each case, the original version of the sentence can be found in one of the reading selections in this chapter. Combine each group of sentences into one sentence. Use the first sentence as the base sentence. Adjectives, adverbs, and prepositional phrases that can be embedded into the base sentence are underlined in the first five groups.

Example

Hunting was a sport. Squirrel hunting was a popular one in West Cald-well. This was in the 1940s.

Squirrel hunting was a popular sport in West Caldwell in the 1940s.

1. I loaded my rifle, cocked the spring, and waited. I was waiting on the steps of the porch, and it was my homemade rifle.

2. When I came in my mother told me that she had seen the suffering I had caused. She told me this reproachfully. I came into the house. She said that she had seen me from the kitchen window.

3. Bill Jacobus's father, to help combat the shortage and to supplement rationing, had built a coop. It was the wartime food shortage he was com-batting. He built a chicken coop. It was in his backyard.

4. Just possibly, she might be the woman. She might be the very wisest of all the women on this planet.

5. I got to thinking one day. I was thinking about all those women who passed up dessert. They were on the Titanic. The dessert was at dinner that fate-ful night. The women had passed it up in an effort to "cut back."

6. We live on a diet. It is a sparse diet, and it is a diet of promises we make to ourselves when all the conditions are perfect.

7. The days get shorter and the list gets longer. It is a list of promises, and they are promises to ourselves.

8. It's just that I might as well apply it directly and eliminate the process. It's as if I applied it directly to my hips with a spatula, and I could just skip the digestive process.

9. On top of Mount Ritter, 13,000 feet above sea level, I was entranced at the sight of the sun as it peeked over the peaks. It was orange-red, and the peaks were glistening. They were far off in the east.

10. Clouds appeared transparent as they glowed. They were cumulous clouds. They glowed bright red in the morning glory. ◼

Chapter 2

Reading for the Central Idea

In Chapter 1, you read that part of the writing process consists of developing a clearly worded statement of your central idea. Such a statement—whether it is a topic sentence or a thesis statement—serves as a guide for your readers, identifying for them the point you are trying to make.

In the "writing-reading conversation," you are a reader as often as you are a writer—and your ability to identify a central idea as a reader is certainly as important as your ability to express a central idea as a writer. In fact, in many college situations you will find that your ability to write a clear central idea depends first upon your ability to identify central ideas in what you read.

In the cartoon on the facing page, Hagar the Horrible and his companion have apparently not identified the central idea of the signs they have just read. (And the writer of the signs has not yet learned how to use *lay* and *lie*.) Of course, the message that Hagar and his friend have overlooked is a fairly clear one. Unfortunately, however, the central ideas of many paragraphs and essays are not always as clear—not necessarily because the paragraph or essay is written poorly, but because it is complex and demands close attention.

In this chapter, you will practice reading to identify and to summarize central ideas, and you will practice writing in response to those ideas.

Paragraphs and Topic Sentences

In a paragraph, the sentence that states the central idea is called the **topic sentence.** It is often the first sentence (or two) of the paragraph, although a paragraph often has its topic sentence in the middle or at the end. Look at the following paragraphs. Their topic sentences are in italics. Following each paragraph is an example of how you could state its central idea in your own words.

> *Football has replaced baseball as the favorite American spectator sport largely because of television.* A comparison between a telecast of a football game on one channel and a baseball game on another could reveal baseball as a game with people standing around seemingly with little to do but watch two men play catch. Football would appear as twenty-two men engaged in almost constant, frenzied action. To watch baseball requires identification with the home team; to watch football requires only a need for action or a week of few thrills and the need for a touch of vicarious excitement.
>
> —*Jeffery Schrank, "Sport and the American Dream"*

Summary of Central Idea

Television has helped football to replace baseball as the favorite American spectator sport.

In the next paragraph, the "topic sentence" actually consists of more than one sentence.

✓

*Some people say the business about the jolly fat person is a myth, that all of us chubbies are neurotic, sick, sad people. I disagree. Fat people may not be chortling all day long, but they're a hell of a lot **nicer** than the wizened and shriveled.* Thin people turn surly, mean, and hard at a young age because they never learn the value of a hot-fudge sundae for easing tension. Thin people don't like gooey soft things because they themselves are neither gooey nor soft. They are crunchy and dull, like carrots. They go straight to the heart of the matter while fat people let things stay all blurry and hazy and vague, the way things actually are. Thin people want to face the truth. Fat people know there is no truth. One of my thin friends is always staring at complex, unsolvable problems and saying, "The key thing is . . . ." Fat people never say that. They know there isn't any such thing as the key thing.

—*Suzanne Britt, "That Lean and Hungry Look"*

Summary of Central Idea

The writer of this paragraph thinks that fat people are more pleasant to be around than thin people.

Paragraphs Without Topic Sentences

✓

Some paragraphs that you read will not have topic sentences. In these paragraphs, the topic sentence is *implied* (that is, it is not stated), but you can tell what the central idea is without it. Here is an example:

The loose bones of Lincoln were hard to fit with neat clothes; and, once on, they were hard to keep neat; trousers go baggy at the knees of a story-teller who has the habit, at the end of a story, where the main laugh comes in, of putting his arms around his knees, raising his knees to his chin, and rocking to and fro. Those who spoke of his looks often mentioned his trousers creeping to the ankles and higher; his rumpled hair, his wrinkled vest. When he wasn't away making speeches, electioneering or practicing law on the circuit, he cut kindling wood, tended to cordwood for the stoves in the house, milked the cow, gave her a few forks of hay, and changed her straw bedding every day.

—*Carl Sandburg,* Abraham Lincoln: The Prairie Years

Summary of Central Idea

Abraham Lincoln was an ordinary man who was not concerned about his appearance and who was willing to do ordinary work.

Many paragraphs in newspapers also do not have topic sentences. The columns in newspapers are so narrow that every third or fourth sentence is indented—not because a new topic idea has started, but because an article is easier to read that way. Look at the following three paragraphs from a newspaper and notice how they all support the same topic sentence in the first paragraph:

> *First, economists are virtually unanimous on the fact that jobs will be lost if the minimum wage is increased.* The Minimum Wage Study Commission concluded in 1981 that every 10 percent increase in the minimum wage could eliminate 70,000 to 200,000 jobs for teenagers alone. Total job loss could be substantially higher.
>
> Given a 40 percent increase, the legislation proposed by Kennedy and Hawkins would jeopardize an additional 400,000 to 800,000 jobs, denying opportunities to thousands more.
>
> Simply put, the minimum wage won't mean a thing—whatever the rate is—if people are forced out of their jobs. A higher wage is little consolation for someone who doesn't have a job.
>
> —*Senator Orrin G. Hatch, "Raising the Minimum Wage Will Put People Out of Work"*

Summary of Central Idea

If the minimum wage is increased, fewer jobs will be available.

Exercise 2.1

Read each of the following paragraphs. For each one, underline the topic sentence. Then, summarize its central idea in your own words. Remember that the topic sentence might be the first sentence, or it might occur later in the paragraph; it might consist of more than one sentence, or it might be implied.

1. Don't meddle with old unloaded firearms, they are the most deadly and unerring things that have ever been created by man. You don't have to take any pains at all with them; you don't have to have a rest, you don't have to have any sights on the gun, you don't have to take aim, even. No, you just pick out a relative and bang away, and you are sure to get him. A youth who can't hit a cathedral at thirty yards with a Gatling gun in three-quarters of an hour, can take up an old empty musket and bag his grandmother every time at a hundred.

   —*Mark Twain, "Advice to Youth"*

2. In the warmth of the inner Solar System a comet releases clouds of vapor and dust that form the glowing head and then leak into the tail, which is the cosmic equivalent of an oil slick. Pieces of the dust later hit the Earth, as meteors. A few survivors among the comets evolve into menacing lumps of dirt in tight orbits around the Sun. For these reasons comets are, in my opinion, best regarded as a conspicuous form of sky pollution.

   —*Nigel Calder,* The Comet Is Coming

3. A TV set stood close to a wall in the small living room crowded with an assortment of chairs and tables. An aquarium crowded the mantelpiece of a fake fireplace. A lighted bulb inside the tank showed many colored fish swimming about in a haze of fish food. Some of it lay scattered on the edge of the shelf. The carpet underneath was sodden black. Old magazines and tabloids lay just about everywhere.

—*Bienvenidos Santos, "Immigration Blues"* ■

Essays and Thesis Statements

The central idea of a complete essay is called its **thesis statement.** Usually, it appears toward the start of the essay (in the introduction), although, like a topic sentence in a paragraph, it can appear in the middle or at the end of an essay, or it might not appear at all because it is implied.

Sometimes a thesis statement is quite straightforward and easy to see. For example, in the following brief essay, the thesis (shown in italics) is clearly stated in the first paragraph:

Three Passions I Have Lived For

Bertrand Russell

Three passions, simple but overwhelmingly strong, have governed my life: the longing for love, the search for knowledge, and unbearable pity for the suffering of mankind. These passions, like great winds, have blown me hither and thither, in a wayward course over a deep ocean of anguish, reaching to the very verge of despair. 1

I have sought love, first, because it brings ecstasy—ecstasy so great that I would often have sacrificed all the rest of my life for a few hours of this joy. I have sought it, next, because it relieves loneliness—that terrible loneliness in which one shivering consciousness looks over the rim of the world into the cold unfathomable lifeless abyss. I have sought it, finally, because in the union of love I have seen, in a mystic miniature, the prefiguring vision of the heaven that saints and poets have imagined. This is what I sought, and though it might seem too good for human life, this is what—at last—I have found. 2

With equal passion I have sought knowledge. I have wished to understand the hearts of men. I have wished to know why the stars shine. . . . A little of this, but not much, I have achieved. 3

Love and knowledge, so far as they were possible, led upward toward the heavens. But always pity brought me back to earth. Echoes of cries of pain reverberate in my heart. Children in famine, victims tortured by oppressors, helpless old people a hated burden to their sons, and the 4 whole world of loneliness, poverty, and pain make a mockery of what human life should be. I long to alleviate the evil, but I cannot, and I too suffer.

This has been my life. I have found it worth living, and would gladly   5
live it again if the chance were offered me.

From The Autobiography of Bertrand Russell. *Reprinted by permission of the Bertrand Russell Peace Foundation c/o Routledge Publishing Co.*

Summary of Central Idea

Bertrand Russell states that his life has been governed by the search for love and for knowledge and by a sense of pity for those who suffer.

Unfortunately, not everything you read will have a thesis statement as clear as the one above. Sometimes essays, articles, or chapters in texts will have their thesis statements in the second or third paragraph—or even later in the work. Sometimes the thesis statement will be most clearly worded in the conclusion. And sometimes it will not be directly stated at all. The point is that you need to read college material carefully and closely. Certainly one of the most important reading skills you will need to develop in college classes is the ability to recognize the central idea of what you read even when it is not directly stated.

Readings

Read the two articles below. After you have read each one, write a sentence that briefly summarizes its central idea. Underline any sentences that seem to state the thesis of the article.

Before You Read

1. Consider the title. In what sense might a marriage be called a "jailbreak"?
2. As you read this selection, watch for sentences that will express the author's central idea about "jailbreak" marriages.

Jailbreak Marriage

Gail Sheehy

Although the most commonplace reason women marry young is to   1
"complete" themselves, a good many spirited young women gave another reason: "I did it to get away from my parents." Particularly for girls whose educations and privileges are limited, a *jailbreak marriage* is

the usual thing. What might appear to be an act of rebellion usually turns out to be a transfer of dependence.

A lifer: that is how it felt to be Simone at 17, how it often feels for girls in authoritarian homes. The last of six children, she was caught in the nest vacated by the others and expected to "keep the family together." Simone was the last domain where her mother could play out the maternal role and where her father could exercise full control. That meant goodbye to the university scholarship. **2**

Although the family was not altogether poor, Simone had tried to make a point of her independence by earning her own money since the age of 14. Now she thrust out her bankbook. Would two thousand dollars in savings buy her freedom? **3**

"We want you home until you're 21." **4**

Work, her father insisted. But the job she got was another closed gate. It was in the knitting machine firm where her father worked, an extension of his control. Simone knuckled under for a year until she met Franz. A zero. An egocentric Hungarian of pointless aristocracy, a man for whom she had total disregard. Except for one attraction. He asked her to marry him. Franz would be the getaway vehicle in her jailbreak marriage scheme: "I decided the best way to get out was to get married and divorce him a year later. That was my whole program." **5**

Anatomy, uncontrolled, sabotaged her program. Nine months after the honeymoon, Simone was a mother. Resigning herself, she was pregnant with her second child at 20. **6**

One day, her husband called with the news, the marker event to blast her out of the drift. His firm had offered him a job in New York City. **7**

"Then and there, I decided that before the month was out I would have the baby, find a lawyer, and start divorce proceedings." The next five years were like twenty. It took every particle of her will and patience to defeat Franz, who wouldn't hear of a separation, and to ignore the ostracism of her family. **8**

At the age of 25, on the seventh anniversary of her jailbreak marriage (revealed too late as just another form of entrapment), Simone finally escaped her parents. Describing the day of her decree, the divorcée sounds like so many women whose identity was foreclosed by marriage: "It was like having ten tons of chains removed from my mind, my body— the most exhilarating day of my life." **9**

From Passages, *by Gail Sheehy, © 1974, 1976 by Gail Sheehy. Used by permission of Dutton Signet, a division of Penguin Books, USA, Inc.*

Before You Read

1. Read the title. What does it suggest will be the topic of this reading selection? What might be the central idea?

2. Read the first four words of this selection. What do they suggest to you?

Art Hoppe

Once upon a time there was a man named Snadley Klabberhorn who was   1
the healthiest man in the whole wide world.

Snadley wasn't always the healthiest man in the whole wide world.   2

When he was young, Snadley smoked what he wanted, drank what   3
he wanted, ate what he wanted, and exercised only with young ladies
in bed.

He thought he was happy. "Life is absolutely peachy," he was fond   4
of saying. "Nothing beats being alive."

Then along came the Surgeon General's Report linking smoking to   5
lung cancer, heart disease, emphysema and tertiary coreopsis.

Snadley read about The Great Tobacco Scare with a frown. "Life is so   6
peachy," he said, "that there's no sense taking any risks." So he gave up
smoking.

Like most people who went through the hell of giving up smoking,   7
Snadley became more interested in his own health. In fact, he became
fascinated. And when he read a WCTU tract which pointed out that
alcohol caused liver damage, brain damage, and acute *weltanschauung,*
he gave up alcohol and drank dietary colas instead.

At least he did until The Great Cyclamate Scare.

"There's no sense in taking any risks," he said. And he switched to   8
sugar-sweetened colas, which made him fat and caused dental caries. On
realizing this he renounced colas in favor of milk and took up jogging,
which was an awful bore.

That was about the time of The Great Cholesterol Scare.   9

Snadley gave up milk. To avoid cholesterol, which caused athero-   10
sclerosis, coronary infarcts and chronic chryselephantinism, he also gave
up meat, fats and dairy products, subsisting on a diet of raw fish.

Then came The Great DDT Scare.   11

"The presence of large amounts of DDT in fish . . ." Snadley read   12
with anguish. But fortunately that's when he met Ernestine. They were
made for each other. Ernestine introduced him to homeground wheat
germ, macrobiotic yogurt and organic succotash.

They were very happy eating this dish twice daily, watching six   13
hours of color television together and spending the rest of their time
in bed.

They were, that is, until The Great Color Television Scare.   14

"If color tee-vee does give off radiations," said Snadley, "there's no   15
sense taking risks. After all, we still have each other."

And that's about all they had. Until The Great Pill Scare.   16

On hearing that The Pill might cause carcinoma, thromboses and lin-   17
gering stichometry, Ernestine promptly gave up The Pill—and Snadley.
"There's no sense taking any risks," she said.

Snadley was left with jogging. He was, that is, until he read some-where that 1.3 percent of joggers are eventually run over by a truck or bitten by rabid dogs. 18

He then retired to a bomb shelter in his back yard (to avoid being hit by a meteor), installed an air purifier (after The Great Smog Scare) and spent the next 63 years doing Royal Canadian Air Force exercises and poring over back issues of The Reader's Digest. 19

"Nothing's more important than being alive," he said proudly on reaching 102. But he never did say anymore that life was absolutely peachy. 20

© 1970 by the Chronicle Publishing Company. Reprinted by permission of the author.

Participating Actively in the Writer-Reader Dialogue

What would you do if a friend showed up at your door with something important to tell you? Would you tell her to go ahead and talk while you finished watching a television show? Probably not. If you believed what she had to say was important, you'd invite her in, turn off the TV, and sit down to talk to her. If her message was complicated, you might find yourself asking her to repeat parts of it, or you might repeat to her what you thought she had said. Perhaps you would nod your head as she spoke to show that you were listening to her and understood her.

The point is, when you think something is important, you listen to it *actively*. You ask questions; you look for clarification; you offer your own opinions. Above all, you *participate* in the conversation.

As we said earlier, reading and listening are very similar. Sometimes we read very casually, just as sometimes we listen very casually. After all, not everything needs (or deserves) our rapt attention. But some reading, like some listening, *does* demand our attention. The reading that you will do in college classes will, of course, demand active participation from you. So will reading related to your job or to major decisions that you must make in your life. In each of these cases, you must read in a way that is quite different from the casual way you might read a newspaper in the morning.

So what is active reading? How does one go about it? Here are some steps that you should learn to apply to all the reading you do in your college classes.

Steps for Active Reading

Establish your expectations.   Before you read an article or chapter or book, look at its title. Does it give you an idea of what to expect? Does it sound as if it is announcing its central idea? Read any background information that comes with the reading material. Does it tell you what to expect?

First reading: underline or mark main points.   With a pen, pencil, or highlighter in hand, read the material from start to finish, slowly and carefully. During the first reading, you're trying to get an overall sense of the central idea of the selection.

Don't try to take notes during this first reading. Instead, just underline or highlight sentences or ideas that seem significant to you as you read. Often these sentences will express the thesis of the reading selection or the topic ideas of individual paragraphs. In addition, mark any details or explanations that seem more important than others.

Second reading: annotate.   This step is of major importance if you intend to fully understand what you have read. *Reread* what you underlined. As you do, briefly summarize those points in the margin. If you think a point is especially important, make a note of it in the margin. If you have questions or disagree with something, note that in the margin.

Summarize the reading.   Briefly write out the central idea of the reading. In your own words, state the thesis of the entire essay and the supporting topic ideas of the paragraphs.

Respond to the reading.   Write out your own response to what you have read. Do you agree with the writer's idea? Did it remind you of anything that you have experienced? Did it give you a new insight into its topic? You might write this response in a journal or as an assignment to be used for class discussion. Your instructor will guide you here.

Should you go through these five steps every time you read? Absolutely not. Who would want to underline, annotate, and summarize when relaxing with a good novel on a Saturday afternoon? However, you should take these steps when what you are reading demands close attention—when you read material you must analyze for a report or a paper, for example.

Here is an example of an article that has been read by an active reader:

Printed Noise   — *see last line*

George Will

> The flavor list at the local Baskin-Robbins ice cream shop is an (anarchy) of names like "Peanut Butter 'N Chocolate" and "Strawberry Rhubarb Sherbet." These are not the names of things that reasonable people consider consuming, but the names are admirably businesslike, briskly descriptive.

cuteness in commerce

> Unfortunately, my favorite delight (chocolate-coated vanilla flecked with nuts) bears the unutterable name "Hot Fudge Nutty Buddy," an example of the plague of cuteness in commerce.

a gentleman won't say "Nutty Buddy"!

> There are some things a gentleman simply will not do, and one is announce in public a desire for a "Nutty Buddy." So I usually settle for a plain vanilla cone.

I am not the only person suffering for immutable standards of propriety. The May issue of *Atlantic* contains an absorbing tale of lonely heroism at a Burger King. A gentleman requested a ham and cheese sandwich that the Burger King calls a Yumbo. The girl taking orders was bewildered.

"Oh," she eventually exclaimed, "you mean a Yumbo."

Gentleman: "The ham and cheese. Yes."

Girl, nettled: "It's called a Yumbo. Now, do you want a Yumbo or not?"

Gentleman, teeth clenched: "Yes, thank you, the ham and cheese."

Girl: "Look, I've got to have an order here. You're holding up the line. You want a Yumbo, don't you? You want a Yumbo!"

Whereupon the gentleman chose the straight and narrow path of virtue. He walked out rather than call a ham and cheese a Yumbo. His principles are anachronisms but his prejudices are impeccable and he is on my short list of civilization's friends.

That list includes the Cambridge don who would not appear outdoors without a top hat, not even when routed by fire at 3 A.M., and who refused to read another line of Tennyson after he saw the poet put water in fine port. The list includes another don who, although devoutly Tory, voted Liberal during Gladstone's day because the duties of prime minister kept Gladstone too busy to declaim on Holy Scripture. And high on the list is the grammarian whose last words were: "I am about to—or I am going to—die: either expression is correct."

Gentle reader, can you imagine any of these magnificent persons asking a teenage girl for a "Yumbo"? Or uttering "Fishamagig" or "Egg McMuffin" or "Fribble" (that's a milk shake, sort of)?

At one point in the evolution of American taste, restaurants that were relentlessly fun, fun, fun were built to look like lemons or bananas. I am told that in Los Angeles there was the Toed Inn, a strange spelling for a strange place shaped like a giant toad. Customers entered through the mouth, like flies being swallowed.

But the mature nation has put away such childish things in favor of menus that are fun, fun, fun. Seafood is "From

Neptune's Pantry" or "Denizens of the Briny Deep." And "Surf 'N Turf," which you might think is fish and horsemeat, actually is lobster and beef.

Hamburger names

To be fair, there are practical considerations behind the asphyxiatingly cute names given hamburgers. Many hamburgers are made from portions of the cow that the cow had no reason to boast about. So sellers invent distracting names to give hamburgers cachet. Hence "Whoppers" and "Heroburgers."

Howard Johnson's menu - no excuse

But there is no excuse for Howard Johnson's menu. In a just society it would be a flogging offense to speak of "steerburgers," clams "fried to order" (which probably means they don't fry clams for you unless you order fried clams), a "natural cut" (what is an "unnatural" cut?) of sirloin, "oven-baked" meat loaf, chicken pot pie with "flaky crust," "golden croquettes," "grilled-in-butter Frankforts [sic]," "liver with smothered onions" (smothered by onions?), and a "hearty" Reuben sandwich.

Verbal litter = language becomes printed noise

America is marred by scores of Dew Drop Inns serving "crispy green" salads, "garden fresh" vegetables, "succulent" lamb, "savory" pork, "sizzling" steaks, and "creamy" or "tangy" coleslaw. I've nothing against Homeric adjectives ("wine-dark sea," "wing-footed Achilles") but isn't coleslaw just coleslaw? Americans hear the incessant roar of commerce without listening to it, and read the written roar without really noticing it. Who would notice if a menu proclaimed "creamy steaks and "sizzling" coleslaw? Such verbal litter is to language as Muzak is to music. As advertising blather becomes the

thesis →

nation's normal idiom, language becomes printed noise.

Summary of the Reading

George F. Will calls advertising language, especially the kind we see on menus, "printed noise." He gives examples of many silly or unnecessary names given to food (like the "Yumbo"), and he admires people who resist what he calls "verbal litter."

Personal Response to the Reading

I thought this article was really funny. I remember feeling stupid the first time I had to ask for an "Egg McMuffin." The name sounds like something on a kindergarten menu. But I don't really think about those names anymore. I guess I've just gotten used to them. The article reminded me how much they are all around us, even though I don't notice them. How about "Wienerdude"? That's the stupidest name I've ever heard. When I first heard it, I thought I'd never order one of those, just because the name is so insulting to any intelligent person. But maybe it's really a good hot dog—so I guess I really would order one. I suppose I agree with the article's point that after a while you don't even notice these things anymore. They are like "verbal litter."

Readings

Read each of the following essays *actively*. That is, as you read each essay, *underline or highlight* its thesis statement, topic sentences, and any examples or ideas that seem important to you. Then reread the parts you have marked and *annotate* the essay. Finally, write a brief *summary* of the article and a brief *personal response paragraph*.

Before You Read

1. What are the "freshman blues"? Define what they might mean to you.

2. Have you taken any courses designed to help you through your first year of college? What were they? How did they affect you?

A Required Course in Beating the Freshman Blues

Rene Sanchez

It's early morning in Gerri Strumpf's class at the University of Maryland, and a batch of bleary-eyes freshmen is busy taking notes. Today's lesson: surviving college.   1

Strumpf begins by collecting her students' latest diary entries about campus life. An assistant dean stops by with tips on how to study and pleads, "We really want to get to know you." Then Strumpf details the tasks ahead: a seminar on date rape, assignments on cultural diversity, outlines of every student's academic goals for the next two years.   2

This is "The Student and the University," a semester-long course in which Maryland freshmen earn college credit simply by examining issues in their academic and personal lives. The idea is not unique. At universities across the nation, it has become a prime tactic in ever more elaborate campaigns to keep students happy, improve their social skills and prevent them from quitting or transferring.   3

By some estimates, about one-third of college freshmen nationally don't return for their sophomore years. Many universities have long looked upon the loss of students as either a fact of life or a testament to their academic rigor, but from the Ivy League to large state universities that attitude is being discarded.   4

An age of sensitivity has begun on American campuses, and it is   5
changing how many of them are run. Stung by persistent criticism that
they are indifferent to undergraduates—and competing like never
before to attract and keep students, particularly minorities—hundreds
of universities are creating courses, revamping orientation programs,
redesigning dormitories, and hiring counselors and tutors in an attempt
to ease students' transition to college life.

"What you're seeing is a profound rethinking of a habit and an   6
attitude that has guided how undergraduates have been treated for
generations," says John Gardner, director of freshman programs at the
University of South Carolina. "Colleges are admitting that they have not
done enough to help students. Now they're taking the initiative. They're
being much more intrusive in student lives."

At Maryland, there are 60 sections of the freshman seminar course,   7
including one taught by the university president. At the University of
Michigan, hundreds of freshmen are in a program that requires them to
live in the same dormitory, take the same seminar course on personal
and campus issues and have regular evening talks about it led by staff
members. At the University of Pennsylvania, students attend "life
sketches," skits that promote racial diversity and sexual health and discourage drinking. Students also are taught how to report a crime and use
the campus peer crisis hot line.

For the first time this fall, new students at Florida A&M University   8
could take workshops about dating relationships. There also are men-
only and women-only sessions with topics that range from academics to
the problems in African American communities.

At the University of South Carolina, there's a course called "Uni-   9
versity 101." To forge a common academic experience, all freshmen are
assigned the same novel, which they later discuss in small groups led by
faculty members. At the University of Colorado, which has a "First Year
Experience" office, faculty and administrators are even telephoning new
students a few weeks into the semester to see how they're doing.

An important part of many initiatives is to get senior faculty to   10
devote more time to undergraduates and less to research and writing
projects. That focus reflects the growing concern among university leaders that students need more academic and personal guidance from experienced faculty members and get bored with large lecture classes taught
by graduate students.

One of the freshmen in Strumpf's class illustrated that problem the   11
other day when she explained why she had not completed an assignment
to interview a professor on Maryland's campus. "I don't have one, and
it's hard to find one," she says.

In a recent survey of more than 2,500 colleges, American College   12
Testing, a group that administers a widely used college entrance exam,
reported that one-third of freshmen did not return for their sophomore
years, the highest rate since the survey began in 1983. In a report this
summer, the American Association of State Colleges and Universities
said its members graduate only 40 percent of their freshman after six

years. The report also noted that for years colleges have used the freshman year as a "gatekeeping experience" and judged their academic quality in part by how many students "washed out."

"Now it's considered irresponsible to think that way," says Joyce 13
Jones, an assistant dean of students at Northwestern University.

It's also costly. The drive to make students more comfortable on 14
campus is not merely a matter of conscience. Many universities simply can no longer afford to lose them.

The nation's pool of college-aged students has declined this decade, 15
forcing universities to compete more vigorously against each other. In many states, lawmakers struggling to cut budgets also are taking a hard look at why colleges lose so many students and questioning whether state higher education aid is being used wisely.

"We've been a revolving door," says Strumpf, who directs Mary- 16
land's student orientation programs. "For a long time here at Maryland and other places, people did not care much about how many freshmen stayed or left. But they're worried about it now."

"The bottom line is retention," says Richard Mullendore, vice chan- 17
cellor for student affairs at the University of North Carolina-Wilmington. "Colleges need the tuition."

Others suggest that the new courses and coping programs are sim- 18
ply a sign of the times. With campuses more racially diverse than ever before, there are concerns that minority students in particular are at risk of being ignored, feeling isolated and leaving. Students are also facing difficult questions on other issues—such as AIDS or date rape—that were not cause for alarm a generation ago. For all of those reasons, universities are trying to do more parenting than ever before.

Still, there are worries that the new approaches could coddle stu- 19
dents too much. "There's definitely that risk," Gardner says. Others contend that an important role of college has long been to allow young adults to fend for themselves for the first time, not to have faculty members hold their hands whenever they confront a new problem.

Strumpf insists that's not the intent. "These students still have trem- 20
endous freedoms," she said. "We're only trying to help with some of it. When they first come to campus, they're totally optimistic. But as the semester goes on, and reality sets in, it can be much different than what they expected."

Strumpf's class meets once a week for nearly two hours. She has 21
about two dozen students, all freshmen. The course lasts for three months. Students are graded and earn one college credit. That's standard practice at other universities with similar seminars; most other academic courses are worth three credits. Once a week, either in writing or through electronic mail, students turn in journal entries in which they are supposed to reflect on their campus experiences.

Already this fall, the freshmen in Strumpf's course have taken per- 22
sonality tests to help them decide what kind of career to choose. There

also have been class sessions on time management and studying skills. One session included tips on how using a highlighting pen while reading or working past 8 p.m. might be bad habits.

Soon, as part of a lesson in racial diversity and prejudice, the class will be required to read "The Diary of Anne Frank" and will visit the Holocaust Museum to learn how intense hatred can be.   23

Many other universities have designed similar courses. The University of South Carolina's "University 101," for example, includes sessions on public speaking, study skills, campus diversity, and "sex and the college student."   24

The students in Strumpf's class say they welcome the help. Midway through their first semester, many are facing problems they never anticipated a few months ago—such as struggling in courses that seemed easy in high school, second-guessing the major they selected, getting little sleep, or sitting in classes for the first time with many students of other races or from other countries.   25

"There's so much going on in your head all of a sudden—it's draining," says Kevin Davidson, 18, a freshman from southern Maryland. "Managing your time is hard. You have so many new things to worry about."   26

"It can be intimidating," says Anna Paule, 18, a freshman from Olney, Maryland. "It's nothing like high school. Everything was basically done for you there. Being on your own like this can be tough. But this class gives good directions."   27

Chanda Littlefield, a freshman from Hyattsville, Maryland, says that at first the size of the campus community and its racial diversity can be daunting. "It's good to have a class like this where you can ask questions and try to figure things out," she says.   28

Some universities are going beyond course work to help undergraduates by hiring more counselors and tutors. Others, like Michigan, are trying to create "learning communities" of freshmen by placing them in the same seminar class and the same dormitory wing staffed with veteran students trained to lead discussion groups.   29

Several hundred randomly chosen students are taking part in Michigan's housing program, which began several years ago and is rapidly being expanded. More than 1,000 students are also taking freshman seminar courses there.   30

To keep class sizes small and have senior professors to teach them, the university is spending several hundred thousand dollars to hire more faculty and staff members.   31

"This has become a priority," says Mary Hummel, who directs the program. "Large colleges are always accused of not paying enough attention to their students, especially the new ones. That's what we're trying to break down. We've finally realized that helping students succeed takes much more than what we've been doing."   32

Suggestions for Summarizing

1. Does this article seem to be *explaining* what colleges are now doing or *arguing* a point about what they should be doing? As you summarize the article's central idea, write a sentence that reflects which approach the article is taking.

2. After you state the central idea of the article, write one sentence of summary for each major supporting section of the article.

Suggestions for Personal Responses

1. In what ways do your own experiences during your first semester in college correspond to those described in this article?

2. Have you taken any courses similar to the University of Maryland's "The Student and the University," courses designed to help you adjust to college life? If you have, what was your reaction to them?

3. Did you feel isolated and ignored during your first few months in college? Why or why not? What might have helped to change that experience?

4. Talk to other members of the class or to people you know about their early experiences in college. Were their experiences difficult ones? Would programs such as those described in Sanchez's article have helped them?

Before You Read

1. Consider the title. Define what "living mindlessly" might mean.

2. What is your answer to the question in the title? Explain why you respond as you do.

Are You Living Mindlessly?

Michael Ryan

Have you ever been mindless?   1

That's not thoughtless, it's mindless—and we all have been. You've   2
been mindless if you've ever "zoned out" and missed a highway exit; if
you've put the cereal in the refrigerator and the milk in the cupboard; or
if you've mumbled "you too" when the airport cab driver wishes you a
good flight—even though you knew you were catching a plane and he
wasn't. Psychologists call this "automaticity"—putting your brain on
autopilot and giving the usual responses, even if you aren't in the appropriate situation.

"Being mindless means you're not there," said Ellen Langer, a pro-   3
fessor of psychology at Harvard who is the author of *Mindfulness* and
The Power of Mindful Learning. "You're not in the moment and aware of
everything going on around you." I had gone to Cambridge, Massachuestts, to talk with Langer about mindlessness and its opposite, mindfulness, and how switching from one to the other can enrich our lives.

The penalty for mindlessness—letting ourselves operate without thinking in a situation we think we're familiar with—can be as minor as missing our highway exit or finding warm milk in the cupboard. But mindlessness also can lead to failure, frustration—even tragedy.

Many of us learn to live mindlessly in our earliest schooldays. "Too often, we teach people things like, 'There's a right way and a wrong way to do everything, regardless of the circumstances,'" Langer explained. "What we should be teaching them is how to think flexibly, to be mindful of all the different possibilities of every situation and not close themselves off from information that could help them."

"I love tennis," Langer continued. "When I was younger, I went to a tennis camp, and they taught me how to hold a racket when I served. Years later, I was watching the U.S. Open, and I realized that not one of the players held the racket that way." Langer saw that the world's best players had put thought and energy into developing a grip and a serve best suited to their individual talents.

"The problem comes in the way we learn," Langer said. "We are rarely taught conditionally: 'This might be a good grip for you.' Usually, we're taught: 'This is the right grip.'" Being mindful—using imagination and creativity to learn what works best for you—is what makes the difference between an average player and a champ.

Langer served up other examples, like the woman who always cut one end off her holiday roasts before putting them into the oven. The woman explained that her mother had always done it that way. The mother, in turn, said it was what her own mother did. When they approached the matriarch, the old woman told them that, as a young bride, she had a very small oven and had been forced to cook her meat in two parts. Mindlessly, the habit had been passed down for generations, long after the need for it had disappeared.

"If you ask most people, 'Is there more than one way to look at anything?' they'll say, 'Of course,'" Langer said. "But it's remarkable that so many go through life with a single-minded lens. It's not that they wouldn't agree with other perspectives. It just doesn't occur to them to look."

In one experiment, psychologists provided a group of subjects with simple objects and asked them to explain their use. The answers were straightforward: a screwdriver turned screws, a sheet covered a bed, etc. But when they were asked what else the items could be used for, people's creativity burst forth: the sheet could be used as a tent for someone shipwrecked; the screwdriver could be a tent peg, and so on. "When people see that there's more than one way of looking at things, they become mindful," Langer said.

Langer and her colleagues have conducted a wide range of experiments, which she documents in her two books. In one experiment, students were given a reading assignment: Half were told simply to learn the material, while the other half were told to think about what they were reading in ways that made it meaningful to their own lives. When they were tested later, the second group—the ones who thought about what they had read instead of just "learning" it the old-fashioned way—scored far higher.

"The way you cultivate mindfulness," Langer said, "is to realize that information about the world around you is endlessly interesting, and it looks different from different perspectives." But many people operate mindlessly, pursuing routines rather than looking for new details around them. The results can be disastrous. 12

Investigations of both the Three Mile Island and Chernobyl nuclear accidents found evidence that technicians—numbed into mindlessness by years of routine—had failed to respond in time to changes in instrument readings that would have told them accidents were about to happen. The most widely accepted theory of how Korean Air Lines Flight 007 went astray—it flew into Soviet airspace and was shot down by an air-to-air missile—holds that the pilots entered incorrect coordinates into their compass. Then, literally on autopilot, they ignored cues from the 747's computers to reconsider their course. Like a driver who has traveled the same highway a hundred times, they expected no problems and saw none. 13

At its worst, mindlessness can help to destroy people's lives, as Langer found in 1974, when she was studying patients and workers in nursing homes. "I argued that we should go around nursing homes making life more complex, not easier," she said. "It's important for people to be in control of their lives, and the way to be in control is to be in the active process of mastering something. It's in the mastering that mindfulness comes in." Langer found that patients who lived in the wards where they were required to take charge of much of their daily routine—dressing themselves or choosing food—had lower mortality rates than people in comparable health who lived in the wards where attendants and nurses saw to all their needs. Langer also found that nursing-home workers who were taught to think mindfully about their work were less likely to quit. "If the workers realize that much of the burnout they experience is the result of mindless over-rhythmization, turnover goes down by a third," she reported. 14

Langer told me that mindlessness is also at the root of prejudice—but she said the way to solve it was with *more* discrimination, not less. "Prejudice comes from the mindless assumption that there are nonoverlapping categories," she explained. "You're either black or white, Jew or non-Jew. Most people, if they go far enough into their backgrounds, will find that they are not purebreds. The mistake we make in dealing with prejudice is trying to counter it by saying we're all one big human group, we're all the same." 15

Langer reasoned that, if we are mindful of each other's individual characteristics—not just race and religion but also height, weight, talent, even hair color—we will understand that each human being is unique. 16

We can be mindful in any situation, Langer said—even when faced with huge challenges. "If all you think about is how you're likely to fail at a challenge, you probably will," she said. "But if you ask yourself, 17

'What are 10 ways I could succeed at this?' your chances of success are much greater. Just noticing new things keeps you alive."

First published in Parade. *Copyright © 1998 by Michael Ryan. Reprinted by permission of* Parade *and Scovil Chichak Galen Literary Agency on behalf of the author.*

Suggestions for Summarizing

1. Is the central idea of this article concerned with the way we should live or the way we *do* live? Or both? Write a sentence that states the central idea of the article.

2. Write three or four more sentences to summarize the major supporting ideas that are presented in the article.

Suggestions for Personal Responses

1. Have you ever acted mindlessly or observed people who did? Describe some examples from your experiences or observations. What were the consequences of such actions?

2. Describe situations from your experiences or observations that could illustrate acting mindfully. Explain why they illustrate mindful actions.

3. Talk to other members of the class about the concepts of acting mindlessly and mindfully. Do you understand what Ellen Langer means by the terms? Develop more examples to illustrate each term.

Assignments: Writing a Personal Response

1. Write a paper that responds to one of the following questions about "A Required Course in Beating the Freshman Blues."

   a. Analyze your first semester at college. Was it a pleasant, successful experience, a difficult, disconcerting one, or a little of both? As you develop examples to illustrate your points, explain your thoughts and reactions in an effort to help your reader understand why you reacted the way you did.

   b. What do you see as the most serious problems an entering college student faces? Write a paper in which you use your own experiences or those of people you know to illustrate and explain your points.

   c. Have you taken any courses similar to those described in the article? If you have, explain why they were or were not helpful, illustrating your points with examples. If you have not taken such courses, do you think they might have helped you? Explain why or why not, using examples to support your points.

2. Write a paper that responds to one of the following questions about "Are You Living Mindlessly?"

   a. According to Ellen Langer, acting mindlessly "can lead to failure, frustration—even tragedy." Think about your own experiences and observations. Are you aware of situations in which acting mindlessly resulted in serious consequences? Are failure, frustration, and tragedy the only serious consequences of mindless behavior? Write a paper in which you illustrate and explain the results of acting mindlessly. Explain your examples and ideas as clearly and as thoroughly as you can.

    b. Langer defines "mindfulness" a number of ways. Write a paper in which you consider several different ways of understanding the term. Illustrate each idea with examples and explanations drawn from your own experiences and observations.

    c. Considering what mindfulness means to you, write a paper in which you identify areas of life that could be improved if you or others acted more "mindfully." Use specific examples to illustrate your points, and explain your ideas fully and clearly.

3.   Write a paper that responds to one of the following questions about "Printed Noise."

    a. George Will describes some of the ridiculous ways restaurants will name or advertise their food. If you think his observations have merit, write a paper that gives examples of your own. If you would like to, use a different type of product, such as cigarettes, liquor, cars, or grocery items. If you think Will is overreacting or has missed the purpose of such advertising, write a paper that explains why, and illustrate your points with examples of actual products.

    b. George Will has focused on one specific change in our culture—the trend toward silly names of food items in restaurants. Are there other specific cultural changes that you object to? Think of the places you visit, the people you see, the situations you encounter. Choose one particular change that you object to and illustrate it with examples from your own experiences and observations. Explain what you find objectionable as you present each example.

Evaluating Sample Papers

Using the Student Model Checklist on pages 24 and 25, evaluate the effectiveness of the following student essays.

Student Essay 1

Reading George Will's article made me realize that I am bothered by many changes in our culture. I don't like the way that people have changed the way they drive around ambulances. As a driver on the road I have seen ambulance drivers experience rudeness in the worst ways.

For example one day I heard sirens and immediately looked for the direction the ambulance was coming in so to be prepared. A car coming to the left of me seemed to do nothing to prepare, so the driver either did not hear the sirens or did not care. He continued to drive but at the last minute he panicked, for now the ambulance was directly behind him, and he didn't know where to go. The driver is entirely rude because it slows down the ambulance from getting to its destination.

Another time I witnessed a car that had to have seen the ambulance coming in the drivers' direction, but still kept on driving as he watched the ambulance speed by. What I had just witnessed left me in awe wondering if these kinds of drivers think they are excluded from the pull over and wait law! I see many drivers do this but have never seen anyone be cited. The law needs to be enforced to act as a reminder to those who are not just rude but endangering lives.

Finally the worst rudeness I have seen on the road is the drivers who think they can make it through an intersection before the ambulance, so they do not have to wait. I actually have witnessed this near miss myself. I saw a black pick-up in front of me and the driver looking to see where the sirens were coming from. The ambulance was speeding towards us from the right hand side of the road. I pulled over, but to my dismay the pick-up hit the gas and flew through the intersection just seconds before the ambulance. How the driver made it without causing an accident I still do not know.

These kinds of people also have no idea to the lives they are putting endanger. The endangerment is more than the life in question or the ambulance drivers but also the idiots who impose this potential hazard. This type of driving should not be tolerated and the drivers need to be reminded of the dangers involved when not following the rules of the road.

Student Essay 2

In the article "A Required Course in Beating the Freshman Blues" Rene Sanchez gave her opinions of how colleges are reevaluating their roles in keeping freshman college students enrolled. I was reminded how I reacted to my first semester at college, and I can see that I was full of many different emotions. I was bewildered by the entire experience, and was amazed by the constant flow of homework thrown at me, which gave me no time for working or a social life.

On my first day of the semester I had become bewildered and forgot my entire schedule, so I ran up to my counselor and asked Mary if she could provide me with a copy of my schedule of classes. She quickly handed me my schedule and sent me on my way. As I walked into English class other students starred at me, making me feel very uncomfortable, and I was hoping class would be over quickly. Other students in the class quickly melted the thick layer of ice I felt as I walked in, and I became happy with my choice of class. I was weary of my English instructor, a very strict and precise teacher. As I walked bewildered into my math class I was greeted by another gauntlet of students with hard stares. The teacher was very prompt and came quickly to the front of the classroom. She looked heavily at the students and took attendance; in addition, she stated if we were there to waste time then leave now. I became tense after looking at the syllabus, noticing that I was going to need a lot of help. I soon realized that I had taken too many classes that summer semester, and quickly opted to take the credit/no credit option offered at the college. I stayed in the class throughout the semester. I was amazed and irritated at the constant flow of homework that never seemed to disappear.

In the following weeks I became terrified of failing and trying to keep current on assignments. I seeked the help of tutors because I was getting further and further behind in my math studies. I turned in my English assignments on time, but I needed additional help. I studied with two fellow students named Laura and Loretta who were finding English just as difficult as I did. We tried to help each other on occasions with our studies, yet we just became more confused and irritated. Still failing math class and getting a chronic cough due to stress. I strived not to give up on my classes. During the semester I was finding it difficult to do much more than study and sleep; consequently my social life took a deep drop. I questioned my goals of continuing with my education, but decided to continue after many friends rallied me on to finish what I had begun. Overall I found the semester to be a rewarding and difficult challenge. I became confused, terrified, and anxious about my classes.

By my next semester I had begun to feel the financial aspect of not working full time, so I started to inquire around campus for part time work. I received an invitation to work for Disabled Students Program and Services; and became a part time employee at the college. I have learned to interact with fellow students and to assist when I see a person who looks puzzled or irritated. I have learned how to deal with many different people and situations around campus and the work has provided enough extra money to keep me in school. The teachers who pushed me have given me the tools for learning, but only I can use the tools. Looking back on my first semester, I found that I am learning now because of the difficulty put upon me by those teachers who did care about my education.

Student Essay 3

In the article "Are You Living Mindlessly?," Michael Ryan explains that "mindlessness" is lacking control of our responses in particular situations that we believe are familiar to us. A simple example of mindless behavior is putting milk in the cupboard and cereal in the refrigerator without thinking about it. Michael Ryan cites several examples from a psychology professor, Ellen Langer, to indicate different mindless behaviors. Ryan and Langer believe mindlessness can cause problems in our lives because it limits our minds from seeing different possibilities. Langer suggests that we should always think creatively and flexibly to prevent mindless behavior. I agree with Langer that acting mindlessly is a dangerous human behavior which confines our creativity and makes us narrow-minded; however, we may defeat narrow-mindedness by thinking creatively and flexibly.

Mindlessness makes us narrow-minded by limiting our behavior and creativity, but these limiting behaviors and creations may be overcome by using our imaginations. Ellen Langer's example of one woman who habitually would cut one end of her holiday turkey before putting it in the oven just because her mother had done it that way demonstrated narrow-mindedness. This example reminded me of the time when I could not accept how my roommate, Natalie, made miso soup. The way she was making it did not seem right to me since it was not the way that I had learned to make it from my mother. Miso soup is a Japanese tradition that is a simple side dish with one or two vegetables in it; however, Natalie cooked it with garlic, tomatoes, bell peppers, carrots and cabbage and called it "miso soup." I instantly said "It is not miso soup." Because of my cultural tradition, I could not see any other way to make it. Even though Natalie's soup did not look like miso soup to me, it ended up tasting better than mine; as a result, now I have started making miso soup in my own creative way. I have become more open minded and creative after this experience, and it has helped me to improve my cooking skills. The way I reacted made Natalie feel uncomfortable. I agree with Langer, and I think that I can try to improve my behavior by being more flexible.

In addition to narrow-minded behavior regarding recipes and eating traditions, mindlessness can cause misunderstandings in relationships, but these misunderstandings may be overcome by thinking flexibly and seeing everyone as unique. Langer says that mindlessness assumption can cause prejudice; for example, people see either "black or white, Jew or non-Jew." This example led me to think about the times when I could not think any other possible situations except "black or white." One of my situations was when I noticed my food was disappearing almost every time I came home. I was mad and just assumed that my roommate was eating my food to take advantage of me. I could not accept another cause for the food's disappearance. I found out later that she'd had a head injury from a car accident; consequently, it became a struggle for her not to eat the food around her whenever she felt lonely. I realized how inflexible I was in judging my friend. My false judgment caused me to misunderstand my roommate. This experience proved to me that mindless behavior can hurt relationships. I agree with Langer, and I think that I want to be more flexible to see individuals' unique personalities.

Thinking creatively and flexibly helped me to improve my cooking skills and to have better friendships. These experiences opened up my eyes to see different possibilities in similar situations. I agree with Langer that acting mindlessly limits our views to familiar things and damages our lives because it prevents us from living creatively and flexibly.

Sentence Combining: Coordination

In Chapter 1, you practiced *embedding* simple modifiers (adjectives, adverbs, and prepositional phrases) next to the words they modify in a sentence. Such embedding may have seemed rather easy to you, for it is something we all learned to do quite automatically at an early age. (Almost everyone would automatically change "I wrote a letter. It was long." to "I wrote a long letter.") However, not all combining of related ideas is as easily performed. As writers become more and more proficient, they develop the ability to create quite sophisticated sentence structures as well as very simple ones—but they develop that ability gradually, after much practice.

In this section, you will practice *coordinating* ideas. Like embedding simple modifiers, the process of coordination can be natural and easy. However, effective coordination also has its complexities, which we will take up in this section.

Using Coordinating Conjunctions

Coordination consists of joining ideas that are grammatically alike, usually by using one of the seven **coordinating conjunctions:** *and, but, or, nor, for, so,* and *yet.* You can easily memorize these seven conjunctions by learning the acronym BOYSFAN. (An acronym is a word made up from the first letters of other words.)

But Or Yet So For And Nor

Of course, when we talk, we use each of these seven words all of the time. They are so common to our language, in fact, that we rarely think about them. When we want to join two ideas, it takes practically no thought at all to stick an *and* or a *but* or some other coordinating conjunction into our speech and to go on.

Writing, however, is more precise than speech. When someone else reads what we have written, we are usually not there to clarify things that might be confusing, so a careful choice of words the first time through is much more important in writing than in speech. For instance, is there a difference between these two sentences?

> Huck Finn was very superstitious, and he knew he was in trouble when he spilled the salt.

> Huck Finn was very superstitious, so he knew he was in trouble when he spilled the salt.

Both sentences suggest a relationship between the ideas of Huck's being superstitious and of his spilling the salt, but only the second sentence is *precise* in stating the relationship clearly. By using the word *so,* the second sentence makes it clear that Huck's belief about spilling salt was a *result* of his being superstitious.

When you use the coordinating conjunctions, keep their *precise* meanings in mind:

> **And** suggests *addition.* It is used to "add" one idea to a similar one.
>
> My grass needs to be mowed, <u>and</u> my garden needs to be weeded.

> **Nor** also suggests *addition,* but it adds two negative ideas.
>
> I have not mowed my lawn in the past two weeks, <u>nor</u> have I weeded the garden.

> **But** suggests a *contrast* or *opposition.*
>
> I should mow the lawn today, <u>but</u> I think I'll watch a movie instead.

> **Yet** also suggests a *contrast* or *opposition.*
>
> I feel guilty about not mowing the lawn, <u>yet</u> I really don't want to work today.

Or suggests *alternatives.*

> I will mow the lawn tomorrow, <u>or</u> perhaps I'll wait until next weekend.

For suggests a *cause.*

>   *(cause)*
> My yard is becoming the neighborhood eyesore, <u>for</u> I hate to do yardwork.

So suggests a *result* relationship.

>   *(result)*
> My neighbors have stopped talking to me, <u>so</u> maybe I should clean up my yard today.

Exercise 2.2

Combine the following sentences using the coordinating conjunctions that most accurately express the relationship between them.

Example

> The forecast was for rain with strong winds. I decided to cancel our picnic.

> The forecast was for rain with strong winds, <u>so</u> I decided to cancel our picnic.

1. Many ideas have been suggested to improve automobiles. Some are much stranger than others.

2. In 1926, Leander Pilton decided to design a car that could be parked almost anywhere. He had grown tired of looking for a parking space.

3. He added a platform with rollers to the back of his car. Then he tried to tip the car onto its end.

4. His plan was to roll the car into a parking space that was slightly larger than the size of a refrigerator. His plan had some flaws.

5. He never explained how he would tip the car onto its end. He did not say how he would prevent the gas, oil, and water from draining out of the car while it was standing on end.

6. Charles Ramage was terribly bored with normal driving. He invented a somersaulting automobile.

7. He combined an engine with a simple chassis. Then he placed a semicircular roll bar around the entire vehicle.

8. He could drive down the street like any ordinary driver. He could flip a lever that would turn the car over onto its front end.

9. The vehicle's momentum would keep it rolling forward. It was able to turn a complete somersault in the middle of the street.

10. Ramage's automobile was fun to watch. It was not very welcome on city streets. ■

Exercise 2.3

Each of the following sentences uses *and* as a coordinating conjunction. Where needed, change the *and* to a more precise and accurate coordinating conjunction. Some of the sentences may not need to be changed.

Example

> Last year I spent $300 on a membership to a local gym, <u>and</u> I used the gym only two times all year long.
>
> Last year I spent $300 on a membership to a local gym, but I used the gym only two times all year long.

1. The horn of a rhinoceros is one of its unique features, <u>and</u> the commercial value of that feature threatens the survival of the rhinoceros.

2. Rhino horns are sought by many poachers, <u>and</u> they are currently worth more than their weight in gold.

3. In some cultures rhino-horn walking sticks are symbols of prestige, <u>and</u> in other cultures rhino-horn products are used for everything from headaches to labor pains.

4. In North Yemen, daggers carved from rhino horns were so expensive, costing as much as $12,000, that very few people could buy them, <u>and</u> today oil wealth has put that price within reach of many Yemeni.

5. Today, an East African farmer can double his annual income by killing a single rhino, <u>and</u> the temptation to hunt rhinos illegally is hard to resist.

6. Game wardens may try to stop poachers, <u>and</u> they may themselves be lured into this very lucrative activity.

7. Rhinos are not difficult to approach, <u>and</u> they are not hard to kill with today's advanced weapons.

8. Professional poachers today use many sophisticated hunting techniques, <u>and</u> they are able to decimate entire populations of rhinos with very little effort.

9. One can tell that the mature rhino is disappearing, <u>and</u> the average size of the illegal rhino horn has dropped 60% since 1973.

10. The poachers cut off the horns of the dead rhinos, <u>and</u> then they ship the horns out of the country. ▪

In each of the above exercises and examples, a comma has been placed before the coordinating conjunction because the statements being combined could stand alone as separate sentences. However, when a coordinating conjunction joins two sentence parts that can *not* stand alone as separate sentences, do not use a comma before the conjunction. (For a further discussion of this comma rule, see Chapter 17.)

Example

Comma

Mario worked all night on the new computer program, and his brother worked with him.

No comma

Mario worked all night on the new computer program and all the next day on his accounting work.

Using Semicolons

So far, we have seen that using a comma and a coordinating conjunction is one way to combine related sentences. Another way to combine sentences is to use a *semicolon,* usually (but not always) with a conjunctive adverb. Here are some common **conjunctive adverbs:**

accordingly	however	otherwise	for example
also	instead	similarly	for instance
besides	meanwhile	still	in addition
consequently	moreover	then	in fact
finally	namely	therefore	on the other hand
further	nevertheless	thus	
furthermore	next	undoubtedly	
hence	nonetheless	as a result	

Examples

Henry ate all of the potato chips; however, he was still hungry.

Tuan knew that he should buy a new car; on the other hand, he really wanted a motorcycle.

The movie was too violent for Sabrina; the concert was too dull for Rocky.

If you use a semicolon to combine related sentences, remember these points:

1. Most writers—professional and nonprofessional—use semicolons *much less frequently* than the other methods of combining sentences that are discussed in this and other sections.

2. Conjunctive adverbs *are not* coordinating conjunctions and should *not be used to combine sentences with commas.*

Examples

Incorrect

Sylvia had always wanted to visit the Far East, however she never had enough money to do so.

Correct

Sylvia had always wanted to visit the Far East; however, she never had enough money to do so.

3. It is the *semicolons* that join sentences, not the conjunctive adverbs. As a result, conjunctive adverbs may appear *anywhere that makes sense* in the sentence.

Examples

It rained for fifteen straight days. <u>Nevertheless</u>, my father jogged every day.

It rained for fifteen straight days; my father, <u>nevertheless</u>, jogged every day.

It rained for fifteen straight days; my father jogged every day, <u>nevertheless</u>.

Exercise 2.4

Combine the following sentences, either by using a comma with a coordinating conjunction or by using a semicolon with or without a conjunctive adverb.

Example

Hillary wanted to attend college full-time. She needed to work forty hours a week to support her family.

Hillary wanted to attend college full-time, but she needed to work forty hours a week to support her family.

or

Hillary wanted to attend college full-time; however, she needed to work forty hours a week to support her family.

1. For hundreds of years, people have considered the number thirteen to be unlucky. Surveys have shown that the fear of the number thirteen is the most widespread of all bad-luck superstitions.

2. The French, for instance, never issue the house address thirteen. The Italian national lottery omits the number thirteen.

3. Americans also fear the number thirteen. Modern skyscrapers, condominiums, and apartment buildings label the floor that follows twelve as fourteen.

4. When a new luxury apartment building labeled a floor thirteen, it rented units on all other floors. It could rent only a few units on the thirteenth floor.

5. The owners recognized the problem. They changed the floor number to twelve-B and were soon able to rent out the rest of the apartments.

6. Fear of the number thirteen has been attributed to the Last Supper, when Christ with his apostles numbered thirteen. It has an older source in Norse mythology.

7. According to Norse mythology, the evil god Loki grew angry when he was not invited to a banquet with twelve other gods. He decided to attend anyway, bringing the total to thirteen.

8. The other gods battled Loki. Balder, the favorite of the gods, was killed.

9. In the United States, thirteen should be considered a lucky number. The nation started with thirteen colonies.

10. On the Great Seal of the United States, the bald eagle holds in one claw an olive branch with thirteen leaves and thirteen berries. It holds in the other claw thirteen arrows. ◼

Combining Parts of Sentences

So far, we have focused on using coordination to combine *separate sentences*. Another way to improve your writing is to use a coordinating conjunction to join *part* of one sentence to *part* of another sentence. This type of sentence combining is more difficult than the simple joining of entire sentences, but it usually results in more concise and direct writing. For instance, here are two sentences as they might have been written by Gail Sheehy in "Jailbreak Marriage." The parts of each sentence that could be combined are underlined.

> Simone was the last domain <u>where her mother could play out the maternal role</u>. She was also the last place <u>where her father could exercise complete control</u>.

Of course, Sheehy recognized that these two ideas could really be expressed as one sentence, so she wrote this:

> Simone was the last domain <u>where her mother could play out the maternal role</u> and <u>where her father could exercise complete control</u>.

Here is another example, taken from "A Required Course in Beating the Freshman Blues," by Rene Sanchez. When discussing the program at the University of Michigan, Sanchez could have written three sentences. The parts of each sentence that could be combined are underlined.

> At the University of Michigan, hundreds of freshmen are in a program that requires them to <u>live in the same dormitory</u>. These freshmen must also <u>take the same seminar course on personal and campus issues</u>. Finally, to help them make good use of each seminar, they <u>have regular evening talks about it led by staff members</u>.

Here is how Sanchez actually wrote the sentence:

> At the University of Michigan, hundreds of freshmen are in a program that requires them to <u>live in the same dormitory</u>, <u>take the same seminar course on personal and campus issues</u> and <u>have regular evening talks about it led by staff members</u>.

Note When joining three or more items, as has been done here, you need to use the coordinating conjunction only before the last item.

Parallel Sentence Structure

When you use coordination to join ideas, you should do your best to word those ideas similarly so they are clear and easy to read. Coordinate ideas that are worded similarly are said to be parallel in structure. Notice the difference between the following two examples:

Nonparallel Structure

> My favorite sports are <u>swimming</u> and <u>to jog</u>.

Parallel Structure

> My favorite sports are <u>swimming</u> and <u>jogging</u>.

Do you see how much clearer the parallel sentence is? Now let's look once more at the examples from the articles by Gail Sheehy and Rene Sanchez. Notice how the coordinate ideas have been written so that they are parallel in structure.

> Simone was the last domain
>
>   <u>where her mother could play out the maternal role</u>
>
> and <u>where her father could exercise complete control</u>.

> At the University of Michigan, hundreds of freshmen are in a program that requires them to
>
>   <u>live in the same dormitory</u>,
>
>   <u>take the same seminar course on personal and campus issues</u>
>
> and <u>have regular evening talks about it led by staff members</u>.

As you can see, recognizing related ideas and combining them in parallel structure can result in sentences that are more direct and less repetitious than the original sentences.

Note For a more thorough discussion of parallel sentence structure, see Chapter 6.

Exercise 2.5

Combine each group of sentences into one sentence by using coordinating conjunctions to join related ideas. Wherever possible, use parallel sentence structure. Parallel ideas that can be combined are underlined in the first three groups.

Example

> People <u>who stereotype others</u> are often insensitive to the pain they cause. The same is true for people <u>who tell ethnic jokes</u>.

> People <u>who stereotype others</u> or <u>who tell ethnic jokes</u> are often insensitive to the pain they cause.

1. According to legend, Calamity Jane was <u>a fierce Indian fighter</u>. She also was <u>a brave scout</u>. In addition, legend describes her as <u>a beautiful, vivacious tamer of the Old West</u>.

2. In reality, however, she often brought misfortune <u>into her own life</u>. She brought misfortune <u>into the lives of others</u>, too.

3. Although born in Princeton, Missouri, she spent most of her life in Deadwood, South Dakota, a town notorious for its collection of <u>miners</u> and <u>Civil War veterans</u>. It was also full of <u>gamblers</u> and <u>outlaws</u>, and it was the home of many <u>prostitutes</u>.

4. It is said that she drank as heavily as any mule skinner. In addition, she cursed as coarsely as the roughest of men.

5. Calamity's life was characterized by drunkenness. It was also full of lawlessness. It even included prostitution.

6. Dime-store novels helped to spread her legend by describing her as a natural beauty. She was referred to as the sweetheart of Wild Bill Hickok.

7. Calamity Jane did know Wild Bill Hickok. She was part of his gang for a while, but there is no evidence that he romanced her. There is also no evidence that he even paid much attention to her.

8. Easterners viewed the westward movement as adventurous. To them, it was romantic. It was exciting, so they preferred stories that idealized the West. They also liked stories that made their heroes seem larger than life.

9. Calamity Jane may have received her nickname from her many hard-luck experiences. It may also have come from the problems she caused others. It may even have resulted from her willingness to help victims of smallpox during an epidemic in Deadwood.

10. In her last years, Calamity drifted from place to place, selling a poorly written leaflet about her life. She also could be found performing as a sharpshooter in Wild West shows. In addition, she performed as a wild driver of six-horse teams in these same shows. ■

Chapter 3

Supporting the Central Idea

Poor Irving! He wants a nice, fuzzy, somewhat vague relationship, but Cathy wants specifics. She wants Irving to explain *why* he had a great time, to elaborate upon what was great about it. We're often the same way, aren't we? If we ask a friend how he or she liked a movie, we're not usually satisfied with answers like "Great!" or "Yuck!" We want to know specifically *why* the person liked or disliked it. Was it the plot or the acting or the special effects or the quality of the popcorn that caused our friend to react in a certain way? The more specific our friend can be, the more he or she will help us to decide whether we want to see the film too.

The same is true of responses to other media, such as novels and television, or to public issues, such as elections or gun control or capital punishment. The more specific information we have on these issues, the better informed our decisions will be.

In the same way, the more you can support your topic sentence or your thesis statement with specific information, the more convincing your writing will be. The most common types of support are brief or extended examples, statistics, and expert opinion or testimony.

Brief Examples

From Personal Experience or Direct Observation

One of the most interesting and convincing ways to support your ideas is by relating brief examples drawn from your own personal experiences or observations. When we are discussing issues casually with acquaintances, we just naturally share our own experiences. Note how several brief examples are used in the following paragraph to support its central idea.

> People, at least the ones in my town, seem to have become ruder as the population has increased. Twice yesterday drivers came up behind me and gestured rudely even though I was driving ten miles per hour over the speed limit. The other day, as my friend and I were sitting on the seawall watching the sunset and listening to the ocean waves, a rollerblader with a boom box going full blast sat down next to us. When we politely asked him to turn off his radio, he cursed at us and skated off. Every day I see perfectly healthy people parking in spaces reserved for the handicapped, smokers lighting up in no-smoking areas and refusing to leave when asked, and people shoving their way into lines at movie theaters and grocery stores.

Personal examples are usually not enough to prove a point, but they do help to illustrate your ideas and make your writing more specific and interesting. In fact, good writing is always moving from the general to the specific, with the emphasis on the specific, and the use of brief examples is one of the most effective ways of keeping your writing interesting, convincing, and informative. Notice how the lack of examples in the following paragraph results in uninteresting, lackluster writing.

> There are a lot of animals to be found in Carlsbad. They come in all sizes and shapes. There are all kinds of birds and other animals besides dogs and cats.

Now let's see if it can be improved with the addition of brief examples.

> The typical yard in Carlsbad is visited by a wide variety of animals. Birds, especially, are present in abundance. House finches and sparrows flit through the trees and search the ground for seeds. Mockingbirds sing day and night, claiming their territory. The feisty and mischievous scrub jays, with their blue plumage, raid the food set out for cats. The homely California towhee, whose call sounds like a squeaky wheel, rustles among the fallen leaves looking for insects. And the exotic and mysterious ruby-throated hummingbirds go from flower to flower, searching for nectar, or visit feeders hung out for them. At night the slow-witted possum rambles about, getting into garbage cans and dog dishes. The elegant and clever raccoons compete with the possums. Occasionally one can sense that a skunk has visited someone's yard. In some places, bands of escaped domestic rabbits can be seen frolicking and raiding gardens. Lizards and snakes ply the underbrush, searching for insects and small rodents. If one is observant and lucky, one can experience a multitude of critters right in the backyard.

As you can see, the many brief, specific examples in this paragraph improve it immensely, giving it texture, color, and interest. They also make the writing believable. Any reader would easily be convinced that this writer knows what he is talking about and has taken the time to observe the animals in Carlsbad carefully and to report them accurately.

From Other Sources

Brief examples from other sources are quite similar to brief personal examples or anecdotes. They may come from places such as books, magazines, television, films, or lectures, or they may come from the experiences of people you know. Like personal examples, they make your abstract ideas and arguments concrete and therefore convincing.

Here are some brief examples from recent news broadcasts that were offered in support of a gun control bill:

> Larry and Sharon Ellingsen were driving home from their 29th wedding anniversary party in Oakland, California, when a passing driver on the freeway sent a bullet through their window, killing Mr. Ellingsen instantly.

> Mildred Stanfield, a 78-year-old church organist from quiet Broad Ripple, Indiana, was shot twice in the chest at a bus stop when she tried to stop a 15-year-old boy from stealing her purse.

> Cesar Sandoval, a 6-year-old kindergartener, was shot in the head while riding home on a country school bus in New Haven, Connecticut. He and six classmates were caught in drug-related crossfire among three teenagers.

Extended Examples

From Personal Experience or Direct Observation

Extended examples from personal experiences or observations are longer, more detailed narratives of events that have involved you or people you know. Sometimes several brief examples just won't have the emotional impact that an extended example will. Sometimes people need to hear the full story of something that happened to a real person to really understand the point you are trying to make. Suppose, for instance, that you are writing about the senseless violence that seems to be occurring more and more frequently in our society today. You could illustrate that violence with several brief examples, or you could emphasize its heartlessness and brutality with an extended example such as the following:

> The senseless, brutal violence that we read about in the newspapers every day seems very distant from the average person, but it is really not far away at all. In fact, it can strike any of us without any warning— just as it struck my uncle Silas last week. After having dinner with his wife and two children, Silas had driven to the Texaco gas station at the corner of Vista Way and San Marcos Drive, where he was working part-time to earn extra money for a down payment on a house. Some time around 11:00 P.M., two young men carrying Smith and Wesson 38's approached him and demanded money. Uncle Silas was a good, brave man, but he was also a realistic person. He knew when to cooperate, and that's just what he did. He opened the cash register and the safe, then handed the intruders the keys to his new truck. They shot him in the head anyway.

Wouldn't you agree that the above extended example carries an emotional impact that brief examples might not carry? This anecdote might be used in a pro–gun control essay or even in an anti–gun control essay (Uncle Silas should have had his own gun). Or it could be part of an essay on capital punishment. In any case, it would add dramatic interest to a piece of writing. As you can see, examples of personal experience can be brief, perhaps only one sentence long, or extended, taking up several paragraphs.

From Other Sources

Extended examples taken from magazines, newspapers, books, or newscasts can also provide dramatic and persuasive support for your papers. Professional writers know the effect that extended examples can have on the reader, so they use such examples frequently. Notice how Ellen Goodman, a nationally known writer, uses the following extended example in an article debating the right of people to commit suicide:

> It is certain that Peter Rosier wouldn't be on trial today if he hadn't   1
> been on television two years ago. If he hadn't told all of Fort Myers,
> Florida, that "I administered something to terminate her life."

His wife Patricia, after all, a woman whose lung cancer had spread to   2
her other organs, had told everyone that she intended to commit suicide.
Indeed she planned her death as a final elaborate production.

Perhaps it was a dramatic attempt to control, or shape, or choose the   3
terms of her death. Perhaps it was an attempt to win some perverse victory over her cancer. Either way, Patricia Rosier, forty-three, picked the
date, the time, even the wine for her last meal. She picked out the pills
and she swallowed them.

Death, however, didn't play the accommodating role that had been   4
scripted for it. While the Rosier children slept in the next room, the deep
coma induced by twenty Seconal pills began to lighten. Her husband,
Peter, a pathologist, went desperately searching for morphine. And then,
as he said a year later, he "administered something."

—*Ellen Goodman,* Making Sense © *1989 by the Boston Globe Newspaper Co./Washington
Post Writers Group. Reprinted with permission.*

The details of Patricia Rosier's death, particularly the descriptions of the cancer that
had spread throughout her body and of her careful plans to take her own life, help
the reader to understand the complexity of the decision that Peter Rosier had to
make. Is he guilty of murder? Should he have ignored his wife's desire to avoid a
painful death by cancer? In the face of detailed, real experience, answering such
questions is not easy.

Exercise 3.1

Examine "Jailbreak Marriage" on pages 41–42 and "Printed Noise" on pages 45–47
(or examine other articles assigned by your instructor) to determine whether the
authors are using brief or extended examples. Discuss the effectiveness (or ineffec-
tiveness) of the types of examples used in each article. ∎

Exercise 3.2

Choose one of the following sentences and support it with at least three brief examples. Then choose another of the sentences and support it with one extended
example.

1. People who think they can fix anything often end up making things worse.

2. My brother (or other relative or friend) has one particular characteristic that consistently causes problems.

3. Many high school students today lead remarkably busy lives outside of school.

4. Racial intolerance (or religious, gender, or sexual intolerance) is alive and well in our
   community.

5. Ignorance of other cultures and traditions can cause people to act in offensive ways
   even though they don't mean to be offensive. ∎

Statistics

Examples are very effective ways to support your ideas, but sometimes examples just aren't enough. Sometimes you need support that is more objective and measurable than an example. Sometimes you need support that covers more situations than one or even several examples could possibly cover. At times like these, statistics are the perfect support. In fact, if statistics are used fairly and correctly and are drawn from reliable sources, they are just about the most credible and effective type of support. We are impressed, perhaps overly impressed, when a writer can cite clear numbers to support an argument. Notice how the editorial writer Joseph Perkins uses statistics in his article about the effect TV violence has on young people:

> In fact, according to a study by the American Psychological Association, the average American child will view 8,000 murders and 100,000 other acts of violence before finishing elementary school. The average 27 hours a week kids spend watching TV—much of it violent—makes them more prone to aggressive and violent behavior as adolescents and adults. [1]
>
> Of course, TV executives have known this for a long time. One of the most comprehensive studies of the impact of violent TV was commissioned by CBS back in 1978. It found that teenage boys who watched more hours of violent TV than average before adolescence were committing such violent crimes as rape and assault at a rate 49 percent higher than boys who watched fewer than average hours of violent TV. [2]
>
> —Joseph Perkins, "It's a Prime-Time Crime"

As the above paragraphs illustrate, statistics can be quite impressive. It is startling to read that the average child will view over 100,000 acts of violence before he or she leaves elementary school or that children spend an average of 27 hours per week watching television. Be aware, however, that statistics can also be misleading. How many of these acts of violence consist of Wile E. Coyote chasing the Road Runner in Saturday morning cartoons? Is there any difference between that kind of violence and the violence found in police shows or murder mysteries?

Expert Opinion or Testimony

Another kind of support that can be quite convincing is information from or statements by authorities on the subject about which you are writing. Let's suppose that you are trying to decide whether to have your child vaccinated against the measles. You have heard other parents say that a measles vaccination can harm a child, but you have never really known any parents who said their own children were harmed. So what do you do? Probably you call your pediatrician and ask for her expert opinion. After all, she is the one who has studied the field and who has vaccinated hundreds, perhaps thousands, of children.

In the same way, if you are writing a paper about a constitutional issue—such as the relationship of the Second Amendment to the need for gun control—you might decide to consult the experts for their opinions. And who are they? Probably legal scholars, political scientists, and even Supreme Court justices. Of course, you won't call these people on the phone; instead, you'll use quotations that you have found in articles and books from your college library. Here is an example of one such use of expert testimony:

> Parents must strive to find alternatives to the physical punishment of children. Almost every effect of corporal punishment is negative. Dr. Bruno Bettelheim, famous psychologist and professor at the University of Chicago, writes, "Punishment is a traumatic experience not only in itself but also because it disappoints the child's wish to believe in the benevolence of the parent, on which his sense of security rests."

If you do use expert opinion or testimony, don't believe too easily everything you read. When choosing authorities, you should consider not only their expertise but also their reputations for such qualities as integrity, honesty, and credibility. Also, you should determine whether other experts in the same field disagree with the expert whose opinion you have cited. After all, if the experts don't agree, testimony from just one of them won't be very convincing. In fact, since experts often *do* disagree, it is a good idea to use expert testimony only *in combination with* the other types of support discussed in this chapter.

Combining Types of Support

Combining the different types of support is a very effective way to develop your ideas. Rarely will you find professional writers relying only on examples or statistics or expert testimony to support what they have to say. Instead, the more convincing writers provide many different types of support to make their point. Usually, the better and wider the support you use, the better your chance of persuading your reader.

Exercise 3.3

The following excerpt from an article on cheating appeared in the *Los Angeles Times*. Examine it for each type of support discussed in this chapter.

> Cheating, studies show, is pervasive. It involves students struggling for A's and admission to prestigious graduate schools as well as those flirting with academic failure.   1
>
> A landmark survey of 6,000 students in 31 of the country's prestigious colleges and universities two years ago found that nearly 70% had cheated—if all manner of minor infractions were taken into account. The figure approached 80% for non–honor code schools and 60% for those with codes. . . .   2

The move back to honor codes is symptomatic of a larger change on college campuses, said Gary Pavela, president of the National Center for Academic Integrity, a consortium of 60 colleges and universities collaborating on issues involving honor codes, student ethics and academic integrity.

"All across the country, college administrators are beginning to take back authority that they gave up to students in the 60's and 70's," he said. "But the area of academic integrity is the only one where authority is still moving toward the students. . . ."

In 1976, 152 cadets were kicked out of the U.S. Military Academy for cheating on an exam. After a long investigation, 98 were reinstated the following year. In 1984, 19 Air Force Academy seniors were suspended for cheating on a physics exam, and cadet honor boards' handling of academic cheating was temporarily halted.

The most excruciating cheating affair in the history of the military service schools is still being played out on the stately campus of the U.S. Naval Academy at Annapolis. There, a panel of senior officers appointed by the Secretary of the Navy is hearing the last cases of as many as 133 midshipmen involved in cheating on an electrical engineering examination in December, 1992.

From the Los Angeles Times, *April 3, 1994, E1. Reprinted by permission of Rudy Abramson.* ■

Exercise 3.4

Examine "A Required Course in Beating the Freshman Blues" on pages 48–51 (or another article assigned by your instructor). Identify the types of support that have been discussed in this chapter. ■

Explaining the Significance of the Support

Remember that better paragraphs and essays almost always move from the more general topic or thesis to the more specific example, statistic, or expert opinion. Specific, detailed support will give color and life to your papers, and it will help to make your points clear and convincing.

However, once you have provided specific support, you are still not finished if you want your ideas to be as convincing as possible. Now is the time to *explain the significance* of your support. You might explain how your supporting details relate to the central idea of your paper, or you might emphasize the parts of your support that you consider the most significant. The point is that *your ideas* will become clearest when you elaborate upon your support, using your own words to explain the significance of the details you have given.

In the following example, note how the student writer elaborates upon her support.

Sometimes it is very difficult not to respond to rude people with more rudeness of my own. For instance, one day last summer while I was working as a cashier at Rice King, a Chinese restaurant, an old lady came in and said "Give me the damn noodles." I could not believe what she said. I was very angry. When I gave her the food, she opened the box in front of me and started picking through the noodles with her fingers. Then she said, "There is not enough meat." I knew there was more than enough meat in the box, but I ended up giving her more anyway. I suppose what I really wanted to do was to tell her what a disgusting person she was, but I'm glad that I didn't. After all, I didn't know her or what kind of problems she might be having in her life. Was she rude and obnoxious? Yes. Did that give me the right to be mean or hurtful in return? I didn't think so.

Jung Yun Park, student writer

Writing Introductions and Conclusions

So far in this chapter, we have been discussing how to support your ideas. In many ways, however, how you introduce and conclude your paper is as important as how you support it. In the next few pages, we will discuss some strategies you can use to write effective introductions and conclusions.

The Introductory Paragraph

As we all know, first impressions can be deceptive, but they can also be of great importance. The opening paragraph of a paper provides the first impressions of the essay and of the writer. Thus, it is one of the most important paragraphs of your essay. Your introductory paragraph serves a number of important purposes:

- It gains the attention of your reader in the lead-in.
- It informs your reader about such details as the background of your subject and the purpose of your essay.
- It gives the reader some idea of you, the writer, particularly through its tone.
- It presents the thesis statement and often the plan or organization of your essay.

The Lead-in

The lead-in generally consists of the first several sentences of the introduction. It may take any number of forms.

A General Statement

One of the most common ways of developing the introduction is to begin with a general statement and then follow it with ever more particular or specific statements leading to your thesis statement. This introductory strategy is sometimes referred to as a *funnel introduction* because, like a funnel, it is broad at the opening and narrow at the bottom. The following brief introduction from a student essay follows the general-to-particular pattern.

general statement

specific thesis

> When disaster strikes, American people respond with their good hearts and numerous organized systems to help families cope with the disaster and its effects. There is beauty in a neighbor's heartfelt response to a disaster. My children and I discovered just how much caring and assistance Americans will help families with when a disaster strikes.

Here is another general-to-particular introduction. Note that the thesis in this introduction presents two particular points on which the paper will focus.

general statement

specific thesis

> Some time around the middle of November, about half the population seems to begin griping about the "secularization" of Christmas. They become nostalgic for some old, ideal, traditional Christmas that may never have existed. They fume about artificial trees and plastic creches. However, P. H. Terzian, in an article entitled "A Commercial Christmas Is Not So Crass," states that these grouches are wrongheaded, and I agree. Terzian and I feel that the Christmas spirit is alive and well for several reasons: Christmas has always been a healthy mixture of the sacred and profane, and it has always been about joyfully getting, giving, and receiving.

A Question

Many writers open their essays with a question that is meant to attract the interest of the reader. Sometimes writers use a *rhetorical question*—that is, a question for which no answer is expected because the intended answer is obvious. Here is a rhetorical question: "Should we allow child abuse to continue?" Obviously, the answer to this question is no. Even so, a writer might open an essay with such a question to make the reader wonder why she or he is asking it and to draw the reader into the essay. Other times a writer might open an essay with a question that requires an answer—and the need to hear the answer keeps the reader reading. Here is a student's introductory paragraph that begins with a question:

question

specific thesis

> Is Tipper Gore overreacting? In her article "Curbing the Sexploitation Industry," Gore emphasizes the dangers posed for our children by what she calls the sexploitation industry. She claims that entertainment producers do not take our children into consideration when they present violent material. She says we should be concerned about the mental health of our children and the dignity of women. I do not think she is overreacting at all. Our society is facing a serious threat from the sexploitation industry: TV networks show excessive sex scenes, movie producers make films with excessive graphic violence, and rock recordings contain explicit sexual lyrics.

An Anecdote or Brief Story

We all enjoy stories. For most of us, reading about real people in real situations is far more convincing and interesting than reading about general ideas. For that reason, opening an essay with a short description of a person, place, or event can be an effective way of grabbing your reader's attention. The following introduction opens with a short anecdote:

anecdote

> I found a *Penthouse* magazine in my twelve-year-old's room last week, and I panicked. I recalled that Ted Bundy, who roamed the country mutilating, murdering, and raping, had said right before his execution that he had been influenced by pornography. Was my son on his way to a life of violent crime? Probably not. But a recent article, "Ted Bundy Shows Us the Crystallizing Effect of Pornography," raises some serious concerns. We need to be more vigilant about what our children (and our fellow citizens of all ages) are experiencing in all of the media, and we need to make
>
> *specific thesis*
>
> our lawmakers aware of our concern. However, we need to accomplish these missions without weakening the First Amendment to the Constitution and without harming the world of art.

A Quotation

A quotation from someone connected with your topic, from an article you're writing about, or from an expert on your subject can be a good way of opening your introduction. Or you might look up a famous quotation on your subject in a book such as *Bartlett's Familiar Quotations*. Notice how the following student paragraph moves from a quotation to a specific thesis statement:

question

> Martin Luther King, Jr., once said, "I have a dream that my four little children will one day live in a nation where they will not be judged by the color of their skin, but by the content of their character." Dr. King would certainly be disappointed if he could read a recent article by Richard Cohen in the *Washington Post*, entitled "A Generation of Bigots Comes of Age." The author claims that we are seeing an increase in bigotry, especially from the generation just coming of age (those in their twenties). He cites a great deal of information and statistics from the Anti-Defamation
>
> *specific thesis*
>
> League and from a Boston polling firm. I believe Mr. Cohen because lately I have experienced an increase in prejudice at work, at school, at shopping malls, and at many other places.

A Striking Statement or Fact

"Coming soon to your local cable system: VTV, violent television, 24 hours a day of carnage and mayhem." This quotation was the lead-in for a recent article on the amount of violence children see on television and the effects it may be having on them. Later in the article, the writer pointed out that one hundred acts of violence occur on television each hour. This fact could also be used as a striking lead-in to your essay. Once you have captured the attention of your reader through a strategy like this, he or she will tend to keep reading. Here is an introduction based on the above quotation:

striking statement

> "Coming soon to your local cable system: VTV, violent television, 24 hours a day of carnage and mayhem." So writes Joseph Perkins in his article "It's a Prime-Time Crime." Perkins cites the American Psychological Association and the quarterly journal *The Public Interest* to support his

specific thesis

idea that the enormous amount of violence viewed by American children may be doing them irreparable harm. I find the overwhelming evidence that violence on TV is making children overly aggressive and is having a negative effect on their mental health quite convincing, especially because so many of my own observations confirm that evidence.

Exercise 3.5

Examine the introductions to "Live Each Moment for What It's Worth" (pages 6–7), "A View from Mount Ritter" (pages 9–11), "Jailbreak Marriage" (pages 41–42), "A Required Course in Beating the Freshman Blues" (pages 48–51), and "Are You Living Mindlessly?" (pages 52–54). Pay particular attention to the type of lead-in used by each article. Be prepared to discuss which introductions you find to be most effective. ■

The Concluding Paragraph

Final impressions are as important as initial ones, especially if you want to leave your reader with a sense of completeness and confidence in you. Although the content of your conclusion will depend on what you have argued or presented in your essay, here are some suggestions as to what you might include:

- A restatement of your thesis, presented in words and phrases different from those used in your introduction
- A restatement of your supporting points, presented in words and phrases different from those used in your body paragraphs
- Predictions or recommendations about your proposals or arguments
- Solutions to the problems you have raised
- A quotation or quotations that support your ideas
- A reference to an anecdote or story that appeared in your introduction

Following are some concluding paragraphs that use some of these strategies.

A restatement of the main points
A prediction or recommendation

The following is a concluding paragraph from an article on the effects of TV violence on children. The author summarizes his main points and also offers a recommendation.

> Given the overwhelming evidence that violent TV has deleterious effects on children, that it increases the level of violence throughout American society, it hardly seems unreasonable that the government ask that [the] TV industry tone down its violent programming. Those who find that request objectionable should forfeit their privileged use of public airwaves.
>
> —*Joseph Perkins, "It's a Prime-Time Crime"*

A solution to a problem that has been raised

Here is a conclusion from a rather unusual essay. Its thesis is that laws allowing men but not women to go topless at the beach are discriminatory and reflect our male-dominated culture. It offers two possible solutions to the problem.

> It was not too long ago that the law also attempted to shield children from pregnant teachers. But the Supreme Court held pregnancy no grounds for a forced leave of absence. Another court has ruled that unmarried pregnant students cannot be excluded from public schools— not unless unmarried expectant fathers are also excluded. It is time for the same equality to be applied to bathing attire. Whether that is accomplished by allowing all people to go topless or by requiring men to wear tops, the end result will be the same: discarding one more premise of a male-defined society.

A restatement of the main points
A quotation that supports the ideas

The following conclusion to a student essay sums up the writer's ideas on her subject and then presents an effective quotation from the author of the article to which she is responding.

> Diversity, in America, is supposed to be good. This country was formed for freedoms like religion, speech, and sexual preference. America was formed for all ethnic groups and all traditions. When a certain group thinks that they are above all, that is when the problems begin. It is important to educate others on your background and to celebrate your heritage, to a certain extent. It is also important to learn about other cultures so that we feel comfortable and not threatened by others. As Schoenberger says, "I would much prefer them to hate or distrust me because of something I've done, instead of hating me on the basis of prejudice."

A restatement of the main points
A reference to an anecdote or story from the introduction
A solution to a problem that has been raised

This conclusion is drawn from the article "Getting to Know about You and Me," which appears later in this chapter. Its introduction tells the story of the author's being invited to join the Diversity Committee at her high school, an invitation she declined. The conclusion refers again to that invitation.

> I'm now back at school, and I plan to apply for the Diversity Committee. I'm going to get up and tell the whole school about my religion and the tradition I'm proud of. I see now how important it is to celebrate your heritage and to educate others about it. I can no longer take for granted that everyone knows about my religion, or that I know about theirs. People who are suspicious when they find out I'm Jewish usually don't

know much about Judaism. I would much prefer them to hate or distrust me because of something I've done, instead of them hating me on the basis of prejudice.

Exercise 3.6

Examine the conclusions to "Live Each Moment for What It's Worth" (pages 6–7), "A View from Mount Ritter" (pages 9–11), "Jailbreak Marriage" (pages 41–42), "A Required Course in Beating the Freshman Blues" (pages 48–51), and "Are You Living Mindlessly?" (pages 52–54). Be prepared to discuss which conclusions you find to be most effective. ◼

Readings

As you read each of the following selections, pay particular attention to the type of support each writer uses and to the introduction and conclusion of each article.

Before You Read

1. Are you familiar with Dave Barry? If you are not, you may be in for a surprise. Ask some friends or other students who he is.

2. What could the title "Male Fixations" possibly refer to? What is a fixation?

Male Fixations

Dave Barry

Most guys believe that they're supposed to know how to fix things. This is a responsibility that guys have historically taken upon themselves to compensate for the fact that they never clean the bathroom. A guy can walk into a bathroom containing a colony of commode fungus so advanced that it is registered to vote, but the guy would never dream of cleaning it, because he has to keep himself rested in case a Mechanical Emergency breaks out. 1

For example, let's say that one day his wife informs him that the commode has started making a loud groaning noise, like it's about to have a baby commode. This is when the guy swings into action. He strides in, removes the tank cover, peers down into the area that contains the mystery commode parts, and then, drawing on tens of thousands of years of guy mechanical understanding, announces that *there is nothing wrong with the commode*. 2

At least that's how I handle these things. I never actually fix anything. I blame this on tonsillitis. I had tonsillitis in the ninth grade, and I missed some school, and apparently on one of the days I missed, they 3 herded the guys into the auditorium and explained to them about things like carburetors, valves, splines, gaskets, ratchets, grommets, "dado joints," etc. Because some guys actually seem to understand this stuff. One time in college my roommate, Rob, went into his room all alone with a Volvo transmission, opened his toolbox, disassembled the transmission to the point where he appeared to be working on *individual transmission molecules*, then put it all back together, and it *worked*. Whereas I would still be fumbling with the latch on the toolbox.

So I'm intimidated by mechanical guys. When we got our boat trailer, 4 the salesman told me, one guy to another, that I should "re-pack" the "bearings" every so many miles. He said this as though all guys come out of the womb with this instinctive ability to re-pack a bearing. So I nodded my head knowingly, as if to suggest that, sure, I generally re-pack a couple dozen bearings every morning before breakfast just to keep my testosterone level from raging completely out of control. The truth is that I've never been 100 percent sure what a bearing is. But I wasn't about to admit this, for fear that the salesman would laugh at me and give me a noogie.

The main technique I use for disguising my mechanical tonsillitis is 5 to deny that there's ever anything wrong with anything. We'll be driving somewhere, and my wife, Beth, who does not feel that mechanical problems represent a threat to her manhood, will say, "Do you hear that grinding sound in the engine?" I'll cock my head for a second and make a sincere-looking frowny face, then say no, I don't hear any grinding sound. I'll say this even if I have to shout so Beth can hear me over the grinding sound; even if a hole has appeared in the hood and a large, important-looking engine part is sticking out and waving a sign that says HELP.

"That's the grommet bearing," I'll say. "It's supposed to do that." 6

Or, at home, Beth will say, "I think there's something wrong with the 7 hall light switch." So I'll stride manfully into the hall, where volley-ball sized sparks are caroming off the bodies of recently electrocuted houseguests, and I'll say, "It seems to be working fine now!"

Actually, I think this goes beyond mechanics. I think guys have a 8 natural tendency to act as though they're in control of the situation even when they're not. I bet that, seconds before the *Titanic* slipped beneath the waves, there was some guy still in his cabin, patiently explaining to his wife that it was *perfectly normal* for all the furniture to be sliding up the walls. And I bet there was a guy on the *Hindenburg* telling his wife that, oh, sure, you're going to get a certain amount of flames in a dirigible. Our federal leadership is basically a group of guys telling us, hey, *no problem* with this budget deficit thing, because what's happening is the fixed-based long-term sliding-scale differential appropriation forecast has this projected revenue growth equalization sprocket, see, which is connected via this Gramm-Rudman grommet oscillation module to . . .

After You Read

Work with other students to develop responses to these questions or to compare responses that you have already prepared.

1. Now that you've read the article, explain the male fixation referred to in the title.

2. What is Barry's point about this male fixation?

3. What does Barry mean when he says that he has "mechanical tonsillitis"?

4. What is Dave Barry's thesis idea? Identify any sentences that seem to express it.

5. What types of support does Dave Barry use? Identify any brief or extended examples. Does he use any statistics or expert opinions?

6. Examine the introduction and conclusion to this article. How does each accomplish its purpose?

Before You Read

1. Bob Chase is President of the National Education Association. In light of his position and of the title of this article, what point do you expect him to be making?

2. Which person do you worry about more, the C student involved in many extracurricular activities or the A student who spends most of his time studying? Why?

Fear of Heights: Teachers, Parents, and Students Are Wary of Achievement

Bob Chase

Imagine you're a high school chemistry teacher. One of your students is a 1
shy, brilliant girl who routinely does "A" work. Another constantly chats
on her cell phone during lab time. She plays varsity soccer, chairs the
homecoming committee, and earns unspectacular grades.

Which student troubles you more? 2

Shockingly, a majority of teachers say they're more worried about 3
the star pupil than the "C" student. And their sentiments mirror those of
most parents. A recent survey by the research group Public Agenda
found that 70 percent of parents said they'd be upset if their child received excellent grades but had a limited extracurricular life. Only 16
percent wanted their children to get "mostly A's."

Similarly, 53 percent of America's public school teachers worried 4
about "A" students with two or three friends, while only 29 percent worried about "C" students who were popular.

Why? According to the survey, a majority of the population agrees 5
that "People who are highly educated often turn out to be book smart
but lack the common sense and understanding of regular folks." Unsur-

prisingly, this perception filters down to students. Research by Public Agenda also reveals that "most teens view the academic side of school as little more than 'going through the motions.'" Explained one Alabama boy, "My parents don't care if I make a C."

In many communities, after-school activities are more sacrosanct than academics. High school football victories garner more newspaper ink than math decathlons. School plays confer greater status on their participants than spelling bees. In perhaps the most bizarre example, in 1991 a mother in Channelview, Texas, hired a man to murder the mother of her daughter's rival for a spot on the cheerleading squad. The National Honor Society has never generated such feverish (albeit insane) competition!   6

Historically, Americans have embraced a degree of anti-intellectualism as a badge of our populist spirit. But as our economy becomes increasingly reliant on technology, scientific research, and a highly skilled work force, this attitude undermines our best interests.   7

Proof came earlier this year, in the form of the Third International Mathematics and Science Study (TIMSS). A comparison of academic performance in 21 countries, TIMSS showed that U.S. 12th graders ranked at or near the bottom in math and science.   8

TIMSS underscores the need for more rigorous curricula, higher academic standards, and better teacher training. But policy changes alone will not improve students' performance. Our basic values need an overhaul. As long as teachers, parents, and students remain suspicious of intellectual excellence, we will function as a tripod for mediocrity—supporting a system that celebrates "averageness" over achievement.   9

What changes are in order?   10

TIMSS offers some important clues. The test revealed that American students spend less time doing homework and more time at after-school jobs than do their international peers. Indeed, says researcher Gerald Bracey, "The American vision of teenagerdom includes dating, malls, cars, jobs, and extracurricular activities." In the name of being "well rounded," many students are being spread too thin. We need to set new priorities, with academics enshrined as the centerpiece.   11

It's ironic that many teenagers are unenthusiastic about learning at a time in their lives when they're generally passionate about everything else. If we're going to cultivate world-class students, we adults may need some remedial lessons ourselves. Says Kay Armstrong, a public school librarian, "If children go into video arcades, it means they can operate a computer. If they can recite rap songs, they can quote Shakespeare. The problem is that we as educators have not learned what motivates this generation."   12

Poet William Butler Yeats once wrote, "Education is not filling up a pail but lighting a fire." Together, we must kindle the sparks fearlessly—and encourage the flames to burn as high and as bright as they can.   13

After You Read

Work with other students to develop responses to these questions or to compare responses that you have already prepared.

1. Which person does Bob Chase think we should worry about more, the C student with extracurricular activities or the A student with a limited extracurricular life? Explain his reasoning.

2. "In many communities, after-school activities are more sacrosanct than academics." Do your own experiences or observations confirm this statement? Explain why or why not.

3. How would you express the thesis of this article? Use your own words. Then find any sentence(s) in the article that express that idea.

4. What types of support does Bob Chase use?

5. Examine the introduction and conclusion to this article. Explain how each accomplishes its purpose.

Before You Read

1. What do you know about religions or denominations other than your own?

2. Do you feel uncomfortable around people who are different from you? Have you ever felt uncomfortable around any particular group of people?

3. What does the title suggest will be the focus of this article?

Getting to Know about You and Me

Chana Schoenberger

As a religious holiday approaches, students at my high school who will   1
be celebrating the holiday prepare a presentation on it for an assembly.
The Diversity Committee, which sponsors the assemblies to increase religious awareness, asked me last spring if I would help with the presentation on Passover, the Jewish holiday that commemorates the Exodus from Egypt. I was too busy with other things, and I never got around to helping. I didn't realize then how important those presentations really are, or I definitely would have done something.

This summer I was one of 20 teens who spent five weeks at the University of Wisconsin at Superior studying acid rain with a National Science Foundation Young Scholars program. With such a small group in such a small town, we soon became close friends and had a good deal of fun together. We learned about the science of acid rain, went on field trips, found the best and cheapest restaurants in Superior and ate in them frequently to escape the lousy cafeteria food. We were a happy, bonded group.

Represented among us were eight religions: Jewish, Roman Catholic, 3
Muslim, Hindu, Methodist, Mormon, Jehovah's Witness and Lutheran.
It was amazing, given the variety of backgrounds, to see the ignorance
of some of the smartest young scholars on the subject of other religions.

On the first day, one girl mentioned that she had nine brothers and 4
sisters. "Oh, are you Mormon?" asked another girl, who I knew was a
Mormon herself. The first girl, shocked, replied, "No, I dress normal!"
She thought Mormon was the same as Mennonite, and the only thing she
knew about either religion was the Mennonites don't, in her opinion,
"dress normal."

My friends, ever curious about Judaism, asked me about everything 5
from our basic theology to food preferences. "How come, if Jesus was a
Jew, Jews aren't Christian?" my Catholic roommate asked me in all seri-
ousness. Brought up in a small Wisconsin town, she had never met a Jew
before, nor had she met people from most of the other "strange" religions
(anything but Catholic or mainstream Protestant). Many of the other kids
were the same way.

"Do you all still practice animal sacrifices?" a girl from a small town 6
in Minnesota asked me once. I said no, laughed, and pointed out that this
was the 20th century, but she had been absolutely serious. The only Jews
she knew were the ones from the Bible.

Nobody was deliberately rude or anti-Semitic, but I got the feeling 7
that I was representing the entire Jewish people through my actions. I
realized that many of my friends would go back to their small towns
thinking that all Jews liked Dairy Queen Blizzards and grilled cheese
sandwiches. After all, that was true of all the Jews they knew (in most
cases, me and the only other Jewish young scholar, period).

The most awful thing for me, however, was not the benign ignorance 8
of my friends. Our biology professor had taken us on a field trip to the
EPA field site where he worked, and he was telling us about the project he
was working on. He said that they had to make sure the EPA got its
money's worth from the study—he "wouldn't want them to get Jewed."

I was astounded. The professor had a doctorate, various other de- 9
grees and seemed to be a very intelligent man. He apparently had no idea
that he had just made an anti-Semitic remark. The other Jewish girl in the
group and I debated whether or not to say something to him about it, and
although we agreed we would, neither of us ever did. Personally, it made
me feel uncomfortable. For a high-school student to tell a professor who
taught her class that he was a bigot seemed out of place to me, even if he
was one.

What scares me about that experience, in fact about my whole visit to 10
Wisconsin, was that I never met a really vicious anti-Semite or a malig-
nantly prejudiced person. Many of the people I met had been brought up
to think that Jews (or Mormons or any other religion that's not mainstream Christian) were different and that difference was not good.

Difference, in America, is supposed to be good. We are expected—at 11
least, I always thought we were expected—to respect each other's tradi-

tions. Respect requires some knowledge about people's backgrounds. Singing Christmas carols as a kid in school did not make me Christian, but it taught me to appreciate beautiful music and someone else's holiday. It's not necessary or desirable for all ethnic groups in America to assimilate into one traditionless mass. Rather, we all need to learn about other cultures so that we can understand one another and not feel threatened by others.

In the little multicultural universe that I live in, it's safe not to worry 12 about explaining the story of Passover because if people don't hear it from me, they'll hear it some other way. Now I realize that's not true everywhere.

Ignorance was the problem I faced this summer. By itself, ignorance 13 is not always a problem, but it leads to misunderstandings, prejudice and hatred. Many of today's problems involve hatred. If there weren't so much ignorance about other people's backgrounds, would people still hate each other as badly as they do now? Maybe so, but at least that hatred would be based on facts and not flawed beliefs.

I'm now back at school, and I plan to apply for the Diversity Com- 14 mittee. I'm going to get up and tell the whole school about my religion and the tradition I'm proud of. I see now how important it is to celebrate your heritage and to educate others about it. I can no longer take for granted that everyone knows about my religion, or that I know about theirs. People who are suspicious when they find out I'm Jewish usually don't know much about Judaism. I would much prefer them to hate or distrust me because of something I've done, instead of them hating me on the basis of prejudice.

After You Read

Work with other students to develop responses to these questions or to compare responses that you have already prepared.

1. What point is Schoenberger making in her references to the girl who responded that she "dressed normal" when she was asked if she was a Mormon?

2. What is her point about the professor who said he "wouldn't want [the EPA] to get Jewed"?

3. How would you express the thesis of this article? Use your own words. Then find any sentence(s) in the article that express that idea.

4. What kind of support does Schoenberger use? Identify the different types of support that you see.

5. Where does the introduction end? In what way does it introduce the article? Which paragraph(s) make up the conclusion? Why is it an effective conclusion?

Writing Assignments

As you write a paper in response to one of the following assignments, pay particular attention to the support that you use as well as to the paper's introduction and conclusion.

1. Dave Barry's article "Male Fixations" takes a humorous look at the behavior of some males who act as if they can fix everything. Have you ever known such a person? Have you known more than one? Write a paper in which you use examples drawn from personal experiences or observations to illustrate and explain the consequences of one particular kind of behavior practiced by a person (or persons) you know.

2. In "Fear of Heights," Bob Chase suggests that we should worry less about the A student with two or three friends and more about the C student with an active extracurricular life. What do you think? Write a paper in which you use examples drawn from personal experiences or observations to illustrate and explain your response.

3. Chase writes that "teachers, parents, and students [are] suspicious of intellectual excellence . . . supporting a system that celebrates 'averageness' over achievement." Write a paper in which you use examples drawn from personal experiences or observations to support or contradict this statement.

4. What do you think of Bob Chase's idea that the American teenager is "spread too thin" and that too much emphasis is placed on extracurricular activities over academics? Write a paper in which you use examples drawn from personal experiences or observations to illustrate and explain your response.

5. In "Getting to Know about You and Me," Chana Schoenberger argues that widespread, often unintentional, religious intolerance exists in the United States. On a broader scale, diversity in various forms—religion, race, gender, sexual preference and so forth—is often not very tolerated in America. Compose an essay in which you use examples drawn from personal experiences or observations to explain the ways you and/or other people have experienced intolerance, whether as victim or perpetrator.

6. Consider Schoenberger's idea that intolerance is often unintentional. Write a paper in which you explain how such unintentional intolerance occurs, supporting your ideas with examples drawn from personal experiences or observations.

Evaluating Sample Papers

Use the following checklist to determine which of the student essays on the next few pages is most effective.

1. Thesis Statement

    Underline the thesis statement of the essay. Does it express a clear and specific central idea?

    1   2   3   4   5   6

2. Introduction

   Does the introduction clearly introduce the central idea of the writer's paper? Does it end with a thesis statement?

   1   2   3   4   5   6

3. Topic Sentences

   Underline the topic sentence of each paragraph. Does each one clearly state the central idea of its paragraph?

   1   2   3   4   5   6

4. Support

   Examine the supporting details in each paragraph. Are they specific and clear? Should they be more detailed, or should more support be included?

   1   2   3   4   5   6

5. Conclusion

   Does the conclusion adequately bring the essay to a close?

   1   2   3   4   5   6

6. Sentence Structure

   Do the sentences combine ideas that are related, using coordination and subordination when appropriate? Are there too many brief, choppy main clauses? (See the Sentence Combining section of this chapter for a discussion of subordination.)

   1   2   3   4   5   6

7. Mechanics, Grammar, and Spelling

   Does the paper contain a distracting number of these kinds of errors?

   1   2   3   4   5   6

8. Overall Ranking of the Essay

   1   2   3   4   5   6

Student Essay 1

"Getting to Know about You and Me" by Chana Schoenberger shows how unaware people are about the differences in religions. Schoenberger says that because of this unawareness/ignorance, people tend to hate or distrust someone because of their background or religion. Schoenberger, a teen, was amazed at the ignorance of even the most intelligent of her fellow students.

Too many people try to force their religion on others. Ever had strange men in suits come to your front door selling their religion? Those men and going to church on a regular basis has made me aware of other religions. According to Schoenberger, "If there weren't so much ignorance about other people's backgrounds, people wouldn't hate each other as badly as they do now." This ignorance leads to prejudice and hatred. Many of society's problems are based on prejudice and hatred. As for those men who go door to door, I believe it is intolerable for people to try to force their religion on you. I understand that they want you to learn about their religion, but I do not like to be pushed or harassed into something I do not agree with. "If people were educated in other backgrounds, then hatred would be based on facts and not flawed beliefs," says Schoenberger.

I became a victim of religious intolerance in my own church. Some members of the church and I went on a weekend trip up north to "spread the word." Although I willingly went, I felt I was pressured into going. I felt as if I was one of those men selling my religion, which I disagree with very much. This incident has made me hesitant to go to church. Do not get me wrong, I know what I believe in I just do not like being pressured into things I do not want to do. My friend took a religious studies course at school, and she said the teacher tried to force his religion on the class. It is good to be proud of your background, but thinking it is best for all is intolerable.

Diversity, in America, is supposed to be good. This country was formed for freedoms like religion, speech, and sexual preference. America was formed for all ethnic groups and all traditions. When a certain group thinks that they are above all, that is when the problems begin. It is important to educate others on your background and to celebrate your heritage, to a certain extent. It is also important to learn about other cultures so that we feel comfortable and not threatened by others. As Schoenberger says, "I would much prefer them to hate or distrust me because of something I've done, instead of hating me on the basis of prejudice."

Student Essay 2

According to the article "Fear of Heights," Public Agenda conducted a survey which found that 53% of America's school teachers worried about "A" students with a couple of friends, while only 29% worried about "C" students who were popular. Most of the current high school students I have spoken to fit in one of these two categories. For example, Shelly Beeby, a senior attending Oceanside High, has a 4.0 GPA and no real social life to speak about. Shelly would like to be a computer engineer in the future. On the other hand, Drew Gillespie, a junior attending La Costa Canyon High, has a 2.4 GPA, plays field hockey and works. In the future she would like to be a social worker. Natalie DelFrancia, a junior attending Carlsbad High, has a 4.3 GPA, works, attends dance classes and plays soccer. Natalie would like to make a career out of teaching math at the college level. What these three girls have in common is that they are all individuals with different capacities. I believe that we need not worry about the "A" student with a minute social life nor the average student with an abundant one, nor should we deny that there are students who can handle both a successful academic life and an active social one.

Most of the "A" students with minute social lives that I have spoken with seem to be geared toward careers that don't have a great amount of emphasis on social skills. Shelly Beeby, future computer engineer, explained to me that she has always felt most comfortable working on her own. In Shelly's case becoming a computer engineer fits her perfectly. She has the smarts to do it, and she enjoys one-sided situations. In high school a boy named Tom, who sat behind me in U.S. history, was a straight "A" student with about two or three friends. Our teacher would give us the option to work in groups; however, Tom always choose to do the projects on his own. He always talked about being some kind of scientist. Tom is another example of a straight "A" student who likes doing things alone. I feel that we do not need to worry about these students. It has been my observation that they often pick careers that fit their intelligence as well as their personality.

Contrary to the "A" students with minute social lives, most average students with abundant social lives that I have come in contact with seem to be interested in careers that focus on social skills. For instance, Drew Gillespie wants to become a social worker. Drew possesses average intelligence, has a passion for people, and loves to be involved; therefore, I believe that one day she will make a fine social worker. My friend Raymond, who was an average high school student, worked, played football, and was a part of the Orange Police Department's Explorer program. Raymond's dream of being a police officer finally came true last March when he was hired to work for the Santa Ana police department. Not only is Raymond good at what he does, but he also enjoys it. I believe we should not worry about these students because they see themselves in positions that require average intelligence with a major focus on people.

What the article failed to mention are those students who can maintain both an academic and social life. These students seem to be drawn to intellectual and prestigious careers. Natalie DelFrancia wants to be a math teacher at the college level. She has everything going for her, a high amount of intelligence and a wide array of people skills. My cousin Mike, who would like to be an international lawyer, graduated this summer with a 3.8 GPA. During his high school years, Mike played football, ran track and worked. He now attends the University of Michigan and is working towards his Master's degree in international law. Again, Mike has the high academic and social skills needed to achieve his dreams. These students should not be left out, for they too play a vital role in America's education system.

All the students I have mentioned in this paper are individual and highly important people. I don't believe that we need to worry that certain percentages of students are smart with no friends or average with many. What we need to focus on are students as individuals with certain capacities. We need to "encourage the flames to burn as high and as bright as they can." After all, if everyone in this world operated on the same level, how could life possibly go on?

Student Essay 3

While reading Dave Barry's article "Male Fixations," I couldn't help but to think of my neighbor's who have different types of fixations. The fixations that I see in some of my neighbors are similar to Barry's because they seem to be know-it-alls who refuse to admit that they really don't know as much as they claim, they will be embarrassed at their mistakes, and go into a state of denial when proven wrong.

Many of my neighbors seems to have a know-it-all attitude when it comes to certain things, only later to learn that they really don't know much about what they were talking about. For example, my neighbor Gabe seems to know everything about the O.J. Simpson trial because he is always telling me what the defense team is going to do everyday in court with the prosecution's witnesses, only later to find that he was only guessing and didn't really know that much about it to begin with. Another example of a know-it-all neighbor is Bob. I remember the time that I had bought my computer, and Bob came over to my house to help get it set up because he believed that he was a computer expert. He said that to set up a computer was a basic thing and that anyone with half a brain should be able to set it up without having to use the enclosed instructions. After an hour of watching him getting frustrated and calling the machine a few choice words, I told him that we could finish it the next day. When he left I referred to the instructions and got the job done in a timely manner, and the next day I just thanked him for his help and gave him lots of credit.

Some of my neighbors seem to get embarrassed when they are wrong about something simple. One morning I went outside to move my car off the street so I wouldn't get fined by the street sweeper. My neighbor Peg was outside, and she told me that the steet sweeper wasn't coming by that day and that it would be crazy for me to move my car. I believed her and later found a ticket on my windshield from the street sweeper for not moving my car. Even though I told her that it was a simple mistake, she was extremely embarrassed about it for weeks to follow.

Finally, the best example of a neighbor going into a state of denial is a situation with Bob in which he just wouldn't accept his wrong verdict of a problem and wouldn't let himself be proved wrong. Even though my washer broke down really late one night, Bob was quick to be on the scene to give his opinion on the mechanics of my washer that wasn't draining. He quickly came to the conclusion that something was in the pipe blocking the drain hose. I took his advice to try to unplug it, but it had then occurred to me that there is a filter on the washer to prevent such a thing from happening. I suggested to him that the problem could be an electrical failure, but he thought that I was kidding around with him. After we unsuccessfully tried looking for the blockage, I broke down and called a repairman the next day. Although it turned out that there was a problem with a switch, Bob just does not accept the fact that he was wrong and goes on by saying that whatever was blocking the pipe had been cleared.

My neighbors are good hearted persons that are eager to please. I believe that they do have practical ideas on how to fix things, but sometimes they are not always correct. It seems that whenever something goes wrong at my house with anything mechanical, a neighbor is there to assist because it is the neighborly thing to do. I guess I just have to accept the fact that they may have an opinion about everything, be embarrassed at their mistakess, and not accept their wrong solutions to certain problems.

Sentence Combining: Using Subordination

In Chapter 2, you practiced using appropriate coordinating conjunctions in your sentences. When you use coordination, you are suggesting that the ideas in your sentences are all of equal importance. On the other hand, when you employ subordination, you indicate to your reader which ideas are more important than others. The subordinate ideas in a sentence are usually the ones of lesser importance. Look at the following pairs of simple statements.

I awoke from my nap.
A burglar was smashing the window in my back door.

The snow was falling lightly on the mountain road.
A huge truck barreled straight at us.

The professor stomped towards me and began to yell.
I would not stop talking.

A very dear friend recently sent me a baby alligator.
She lives in Pittsburgh.

As you can see, in each pair of sentences, one sentence contains much more important information than the other. In the first two pairs, the second sentences convey the more important ideas. In the last two pairs, the first sentences seem to be more important. (Admittedly, deciding which sentences are more "important" can be rather subjective, yet you must attempt to make such distinctions when you combine related ideas.)

Subordinating Conjunctions and Relative Pronouns

One way to combine ideas is to write the less important information as a **subordinate clause.** Doing so will emphasize the relative importance of the ideas as well as clarify *how* the words are related. To write a subordinate clause, begin the clause with a **subordinator** (either a **subordinating conjunction** or a **relative pronoun**). Here is a list of subordinating conjunctions and relative pronouns that you can use to start subordinate clauses.

Subordinating Conjunctions			Relative Pronouns	
after	even though	until	that	who(ever)
although	if	when	which	whom(ever)
as	since	whenever	whose	
as if	so that	where		
as long as	than	wherever		
because	though	while		
before	unless			

You can combine the above four pairs of sentences by using subordinators. Here is how the sentences look when the less important sentences are written as subordinate clauses. Each subordinate clause is underlined.

When I awoke from my nap, a burglar was smashing the window in my back door.

As the snow was falling lightly on the mountain road, a huge truck barreled straight at us.

The professor stomped toward me and began to yell **because** I would not stop talking.

A very dear friend **who** lives in Pittsburgh recently sent me a baby alligator.

As you can see, each subordinate clause begins with a subordinator that expresses the relationship between the main clause and the subordinate clause. Notice also that the subordinate clause can appear at the start, at the end, or in the middle of the sentence.

Exercise 3.7

Each of the following sentences is drawn from one of the reading selections in this chapter. Underline each subordinate clause and circle its subordinator. Some sentences may contain more than one subordinate clause.

Example

(If) they can recite rap songs, they can quote Shakespeare.

1. One of your students is a shy, brilliant girl who routinely does "A" work.

2. As long as teachers, parents, and students remain suspicious of intellectual excellence, we will function as a tripod for mediocrity—supporting a system that celebrates "averageness" over achievement.

3. If we're going to cultivate world-class students, we adults may need some remedial lessons ourselves.

4. As a religious holiday approaches, students at my high school who will be celebrating the holiday prepare a presentation on it for an assembly.

5. This summer I was one of 20 teens who spent five weeks at the University of Wisconsin at Superior studying acid rain with a National Foundation Young Scholars program.

6. He apparently had no idea that he had just made an anti-Semitic remark.

7. Rather, we all need to learn about other cultures so that we can understand one another and not feel threatened by others.

8. If there weren't so much ignorance about other people's backgrounds, would people still hate each other as badly as they do now?

9. He said this as though all guys come out of the womb with this instinctive ability to re-pack a bearing.

10. So I'll stride manfully into the hall, where volley-ball sized sparks are caroming off the bodies of recently electrocuted houseguests, and I'll say, "It seems to be working fine now!" ■

Punctuating Subordinate Clauses

There are a few rules you need to know in order to punctuate sentences with subordinate clauses correctly.

1. Use a comma after a subordinate clause that precedes a main clause.

   <u>Because I have a meeting in the morning</u>, I will meet you in the afternoon.

2. In general, do not use a comma when the subordinate clause follows a main clause.

   I will meet you in the afternoon <u>because I have a meeting in the morning</u>.

3. Use commas to set off a subordinate clause beginning with *which, who, whom,* or *whose* if the information in the subordinate clause is not necessary to identify the word the clause modifies.

   Dave Barry, <u>who is a very funny man</u>, writes for the Miami Herald.

   (Because the information contained in the subordinate clause is not necessary to identify Dave Barry, it is set off with commas.)

4. On the other hand, do not use commas to set off a subordinate clause beginning with *which, who, whom,* or *whose* if the information in the subordinate clause is necessary to identify the word it modifies.

   The woman <u>who stepped on my toes in the theater</u> apologized profusely.

   (The clause "who stepped on my toes in the theater" is necessary to identify which "woman" you mean.)

5. No commas are used with subordinate clauses that begin with *that.*

   Subordinate clauses <u>that begin with</u> *that* are never enclosed in commas.

Exercise 3.8

Combine each of the following sets of sentences by changing at least one of the sentences in each set into a subordinate clause. Use commas where they are needed.

Example

> I was anxious. I prepared my tax return.
>
> I was anxious after I prepared my tax return.
>
> or
>
> Because I was anxious, I prepared my tax return.

1. I always thought that my friends and I weren't prejudiced. I now know that we have our share of biases.

2. My cousin came over to my house. She didn't feel comfortable talking to her parents.

3. One night I was extremely happy and in good spirits. I felt I could not contain my energy.

4. I would describe myself as an energetic person. I don't like to sit around doing nothing.

5. *Neurotic* is another word I would use to describe myself. I am embarrassed to admit it.

6. My neighbor Gabe thinks he knows everything about the judicial system. He tells me what he thinks the verdict will be whenever there is a major trial.

7. Last week I bought a new computer. Bob came over to my house to help me set it up. He thinks he is a computer expert.

8. A friend of mine works as a mechanic at a local garage. He told me that my battery was weak and needed to be recharged.

9. One of my neighbors can no longer drive. She gave me a list and some money and asked me to pick up some groceries for her.

10. He told me that he was going to do the dishes. I became upset with him. We were late for the party.

11. Josefina had always lived along the coast. She moved to Nevada. Her company offered her a better position there.

12. Snowboarding is a popular sport in our local mountains. It makes a person feel as if she were surfing on snow.

13. I attended a trade school after high school. I met a student named Jack. He owned a black 1975 Corvette.

14. A couple of weeks ago a close friend and I were talking on the phone. He asked me a question. Would I consider dating someone of a different race?

15. Edna was driving home in the pouring rain. She decided to stop at Home Depot. She picked up fifteen pounds of lawn seed. ■

Exercise 3.9

Combine each of the following groups of sentences into one sentence. Use subordination and coordination where appropriate. Embed adjectives, adverbs, and prepositional phrases. Use commas where they are needed.

1. Capital punishment today is reserved for "serious" crimes.
   They may be crimes such as murder, treason, espionage, or rape.
   In ancient and medieval times, people were executed for many crimes.
   We would consider these crimes trivial.

2. In India, people could be executed for killing a cow.
   They also could be executed for stealing a royal elephant.
   In Egypt, death was once the punishment for injuring a cat.

3. In ancient Babylon, you could be sentenced to death for selling bad beer.
   In Assyria, a good haircut was a sign of nobility.
   In Assyria, you might be executed for giving a bad haircut.

4. For many centuries the early Christian Church burned heretics alive.
   It kept the definition of heresy broad.
   Anyone with a new idea might find himself going up in flames.

5. For a while in colonial America, women were branded as witches.
   They were executed.
   This occurred if they possessed a demonic gaze.
   This occurred if they kept a black cat.
   This occurred if they were sexually attractive.
   This occurred if they raised the suspicions of almost anyone who wanted to accuse them of witchcraft.

6. Throughout history, executions have been held in public view.
   The executions were cruel and painful.
   They were a way to deter other crimes.

7. Public executions were meant to terrify the average citizen.
   In England they turned into weekly festivals.
   They also became family outings.
   They were full of merrymaking, drunkenness, and more crime.

8. In Babylon, a poorly built house collapsed on its owner and killed him.
   The architect of the house would be executed. The owner's wife was killed.
   The architect's wife would be executed too.

9. Noble men or women were sentenced to death.
   They were often allowed to select their own means of execution.
   Socrates did.
   He drank poison in the presence of his family and friends.

10. For thousands of years, hanging was considered a lowly way to die.
    It involved humiliating kicking, gasping, and flailing.
    Beheading was considered an honorable way to be executed.
    The death came swiftly and cleanly. ■

Chapter 4

Unity and Coherence

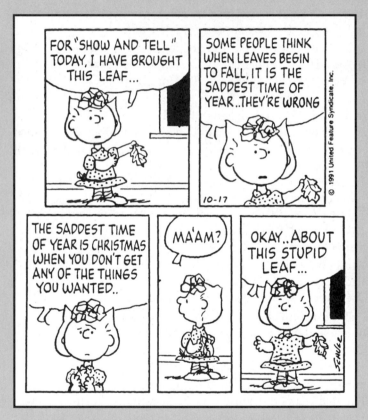

From PEANUTS. Reprinted by permission of United Features Syndicate, Inc.

Unity

As you can see from the "Peanuts" cartoon on the facing page, Sally is having trouble staying focused on her topic. Her tendency to drift from the subject of her report ("this stupid leaf") to why Christmas is the saddest time of year is called a break in **unity.**

Think about the word *unity* for a moment. It means *oneness* or *singleness of purpose*. A *unified* paragraph or essay is one that stays focused on its central idea. It does not wander into areas that are unrelated to that central idea. To put it another way, all the details, facts, examples, explanations, and references to authorities with which you develop a unified paper should clearly relate to and develop the central idea of that paper. If they do not do so the paper lacks **unity.**

A good time to check the unity of your writing is after you have written the first draft. Until that time, you are still prewriting, and during the prewriting stage you really should not worry too much about unrelated material that creeps into your writing. Remember, when you prewrite, you concentrate on getting as many ideas on paper as you can. When you write, you produce your draft. And when you revise, you improve that draft. Checking your paper for unity will usually occur as you revise—before you submit your paper to your instructor but after you have produced a first draft.

Exercise 4.1

Read the following paragraphs and identify the topic sentence of each one. Then identify any sentences that break the unity of the paragraph.

A.   **1** The names of the seven days of the week have some rather interesting origins. **2** The names *Sunday* and *Monday*, for example, come from Old English words that refer to the sun (*sunne*) and moon (*mona*), respectively. **3** *Tuesday, Wednesday, Thursday,* and *Friday* all refer to gods in Germanic mythology. **4** Tiu (for Tuesday) was a god of war. **5** Most cultures have some kind of name for a war god. **6** The Roman name was Mars; the Greek name was Ares. **7** Woden (for Wednesday) was the chief Germanic god. **8** He is known to many people as Odin. **9** The corresponding chief god in Roman mythology is Jupiter, and in Greek mythology it is Zeus. **10** Thor (for Thursday) was the Germanic god of thunder; Freya (for Friday) was the goddess of love and beauty. **11** Interestingly, *Saturday* comes from the name of a Roman god, not a Germanic one. **12** Saturn was the Roman god of agriculture. **13** How agriculture is related to the huge planet we know as Saturn may be confusing to some people, but it obviously did not worry the Romans very much.

B.   **1** Folk remedies, which are passed on from one generation to another, are sometimes quite effective and at other times absolutely worthless. **2** One example of effective folk wisdom is the advice to eat chicken soup when you have the flu. **3** Many people love the taste of chicken soup, especially during cold weather. **4** Several scientific studies have shown that chicken soup improves the functioning of the fibers in the upper respiratory tract that help people get rid of congestion. **5** Usually, people buy over-the-counter drugs to alleviate the symptoms of the flu, and today generic brands are much more popular than name brands. **6** Unfortunately, not all folk remedies are as effective as chicken soup. **7** Scientists say, for example, that slices of raw potato placed on the forehead will do nothing for a fever, although many people believe otherwise. **8** In fact, many people believe almost anything they are told. **9** A friend of mine once told some children that the world used to have only two colors—black and white—and that was why old movies looked that way. **10** And the children believed him! **11** Another bit of folk advice that scientists say is untrue is that taping a child's ears back at night will change the positions of ears that stick out too much. **12** Finally, scientists say that boiling skim milk for children with diarrhea is dangerous as well as ineffective.

C.   **1** For many years, ice cream was a treat enjoyed only by the nobility. **2** When Marco Polo returned to Italy from China in 1271 with a recipe for a new dessert made of fruit mixed with ice and milk, the dish quickly became a favorite of the Italian nobility. **3** However, the nobility did not share the recipe with the common people. **4** Marco Polo went on to become one of the most famous travelers in history. **5** His book, *The Travels of Marco Polo*, describes China as a country far superior to his own in culture and technology. **6** Several hundred years later, in 1533, Catherine de Medici of Italy introduced the recipe to the French nobility when she married a son of the King of France. **7** A creative French chef experimented with the recipe, beating a mixture of fruit and cream in a bowl surrounded by ice. **8** Of course, French chefs are known for their creativity and imagination, which is why French restaurants are regarded as special, expensive places by most Americans. **9** The result was a dessert much like our ice cream of today, but the recipe was still kept a closely guarded secret. **10** When King Charles I of England brought the dessert to his country in 1625, he was so determined to keep the recipe secret that he even refused to tell his own nobility how to make it. **11** That is just like the English, though. **12** They are known for keeping things to themselves. **13** Finally, in 1670, ice cream appeared for the first time on the menu of a Paris restaurant, and soon people throughout the world were sharing this "new" taste treat. ■

Coherence

Another way to improve the clarity of your writing is to work on its **coherence,** which involves clarifying the *relationships* between ideas. When ideas (or sentences) are *coherent*, they are understandable. And when they are understandable, one sentence makes sense in relation to the sentence before it. When ideas (or sentences) are *incoherent*, they do not make much sense because they are not clearly related to each other or to the central idea of the paper.

For example, imagine someone passing you a note that read "Snow! Last winter! Trees! Gone!" What in the world could such a person possibly be trying to tell you? That the snow that fell on the trees last winter is gone? That the trees that were snowed on last winter are gone? That last winter's snow killed the trees? What is missing here is **coherence,** the connections between the ideas.

Of course, a person's writing is rarely as incoherent as the above example, but all writers—from students who are taking their first writing classes to professionals who make their living by writing—must consistently work on the clarity of what they have written. Here is an example of a paragraph that needs more work in coherence.

> **1** Some television viewers claim that Donald Duck cartoons are immoral. **2** For fifty years, Donald has kept company with Daisy. **3** Donald's nephews—Huey, Dewey, and Louie—are apparently the children of a "Miss Duck," who was last seen in a comic book in 1937. **4** Donald is drawn without pants. **5** The opinions of these persons have been largely ignored by the general public.

The above paragraph lacks coherence because each sentence seems to jump from one unrelated detail to the next. A careful reader will probably be able to figure out that each sentence is meant to be an example of the "immorality" of Donald Duck cartoons, but the relationship of each sentence to that central idea and to the idea in the sentence before it needs to be made much clearer. Clarifying such relationships involves working on the coherence of the paper.

There are a number of techniques that will help you improve the coherence of your writing.

Improving Coherence

Refer to the central idea.   One of the most effective ways to improve coherence is to use words that refer to the central idea of your paper as you write your support. In the above paragraph about Donald Duck cartoons, the central idea is that some people think they are "immoral," but none of the supporting sentences clearly refer to that idea. The relationship between the supporting sentences and the central idea will be clearer—and the coherence improved—if the writer uses words that connect her support to the central idea of immorality.

> **1** Some television viewers claim that Donald Duck cartoons are immoral. **2** For example, for fifty years, Donald has kept company with Daisy, a relationship that to some seems **suspicious and dishonorable. 3** In addition, Donald's nephews—Huey, Dewey, and Louie—are apparently the **illegitimate** children of a "Miss Duck," who was last seen in a comic book in 1937. **4** Finally, it seems **improper and indecent** to these critics that Donald is drawn without pants. **5** Donald's dressing habits **clearly upset** these particular television viewers. **6** However the opinions of these persons have been largely ignored by the general public.

Now the relationship of each supporting idea to the central idea of the paragraph has become much clearer. Notice how the boldfaced words keep the emphasis of the paragraph on the "immorality" of Donald Duck cartoons.

Use common transitional words and phrases.   Transitions tell you what direction a sentence is about to take. When a sentence starts with *However,* you know that it is about to present a contrast; when it starts with *For example,* you know that it is about to move from a general statement to a specific illustration of that statement. Clear transitions will improve the coherence of your paper because they will signal to your readers how the sentence that they are about to read is related to the sentence that they have just finished reading.

Many transitions are so common that they are worded the same way no matter who is doing the writing. They are like road signs (*Stop, Yield, School Zone*) that all drivers are expected to recognize and respond to. These common transitions can improve your paper, but do not overuse them. Too many of them will make your writing sound artificial and awkward.

- To show a movement in time: *first, second, next, finally, then, soon, later, in the beginning, at first, meanwhile*

- To move to an example: *for example, to illustrate, for instance, as a case in point*

- To add another idea, example, or point: *in addition, furthermore, and, also, second, third, next, moreover, finally, similarly*

- To show a contrast: *on the other hand, however, but, yet, instead, on the contrary, nevertheless*

- To show a result: *so, therefore, as a result, consequently, hence, thus*

- To conclude: *finally, in conclusion, as a result, hence, therefore, clearly, obviously*

Notice how the addition of three transitions helps to improve the paragraph about Donald Duck cartoons.

---

1 Some television viewers claim that Donald Duck cartoons are immoral. **2 For example,** for fifty years, Donald has kept company with Daisy, a relationship that to some seems suspicious and dishonorable. **3 In addition,** Donald's nephews—Huey, Dewey, and Louie—are apparently the illegitimate children of a "Miss Duck," who was last seen in a comic book in 1937. **4 Finally,** it seems improper and indecent to these critics that Donald is drawn without pants. **5** Donald's dressing habits clearly upset these particular television viewers. **6 However** the opinions of these persons have been largely ignored by the general public.

Write your own transitional phrases, clauses, or full sentences.   The most effective transitions are those written in your own words as phrases, clauses, or complete sentences. Transitions such as these often **repeat a word or idea** from the previous sentence. They also often **refer to the central idea** of a paper in order to introduce a new element of support.

Note the transitional phrases, clauses, and full sentences in the following paragraph.

> **1** Some television viewers claim that Donald Duck cartoons are immoral. **2 According to these viewers, Donald's relationship with Daisy is an example of his immorality.** **3** For fifty years, Donald has kept company with Daisy, a relationship that to some seems suspicious and dishonorable. **4** In addition, **some people question the morality of a cartoon that features three children of unknown parentage.** **5** Donald's nephews—Huey, Dewey, and Louie—are apparently the illegitimate children of a "Miss Duck," who was last seen in a comic book in 1937. **6** Finally, it seems improper and indecent to these critics that Donald is drawn without pants. **7 Although few people ever expect to see *any* animal in pants,** Donald's dressing habits clearly upset these particular television viewers. **8 Luckily for the famous duck,** the opinions of these persons have been largely ignored by the general public.

In the above paragraph, sentence 2 is a full *transitional sentence*. It replaces the phrase *for example,* and it emphasizes the central idea of the paragraph by using the word *immorality*. Sentence 3 is another *transitional sentence*. Again, this sentence improves the coherence of the paragraph by emphasizing the central idea of *morality*. Sentence 7 now includes a *transitional clause.* Notice that the clause refers to the idea of animals "in pants," which was mentioned at the very end of sentence 6. Sentence 8 contains a *transitional phrase* that allows the reader to move easily into the concluding idea of the paragraph.

Exercise 4.2

Work with several other students in a small group to identify the topic sentence and central idea in each of the following paragraphs. Write "C.I." above all references to the central idea. Circle all words or ideas that are repeated from one sentence to the next. Finally, underline all common transitional words and phrases.

Example

1 Folk remedies, which are passed on from one generation to another, are sometimes quite effective and sometimes absolutely worthless. **2** One example of effective folk wisdom is the advice to eat chicken soup when you have the flu. **3** Several scientific studies have shown that chicken soup improves the functioning of the fibers in the upper respiratory tract that help people get rid of congestion caused by the flu. **4** Unfortunately, not all folk remedies are as effective as chicken soup. **5** Scientists say, for example, that slices of raw potato placed on the forehead will do nothing for a fever, although many people believe otherwise. **6** Another bit of folk advice that scientists say is untrue is that taping a child's ears back at night will change the position of ears that stick out too much. **7** Finally, scientists say that boiling skim milk for children with diarrhea is dangerous as well as ineffective.

A. **1** If you think dainty butterflies are lily-livered weaklings, think again. **2** Most male butterflies are gutsy and aggressive within their own habitat and will pick a fight at the slightest provocation. **3** This trait is often seen when a male is on the prowl for a mate. **4** The European grayling butterfly, for example, will perch on a twig or leaf to wait for Ms. Right. **5** When he scents a female of his own species, he will begin an elaborate courtship dance and emit his own identifying scent. **6** But he will rough up almost anyone else who ventures into his territory, whether it's another butterfly twice his size, a dragonfly or a small bird. **7** He'll even lunge at his own shadow. **8** Black swallowtail butterflies, an especially aggressive species, have been known to chase after terrified birds for as long as half a minute. **9** When vying for the favors of the same female, two male butterflies will repeatedly ram each other in midair until one surrenders and flees.

—*Irving Wallace et al.,* Significa

B. **1** In competition, losing should not necessarily be seen as failing. **2** If a runner finishes behind Bill Rogers in the marathon but runs the race twenty minutes faster than he has ever before, one cannot say that he has failed. **3** If a person enters a city tennis tournament and is eliminated in the third round, he cannot be said to have failed if neither he nor anyone else expected him to survive the first round. **4** The point is simple: failure in competition is not to be identified with losing per se but rather with performing below reasonable expectations. **5** Only when one could reasonably have expected to win does losing mean failing. **6** In most competition, someone wins and someone or many lose, but this does not mean that many (or even *any*) have performed below reasonable expectations and have, therefore, failed.

—*Richard Eggerman, "Competition as a Mixed Good"*

C. **1** When a man and a woman walk together, convention says the man takes the curb side. **2** A common historical explanation of this custom is that in the days when garbage was hurled into the street from upper-story windows, it was the man's duty to bear the majority of the refuse. **3** More reasonable is the explanation that a man on the outside is in a better position to protect his female companion from the hazards of the street itself, which until fairly recently included runaway horses and street brawlers. **4** Though Emily Post dutifully approved the custom, she denied its usefulness in the days of automobiles. **5** Apparently she had never negotiated a New York City sidewalk just after a downpour.

—*Tad Tuleja,* Curious Customs ■

Exercise 4.3

Revise the following paragraphs to improve their coherence by referring more clearly to the central idea, by repeating words and ideas from one sentence to the next, and by adding appropriate transitional words and phrases. You may also need to add complete sentences to emphasize how the details are related to the central idea of the paragraph. Consider working with other students as you revise two of these paragraphs. Then revise one on your own.

A.   **1** Driving on freeways today has become a frightening experience. **2** I glanced into my rear-view mirror to find a blue Ford pickup driving sixty-five miles per hour only two feet from my rear bumper. **3** When I changed lanes, he changed lanes too. **4** He pulled off the freeway at the next exit. **5** The local "freeway skiers" weave in and out of traffic as if they were in an Olympic slalom event. **6** Some small red sportscar will swing onto the freeway, race up the lane next to mine, change lanes, and then repeat the same maneuver as it weaves up the freeway. **7** There are the people who are much too busy to be driving. **8** They are reading reports, checking makeup, combing mustaches, drinking soft drinks, or talking on the telephone. **9** People have changed the nature of freeway driving.

B.   **1** Most fathers that I know seem to be much more awkward and nervous than mothers when it comes to caring for their babies. **2** My brother's baby, Kaori, had a slight cold. **3** My brother insisted that she should be taken to the hospital. **4** His wife said that Kaori would be fine in a day or so. **5** The child recovered completely. **6** My brother became sick because he hadn't slept all night. **7** My father would always avoid holding my little brother when we were younger. **8** At Disneyland, my mother asked him to hold my brother while she used the restroom. **9** The entire time, my dad paced back and forth. **10** Whenever my mother held the child, she seemed completely at ease. **11** I suppose it is natural for mothers to feel comfortable with their young children. **12** I don't see any reason for fathers to be as awkward as they are.

C.   **1** After reading G. Gordon Liddy's "Without Emotion," I was reminded of times in my own life when I felt that I had to act without emotion just to make it through an unpleasant experience. **2** I had to go through a divorce. **3** I had no financial support, and I had an eleven-month-old son to take care of. **4** I had to think about handling the pressing issues of finding food, clothing, shelter, and a job. **5** Another time, I was laid off from a typesetting position with a local newspaper. **6** I immediately busied myself with the task of finding another job. **7** I think Liddy was trying to get to the point where he could act without emotion if he ever really had to. **8** For me, it was either act without letting my emotions get to me or allow myself to be defeated by my circumstances. ■

Improving Unity and Coherence
with Thesis Statements and Topic Sentences

So far we have discussed unity and coherence *within* paragraphs, but these elements of clear writing affect the entire essay, not just the single paragraph. Remember, *unity* refers to a writer's ability to stay focused on one central idea. *Coherence* involves clarifying relationships between ideas. When you move from one paragraph to another within an academic essay, you can stay focused on the central idea of the essay (unity) and clarify the relationships between paragraphs (coherence) by paying particular attention to the thesis statement of the essay and the topic sentence of each paragraph.

Thesis Statements and Topic Sentences

Write a thesis statement that clearly expresses the central idea of the essay.   As we discussed in Chapters 1 and 2, academic essays need thesis statements that carefully and accurately state the central idea of the paper. Unless your instructor tells you otherwise, place the thesis statement at the end of your introductory paragraph.

Write topic sentences that clearly express the central idea of each paragraph.   Again, this point has been discussed in Chapters 1 and 2. Unless your instructor tells you otherwise, place your topic sentences at the start of each body paragraph.

Write topic sentences that clearly develop the central idea of the thesis statement. This point relates to both the *unity* and the *coherence* of your essay. One way to emphasize the relationship between each topic sentence and the thesis statement is to repeat words and ideas from the central idea of the thesis statement within each topic sentence. To avoid repetitive wording, don't repeat exact phrases.

Write topic sentences that use transitions to move away from the topic in the previous paragraph.   This point relates the *coherence* of your essay. A transition within a topic sentence might be a brief reference to the central idea of the previous paragraph, a common transitional phrase, or a transitional phrase or sentence of your own.

Sample Student Essay

Examine the following essay and note how the unity and coherence are emphasized as the writer moves from one paragraph to another. The central idea in the thesis and in each topic sentence is in boldface. The transition that opens each paragraph is underlined once. The words in each topic sentence that repeat the central idea of the thesis statement are in parentheses.

The Benefits of Competition

In the article "School Sports—Latest New Age Target," John Leo tells   1 us that many gym teachers across America are opposed to competition in school sports because they think such competition harms the children who aren't outstanding players. He refers to an article from *The New York Times*, which he says "carries the implicit message that win-lose games are dangerous." Leo, however, disagrees with the *Times* article. He believes that one can "lose without humiliation and win without feeling superior." I agree with him. In fact, after the experiences I have had with school sports in my own life, **I believe that the competition in school sports benefits students in many ways.**

One of the (benefits of competition) in school sports is that it **motivates** students to do their best. For example, when I was taking a swim class last semester, I could not swim one hundred yards without stopping. When the teacher said that he was going to time every one of us to see who could finish one hundred yards in the least amount of time, I was worried because I was sure I could not swim that far. During the competition, the only thought that came into my mind was that I did not want to be the last one to finish, and that thought motivated me to continue swimming even though I was very tired. When I reached the finish line, I was astounded to find that I was in fourth place. From this experience and from many others like it, I can say the competition did indeed bring out the best in me. 2

In addition to motivating students, competition in school sports (**prepares young people**) for the competition they will face in real life. My younger brother has (benefited) from school sports this way. Since he is the youngest member of our family, we always used to let him win when we played games with him because that was the only way we could keep him happy. Then one day he came home from school depressed. When I asked him what had happened, he said that he had lost to a friend in a school race. After I heard his story, I realized that my brothers and I had spoiled him and that school sports were giving him a dose of reality. I decided that the next time he wanted to beat me at checkers, he would have to really compete with me because that is the only way to teach him what life is really like. 3

Not only does competition benefit people by motivating them and teaching them about life, but it also (benefits them) by **revealing their own inner strengths and weaknesses.** My friends Minh and Hoa are good illustrations of this point. Minh is a quiet person who never seems very secure about his tennis talent. On the other hand, Hoa, a talkative person, always brags about how well he plays tennis. Hoa was sure that he was a better tennis player than Minh, but one day he had to face Minh in a school tennis tournament. When Hoa lost the game, he realized that he really could not play tennis as well as he thought. This competition pointed out Hoa's weakness, but it also revealed to Minh his own hidden strength. If they had not competed, neither would have discovered the truth about himself. 4

Clearly, competition in school sports can (benefit) people in many ways. It motivates students to do their very best, it teaches them about real life, and it reveals to them their own strengths and weaknesses. Like John Leo, I believe that school sports are a valuable part of school life. 5

Exercise 4.4

Examine the following sets of thesis statements and topic sentences. In each set, consider the following questions.

1. Does each thesis statement present one clear central idea? What is it?

2. Does each topic sentence introduce a central idea? What is it?

3. Does each topic sentence clearly develop the central idea in the thesis statement? What words or ideas from the thesis statement does it repeat?

4. Does each topic sentence open with some kind of transition to move it away from a previous paragragh?

A. thesis statement   Knowing many people myself who have attended college as freshmen, I agree that survival skill courses are extremely helpful in dealing with all the stress that comes along with college life.

    topic sentence   One of the main things that many freshmen stress about is the fact that they will no longer be living under the care of their parents.

    topic sentence   In addition to the stress of being away from home, college also introduces new financial stress.

B. thesis statement   Will the "A" student or the "C" student get farther in life and have what it takes to survive everyday troubles?

    topic sentence   Surprisingly, most people would say that the "A" student would be better off because he puts academics first.

    topic sentence   I feel that the so-called smart kids get far too much praise for excellence in academics.

    topic sentence   Education is a great thing.

    topic sentence   I feel that education is incorrectly defined in other parts of the world, and that our international peers are becoming stupid by their schooling.

C. thesis statement   Thanks to the counseling required by the college prior to registration, the helpful staff, and the job placement office, my first college semester was a success.

    topic sentence   As I analyzed my first college semester, I realized that the success I experienced was the result of the counseling I received before enrolling.

    topic sentence   During this first semester, I also found the staff to be informative and helpful.

    topic sentence   Most important, the job placement assistance I received from the college made it possible to succeed the first semester.

D. thesis statement   Straight "A" students might end up making the most money, but most of them are creating a huge hole for themselves that will only get bigger until they can't get out.

    topic sentence   Many of the prestigious students might be book smart, but they lack social skills.

| topic sentence | One major factor in a happy life is health. |
| topic sentence | America's job force has changed dramatically within the last couple of years, with the type of person they hire for positions. |

E. thesis statement   I agree that going through life "mindlessly" makes a person accept the norm and suppresses the creative side of human behavior.

topic sentence	Being mindful involves forcing ourselves into looking at things from a different point of view.
topic sentence	Being mindful also means using your imagination and creativity to learn what works best for you as an individual.
topic sentence	One last definition of what being mindless means is best portrayed by elderly people at retirement homes. ■

Readings

Before You Read

1. Consider the title of the following article. What does it lead you to expect? Will the article criticize or defend school sports?

2. What is your opinion of school sports? Are they overly competitive?

School Sports—Latest New Age Target

John Leo

If you read *The New York Times,* always look first at the bottom of Page   1
One. That's where the editors sometimes insert a warm and fuzzy article
to get your mind off the real front-page news about Bosnia, famine, Senator Bob Dole and other unsolvable problems.

One day last week, the fuzziness and warmth radiated smartly out of   2
an article headlined "New Gym Class: No More Choosing Up Sides." The
story was that basketball and other games are disappearing from gym
classes across America, mostly because gym teachers think the games
damage the feelings of children who aren't outstanding players.

Even games like dodgeball "have fallen into disrepute," wrote re-   3
porter Melinda Henneberger, who perhaps had a harrowing time in traditional gym class. She described P. E. in the past, with "all but the best athletes hoping the bell would rescue them from some fresh humiliation,"
and says that "now competition is out and cooperation is in."

Sure enough, right above the article was a photo of six children in a   4
gym, each up on one leg doing an interpretive dance. Nearby a grim

phys-ed teacher looks on, perhaps to make sure that none of the kids made a break for it and tried to start an illicit basketball game.

Kids can still shoot some hoops on their own, the *Times* said, but "even then, the goal is not so much to learn to score a basket as to develop body awareness, hand and motion skills and the confidence to try new activities." 5

This is a New Age approach to sports, drained of fun and skill. "Body awareness," "space awareness" and various concepts and feelings are excruciatingly important to this form of basketball. Actually putting the ball in the basket is not. 6

The *Times* article carries the implicit message that win-lose games are dangerous. Losing inevitably means humiliation. Kids have such fragile egos that it's better to avoid any challenge or competition that might send them into a tailspin. (Chalk up much of this attitude to the self-esteem movement.) There's also the hint that these games are vaguely undemocratic because the kids who play them are suddenly separated into winners and losers. 7

A lot of the anti-competition theory made the rounds in the late '60s, when giant balls were pushed around by whole classes so everybody could be on the same team. Later, books of non-competitive games started to appear, with titles like *Everybody Wins*, the first sign that losing at kickball was about to be defined as traumatic. 8

In fairness, the game theorists who stressed group fun and de-emphasized competition had a point. This is a very competitive, hyper-individualistic culture that undervalues cooperation. School sports shouldn't be used to turn out little predators or the screaming Little League parents of tomorrow. 9

The trouble is that the anti-competition people couldn't seem to hold up the ideal of cooperation without going berserk over team games. Alfie Kohn, author of the 1986 book *No Contest*, argues that competition in the classroom and in the gym inevitably has destructive effects. 10

Even a choose-up gain of hoops? Yes, he told me. "There are still destructive effects—anxiety, a sense of failure, and lack of interest in exercise. Fun doesn't require adversarial activities. The way we feel about people is affected by the structure of the game." 11

But kids in a pickup game are not learning the dangerous lesson that "other people are obstacles to my success" (Alfie Kohn's phrase). They are simply playing, and perhaps learning about cooperation, discipline and excellence along the way. 12

The attack on competitive sports in schools comes in two new forms these days. One has to do with gender. Since boys tend to grow up throwing a ball against a wall or a stoop, and most girls may not, there's a feeling that girls reach school age with an athletic disadvantage. The schools are addressing this problem, but some people want to avoid the whole issue by downgrading or eliminating team games. 13

Rita Kramer, author of *Ed School Follies,* a book on theories at schools   14
of education, thinks a feminist argument against competitive sports is
emerging. "This is one of those hidden-agenda items for feminists," she
says. "Some of them don't want masculine skills to be valued too highly
in the schools."

The other, more serious argument comes from the cooperative learn-   15
ing movement and other school movements that promote "equity issues,"
and are less concerned with excellence than with equality. The basic
teaching, that nobody is better than anybody else, leads believers to
oppose any activity that produces winning individuals.

From an "equity" point of view, it's better to have everybody hop-   16
ping up and down on one leg than to risk the inequality of having
winners.

There are many obvious things to say here. The anti-achievement   17
ethic buried in the "equity" argument is a deadly one. People can lose
without humiliation and win without feeling superior. Through sports,
children learn how to handle defeat as well as victory—no sulking, gloating or rubbing it in. Aerobics and interpretive dancing have their place,
but so do team sports. And it's always best to keep ideologues out of the
gym.

Come on. Let's play ball.   18

From U.S. News & World Report. *Reprinted by permission of John Leo.*

After You Read

Work with other students to develop responses to these questions or to compare
responses that you have already prepared.

1. Use your own words to state the thesis of the article. Then identify any sentence or
   sentences in the article that seem to express the idea.

2. Divide the article into sections according to each major point that Leo makes.

3. In three or four sentences, briefly summarize the thesis of the article and its major
   supporting points.

4. Identify the types of support that Leo uses. Does he use brief or extended examples, statistics, expert testimony?

5. Read the first five paragraphs of the article and identify the techniques used to
   maintain coherence from sentence to sentence and from paragraph to paragraph.

Before You Read

1. Look at the title. What is a bigot? What does the title suggest will be the central idea
   of this article?

2. In what age group would you expect to find the most bigotry—older Americans,
   middle-aged Americans, or younger Americans? Why?

A Generation of Bigots Comes of Age

Richard Cohen

There's hardly a politician in the land who, when children are mentioned, 1
does not say they are our future. That's true, of course—and nothing can
be done about it—but the way things are going we should all be worried.
A generation of bigots is coming of age.

The evidence for that awful prognostication can be found in a recent 2
public opinion survey conducted for the Anti-Defamation League by the
Boston polling firm of Marttila & Kiley—two outfits with considerable
credentials in the field of public opinion research.

For the first time, a trend has been reversed. Up to now, opinion polls 3
have always found that the more schooling a person has, the more likely
he is to be tolerant. For that reason, older people—who by and large have
the least education—are the most intolerant age group in the nation.

But no longer. The ADL found a disturbing symmetry: Older and 4
younger white Americans share the same biases. For instance, when
white people were asked if blacks prefer to remain on welfare rather than
work, 42 percent of the respondents 50 years old and over said the statement was "probably true." Predictably, the figure plummeted to 29 percent for those 30 to 49. But then it jumped to 36 percent for respondents
under 30.

Similarly, a majority of younger respondents thought blacks "com- 5
plain too much about racism" (68 percent) and "stick together more than
others" (63 percent). For both statements, the young had a higher percentage of agreement than any other age category.

The pattern persisted for the other questions as well—questions de- 6
signed to ferret out biased attitudes. In the words of Abraham Foxman,
the ADL's national director, the generation that's destined to run this
country is either racist or disposed to racism to a degree that he characterized as "a crisis." It's hard to disagree with him.

What's going on? The short answer is that no one knows for sure. But 7
some guesses can be ventured and none of them are comforting. The first
and most obvious explanation has to do with age itself: The under-30 generation is pathetically ignorant of recent American history.

Younger people apparently know little about—and did not see on 8
television—the civil rights struggles of the 1950s and 1960s, everything
from the police dogs of Birmingham to the murder of civil rights workers.
They apparently do not understand that if blacks tend to see racism
everywhere, that's because in the recent past, it was everywhere and
remains the abiding American sickness.

But historical ignorance is not the only factor accounting for the 9
ADL's findings. Another, apparently, is affirmative action. It has created a
category of white victims, either real or perceived, who are more likely
than other whites to hold prejudicial views.

For instance, when the ADL asked "Do you feel you have ever been a   10
victim of reverse discrimination in hiring or promotion," only 21 percent
said yes. But the percentage rose to 26 percent for college graduates and
23 percent for people with post-graduate degrees. Since the ADL found
that "about one-third" of the self-described victims of reverse discrimination fell into the "most prejudiced" category, these numbers are clearly
worth worrying about.

Too many of the American elite are racially aggrieved—although pos-   11
sibly some of them were bigoted in the first place.

One could argue that not all of the statements represent proof of   12
bigoted attitudes. For instance, white college students who witness vol-
untary self-segregation on the part of black students—demands for their
own dorms, for instance—have some reason to think that blacks "stick
together more than others."

Nevertheless, the data strongly suggests that progress on racial atti-   13
tudes is being reversed—with contributions from both races. Worse, this
is happening at a time when the economic pie is shrinking and competition for jobs increasing. If the economic trend continues, racial intolerance
is likely to grow.

It's nothing less than a calamity that a generation has come of age   14
without a deep appreciation of the recent history of African-Americans.
At the same time, black leaders who advocate or condone separatism had
better appreciate the damage they are doing.

And finally, affirmative action programs, as well-intentioned as they   15
may be, need to be re-examined—and without critics automatically being
labeled as racist. No doubt these programs have done some good. But
there's a growing body of evidence—of which the ADL poll is only the
latest—that they also do some bad.

© 1993, Washington Post Writers Group. Reprinted with permission.

After You Read

Work with other students to develop responses to these questions or to compare
responses that you have already prepared.

1. Use your own words to state the thesis of the article. Then identify any sentence or
    sentences in the article that seem to express the idea.
2. Divide the article into sections according to each major point that Cohen makes.
3. In three or four sentences, briefly summarize the thesis of the article and its major
    supporting points.
4. Paragraphs 2–6 serve a purpose different from paragraphs 7–11. Explain that dif-
    ference.
5. Identify the types of support that Cohen uses.
6. Look at paragraphs 12 and 13 (or other paragraphs assigned by your instructor)
    and explain how the coherence is maintained from sentence to sentence.

1. Consider the title. Does it describe you or people you know? In what way?

2. As a professor of psychiatry and pediatrics, Ronald Dahl focuses his article primarily on children. In what way might children be "burned out and bored"?

Burned Out and Bored

Ronald Dahl

Each summer, no matter how pressing my work schedule, I take off one day exclusively for my son. We call it dad-son day. This year our third stop was the amusement park, where he discovered (at the age of 9) that he was tall enough to ride one of the fastest roller coasters in the world. We blasted through face-stretching turns and loops for 90 seconds. Then, as we stepped off the ride, he shrugged and, in a distressingly calm voice, remarked that it was not as exciting as other rides he'd been on. As I listened, I began to sense something seriously out of balance.

Throughout the season, I noticed similar events all around me. Parents seemed hard pressed to find new thrills for nonchalant kids. I saw this pattern in my family, in the sons and daughters of friends and neighbors and in many of my patients with behavioral and emotional problems. Surrounded by ever-greater stimulation, their young faces were looking disappointed and bored.

By August, neighborhood parents were comparing their children's complaints of "nothing to do" to the sound of fingernails on a chalkboard. They were also shelling out large numbers of dollars for movies, amusement parks, video arcades, camps and visits to the mall. In many cases the money seemed to do little more than buy transient relief from the terrible moans of their bored children. This set me pondering the obvious question: "How can it be so hard for kids to find something to do when there's never been such a range of stimulating entertainment available to them?"

What really worries me is the intensity of the stimulation. I watch my 11-year-old daughter's face as she absorbs the powerful onslaught of arousing visuals and gory special effects in movies. Although my son is prohibited from playing violent videogames, I have seen some of his third-grade friends at an arcade inflicting blood-splattering, dismembering blows upon on-screen opponents in distressingly realistic games. My 4-year-old boy's high-tech toys have consumed enough batteries to power a small village for a year.

Why do children immersed in this much excitement seem starved for more? That was, I realized, the point. I discovered during my own reckless adolescence that what creates exhilaration is not going fast, but going faster. Accelerating from 0 to 60 mph in a few seconds slams the body backward with powerful sensations, but going 60 for hours on the interstate causes so little feeling of speed that we fight to stay awake. At a steady velocity of 600 mph we can calmly sip coffee on an airplane. Thrills have less to do with speed than changes in speed.

Since returning to school, the kids have been navigating ever more densely packed schedules. The morning rush to make the schoolbus is matched by a rapid shuttle through after-school sports, piano, foreign-language programs and social activities. Dinner is, too often, a series of snacks eaten on the run. Then, if they manage to get their homework done, the kids want to "relax" in front of highly arousing images on the television or computer screen. 6

I'm concerned about the cumulative effect of years at these levels of feverish activity. It is no mystery to me why many teenagers appear apathetic and burned out, with a "been there, done that" air of indifference toward much of life. As increasing numbers of friends' children are prescribed medications—stimulants to deal with inattentiveness at school or antidepressants to help with the loss of interest and joy in their lives—I question the role of kids' boredom in some of the diagnoses. 7

My own work—behavioral pediatrics and child psychiatry—is focused on the chemical imbalances and biological underpinnings to behavioral and emotional disorders. These are complex problems. Some of the most important research concentrates on genetic vulnerabilities and the effects of stress on the developing brain. Yet I've been reflecting more and more on how the pace of life and the intensity of stimulation may be contributing to the rising rates of psychiatric problems among children and adolescents in our society. 8

The problem of overstimulation arises frequently in my work on children's sleep. Although I diagnose and treat many unusual neurologically based sleep disorders, the most common is deceptively simple— many kids and adolescents don't get enough sleep. There are myriad factors in delaying bedtime despite the need to get up early for school. Even when tired, children often find stimulation through exciting activities. Fighting off tiredness by going faster can turn into a habit—and habits can be very hard to change. Most important, as thrills displace needed rest, sleep-deprived kids have trouble with irritability, inattention and moodiness. Ironically, stimulants can seem to help children with these symptoms. 9

Our research also suggests that difficulties in turning down one's emotions after a stressful event may be a major factor leading to adolescent mood disorders. Constant access to high stimulation may also create patterns of emotional imbalance. An adolescent moving too fast emotionally for too long can experience the same sense of stillness as the airline passenger traveling at breakneck speed. 10

My wait at the airport for a flight home from a scientific meeting gave me time to think more about this fast-track phenomenon. I fleetingly considered my own need to slow down and the disturbing truth in the cliché that each year goes by more quickly. I realized with sadness 11 how soon my children will be grown, and I sensed the fear that I may miss chapters of their childhood amid my hectic, overfilled life. In these images, I saw clearly the need to help our children find alternatives to the thrill-seeking fast lane by leading a slower version of life ourselves. I became convinced that nothing could be so important as finding a more balanced path, rediscovering slower, simpler pleasures before we all become burned out and bored to death.

After You Read

Work with other students to develop responses to these questions or to compare responses that you have already prepared.

1. Use your own words to state the thesis of the article. Then identify any sentence or sentences in the article that seem to express the idea.
2. Divide the article into sections according to each major point that Dahl makes.
3. In three or four sentences, briefly summarize the thesis of the article and its major supporting points.
4. Identify the types of support that Dahl uses. In what way is it different from the support used by Cohen and Leo?
5. Choose one paragraph from the article and explain how its coherence is maintained from sentence to sentence.

Writing Assignments

1. Discuss the kinds of experiences you or members of your class have had with competition in school sports. Was such competition enjoyable? Was it beneficial or detrimental in any way? Was competition overemphasized? Write a paper in which you briefly respond to John Leo's article "School Sports—Latest New Age Target." Describe your reaction to competitive school sports, using examples drawn from your own experience or from the experiences of people you have talked to.
2. Competition does not have to be restricted to sporting events. Work with members of your class to identify other areas of life in which you find yourself competing. Write a paper explaining whether or not you find that competition beneficial. Use specific examples to illustrate your ideas.
3. According to Richard Cohen, the national director of the Anti-Defamation League believes that "the generation that's destined to run this country is either racist or disposed to racism to a degree that he characterized as 'a crisis.'" Do your own experiences confirm or contradict this view? Write a paper in which you illustrate either in what ways attitudes of younger Americans are racist, intolerant, and bigoted or in what ways they are open, tolerant, and accepting

of other races, religions, lifestyles, or cultures. Support your ideas with examples drawn from your own experiences and observations.

4. Toward the end of his essay, Richard Cohen offers three reasons for the apparent racism of young Americans. Write an essay in which you offer your own explanations for racism among the young. Use examples drawn from your own experiences and observations to support your reasons.

5. In "Burned Out and Bored," Ronald Dahl discusses some of the disturbing consequences of our "fast-paced lives." Consider the pace of your own life and of the lives of people around you. Is a fast-paced life a drawback or a benefit? Can it be a little of both? Write an essay in which you examine the advantages and/or disadvantages of such a lifestyle, illustrating your points with examples drawn from your own experiences and observations.

6. Ronald Dahl closes his article this way: "I became convinced that nothing could be so important as finding a more balanced path, rediscovering slower, simpler pleasures before we all become burned out and bored to death." If this statement is true for you or for people you know, write a paper in which you explain exactly in what way it is true, giving detailed examples from personal experiences or observations.

Evaluating Sample Papers

As you read and evaluate the quality of the essays on the following pages, consider these areas:

1. Thesis Statement

   Underline the thesis statement of the essay. Does it express a clear and specific central idea?

   1   2   3   4   5   6

2. Topic Sentences

   Underline the topic sentence of each paragraph. Does it clearly state the central idea of the paragraph?

   1   2   3   4   5   6

3. Support

   Examine the supporting details in each paragraph. Are they specific and clear? Should they be more detailed, or should more support be included?

   1   2   3   4   5   6

4. Unity

   Does each paragraph clearly relate to and develop the central idea expressed in the thesis statement? Do the supporting details *within* each paragraph clearly relate to and develop the *central idea* expressed in the topic sentence of that paragraph?

   1   2   3   4   5   6

5. Coherence

   Does each paragraph open with a transition, a reference to the central idea of the thesis statement, and an identification of its own central idea? Are the sentences within each paragraph clearly related to each other by the use of transitions or by references to the central idea of the paragraph?

   1   2   3   4   5   6

6. Sentence Structure

   Do the sentences combine ideas that are related, using coordination and subordination when appropriate? Are there too many brief, choppy main clauses?

   1   2   3   4   5   6

7. Mechanics, Grammar, and Spelling

   Does the paper contain a distracting number of errors of these kinds?

   1   2   3   4   5   6

8. Overall Ranking of the Essay

   1   2   3   4   5   6

Student Essay 1

According to John Leo, who wrote "School Sports—Latest New Age Target," competitive games such as basketball and dodgeball are becoming scarce among gym classes across America. He reports that a *New York Times* article suggests that win-lose games are dangerous because losing means humiliation and the breaking of children's fragile egos. Although he believes that competition can be stressed too much, Leo thinks that competition doesn't have to be destructive. My own experiences make me agree with him. In my experience, the competition in team sports teaches kids cooperation and discipline, life skills which every child should learn.

Kids' egos might be fragile, but they are mended just as quickly as they are broken. Two children on my block, each around nine years of age, play little league baseball and are on opposing teams. Their teams both made it to the championship game, which I had the pleasure of watching. The game was close when one of the boys made the mistake of not running all the way to home plate; instead, he stopped half way there and then ran back to third while his teammate was on base. The terrible mistake caused him to get into a pickle and eventually be tagged out. His ego was broken that night on the field, but when I saw him the next day out on our street playing games with the other neighbors, he seemed fine. It seemed as if his ego had mended and he had regained his pride overnight. Later on in life, I'm sure this boy will be able to hold his composure during bad times. Holding one's pride after bad times is a quality I wish many people had.

In the twentieth century, women are having to compete with men all the time. Competition starts at the elementary level in the classroom and team sports. Girls can be just as good athletes as boys or even better. Many a time I have swum with faster girls, lost a game of volleyball against a team of girls, and been beaten by a girl in a game of tennis. Last year, my senior year in high school, my view of students was that girls were better students than boys. Healthy competition of the opposite sex at a young age is an indirect way for these girls to have the confidence they need when they get older and have to compete against men for jobs.

My feelings on competition in school are the same as John Leo's. Kids want to have fun playing games. I think it's the adults who have the problem, not the kids. Competition is present in everyday life in many different forms, and kids need to learn how to deal with competition at a young age so they are ready when they enter the real world. Cooperation and discipline are good features which I hope my kids learn at an early age.

Student Essay 2

Throughout my life I and people I know have experienced intolerance, racism, or bigotry. Richard Cohen explains in his article how people in America are still experiencing bigotry and intolerance for being the race they are. Cohen feels that we should be worried about the way things are going in America because a generation of bigots is coming of age. I feel that he is correct in this assumption.

This intolerance of other races comes from people who have never experienced intolerance in their lives. For example, when I was a little girl, my next door neighbors kids would come out and play with my sister and me, but they'd call us names and put us down by saying bad things about Mexicans, they obviously didn't like people of our race mixing with theirs. So, we tried to stay away from them as much as possible. These kids just didn't know to act any better because of the way they were raised. Some people are just raised to not like certain races and act differently toward them.

The reality of how people may be so intolerant toward other peoples races is being very closed minded. Like Cohen stated in his article "... if blacks tend to see racism everywhere ... it was everywhere and remains the abiding American sickness." To live in America you have to get accustomed to their culture and race, but people want to stick to their own. For example, when we visit with the cousins on my moms side of the family, they want us to leave our Mexican customs and heritage behind because they want us to be like they are which is having a white tradition.

Cohen raises this bigotry issue that touches everyone who's been treated with intolerance in the past. But no one wants to have to change themselves to try to fit in more with other races than their own. Like me when I was little and played with my next door neighbors I just wished that we could all just play together without worrying about being a different race, so that meant we couldn't play together. Somehow almost everyone out there is guilty of being a racist or bigot because we don't all get along and we don't all like everyone else. Maybe this is just a part of living in America and it will never change.

Student Essay 3

Since returning to school, I have been navigating a very densely packed schedule. From school, to working full time, to spending time with family and friends there is hardly any time to relax. In his article "Burned Out and Bored," Ronald Dahl discusses the "fast-paced lives" kids lead today; Dahl believes that children are suffering due to their busy lives. Dahl explains that kids today are getting bored easily, and in turn may suffer from sleep disorders as well as emotional problems. It seems that living a "fast-paced" lifestyle is a drawback. There are several disadvantages of living a "fast-paced" life such as, sleep disorders, a rise in stress level, and becoming bored.

Lack of sleep is one drawback to having a "fast-paced" life. Children today are finding "stimulation through exciting activities" and fighting off the tiredness, making them more and more sleep deprived. I've noticed this with my younger sister, Melanie. Even when she complains about being tired she always seems to find another activity to do. Just a couple of nights ago, about 10:30 pm she was whinning about needing to go to sleep. She went into her room, turned on the television, and watch t.v. for another hour and a half.

An increase in stress is also a factor of a "fast-paced" life. With more and more to do but not as much time to do them in, stressfulness is always the outcome. For myself, this statement is quite true. In my first semester of college, I decided to take twelve units, work more hours at my job and try to spend more time with friends and family. Trying to have a "fast-paced" life, to do as much as I possibly could caused my stress level to jump. I constantly wondered whether or not I would get good grades at school and if I would get enough money on my next paycheck to pay the bills. My life became so stressful I stopped spending so much time with my friends, but even that only relieved the stress temporarily.

Boredom is another downfall to living a "fast-paced" life. Every day I hear the words "I'm bored" from the toddler that I baby sit. With every video game ever made, several toys and board games, and various movies kids today are complaining about lack of stimulation. Mitchell, the little boy I baby sit, is only five-years-old and already complaining that he's bored with his toys. I had to ask myself the same question Ronald Dahl asked himself: "How can it be so hard for kids to find something to do when there's never been such a range of stimulating entertainment available to them?" Children are bored with the same old entertainment. The truth is "what creates exhilaration is not going fast, but going faster." Kids need different activities and other forms of entertainment, because they are getting bored too easily.

"Fast-paced" lives can cause several drawbacks including lack of sleep, an increase in stress and boredom. For myself, I noticed that the years pass more quickly as I continue to live a fast-track lifestyle. Amid my hectic life, it is clear that we should slow down to help the children with their fast-track lives and try to find an alternative. Ronald Dahl was correct when he wrote, "I became convinced that nothing could be so important as finding a more balanced path, rediscovering slower, simpler pleasures before we all become burned out and bored to death."

Sentence Combining: Verbal Phrases

The verbal phrase is an easy and effective way to add more information to your sentences without using a full clause to do so. In fact, you already use verbal phrases every day, both in your speech and in your writing. When you write "The man crossing the street waved at the irate motorists," you use a verbal phrase ("crossing the street"). The sentence "The plan to rob the bank was nearly flawless" also contains a verbal phrase ("to rob the bank").

Although people use verbal phrases unconsciously in their speech and writing, learning how to use them in a planned, conscious manner can improve your writing two ways. First, using verbal phrases will allow you to add more action and description to your writing without using additional sentences. As a result, your writing will have a sense of depth and detail that will distinguish it from the prose of the average writer. Second, using these phrases will allow you to vary the structure of the sentences that you write, and a varied sentence structure makes for more interesting reading than sentence after sentence written exactly the same way.

A **verbal** is simply a verb form that is not used as a verb. For example, in the following sentences, the underlined verb forms are used as adjectives, not as verbs.

The <u>singing</u> cowboy made everybody angry.

The police officer assisted the <u>confused</u> motorist.

Each type of verbal has its own specific name. In the above examples, *singing* is a **present participle** and *confused* is a **past participle.**

Present and Past Participles

The **present participle** is the "-ing" form of a verb used as an adjective.

A <u>traveling</u> sales representative decided that he needed a new pair of shoes.

Mr. Ingham did not know what to do about the <u>barking</u> dogs.

The **past participle** is also used as an adjective. Some past participles end in "-d" or "-ed" (*picked, fired, tossed*); others end in "-n" or "-en" (*eaten, thrown, spoken*); still others have their own unique forms (*sung, brought, gone*). To determine the past participle form of any verb, ask yourself how you would spell the word if "have" preceded it.

The <u>exhausted</u> jogger decided to rest for an hour.

The patient with the <u>broken</u> leg was ready to leave the hospital.

Present and Past Participial Phrases

Present and past participial phrases consist of present and past participles with other words added to them to give more details. The following examples are drawn from "Rambos of the Road," "A Generation of Bigots Comes of Age," and "Burned Out and Bored."

> <u>Approaching a highway on an entrance ramp recently</u>, I was strongarmed by a trailer truck. . . .

> A bus had stopped in the cross traffic, <u>blocking our paths</u>: it was normal-for-New-York-City gridlock.

> The evidence for that awful prognostication can be found in a recent public opinion survey <u>conducted for the Anti-Defamation League by the Boston polling firm of Marttila & Kiley</u>. . . .

> <u>Surrounded by ever-greater stimulation</u>, their young faces were looking disappointed and bored.

Infinitive Phrases

The **infinitive** is another type of verbal. It consists of the base form of a verb preceded by "to" (*to throw, to breathe, to eat*). The **infinitive phrase** consists of the infinitive with other words added to it to give more details. Here are some examples from "Burned Out and Bored":

> This year our third stop was the amusement park, where he discovered (at the age of 9) that he was tall enough <u>to ride one of the fastest roller coasters in the world</u>.

> There are myriad factors in delaying bedtime despite the need <u>to get up early for school</u>.

Using Verbal Phrases

Participial and infinitive phrases can be used to improve your writing in several ways:

1. Use verbal phrases to develop sentences by adding details and ideas.

   Participial phrases are particularly effective for adding details to your sentences. Since participles are verbals, they work especially well when you are describing actions. Notice how the writers of the articles in this chapter used verbal phrases to expand their sentences.

   Through sports, children learn how to handle defeat as well as victory.

   Through sports, children learn how to handle defeat as well as victory—<u>no sulking, gloating or rubbing it in</u>.

   An adolescent can experience the same sense of stillness as the airline passenger.

An adolescent <u>moving too fast emotionally for too long</u> can experience the same sense of stillness as the airline passenger <u>traveling at breakneck speed</u>.

2. Use verbal phrases to combine related sentences.

Verbal phrases often can be used to create one sentence from two or more related sentences. Note how the following sentences can be combined using verbal phrases.

Two sentences: Seymour stared at his lottery ticket in amazement. He could not believe that he had just won ten million dollars.

One sentence using a present participial phrase: <u>Staring at his lottery ticket in amazement</u>, Seymour could not believe that he had just won ten million dollars.

Two sentences: A body was found in the Alps last year. It had been frozen for over three thousand years.

One sentence using a past participial phrase: A body <u>frozen for over three thousand years</u> was found in the Alps last year.

Two sentences: Michelle wanted to pass the midterm on Monday. She knew that she should study all weekend.

One sentence using an infinitive phrase: Michelle knew that she should study all weekend <u>to pass the midterm on Monday</u>.

3. Use verbal phrases to be concise.

Many subordinate clauses can easily and more concisely be written as verbal phrases.

The sycamore tree <u>that is growing next to our driveway</u> has started to drop its leaves.

The sycamore tree <u>growing next to our driveway</u> has started to drop its leaves.

<u>Because he thought that he had seen a ghost</u>, Herman began to scream.

<u>Thinking that he had seen a ghost</u>, Herman began to scream.

The person <u>who was accused of shoplifting</u> insisted that she had paid for all her items.

The person <u>accused of shoplifting</u> insisted that she had paid for all her items.

Exercise 4.5

Develop the following sentences by adding verbal phrases to them where indicated. Use verbals derived from the verbs in parentheses.

Example

⌃ Lyle stared at the paper in front of him. (confuse, determine)

Confused by the unclear directions but determined to pass the test, Lyle stared at the paper in front of him.

1. ⌃ Calvin jogged fifteen miles every day. (prepare)
2. ⌃ The mangy alley cat slowly licked its lips. (stare)
3. The driver in the blue Isuzu was driving erratically ⌃ . (honk, cut, weave)
4. ⌃George was not in the mood to shop for Christmas trees. (irritate, bother)
5. My six-year-old daughter ⌃ walked out of the rain and into our living room. (wear, hold)
6. Narcissus stood before the mirror ⌃ . (gaze, wonder)
7. Frankie looked at Annette and told her about his plans ⌃ . (quit, buy, move)
8. The UFO ⌃ flew into space and never returned. (observe, photograph)
9. ⌃ The seven dwarves headed for the mine. (whistle, sing)
10. Last summer we drove over three thousand miles. ⌃ (visit, tour, relax) ■

Exercise 4.6

Combine each of the following groups of sentences* into one sentence. Change each underlined sentence into the type of verbal phrase suggested in parentheses.

Example

The macaw emitted an earsplitting shriek.
It flew from the tree.
(present participial phrase)

Emitting an earsplitting shriek, the macaw flew from the tree.

1. A rogue elephant separates itself from the herd and roams alone.
   It is often quite dangerous.
   (present participial phrase)

2. A solitary rogue elephant can be savage.
   It attacks and kills everyone it can.
   (present participial phrase)

3. A. A. Kinlock, a British authority, wrote that a rogue will often haunt a particular road.
   It will stop traffic for as long as it remains.
   (present participial phrase)

Adapted from Lawrence D. Gadd, The Second Book of the Strange (Amherst, NY: Prometheus Books). © 1981 by Newspaper Enterprise Association. Reprinted by permission of the publisher.

4. One particular rogue in India seemed determined.
   <u>It killed many people and even destroyed their homes.</u>
   (infinitive phrase)

5. <u>Carl Ackley was seized and mutilated by a rogue elephant.</u>
   Carl Ackley, the father of modern taxidermy, became convinced that the elephant was the most dangerous of all animals.
   (past participial phrase)

6. <u>The Asian elephant is considered less temperamental than the African elephant.</u>
   It nevertheless more commonly turns rogue.
   <u>It accounts for the deaths of more than fifty persons per year.</u>
   (past participial phrase and present participial phrase)

7. <u>A rogue elephant wants to destroy its victim.</u>
   It will catch him and dismember him.
   <u>It will smash him against the ground or a tree.</u>
   <u>It will toss him into the air.</u>
   (infinitive phrase and two present participial phrases)

8. An elephant may turn rogue because it is suffering from a wound.
   <u>The wound may have been inflicted by another elephant or by hunters.</u>
   (past participial phrase)

9. In many instances, elephants were found to have been suffering from painful sores and old wounds.
   <u>These elephants had been identified as rogues and killed.</u>
   (past participial phrase)

10. <u>One Indian rogue suffered from a huge sore at the end of its tail.</u>
    It caused great damage.
    <u>It chased travelers.</u>
    <u>It killed several natives.</u>
    (present participial phrases) ■

Avoiding Dangling Modifiers

Since verbal phrases are not verbs, they do not have subjects. However, they do express an action, and the "doer" of that action is usually the subject of the sentence. Whenever you open a sentence with a verbal phrase, be sure that the subject of the sentence is also the "doer." If the subject cannot logically perform the action in the verbal phrase, you have a dangling modifier that needs to be rewritten. (See Chapter 16 for a more thorough discussion of dangling modifiers.)

Dangling modifier

> <u>Sighing with relief</u>, the golf ball rolled into the cup.
> (A golf ball cannot sigh with relief.)

Possible correction

> <u>Sighing with relief</u>, the golfer watched as his golf ball rolled into the cup.
> (A logical subject has now been supplied. A golfer can sigh with relief.)

Possible correction

> As the golfer sighed with relief, the golf ball rolled into the cup.
> (The verbal phrase has been rewritten into a subordinate clause with its own subject and verb.)

Exercise 4.7

Revise any dangling modifiers in the following sentences, either by supplying a logical subject or by rewriting the verbal phrase as a subordinate clause. Some sentences may be correct.

Example

Incorrect

> Surprised by the unexpected rainstorm, our clothing was soon soaked.

Correct

> Surprised by the unexpected rainstorm, we were all soon soaked.

Correct

> Because we were all surprised by the unexpected rainstorm, our clothing was soon soaked.

1. Staring at the boiling noodles, the pasta was almost ready.
2. Damaged by the intense heat, Cheryl threw the videocassette into the trash.
3. Turning green with slime and algae, parts of Lake Elsinore soon became a local eyesore.
4. Breaking in through the kitchen window, the stereo equipment and television set were stolen.
5. Frightened by the low moaning sounds coming from the cellar, Herman's hand reached for the phone. ■

Exercise 4.8

Combine the following sentences using verbal phrases. In each case, the first sentence is the main sentence. Each following sentence should be revised as a verbal phrase and added to the beginning or to the end of the main sentence or, occasionally, within the main sentence. Be careful not to write a dangling modifier when you start a sentence with a verbal phrase.

1. A zombie is the body of a dead person.
   The dead person has been reanimated by a voodoo sorcerer.
   The sorcerer is called a *boko*.
2. Haitian folklore is filled with stories of zombies.
   It cites many cases of people who have reappeared after they were already buried.

3. According to folklore, a *boko* reanimates the corpse.
   He will use it as his slave.

4. The *boko* causes people to think a person has really died.
   He uses certain drugs that induce a state of lethargy similar to death.

5. After the person's burial, the body is recovered by the *boko*.
   The body has been deprived of its soul.
   The body has been reduced to a zombie.

6. The zombie can return to its grave only after the time decreed for its natural death has arrived.
   The zombie serves the *boko* who has reanimated it.

7. Believers in zombies will poison or stab a corpse.
   They want to prevent their relatives from becoming zombies.
   They want to be sure the corpse is really dead.

8. Supposedly, feeding a zombie salt will free it from its condition.
   It will allow the zombie to seek out its grave and die.

9. Some people say that zombies are actually victims of a potent drug that incapacitates them.
   The drug inhibits speech and will power. It allows motion.

10. A *boko* may use hypnosis and suggestion.
    Hypnosis and suggestion may increase the power of the drug.
    Hypnosis and suggestion may further incapacitate the person. ■

Part 2

Writing about Reading

In the first four chapters of this text, you have written papers on topics similar to those in the reading selections. In a sense, you have used the topics in the reading selections as springboards for your own ideas, and then you have supported those ideas with examples drawn from real life experiences.

In the next four chapters, you will move from writing on topics that are similar to those in the reading selections to writing about the reading selections themselves. Often called academic *papers because they are required in many college-level courses, the writing assignments in the next four chapters will introduce you to accurately summarizing what you have read, to evaluating and responding to the ideas in a reading selection, to synthesizing ideas from several articles, and to arguing a point based on information drawn from a number of sources. In other words, you will be asked to write about what you have read.*

Of course, academic writing *does not mean that you will no longer use personal experiences to support your points. As a means of supporting your ideas, the real experiences of real people are just as important as ever. You will find, however, that much of your support will also be drawn from the articles you read. For that reason, the clear and accurate reading you have been practicing in Chapters 1 through 4 will be of critical importance. Obviously, you cannot write thoughtfully about an article if you have not first read it in a thoughtful manner.*

Chapter 5

Summarizing and Responding to Reading

Clear and accurate summarizing is one of the most important skills you can learn in college. Your ability to summarize effectively will help you to study for and take tests, to write reports and papers (particularly papers involving research), and to give thorough, convincing oral presentations. Summarizing is also a skill in demand in the business world, especially when you must report information to other people. The person who can read and *accurately* report what he or she has read will always have an advantage over the person who cannot.

It seems as if summarizing should be such a simple task. After all, when you summarize, you merely explain what you have read to somebody else. And in many ways summarizing *is* simple. Yet it also can be quite a challenging assignment. A good summary demands that you read carefully, that you accurately identify the main points of what you have read, and that you then successfully communicate those ideas to another person. The following explanations should help you to write successful summaries.

Characteristics of a Successful Summary

- A summary accurately communicates the author's ideas.
- It includes all of the author's main points.
- It usually does *not* include supporting details.
- It does *not* include your opinions or reactions.
- It does *not* alter the author's meaning in any way.
- It uses your own words and writing style.

Writing a Brief Summary

Because most summaries present only the central idea and main points of a reading selection, they are usually quite brief, often no more than one or two paragraphs long. To write a summary, follow these steps:

1. As you read the material that you intend to summarize, underline or highlight whatever seems significant to you. Mark statements that seem to express the central idea and the main points of the reading selection. Even particularly vivid facts or other supporting details may be marked.

2. Reread the material, annotating it and dividing it into major sections so that each section reflects one main point.

3. Write the opening sentence of your summary. It should identify the name of the reading selection, the author, and the central idea, purpose, thesis, or topic of the reading.

4. After the opening sentence, briefly summarize each of the author's main ideas. Often you will need no more than one sentence to summarize each main idea.

5. Revise what you have written so that your summary is expressed in your own words and in your own style of writing. Where needed, add transitions that refer to the author between main points.

Reading

Read the following article. As you do, identify its central idea and main points. Then reread the article, annotating it and dividing it into major sections. A sample brief summary follows the article. Note how the central idea and main points of the article are incorporated into the summary.

The Decline of Neatness

Norman Cousins

Anyone with a passion for hanging labels on people or things should have little difficulty in recognizing that an apt tag for our time is the Unkempt Generation. I am not referring solely to college kids. The sloppiness virus has spread to all sectors of society. People go to all sorts of trouble and expense to look uncombed, unshaved, unpressed.

The symbol of the times is blue jeans—not just blue jeans in good condition but jeans that are frayed, torn, discolored. They don't get that way naturally. No one wants blue jeans that are crisply clean or spanking new. Manufacturers recognize a big market when they see it, and they compete with one another to offer jeans that are made to look as though they've just been discarded by clumsy house painters after ten years of wear. The more faded and seemingly ancient the garment, the higher the cost. Disheveled is in fashion; neatness is obsolete.

Nothing is wrong with comfortable clothing. It's just that current usage is more reflective of a slavish conformity than a desire for ease. No generation has strained harder than ours to affect a casual, relaxed, cool look; none has succeeded more spectacularly in looking as though it had been stamped out by cookie cutters. The attempt to avoid any appearance of being well groomed or even neat has a quality of desperation about it and suggests a calculated and phony deprivation. We shun conventionality, but we put on a uniform to do it. An appearance of alienation is the triumphant goal, to be pursued in oversize sweaters and muddy sneakers.

Slovenly speech comes off the same spool. Vocabulary, like blue jeans, is being drained of color and distinction. A complete sentence in everyday speech is as rare as a man's tie in the swank Polo Lounge of the Beverly Hills Hotel. People communicate in chopped-up phrases, relying on grunts and chants of "you know" or "I mean" to cover up a damnable incoherence. Neatness should be no less important in language than it is in dress. But spew and sprawl are taking over. The English language is one of the greatest sources of wealth in the world. In the midst of accessible riches, we are linguistic paupers.

Violence in language has become almost as casual as the possession   5
of handguns. The curious notion has taken hold that emphasis in communicating is impossible without the incessant use of four-letter words.
Some screenwriters openly admit that they are careful not to turn in
scripts that are devoid of foul language lest the classification office
impose the curse of a G (general) rating. Motion-picture exhibitors have a
strong preference for the R (restricted) rating, probably on the theory of
forbidden fruit. Hence writers and producers have every incentive to
employ tasteless language and gory scenes.

The effect is to foster attitudes of casualness toward violence and   6
brutality not just in entertainment but in everyday life. People are not as
uncomfortable as they ought to be about the glamorization of human
hurt. The ability to react instinctively to suffering seems to be atrophying.
Youngsters sit transfixed in front of television or motion-picture screens,
munching popcorn while human beings are battered or mutilated. Nothing is more essential in education than respect for the frailty of human
beings; nothing is more characteristic of the age than mindless violence.

Everything I have learned about the educational process convinces   7
me that the notion that children can outgrow casual attitudes toward brutality is wrong. Count on it: if you saturate young minds with materials
showing that human beings are fit subjects for debasement or dismembering, the result will be desensitization to everything that should produce revulsion or resistance. The first aim of education is to develop
respect for life, just as the highest expression of civilization is the supreme
tenderness that people are strong enough to feel and manifest toward one
another. If society is breaking down, as it too often appears to be, it is not
because we lack the brainpower to meet its demands but because our feelings are so dulled that we don't recognize we have a problem.

Untidiness in dress, speech and emotions is readily connected to   8
human relationships. The problem with the casual sex so fashionable in
films is not that it arouses lust but that it deadens feelings and annihilates
privacy. The danger is not that sexual exploitation will create sex fiends
but that it may spawn eunuchs. People who have the habit of seeing
everything and doing anything run the risk of feeling nothing.

My purpose here is not to make a case for a Victorian decorum or for   9
namby-pambyism. The argument is directed to bad dress, bad manners,
bad speech, bad human relationships. The hope has to be that calculated
sloppiness will run its course. Who knows, perhaps some of the hip
designers may discover they can make a fortune by creating fashions that
are unfrayed and that grace the human form. Similarly, motion-picture
and television producers and exhibitors may realize that a substantial
audience exists for something more appealing to the human eye and
spirit than the sight of a human being hurled through a store-front window or tossed off a penthouse terrace. There might even be a salutary
response to films that dare to show people expressing genuine love and
respect for one another in more convincing ways than anonymous clutching and thrashing about.

Finally, our schools might encourage the notion that few things are more rewarding than genuine creativity, whether in the clothes we wear, the way we communicate, the nurturing of human relationships, or how we locate the best in ourselves and put it to work.

© 1990 by Time, Inc. Reprinted by permission.

A Sample Brief Summary

In "The Decline of Neatness," Norman Cousins argues that a "sloppiness virus" is affecting all areas of our society. According to Cousins, the sloppy clothing that is so fashionable today reflects our desperate need to conform, making us look as if we had been "stamped out by cookie cutters." Our sloppy speech reflects the same need, but it goes beyond the slovenly to the violent. And this sloppily violent speech results in casual attitudes toward all violence and brutality. Cousins claims that we seem to be losing the ability to react to suffering. He says that the violence and brutality in movies and television are "desensitizing" our children and that such casual attitudes toward violence will not be outgrown. Finally, he suggests that our sloppy clothing, speech, and emotions affect human relationships, as is evident in the casual attitude toward sex in films, an attitude that is deadening our feelings and destroying our privacy. Cousins concludes by stating that he does not want to return to Victorian attitudes, although he does hope that our "calculated sloppiness" will soon disappear and that we will all begin to "locate the best in ourselves and put it to work."

Exercise 5.1

Identify the paragraph or paragraphs from "The Decline of Neatness" that are covered in each sentence of the above summary. Are all of the main points of "The Decline of Neatness" clearly and accurately summarized? ■

Writing Paraphrases and Quotations

Paraphrasing

As you can see from the above sample summary, most of what you write in a summary consists of the author's ideas put into your own words. Each time you reword what an author has written so that the *author's idea* is now expressed in *your writing style*, you have **paraphrased** the author. Here are some points to consider when you paraphrase:

1. Paraphrases must reflect your own writing style, not the author's.
2. Paraphrases must not change or distort the author's ideas in any way.
3. Paraphrases must be clearly identified as presenting the author's ideas, not your own.

4. Paraphrases use the present tense when referring to the author.

Here are some paraphrases that appeared in the sample summary of "The Decline of Neatness," along with the original passages.

Original

> The ability to react instinctively to suffering seems to be atrophying.

Paraphrase

> Cousins claims that we seem to be losing the ability to react to suffering.

Original

> Untidiness in dress, speech, and emotions is readily connected to human relationships. The problem with the casual sex so fashionable in films is not that it arouses lust but that it deadens feelings and annihilates privacy.

Paraphrase

> Finally, he suggests that our sloppy clothing, speech, and emotions affect human relationships, as is evident in the casual attitude toward sex in films, an attitude that is deadening our feelings and destroying our privacy.

Note that both of the above paraphrases accurately state the ideas in the original, yet they do so in a writing style quite different from that of the original. Both paraphrases clearly refer to the author of the article, and the words that refer to the author are written in the present tense.

Quoting

A quotation is an exact reproduction of an author's words. To let the reader know that the words are not your own, you must use quotation marks. However, you should be careful to use quotations sparingly in your writing. For the most part, *your* writing should be in *your* style, not in someone else's, so most references to what you have read should appear as paraphrases, not as quotations. In general, quote only those words, phrases, or sentences that you really want to emphasize or that would not be as emphatic if they were paraphrased. In fact, notice how *few* quotations appear in the brief summary of "The Decline of Neatness" above. With that said, let's discuss the points you should keep in mind when you use quotations in your writing.

1. Quotations must be accurate.

Original

> People go to all sorts of trouble and expense to look uncombed, unshaved, unpressed.

Inaccurate

> As Cousins says, "People go to <u>a lot</u> of trouble and expense to look uncombed, unshaven, <u>and</u> unpressed."

2. *Every* quotation should be integrated into your text with a transition that refers to its source.

> Cousins says, "Slovenly speech comes off the same spool."

> Next, Cousins discusses sloppy speech, saying it "comes off the same spool" as sloppy dress.

3. Use correct punctuation to separate transitions from quotations.

   a. Use commas to set off transitional phrases that introduce a complete-sentence quotation.

   > According to Cousins, "The sloppiness virus has spread to all sectors of society."

   > "The sloppiness virus," according to Cousins, "has spread to all sectors of society."

   > "The sloppiness virus has spread to all sectors of society," according to Cousins.

   b. Use a colon to separate a complete-sentence quotation from a complete-sentence transition.

   > Cousins is emphatic in his assertion that sloppiness affects us all: "The sloppiness virus has spread to all sectors of society."

   c. Do not use any punctuation to set off partial quotations unless you would have used punctuation even if the quotation marks were not there.

   > Cousins insists that sloppiness affects "all sectors of society."

4. Use brackets if you need to add one or more of your own words for clarity and an ellipsis (three spaced dots) if you leave out material.

Original

> People go to all sorts of trouble and expense to look uncombed, unshaved, unpressed.

Quotation

> Cousins claims that many people today go to great lengths to appear "uncombed, unshaved, [and] unpressed."

Original

> If society is breaking down, as it too often appears to be, it is not because we lack the brainpower to meet its demands but because our feelings are so dulled that we don't recognize we have a problem.

Quotation

> According to Cousins, "If society is breaking down . . . it is not because we lack the brainpower to meet its demands. . . ."

Note Words added in brackets must *not* alter the author's idea, and words omitted need *not* be replaced with an ellipsis if it is obvious that they have been omitted. Notice that none of the partial quotations in any of the above examples need ellipses. Also notice that the last example has *four* spaced dots. The fourth dot is a period.

5. Use single quotation marks to indicate a quotation that appears within another quotation.

   Cousins states that people today speak in "chopped-up phrases, relying on grunts and chants of 'you know' or 'I mean' to cover up a damnable incoherence."

6. Punctuate the end of a quotation correctly.

   a. Place periods and commas within quotation marks.

      Cousins also states, "Nothing is wrong with comfortable clothing."

      "Nothing is wrong with comfortable clothing," Cousins states.

   b. Place semicolons and colons outside quotation marks.

      Cousin also states, "Nothing is wrong with comfortable clothing"; however, he does object to our "slavish conformity."

   c. Place question marks and exclamation points within quotation marks if the quotation is a question or exclamation. In all other situations, place them outside.

      Do you agree when Cousins writes, "Violence in language has become almost as casual as the possession of handguns"?

      In "Burned Out and Bored," Ronald Dahl asks, "Why do children immersed in this much excitement seem starved for more?"

Exercise 5.2

Write a brief summary of Michael Ryan's "Are You Living Mindlessly?" which appears on pages 52–54, or an article assigned by your instructor. Your summary should identify the central point and main ideas of the article. Follow the above suggestions for writing paraphrases and quotations in your summary. ■

Writing an Extended Summary

Although brief summaries are handy for expressing the main ideas of something you have read, many papers, reports, or presentations will require a more detailed summary of your source, one that explains the main ideas more thoroughly, pointing out which ideas the author has emphasized and how the author has supported those ideas. Writing an extended summary is excellent practice for such assignments. To write a successful extended summary, you need to read carefully and accurately and to communicate what you have read clearly and completely to someone else.

The steps in the writing of an extended summary are essentially the same as those in the writing of a brief summary. However, the extended summary is written as a brief essay, with individual paragraphs explaining the author's points in more detail than in a brief summary. Below is an extended summary of "The Decline of Neatness." Notice how each paragraph focuses on one of the article's main points.

Sample Extended Summary

In his article "The Decline of Neatness," Norman Cousins claims that a "sloppiness virus" has infected all areas of our society. His evidence focuses specifically on our style of dress, our casual speaking habits, our apathetic attitude toward violence and brutality, and our ineffective human relationships.

Cousins first examines the way we dress. He points out that the torn, sloppy jeans worn by so many people today can stand as a symbol of our times. According to Cousins, today it is fashionable to look disheveled, but such sloppiness is really not much more than a "slavish conformity." In fact, he says that today's sloppy dress makes people look as if they had been "stamped out by cookie cutters." It suggests, he says, a phoniness, as if the mere "appearance of alienation" were our goal.

In addition to the sloppiness in our dress, Cousins discusses the sloppy speech so common today. He says that people today speak in "chopped-up phrases," rarely use complete sentences, and lack the ability to use the English language effectively. Our speech, he says, is violent and foul, so foul in fact that screenwriters today resist turning in scripts that are too tame in order to avoid receiving any rating lower than an R (restricted).

Our foul and violent speech, according to Cousins, results in casual attitudes towards all violence and brutality. Cousins claims that we seem to be losing the ability to react to suffering, that "mindless violence" is the characteristic of our age. He says that the violence and brutality in movies and television are "desensitizing" our children and that such casual attitudes toward violence will not be outgrown.

Cousins's final point concerns human relationships. He suggests that our sloppy clothing, speech, and emotions affect human relationships, as is evident in the casual attitude toward sex in films. Our willingness to accept such casual sex, he says, deadens our feelings and destroys our privacy. It turns us not into lustful people, but into people who are incapable of feeling anything. Norman Cousins closes his article by stating that he does not want to return to Victorian attitudes, although he does hope that our "calculated sloppiness" will eventually disappear. He suggests that fashion designers and movie or television producers might someday discover that people would respond to clothes and movies that show respect for the human form and spirit, and he hopes that schools will find ways to encourage students to pursue "genuine creativity" in all areas of their lives.

Exercise 5.3

Work with other students to develop responses to these questions or to compare responses that you have already prepared.

1. Examine the introductory paragraph of the sample extended summary above. Where does it state the central idea of "The Decline of Neatness"? What other information does it include?

2. Identify the topic sentence of each body paragraph. Which paragraph or paragraphs from "The Decline of Neatness" does that topic sentence introduce?

3. Identify the transitions between paragraphs.

4. Examine the support within each paragraph. Have any points been left out of it that you think should have been included? ■

Writing a Summary-Response Essay

Many college writing assignments will ask you both to summarize what you have read and to respond to it. After all, your ability to express your own reaction to a topic is certainly as important as your ability to summarize that topic. Although the structure of such an essay will vary, depending on the topic and the expectations of your instructor, one common format consists of a brief summary in your introductory paragraph, followed by a clear thesis statement of your own in the same introductory paragraph, followed by several body paragraphs that support and develop your thesis statement. When you write a summary-response essay, keep the following points in mind:

1. The introduction should include a brief summary of the article and its main points.

2. The introduction should include a thesis statement that expresses your response to the topic.

3. Each body paragraph should open with a topic sentence that clearly refers to and develops the thesis statement.

4. Each body paragraph should support its topic sentence with explanations, facts, examples, statistics, or references to authority.

5. Each sentence should reflect a sense of coherence by exhibiting a clear relationship to the sentence before it or to the topic sentence of the paragraph.

Sample Summary-Response Essay

In "The Decline of Neatness," Norman Cousins argues that a "sloppiness virus" is affecting all areas of our society. According to Cousins, the sloppy clothing that is so in fashion today reflects our desperate need to conform, making us look as if we had been "stamped out by cookie cutters." Our sloppy speech reflects the same need, but it is more than just sloppy: it is foul and violent. He says that our sloppy language results in casual attitudes toward all violence and brutality and that, as a result, our children are losing the ability to react to suffering. Finally, he suggests that our sloppy clothing, speech, and attitudes affect human relationships, resulting in a sexual exploitation that "deadens feelings and annihilates privacy." I believe that Cousins's points are well worth considering. In fact, I have found that his "sloppiness virus" has affected my life and the lives of people I know in a number of significant areas.

A quick jaunt down the freeway will reveal the sloppiness virus at work in the way we drive our cars. Many drivers today either do not care about other people on the road or do not realize how dangerous their sloppy driving habits really are. Cars switch from one lane to the other and back again without signaling; they weave in and out of traffic; they race up to the rear bumper of the car in front of them—even if both cars are in the right lane—and tailgate for miles. Not too many months ago I was nearly killed by a sloppy driver in a white Celica. Traffic was heavy, moving at only about forty-five miles per hour, when he raced up behind me and began to flash his brights—as if there were anywhere I could go. As soon as he had the chance, he changed lanes to the left, raced past me, changed lanes again so that he was now in front of me, and then plowed into the rear of a bus. I had just enough time to brace myself before I smashed into him. I awoke in the hospital with a broken hip and a smashed ankle—all because of one person's sloppy driving habits.

As well as turning drivers into life-threatening idiots, the sloppiness virus affects our attitudes toward relationships. Many people today (myself included) act as if relationships should be easy, as if "love" should smooth out all the rough spots and keep us comfortable. I know of couple after couple who have separated or divorced or broken up after their relationship became more work than romance. But I also know a few couples who have managed to drop the sloppy expectation that relationships should be easy. One person in particular, a friend named Bob, nearly walked out of a sixteen-year marriage last year, but today he and his wife are closer than I have ever seen them. When I asked him what made the difference, he said that he decided to act *as if* he still loved his wife until he really did feel love for her again. He said, "I faked it until I made it." Don't misunderstand me. I'm not saying that we should never have the courage to end unhealthy relationships, but something is wrong when more than 50% of all marriages end in divorce.

Finally, I see the sloppiness virus at work every day in my own thinking and in the thinking of people I know. When a person is faced with a situation that is uncomfortable or that challenges his or her beliefs, it is easier *not* to think. It is easier to grab hold of the nearest, safest stereotype and believe in that. When the issue of gays in the military recently arose, for example, I had to laugh at how many people refused to consider the issues and took refuge in their stereotypical fears that gays are some sort of moral deformity that will invade the barracks and seduce all of our helpless young boys, destroying the "morale" of our troops. I see the same sort of thing happen when people from different races marry. When our new neighbors moved in—a recently married white woman and black man—many people around us were appalled (and yet these same people would never consider themselves racists). Unfortunately, it is just too easy for many of us to retreat into our sloppy thinking and hasty moral judgments.

Norman Cousins has raised an issue that touches us all, for all of us, in our sloppiness, want things to go *our* way. We do not want to have to change ourselves. The driver on the freeway wishes cars would part before him so he can be as reckless as he wants to be; the lover in a relationship wishes the other person would change so that he or she does not have to; and all people wish life itself would stop challenging them with situations that force them to think for themselves. We are, indeed, all victims of the sloppiness virus. Perhaps that virus is part of being a human being.

Exercise 5.4

Work with other students to develop responses to these questions or to compare responses that you have already prepared.

1. The introduction to the summary-response essay is much more developed than the introduction to the extended summary essay. Why? What is it doing that is different?
2. Identify the thesis statement of the essay.
3. Identify the topic sentence of each body paragraph. Does it clearly introduce the topic of the paragraph?
4. Identify the transitions between paragraphs. Also, explain how each topic sentence is clearly connected to the thesis statement.
5. Examine the support in each paragraph. Point out which sentences are generalized explanations and which are specific examples.
6. Examine the concluding paragraph and explain what it does to bring the essay to a satisfactory close. ■

Readings

Before You Read

1. Consider the title. Does it make sense to you? In what way is "killing women" a tradition in pop-music?
2. Do you think lyrics in popular music affect the attitudes of the audience? Or do they merely reflect attitudes that are already there?

Killing Women: A Pop-Music Tradition

John Hamerlinck

If there has been anything positive about the flood of media coverage of   1
the O. J. Simpson trial, it has been an increased public awareness of the

disturbing incidence of violence against women in our society. According to the Family Violence Prevention Fund, an act of domestic violence occurs every nine seconds in the United States. Even though the mainstream press seems to have only recently recognized this horrible reality, the signs of our tolerance toward domestic violence have long had a prominent profile in popular culture. This tragic phenomenon has often been reflected in novels and on film, but perhaps the most common occurrence of depictions of violence against women comes in popular music. Indeed, the often innocuous world of pop music has cultivated its own genre of woman-killing songs.

2 Violent misogyny in popular song did not begin with recent controversial offerings from acts like Guns 'N' Roses and 2 Live Crew. There's an old, largely southern, folk genre known as the "murder ballad." And as long as men have sung the blues, they have told stories of killing the women who have "done them wrong." In a common scenario, a man catches "his" woman with another man and kills them both in a jealous rage. In the 1920s, Lonnie Johnson sang a song called "Careless Love," in which he promises to shoot his lover numerous times and then stand over her until she is finished dying. In "Little Boy Blue," Robert Lockwood threatens to whip and stab his lover; while Robert Nighthawk's "Murderin' Blues" suggests a deliberate values judgment in the premeditation: the song says that prison chains are better than having a woman cheat and lie to you.

3 In many of the songs in this genre, the music belies the homicidal lyrics. A song like Little Walter's "Boom, Boom, Out Go the Lights" (later turned into an arena-rock anthem by Pat Travers) features a smooth, catchy, danceable blues riff. Little Walter caresses the song's famous hook so softly that one gets the feeling that perhaps his bark is worse than his bite. There is, however, no doubt that retribution for emotional pain is going to come in the form of physical violence.

4 This theme is not limited to blues artists. The Beatles provide harsh and frightening imagery in "Run for Your Life," a song which features premeditation along with traditional blues lines. It also incorporates stalking and threats sung directly to the target. The stalking transcends the mind-game variety we find in a song like the Police's "Every Breath You Take"; "Run for Your Life" is pure terror. Charles Manson aside, this Beatles offering is considerably more frightening than "Helter Skelter."

5 Another song in this vein is "Hey Joe," which was a minor hit for a band called the Leaves in the 1960s and was later covered by numerous artists, including an electrifying version by Jimi Hendrix. Thanks to Hendrix, the song became a garage-band staple in the sixties and seventies: many a young vocalist cut his rock-and-roll teeth singing that musical question: "Hey, Joe/Where you goin' with that gun in your hand?" (The same bands probably also played Neil Young's contribution to the genre, "Down by the River.")

The woman-killing genre has also been embraced by the MTV generation. One of the video age's most recent additions to the catalog of murder songs comes from the "man in black," Johnny Cash, who is only one of many country artists to record such songs. Cash recently released a single called "Delia's Gone" from his latest album, *American Recordings*. The stark and eerie video, which features Cash digging a grave for his victim, even made its way into an episode of MTV's "Beavis and Butt-Head." 6

Occasionally the genre attempts to even the odds by arming the victim: for example, in Robert Johnson's "32-20 Blues," the heartbroken man gets his revenge despite the fact that the victim had a "38 Special." And sometimes the gender tables are turned: for example, Nancy Sinatra covered "Run for Your Life" shortly after the Beatles recorded it, changing the prey from "little girl" to "little boy." In real life, however, the victims are overwhelmingly women, and their primary form of defense usually consists of a mere piece of paper called a restraining order. 7

It should quickly be pointed out, however, that these songs do not *cause* violence. Their singers are not wicked, evil people. The perseverance of this genre, however, certainly reflects a disturbingly casual level of acceptance in society when it comes to so-called "crimes of passion." When we hear tales of real domestic abuse, we are appalled. Often, however, we rationalize the perpetrator's actions and say that we can understand how he was driven to commit such a crime. Shoulders shrug and someone ubiquitously adds, "Well, we live in a violent society." Just as metal detectors and X-rays have become an unquestioned, accepted part of the airport landscape, our culture comfortably places violence and terror in pop music's love-song universe. 8

"I-loved-her-so-much-I-had-to-kill-her" songs are not about love; they are about power and control. But if the beat is good and the chorus has a catchy hook, we don't need to concern ourselves with things like meaning, right? We can simply dance on and ignore the violence around us. 9

After You Read

Work with other students to develop responses to these questions or to compare responses that you have already prepared.

1. State the thesis of the article in your own words. What sentences in the article, if any, best express the idea?

2. Divide the article into sections according to each major point that Hamerlinck makes.

3. Briefly summarize the thesis of the article and its major supporting points.

4. Hamerlinck refers to "a disturbingly casual level of acceptance in society when it comes to so-called 'crimes of passion.'" What does he mean by this? In what way do we casually accept violence?

5. What other attitudes toward women does popular music reflect?

Before You Read

1. Consider the title. What do you assume the "changing face" of America refers to?

2. Friedrich discusses the concerns that many Americans have about the changing population. Do you have such concerns? Why or why not?

The Changing Face of America

Otto Friedrich

Reina came from El Salvador because of "horrible things." She says simply, "I got scared." When she finally reached Los Angeles and found a job as a housekeeper at $125 a week, her new employer pointed to the vacuum cleaner. Vacuum cleaner? Reina, 24, had never seen such a thing before. "She gave me a maid book and a dictionary," says Reina, who now writes down and looks up every new word she hears. "That's how I learn English. I don't have time to go to school, but when I don't speak English, I feel stupid, so I must learn. . . ." 1

Lam Ton, from Viet Nam, is already a U.S. citizen, and he did well with a restaurant, the Mekong, at the intersection of Broadway and Argyle Street in Chicago. "When I first moved in here, I swept the sidewalk after we closed," he recalls. "People thought I was strange, but now everyone does the same." Lam Ton's newest project is to build an arch over Argyle Street in honor of the immigrants who live and work here. "I will call it Freedom Gate," he says, "and it will have ocean waves with hands holding a freedom torch on top. It will represent not just the Vietnamese but all the minorities who have come here. Just look down Broadway. That guy is Indian, next to him is a Greek, next to him is a Thai, and next to him is a Mexican." 2

They seem to come from everywhere, for all kinds of reasons, as indeed they always have. "What Alexis de Tocqueville saw in America," John F. Kennedy once wrote, "was a society of immigrants, each of whom had begun life anew, on an equal footing. This was the secret of America: a nation of people with the fresh memory of old traditions who dared to explore new frontiers." It was in memory of Kennedy's urging that the U.S. in 1965 abandoned the quota system that for nearly half a century had preserved the overwhelmingly European character of the nation. The new law invited the largest wave of immigration since the turn of the century, only this time the newcomers have arrived not from the Old World 3 but from the Third World, especially Asia and Latin America. Of the 544,000 legal immigrants who came in fiscal 1984, the largest numbers were from Mexico (57,000 or more than 10%), followed by the Philippines (42,000) and Viet Nam (37,000). Britain came in ninth, with only 14,000. . . .

In addition to the half-million immigrants who are allowed to come 4 to the U.S. each year, a substantial number arrive illegally. Estimates of the total vary widely. The Immigration and Naturalization Service apprehended 1.3 million illegal immigrants last year and guessed that several times that many had slipped through its net. . . .

The newest wave raises many questions: How many immigrants can 5 the country absorb and at what rate? How much unskilled labor does a high-tech society need? Do illegals drain the economy or enrich it? Do newcomers gain their foothold at the expense of the poor and the black? Is it either possible or desirable to assimilate large numbers of immigrants from different races, languages and cultures? Will the advantages of diversity be outweighed by the dangers of separatism and conflict?

When asked about such issues, Americans sound troubled; their an- 6 swers are ambiguous and sometimes contradictory. In a *Time* poll taken by Yankelovich, Skelly & White Inc., only 27% agreed with the idea that "America should keep its doors open to people who wish to immigrate to the U.S. because that is what our heritage is all about." Two-thirds agreed that "this philosophy is no longer reasonable, and we should strictly limit the number." Some 56% said the number of legal immigrants was too high, and 75% wanted illegal immigrants to be tracked down. On the other hand, 66% approved of taking in people being persecuted in their homelands.

"One of the conditions of being an American," says Arthur Mann, 7 professor of history at the University of Chicago, "is to be aware of the fact that a whole lot of people around you are different, different in their origins, their religions, their life-styles." Yet most Americans do not know exactly what to make of those differences. . . . Much of the concern comes from people who favor continued immigration, but who fear the consequences if a slowdown in the economy were to heighten the sense that immigrants, especially illegal ones, take jobs away from Americans. . . .

The number of newcomers is large in itself, . . . but their effect is 8 heightened because they have converged on the main cities of half a dozen states. Nowhere is the change more evident than in California, which has become home to 64% of the country's Asians and 35% of its Hispanics. Next comes New York, followed by Texas, Florida, Illinois and New Jersey. Miami is 64% Hispanic, San Antonio 55%. Los Angeles has more Mexicans (2 million) than any other city except metropolitan Mexico City, and nearly half as many Salvadorans (300,000) as San Salvador.

These population shifts change all the bric-a-brac of life. A car in Los 9 Angeles carries a custom license plate that says *Sie sie li*, meaning, in Chinese, "Thank you." Graffiti sprayed in a nearby park send their obscure signals in Farsi. A suburban supermarket specializes in such Vietnamese delicacies as pork snouts and pickled banana buds. The Spanish-language soap opera *Tu o Nadie* gets the top ratings among independent stations every night at 8.

Such changes require adaptation not only in the schools and the marketplace but throughout society. The Los Angeles County court system now provides interpreters for 80 different languages from Albanian and Amharic to Turkish and Tongan. One judge estimates that nearly half his cases require an interpreter.

These changes do not represent social decline or breakdown. The newcomers bring valuable skills and personal qualities: hope, energy, fresh perspectives. But the success stories should not blot out the fact that many aliens face considerable hardships with little immediate chance of advancement. Avan Wong, 20, came from Hong Kong in 1983 and hoped to go to college. She lives in the Bronx with her aged father, commutes two hours by bus to a job of up to twelve hours a day in a suburban restaurant. "I don't even read the newspapers," she says. "You don't have time. Once you go home, you go to sleep. Once you get up, you have to go to work. The only thing I'm happy about is that I can earn money and send it back to my mother. Nothing else. You feel so lonely here." College is not in sight. . . .

Even with the best intentions on all sides, the question of how to fit all these varieties of strangers into a relatively coherent American society remains difficult. Linda Wong, a Chinese-American official of the Mexican-American Legal Defense and Education Fund, sees trouble in the racial differences. "There is concern among whites that the new immigrants may be unassimilable," says Wong. "Hispanics and Asians cannot melt in as easily, and the U.S. has always had an ambivalent attitude toward newcomers. Ambivalent at best, racist at worst."

Many historians disagree. Hispanics, says Sheldon Maram, a professor of history at California State University at Fullerton, "are moving at about the same level of acculturation as the Poles and Italians earlier in the century. Once they've made it, they tend to move out of the ghetto and melt into the rest of society." Asians often have it easier because they come from urban middle-class backgrounds. "They are the most highly skilled of any immigrant group our country has ever had," says Kevin McCarthy, a demographer at the Rand Corp. in Santa Monica, Calif. . . .

How long, how complete and how painful the process of Americanization will be remains unclear. It is true that ethnic elitists have bewailed each succeeding wave of Irish or Germans or Greeks, but it is also true that the disparities among Korean merchants, Soviet Jews, Hmong tribesmen, French socialites and Haitian boat people are greater than the U.S. or any other country has ever confronted. On the other hand, Americans are probably more tolerant of diversity than they once were. . . .

The question is not really whether the new Americans can be assimilated—they must be—but rather how the U.S. will be changed by that process.

© 1985, Time, Inc. Reprinted by permission.

After You Read

1. State the thesis of the article in your own words. What sentences in the article, if any, best express the idea?

2. Divide the article into sections according to each major point that Friedrich makes.

3. Briefly summarize the thesis of the article and its major supporting points.

4. "Will the advantages of diversity be outweighed by the dangers of separatism and conflict?" What does Friedrich mean by this question? Explain the advantages and dangers that he seems to have in mind.

5. What changes in American life does Friedrich discuss in paragraphs 8-11? What sentences suggest his attitude toward these changes?

Before You Read

1. What do you think are the major drawbacks of lecture classes as opposed to discussion classes?

2. What are the benefits of lecture classes?

College Lectures: Is Anybody Listening?

David Daniels

A former teacher of mine, Robert A. Fowkes of New York University, likes   1
to tell the story of a class he took in Old Welsh while studying in Germany during the 1930s. On the first day the professor strode up to the podium, shuffled his notes, coughed, and began, *"Guten Tag, Meine Damen und Herren"* ("Good day, ladies and gentlemen"). Fowkes glanced around uneasily. He was the only student in the course.

Toward the middle of the semester, Fowkes fell ill and missed a class.   2
When he returned, the professor nodded vaguely and, to Fowkes's astonishment, began to deliver not the next lecture in the sequence but the one after. Had he, in fact, lectured to an empty hall in the absence of his solitary student? Fowkes though it perfectly possible.

Today, American colleges and universities (originally modeled on   3
German ones) are under strong attack from many quarters. Teachers, it is charged, are not doing a good job of teaching, and students are not doing a good job of learning. American businesses and industries suffer from unenterprising, uncreative executives educated not to think for themselves but to mouth outdated truisms the rest of the world has long discarded. College graduates lack both basic skills and general culture. Studies are conducted and reports are issued on the status of higher education, but any changes that result either are largely cosmetic or make a bad situation worse.

One aspect of American education too seldom challenged is the lecture system. Professors continue to lecture and students to take notes much as they did in the thirteenth century, when books were so scarce and expensive that few students could own them. The time is long overdue for us to abandon the lecture system and turn to methods that really work.

4

To understand the inadequacy of the present system, it is enough to follow a single imaginary first-year student—let's call her Mary—through a term of lectures on, say, introductory psychology (although any other subject would do as well). She arrives on the first day and looks around the huge lecture hall, taken a little aback to see how large the class is. Once the hundred or more students enrolled in the course discover that the professor never takes attendance (how can he?—calling the role would take far too much time), the class shrinks to a less imposing size.

5

Some days Mary sits in the front row, from where she can watch the professor read from a stack of yellowed notes that seem nearly as old as he is. She is bored by the lectures, and so are most of the other students, to judge by the way they are nodding off or doodling in their notebooks. Gradually she realizes the professor is as bored as his audience. At the end of each lecture he asks, "Are there any questions?" in a tone of voice that makes it plain he would much rather there weren't. He needn't worry—the students are as relieved as he is that the class is over.

6

Mary knows very well she should read an assignment before every lecture. However, as the professor gives no quizzes and asks no questions, she soon realizes she needn't prepare. At the end of the term she catches up by skimming her notes and memorizing a list of facts and dates. After the final exam, she promptly forgets much of what she has memorized. Some of her fellow students, disappointed at the impersonality of it all, drop out of college altogether. Others, like Mary, stick it out, grow resigned to the system and await better days when, as juniors and seniors, they will attend smaller classes and at last get the kind of personal attention real learning requires.

7

I admit this picture is overdrawn—most universities supplement lecture courses with discussion groups, usually led by graduate students, and some classes, such as first-year English, are always relatively small. Nevertheless, far too many courses rely principally or entirely on lectures, an arrangement much loved by faculty and administrators but scarcely designed to benefit the students.

8

One problem with lectures is that listening intelligently is hard work. Reading the same material in a textbook is a more efficient way to learn because students can proceed as slowly as they need to until the subject matter becomes clear to them. Even simply paying attention is very difficult: people can listen at a rate of four hundred to six hundred words a minute, while the most impassioned professor talks at scarcely a third of that speed. This time lag between speech and comprehension leads to daydreaming. Many students believe years of watching television have

9

sabotaged their attention span, but their real problem is that listening attentively is much harder than they think.

Worse still, attending lectures is passive learning, at least for inexperienced listeners. Active learning, in which students write essays or perform experiments and then have their work evaluated by an instructor, is far more beneficial for those who have not yet fully learned how to learn. While it's true that techniques of active listening, such as trying to anticipate the speaker's next point or taking notes selectively, can enhance the value of a lecture, few students possess such skills at the beginning of their college careers. More commonly, students try to write everything down and even bring tape recorders to class in a clumsy effort to capture every word.

Students need to question their professors and to have their ideas taken seriously. Only then will they develop the analytical skills required to think intelligently and creatively. Most students learn best by engaging in frequent and even heated debate, not by scribbling down a professor's often unsatisfactory summary of complicated issues. They need small discussion classes that demand the common labors of teacher and students rather than classes in which one person, however learned, propounds his or her own ideas.

The lecture system ultimately harms professors as well. It reduces feedback to a minimum, so that the lecturer can neither judge how well students understand the material nor benefit from their questions or comments. Questions that require the speaker to clarify obscure points and comments that challenge sloppily constructed arguments are indispensable to scholarship. Without them, the liveliest mind can atrophy. Undergraduates may not be able to make telling contributions very often, but lecturing insulates a professor even from the beginner's naive question that could have triggered a fruitful line of thought.

If lectures make so little sense, why have they been allowed to continue? Administrators love them, of course. They can cram far more students into a lecture hall than into a discussion class, and for many administrators that is almost the end of the story. But the truth is that faculty members, and even students, conspire with them to keep the lecture system alive and well. Lectures are easier on everyone than debates. Professors can pretend to teach by lecturing just as students can pretend to learn by attending lectures, with no one the wiser, including the participants. Moreover, if lectures afford some students an opportunity to sit back and let the professor run the show, they offer some professors an irresistible forum for showing off. In a classroom where everyone contributes, students are less able to hide and professors less tempted to engage in intellectual exhibitionism.

Smaller classes in which students are required to involve themselves in discussion put an end to students' passivity. Students become actively involved when forced to question their own ideas as well as their instructor's. Their listening skills improve dramatically in the excitement of

10

11

12

13

14

intellectual give and take with their instructors and fellow students. Such interchanges help professors do their job better because they allow them to discover who knows what—before final exams, not after. When exams are given in this type of course, they can require analysis and synthesis from the students, not empty memorization. Classes like this require energy, imagination, and commitment from professors, all of which can be exhausting. But they compel students to share responsibility for their own intellectual growth.

Lectures will never entirely disappear from the university scene both   15 because they seem to be economically necessary and because they spring from a long tradition in a setting that rightly values tradition for its own sake. But the lectures too frequently come at the wrong end of the students' educational careers—during the first two years, when they most need close, even individual, instruction. If lecture classes were restricted to junior and senior undergraduates and to graduate students, who are less in need of scholarly nurturing and more able to prepare work on their own, they would be far less destructive of students' interests and enthusiasm than the present system. After all, students must learn to listen before they can listen to learn.

After You Read

Work with other students to develop responses to these questions or to compare responses that you have already prepared.

1. State the thesis of the article in your own words. What sentences in the article, if any, best express the idea?

2. Divide the article into sections according to each major point that Daniels makes.

3. Briefly summarize the thesis of the article and its major supporting points.

4. Describe your own experiences in lecture classes. Are they similar to the experiences of other members of your class?

5. Explain what you think the student's responsibility is in the learning process. Does this article address that responsibility?

Writing Assignments

1. Write a brief summary of one of the reading assignments in this chapter or of a reading assignment from Part Four of this text.

2. Write an extended summary of one of the reading assignments in this chapter or of a reading assignment from Part Four of this text.

3. Write a summary-response essay in reaction to John Hamerlinck's "Killing Women: A Pop-Music Tradition." After briefly summarizing his article, your

introduction should include a thesis of your own that responds to one of the following topics or to a topic assigned by your instructor:

a. John Hamerlinck is careful not to claim that these "women killing" songs *cause* violence. Rather, he writes that they *reflect* "a disturbingly casual level of acceptance in society when it comes to so-called 'crimes of passion.'" Do the lyrics of popular music reflect other attitudes toward women as well? Write a paper in which you analyze any other attitudes that such music reflects, supporting your points with specific examples and clear explanations.

b. Although Hamerlinck suggests that violent lyrics do not cause violence, most people might agree that they are affected one way or another when they listen to music, whether the effect comes from the lyrics or the music. Consider many types of pop music. Write a paper in which you analyze ways that different types of pop music and/or its lyrics might affect the attitudes of its listeners, supporting your points with specific examples and clear explanations.

c. Hamerlinck focuses on depictions of violence against women, but on a more general level his article suggests that we have developed a casual attitude toward many instances of violence in our society. What do you think of that idea? Write a paper in which you analyze different types of violence toward which people have developed casual attitudes, supporting your points with specific examples and clear explanations.

4. Write a summary-response essay in reaction to Otto Friedrich's "The Changing Face of America." After briefly summarizing his article, your introduction should include a thesis of your own that responds to one of the following topics or to a topic assigned by your instructor:

a. Throughout his article, Friedrich says that Americans are "troubled" and "concerned" about the changes they see. Talk to other students about these concerns and examine your own (if you have any). What concerns do people have? Write a paper in which you identify those concerns, explaining them as clearly and specifically as you can.

b. Choose one of the following statements from Friedrich's article (or a statement provided by your instructor) and respond to it with examples and explanations of your own.

   i. These population shifts change all the bric-a-brac of life.

   ii. Such changes require adaptation not only in the schools and the marketplace but throughout society.

   iii. These changes do not represent social decline or breakdown. The newcomers bring valuable skills and personal qualities: hope, energy, fresh perspectives.

c. If you or your parents are immigrants to the United States, explain whether or not you have found the process of adapting to this society a difficult or painful one. Give specific examples to illustrate your points.

5. Write a summary-response essay in reaction to David Daniels's "College Lectures: Is Anybody Listening?" After briefly summarizing his article, your introduction should include a thesis of your own that responds to one of the following topics or to a topic assigned by your instructor:

   a. Daniels provides several reasons to support his contention that larger lecture classes are less effective than smaller discussion classes. What have your experiences been? Have you found smaller discussion classes more effective? Are larger lecture classes sometimes preferable? Write a paper in which you support your response with specific examples and clear explanations.

   b. Daniels focuses on the lecture system in his criticism of our current educational system. Are there other areas that you think should be improved, areas that have caused trouble for you or for people you know? Choose one problem area and write a paper in which you explain exactly why it is a problem. Support your ideas with specific examples and clear explanations.

6. Write a summary-response essay in reaction to one of the reading assignments in Part Four of this text. After briefly summarizing the article, your introduction should include a thesis of your own that responds to a topic assigned by your instructor.

Evaluating Sample Papers

Extended Summaries

As you read and evaluate the following extended summaries, consider these areas:

1. Introduction

   Underline the sentence(s) that states the central idea of the article. Is it accurate and clear? Does the introduction prepare the reader for an extended summary and not for a summary-response?

   1   2   3   4   5   6

2. Unity

   Does each paragraph have a clear and specific topic sentence that accurately introduces one of the major sections of the article? Does the material in each paragraph clearly relate to its topic sentence?

   1   2   3   4   5   6

3. Support

   Are all of the major points in the article summarized? Is each point accurately and fully explained?

   1   2   3   4   5   6

4. Coherence

   Are transitions used between paragraphs? Where needed, are transitions used between sentences within each paragraph?

   1   2   3   4   5   6

5. References to the Text

   Are direct quotations and paraphrases correctly introduced and smoothly incorporated into the text? Do they reflect the author's points accurately?

   1   2   3   4   5   6

6. Sentence Structure

   Do the sentences combine ideas that are related, using coordination, sub-ordination, or verbal phrases when appropriate? Are there too many brief, choppy main clauses?

   1   2   3   4   5   6

7. Mechanics, Grammar, and Spelling

   Does the paper contain a distracting number of errors of these kinds?

   1   2   3   4   5   6

8. Overall Ranking of the Essay

   1   2   3   4   5   6

Student Summary 1

In his article, "The Decline of Neatness," Norman Cousins explains that a "sloppiness virus" has spread to all categories of life. His evidence of this virus is directed towards the way we dress, the way we speak, the way we treat one another, and the way we act in relationships.

In his first point, Norman Cousins speaks of our clothing. According to Cousins, "The symbol of the times is blue jeans." He describes our blue jeans as frayed, torn, and discolored, and he shows that the more worn and "ancient" the jeans look, the higher the price on the tag will be. Cousins writes, "Disheveled is in fashion; neatness is obsolete." He implies that this generation tries desperately to appear as individuals, but we come out looking like we stepped off an assembly line. He shows that in order to be different, we must be well groomed and even neat.

In the next section of his article, Cousins shows that our vocabulary has been "drained of color as well," and communication has progressed into grunts, chants, chopped up phrases, and "the incessant use of four letter words." He demonstrates this point by mentioning that screenwriters will not turn in a script without at least a handful of obscene words because they do not want to receive a "'G' rating." These screenwriters "employ tasteless language and gory scenes" so that they receive the strongly preferred "'R' rating."

Next, Cousins moves into the idea that our sloppiness in attitudes is directly related to our casualness toward violence. He states," People are not as uncomfortable as they ought to be about the glamorization of human hurt." He suggests that we take "debasement and dismembering" of human beings for granted and that if we continue to let this happen, the younger generation will be desensitized "to everything that should produce revulsion or resistance." He says our aim should be to educate the younger people to respect and cherish life.

Cousins' final point helps summarize the article by showing that our shortcomings in other aspects in life, such as clothing and vocabulary, have a direct impact on how we view our relationships. Cousins states, "Untidiness in dress, speech, and emotions is readily connected to human relationships." He implies that we have become apathetic because we have seen too much and have become immune to our feelings. He reminds us that because we are so casual with our feelings and our privacy, casual sex is as "fashionable" as our clothing.

In conclusion, Cousins points out that the outlook may be positive. Maybe a fashion designer will create a fashion that is not frayed and "grace[s] the human form." Maybe a screen writer will write a movie "to show people expressing genuine love and respect for one another." Maybe our schools could "encourage the notion that fewer things are more rewarding than genuine creativity." Cousins implies that the choice is ours: do we want to be "cookie cutters" or do we want to be unique?

Student Summary 2

According to Norman Cousins in his article, "The Decline of Neatness," the sloppiness virus has spread to all sectors of society. He thinks people go to great lengths and expense to look uncombed, unshaved, and unpressed. Anyone who is passionate about labels, he says, can tag us the Unkempt generation. He certainly makes us think about our appearance.

One factor he uses as a basis for that opinion is the fashion in blue jeans today. They are torn, discolored and look as though they have been discarded by a house painter. The fashion of today is disheveled. The author is not opposed to comfortable clothing. He thinks the desire for nonconformity has created people like cookie cutters. They are desperate not to be well groomed, their appearance takes on an uncaring quality.

Mr. Cousins attacks the modern day slovenly speech. He compares it to the blue jeans, and it is drained of color, with chopped up phrases, grunts, and chants. The violence in our language and the four letter words are a sign of decline. Some screen writers use four letter words so they don't get rated G. Violence is also affecting people. Battering and mutilations on TV and in movies leave us desensitized to the dismembering of humans. It also fosters attitudes of casualness, and children cannot outgrow the casualness.

Human relationships are connected to the lack of tidiness in dress, speech, and emotions. Sexual exploitation, which is fashionable in films today, does not create sex fiends, on the contrary, it deadens feelings. "People who have the habit of seeing everything and doing anything run the risk of feeling nothing.'

He goes on to say that his purpose is not to make a case for the return to Victorian decorum, but rather to examine bad dress, manners, speech, and human relationships. He hopes fashion designers and motion picture producers will realize that there are people who want something better. Films that show genuine love and respect.

In conclusion, Norman Cousins says that schools may begin to encourage genuine creativity in clothes fashion, communication and human relationships. Perhaps, he says, we can locate the best in ourselves and put it to work.

Summary-Response Essays

As you read and evaluate the following summary-response essays, consider these areas:

1. Introduction

    Does the introduction contain a clear and accurate brief summary of the central idea and major supporting points of the article? Does it prepare the reader for a summary-response essay by moving to a thesis of the writer's own?

    1   2   3   4   5   6

2. Thesis Statement

    Underline the thesis statement of the essay. Does it express a clear and specific central idea?

    1   2   3   4   5   6

3. Topic Sentences

    Underline the topic sentence of each paragraph. Does it clearly state the central idea of the paragraph?

    1   2   3   4   5   6

4. Support

    Examine the supporting details in each paragraph. Are they specific and clear? Should they be more detailed, or should more support be included?

    1   2   3   4   5   6

5. Unity

    Does each paragraph clearly relate to and develop the *central idea* expressed in the thesis statement? Do the supporting details *within* each paragraph clearly relate to and develop the *central idea* expressed in the topic sentence of that paragraph?

    1   2   3   4   5   6

6. Coherence

   Does each paragraph open with a transition, a reference to the central idea of the thesis statement, and an identification of its own central idea? Are the sentences within each paragraph clearly related to each other by the use of transitions or by reference to the central idea of the paragraph?

   1   2   3   4   5   6

7. Sentence Structure

   Do the sentences combine ideas that are related, using coordination, subordination, and verbal phrases when appropriate? Are there too many brief, choppy main clauses?

   1   2   3   4   5   6

8. Mechanics, Grammar, and Spelling

   Does the paper contain a distracting number of errors of these kinds?

   1   2   3   4   5   6

9. Overall Ranking of the Essay

   1   2   3   4   5   6

Student Essay 1

In "Killing Women: A Pop-Music Tradition," John Hamerlinck writes that accepting violence towards women in pop music has somehow made society less sensitive to domestic abuse. Hamerlinck believes many artist have incorporate these kinds of 1yrics into their songs. Even the MTV generation is not concerned with these disturbing images that can be produced by these kinds of woman-killing lyrics. He also points out that these songs do not cause violence but "reflect a disturbingly casual level of acceptance in society when it comes to so-called crimes of passion." We as a society have let ourselves understand and rationalize with why people commit these types of crimes. I believe Hamerlinck's view of woman in pop music is accurate. I feel music is extremely powerful and certain lyrics in songs can glamorize drug-induced lifestyles, while other lyrics in songs embrace drinking as a part of everyday life. Even a person's style of dressing and attitude can change.

Music lyrics have been known through the ages to glamorize drug-induced lifestyles. In Eric Clapton's "Cocaine" Clapton sings "If you wanna hang out, you've gotta take her out—cocaine," or "If you got that lose, you wanna kick them blues—cocaine." These lyrics could suggest that, if you want to have a good time or if you want to hang out and be cool you should take cocaine. I feel these lyrics send a false representation of drug use to people. These lyrics just mention the glamorous side of drugs use and not the deadly addiction it can have on a person. Another example are the musicians who lived drug-induced lifestyles. Janis Joplin and Jimi Hendrix are always being portrayed as wild drug-loving hippies that lived fast glamorous lives. On the cover of *Pearl*, Janis Joplin has a bottle of whiskey in one hand and a smoke in the other. This might send a negative message to people who want to be like their favorite musician. They could decide that they want to drink and use drugs like Janis Joplin did. I enjoy listening to these artists, but I do not feel we should glamorize their lifestyles.

In addition to lyrics that glamorize drug-induced lifestyles, there are also the lyrics in songs that seem to say, It's alright to have a drink or to get drunk whenever you feel like it. Country music is always portraying booze and bars as just a natural part of life. David Allan Coe writes "Mamma, train, truck, prison, and getting drunk, is the perfect country western song." I personally listen to country music and I realize that most of my country CD's I own have at least one song about getting drunk. People might get carried away with the lyrics and drink whenever they feel like it because the CD they are listening to promotes drinking. Country music can be good music, but I think some of these artists need to stop using alcohol as a way to fix problems. Next is another example of lyrics in pop music promoting drinking. In the famous song "Margaritaville" Jimmy Buffett tells the story of a man who is constantly drunk in order to forget about his lost love. I do not feel these lyrics will turn a person into an alcoholic, but these lyrics could urge someone to drink if they have had a fight with their boyfriend or girlfriend. The lyrics seem to say it's alright to drink when you are depressed and have problems in life.

Finally, some types of lyrics can influence people to dress a certain way and can change a person's attitude. Some people like to dress in clothes that reflect what kind of music they like. People who listen to country like to wear cowboy hats, Wrangler jeans, and ropers while rap music lovers like to dress in baggy, loose, hip-hop clothes. I think dressing this way is fine, but sometimes people attitudes reflect negatively on the music they listen to. When I worked in a music shop in high school young kids that listen to rap would come in and act rude. On some occasions they used vulgar language when they talked. Some of theses boys had no respect for women because many of the rap artists use insulting language about women in their music. This is not a message that we want to be sending our youth. Artist should be more careful when they write music because they have the power to mold young people in our society.

Clearly, music is powerful and wonderful today, but I feel artist need to be more observant when writing lyrics that could have negative effects on people that are looking for role models and are trying to deal with problems in their life.

Student Essay 2

In the article "The Changing Face of America" Otto Friedrich talks about American people's concern that new group of immigrants is changing American society in positive and negative ways. Friedrich discusses the new wave of immigrants from Asia and Latin America especially those immigrants who have come since 1965. According to Friedrich, immigration raises all sorts of questions that trouble and confuse American society because Americans do not know if the immigrants are positive or negative for our society. One expert states that America is a lot of different societies combined together. Friedrich explains that immigrants bring changes in "bric-a-brac of life" that require adaptation; however, changes might be good for American society to improve "valuable skills and personal qualities." Friedrich questions whether different people can fit in one society. He explains that one expert sees differences as a problem, but other experts don't see them as a problem. Friedrich concludes that new Americans are assimilated just as in the past. I believe that many American immigrants go through painful experiences to assimilate in American society as they adapt a new culture. I am an immigrant from Japan who came to live and study in America in 1995. As I have adapted to a new culture, I have had a number of painful experiences that caused confusion, frustration, and fear about myself.

One of my painful experiences while adapting to a new culture was speaking English with American people. I felt awkward speaking English in the beginning because I noticed that people avoided talking to me right after they found out I spoke different or funny. For example, one of the girls in my first semester of dance class asked me if she missed anything or not because she came in late. I tried to explain about the things that she needed to know, but she couldn't understand me. She kept saying "What? . . . Ha? . . . What? . . ." and then she said, "Never mind. It's OK" and went to ask different people. She never came back to talk to me after this happened. This experience made me nervous to talk to American people and hurt my feelings. Another example happened when my host family had a party and introduced me to their friends. When one guy came to ask me some questions, I tried to have a fun conversation with him, but he didn't want to stay and talk to me. I felt my English was too basic and boring, but I didn't really know what I was doing wrong. I was frustrated because I felt that I was out of place even though I wanted to fit in these circles and have fun just like native Americans.

Adapting to American culture caused me to discover difficulty in my own country. When I went back to Japan, it was hard for me to communicate with my family and my friends because they didn't accept me since I had become a different person. I discovered that I liked speaking English better than Japanese even though I didn't speak perfect English. I was confused because I felt awkward speaking my native language, Japanese, to my family and my friends. I do not know why, but it just didn't feel right to me to speak Japanese anymore. I was uncomfortable because I was forced to speak Japanese, and I felt that people did not accept me if I did not speak Japanese as my native language. I also found difficulty in my own culture when my family didn't accept my looks: my new clothes, my makeup, and my new hairstyle. They made funny comments about my new American appearance to make me feel uncomfortable. For example, my mom told me "Stop wearing those American clothes and makeup in Japan because you look funny. I do not have an American daughter." Another time my sister told me "Sis, you look like you are copying American style. You put makeup on just like your host sister, Lisa." I felt that I no longer fit in my own society any more. I found out that I liked myself more in America and American culture because I could express the best of me with English language, clothes, makeup and hair style.

My last painful experience while adapting to American society was when my roommate Natalie and I took a trip to visit her family in Montana. I discovered that some places in America are close minded and prejudice to different races. People in Montana treated me differently than American people and that hurt my feelings. One example is when I went into a restaurant in Montana with Natalie and her family. The waitress took orders from Natalie, her mom Ruth, her brother Jed, and then me. I never had to wait to be the last person to order, especially when a guy was with me. I felt uncomfortable and started to worry about my different culture appearances. I was sad and felt awkward because I was the last one to order after all the American people had ordered. Likewise, when Ruth introduced Natalie and me to Ruth's friends from work, her friends paid attention only to Natalie and didn't even look at me to introduce themselves. I know that people in California would have said something to me even if it was just to be polite. I felt out of place being there because of the way I looked was a different look from the American people. These are some of the experiences that hurt my feelings and left me confused.

In this essay I gave some examples of the painful experiences I had faced in American culture. Some of the experiences were dealing with the students in my class who did not understand my speech, not fitting in to the Japanese culture when I returned because of my actions and looks, and not being treated the same as Americans. Even though I fit into American culture, I still feel confused by the way the closed minded people treat me.

Student Essay 3

This is an important article that expresses Mr. Daniels idea that the lecture approach to education leaves education sadly lacking. He expresses the idea that lectures only do not teach the subject; there is no opportunity to ask questions on areas the student does not understand. He feels that listening is an art, that students do not always possess and that they miss a great deal of information while they are trying to write down all that is said. Some students can't get the information so there for they lose intrest in the subject matter. The other point that is important in this article is that the teacher loses his own teaching ability by not receiving the feedback from students that help the teacher improve his teaching skills.

I can confirm that this articles main ideas are true from my own personal experience. I took a psychology class at Lane College that was given in an amphitheater in Eugene. When I arrived the only seats left were at the third level and the stage was straight down below. The teacher looked like an ant and all the sound was via a microphone that the teacher wore around his neck. Sometimes during the lecture the teacher would drop his voice, and it was difficult to hear. Also with that many students they would get restless and somewhat noisy so you couldn't hear When I stopped to think about what the teacher was then on, it was very frustrating to try and keep up. Many of the students that had tape recorders at the lectures, but I feel how can you understand the material on a tape better than you did at the lecture?

There was a joke in the school newspaper once that showed this large lecture hall with the teacher up in front and the rest was a series of desks that each had a tape recorder on but no people. At least in a discussion class you can ask questions and clear things you don't understand. In the article one of the points Mr. Daniels brought out was that the school administration liked the large lecture classes because they could enroll more paying students into one class.

For a while I felt I was the only one who didn't get it, but after talking to my fellow class mates I heard the same complaint from them. I don't know what the alternative is, but I think that a student has the obligation to try to find the classes which give him the best opportunity to learn, and a large lecture class is not one of them.

Sentence Combining: Appositives

As you know from the earlier sentence-combining sections of this text, in English there are many ways to add information to the basic sentence. So far, you have practiced using adjectives, prepositional phrases, main clauses, subordinate clauses, and verbal phrases in your sentences. The **appositive** is yet another way to add interest and depth to your writing. Like most of the other sentence-combining methods you have studied, the appositive allows you to consolidate ideas into one sentence that otherwise might be expressed in two or more separate sentences.

At its simplest level, an **appositive** is simply a noun or a pronoun renaming or identifying another noun or pronoun. Usually the appositive is set off by commas, and it normally follows the noun or pronoun it is renaming. Here are some examples from the articles you have read in this chapter:

> A former teacher of mine, **Robert A. Fowkes of New York University,** likes to tell the story of a class he took in Old Welsh while studying in Germany during the 1930s.

> Cash recently released a single called "Delia's Gone" from his latest album, ***American Recordings.***

Notice that in each of the above examples a noun renames a noun. The noun *Robert A. Fowkes* renames *teacher* in the first sentence, and *American Recordings* renames *album* in the second. As is usually the case, each appositive follows and is set off from the noun it renames by commas.

Another characteristic of the appositive is that it usually includes modifiers of its own—adjectives, adverbs, or other modifiers that add information to the appositive word. Notice the modifiers of the appositive word in the following examples from "College Lectures: Is Anybody Listening?" and "Killing Women: A Pop-Music Tradition":

> Nevertheless, far too many courses rely principally or entirely on lectures, **an arrangement much loved by faculty and administrators but scarcely designed to benefit the students.**

> The Beatles provide harsh and frightening imagery in "Run for Your Life," **a song which features premeditation along the traditional blues line.**

Punctuating Appositives

As in the above examples, most appositives are set off with commas. However, occasionally they are set off with dashes or with a colon. In general, follow these guidelines:

1. Use commas to set off most appositives.

   Two dogs, **an Irish setter and a German shepherd,** ran into the lobby of the hotel.

2. Use dashes to set off an appositive that consists of a series or that already uses internal commas.

   Only three people—**a real estate agent, the manager of the local grocery store, and the town's only banker**—attended the Chamber of Commerce mixer.

3. Use a colon to set off an appositive at the end of a sentence if you want to establish a formal tone.

   Last Christmas, Jason visited only one person: **his father.**

   (Note that the above appositive could also have been set off with a comma or with a dash.)

Recognizing When to Use Appositives

You have the opportunity to use an appositive almost any time you have a sentence consisting of a form of the verb *be* followed by a noun or pronoun. If you omit the verb, set off the resulting phrase with commas, and then continue with your sentence, you have created an appositive.

Original Sentence with Form of Be

   Alex Haley was the author of *Roots.*

Omit the Verb and Set Off the Resulting Phrase with Commas

   Alex Haley, the author of *Roots,*

Complete the Sentence

Alex Haley, the author of *Roots*, died in 1992.

If you watch for them, you will find many opportunities to create appositives when you have written sentences using a form of the verb *be* followed by a noun or pronoun. Notice, for example, how two of the following three sentences use *was* and *is* to introduce a noun.

Mr. Erickson **was** the winner of the Florida lottery. He gave all of his money to Helping Hands. Helping Hands is a small orphanage in New York.

Now notice how those same three sentences can be written as one sentence with two appositives.

Mr. Erickson, **the winner of the Florida lottery,** gave all of his money to Helping Hands, **a small orphanage in New York.**

Exercise 5.5

Use appositives and appropriate punctuation to combine the following sentences. In each case, the words to be made into an appositive are underlined.

Examples

Robert Louis Stevenson was a British novelist. He wrote *Treasure Island*.

Robert Louis Stevenson, a British novelist, wrote *Treasure Island*.

Johann von Goethe lived from 1749 to 1832. He was a poet, dramatist, and novelist.

Johann von Goethe—a poet, dramatist, and novelist—lived from 1749 to 1832.

1. Jean-Baptiste Sanson was the official executioner of France in the early 1700s. He was only seven years old when he was appointed to the post.

2. He inherited the position from his father, who had inherited it from Jean-Baptiste's grandfather. Jean-Baptiste's grandfather was the first member of the Sanson family to be the nation's executioner.

3. At first Jean-Baptiste was too young to behead anybody, so his deputy performed the task. His deputy was François Prud'homme.

4. Two kinds of weapons were used. They were an ax (for commoners) and a sword (for aristocrats).

5. Jean-Baptiste's eldest son, who was executioner during the French Revolution, beheaded over 2,700 persons. His eldest son was Charles-Henri Sanson, and beheading over 2,700 persons was a family record. ■

Changing Adjective Clauses to Appositives

Another opportunity to use an appositive arises whenever you write an adjective clause containing a form of the verb *be* followed by a noun or pronoun. In such cases, you can omit the relative pronoun that starts the adjective clause and the verb. The result will be an appositive.

Example:

Using an Adjective Clause

Amoxil, **which was** the most frequently prescribed drug in 1991, is an antibiotic.

Using an Appositive

Amoxil, the most frequently prescribed drug in 1991, is an antibiotic.

Exercise 5.6

Use appositives and appropriate punctuation to combine the following sentences or to change adjective clauses to appositives. In each case, the words to be made into an appositive are underlined.

1. In the United States, legal help for battered children came originally from an unexpected source, which was the Society for the Prevention of Cruelty to Animals.
2. In 1874, Etta Wheeler, who was a church worker, heard about Mary Ellen. She was a nine-year-old child who was being whipped daily, stabbed with scissors, and tied to a bed by her guardians.
3. There was no legal way to rescue Mary Ellen, so Wheeler called Henry Bergh. Bergh was a member of the SPCA.
4. Bergh had the child removed from her home by arguing that she was a member of the animal kingdom, and that was the area over which the SPCA had jurisdiction.
5. A picture of Mary Ellen still hangs at the New York SPCA. She was a pathetic waif when she was rescued. ∎

Exercise 5.7

Use appositives and appropriate punctuation to combine the following sentences or to change adjective clauses to appositives.

1. The Great Pyramid of Khufu contains 2.3 million blocks of limestone averaging $2\frac{1}{2}$ tons each. It is the largest of all the pyramids.
2. Both Hansel and Gretel looked politely at the little old lady's new appliance, which was an extra-large General Electric oven.
3. More than 75% of the world's 850 active volcanoes lie within the "Ring of Fire." It is a zone running along the west coast of the Americas and down the east coast of Asia.
4. Medusa could not do a thing with her hair, but Perseus, who was the son of Zeus, soon solved that problem.
5. The first toothbrush was the "chew stick." It was a twig with one end frayed to a soft, fibrous condition.

6. Achilles stared in irritation at his heel, which was the only sore spot on his body.

7. Mercury is the nearest planet to the sun. It is the second smallest of the planets known to be orbiting the sun.

8. Henry watched the battle between two armies of tiny combatants while he ate his favorite food. The combatants were red ants and black ants, and the food he ate was freshly baked bread.

9. Paul was uncomfortable around his father, who was a rough, drunken coal miner, but not around his mother. She was a woman who now regretted her marriage.

10. Amanda recalled the high point of her life while Laura stared at her favorite possession, which was a small glass unicorn. Amanda's high point was the time she had seventeen gentlemen callers. ■

Exercise 5.8

Combine the following sentences, using coordination, subordination, verbal phrases, or appositives.

1. The "Trail of Tears" refers to one of the many forced "removals" of Native Americans from their native lands.

   These "removals" resulted in the deaths of thousands of men, women, and children.

2. In the 1830s, these so-called removals focused on what are generally referred to as the Five Civilized Tribes of the Southeast.

   These were the Choctaw, Chickasaw, Creek, Cherokee, and Seminole nations.

3. Each of these Native American societies had developed a culture.

   The culture was compatible with white society.

   It even emulated European styles in many respects.

4. There was a problem, however.

   It was that these tribes resided in valuable territory.

   The territory was cotton-growing land.

5. The Indian Removal Act was passed in 1830.

   Thousands of Choctaws, Chickasaws, and Creeks were forced to move.

   They moved from the Southeast to territory west of Arkansas.

6. The forced move caused many hardships.

   Hundreds and eventually thousands of Native Americans died.

   They suffered from pneumonia, cholera, and other diseases.

7. Gold was discovered in Cherokee country in Georgia.

   The state of Georgia tried to force the Cherokee to leave.

   The Cherokee took their case to the United States Supreme Court.

8. At this time, the Cherokee were not nomads.

   They were a nation of Native Americans.

   They had built roads, schools, and churches.

   They even had a system of representative government.

9. The Supreme Court ruled against them.

   Seventeen thousand Cherokee were forced to travel the "Trail of Tears" to Oklahoma.

10. Along the way, 4,000 of the 17,000 died.

    Another 1,000 escaped.

    They hid in the Great Smoky Mountains.

11. In the following years, the Cherokee eventually won back 56,000 acres. Seven million acres of land had been taken from them.

Evaluating Reading Selections

The students in the Trudeau cartoon seem to be doing an excellent job of recording what their instructor has to say. Since they are listening carefully, their notes will probably be accurate summaries of the lecture. However, wouldn't you agree that something is missing from the students' activities in this cartoon? Shouldn't they have some reaction to the statements "Jefferson was the Antichrist! Democracy is Fascism! Black is white! Night is Day!"? The problem, of course, is that taking careful notes is just not enough. These students need to **evaluate** as well as record.

Evaluating what you read (or hear) is a valuable skill. We have all heard the old saying "Don't believe everything that you read," and certainly most people follow that advice. Unfortunately, what we do or do not believe is often not based on careful evaluation. Instead, many people merely accept material that confirms what they *already* believe and reject material that does not confirm their previously held beliefs.

Evaluation demands that you approach an idea with an open mind, that you be willing to consider its validity on the basis of the evidence presented, not on the basis of any preconceptions you might have. It demands that you be willing to change your ideas if the evidence suggests that you should. And it demands that you make an effort to understand the purpose of what you are reading so that you not criticize something for failing to do what it was not intended to do in the first place.

Audience and Purpose

Perhaps the first step in evaluating anything that you read is to determine the audience and the purpose of the article. The **audience** of an article is its intended readers. Obviously, an article in *Ms.* magazine on the sexual exploitation of women will have a different audience from an article on the same subject published in *Playboy*, and those different audiences may influence the authors' choices of ideas to be covered. Of course, no matter who the audience is, a writer must still provide reasonable support for his or her points.

An evaluation should also consider the **purpose** of any article that you read. Clearly it would be unfair to criticize a writer for failing to discuss the responsibilities of parenthood if that writer's purpose was to entertain you with humorous stories about the frustrations of living with a teenager. Here are four common purposes that you should consider whenever you read.

To Inform

This type of writing is often called *expository*. It generally consists of facts rather than opinions or arguments. Most newspaper reporting has *informing* as its purpose, as does most of the material that you read in textbooks.

To Entertain

Generally, nonfiction *entertainment* writing tends to be humorous and often focuses on situations that are common to the average person. Dave Barry, for example, is a nationally syndicated entertainment columnist.

To Persuade

Persuasive writing tends to focus on controversial issues, presenting opinions and arguments that are supported (effectively or ineffectively) with facts, examples, explanations, statistics, and/or references to authority. Editorials in newspapers and magazines are common examples of persuasive writing.

To Raise an Issue or Provoke Thought

This type of writing is similar to persuasive writing in that it examines controversial issues, but its purpose is not necessarily to persuade the reader that the writer's particular argument is the correct one. Instead, its intent is often to unsettle the reader, to raise questions that need to be answered but that are not fully answered in the article itself. Such articles are often found in newspaper and magazine editorials.

In this chapter, you will write evaluations of articles designed to persuade, to raise an issue, or to provoke thought. As you read each article in this chapter, you must ask yourself if the article's purpose is to convince you of a particular argument or if it is merely to get you to think about the issue at hand. Of course, at times, the purpose may be a little of both, so you should consider that possibility too.

Evaluating Support

In addition to considering the audience and the purpose of what you read, you need to examine the evidence or support that is presented to you. For example, if a writer claims that we should do away with the minimum wage, you should look to see not only what reasons he gives but also what facts, statistics, examples, or references to authority he offers to explain his reasons.

When you do look closely at a written argument—especially an editorial in a newspaper or magazine—you will often find that the support is quite sketchy. Much of the argument may consist of opinions or explanations rather than facts or other specific types of support. In such cases, you must decide if more support is needed or if the argument is reasonably convincing as it stands. However, an argument without sufficient support should be looked at skeptically, no matter how well it is written.

Facts

Facts are tricky things. Most people consider a fact to be something "true" or "correct" or "accurate." But not everyone agrees about what is or is not true. For example, is it a fact that drinking coffee is bad for your health? Some people might *claim* that such a statement is accurate, but as many others would say it is not. And science itself has provided few answers about the long-term effects of coffee drinking. So is it or is it not true that coffee is bad for your health? Surely such a statement cannot be treated as a fact if there is so much disagreement about it.

The best way to define a fact is to move away from the idea of "truth" or "correctness" and toward the idea of objective, physical verification. Treat as a fact any statement that has been objectively verified through direct experience, measurement, or observation. Statistics, then, are facts, as are historical or current events, scientific observations, and even personal experience. If it has been verified that caffeine increases a person's blood pressure, then such a statement is a fact. If you visited a Toyota dealership yesterday and felt uncomfortable talking to the salesperson, your statement that such an event occurred and that you reacted the way you did are facts. If the distance between the sun and the earth has been measured as 92,900,000 miles, such a statement is a fact.

Of course, even using objective verification, you cannot assume all facts are always accurate. For many years, people believed it was a fact that the sun circled the earth, not vice versa. After all, anyone could see that each day the sun rose in the east and set in the west. In this case, objective verification was not accurate enough to lead us to the fact that the earth circled the sun. So how do you know which facts have been accurately verified and which have not? Often you must consider the source. If the writer of an article says that 24,700 murders were committed in the United States in 1991, you will probably accept that statement as a fact if the writer is a professional reporter or columnist whose career is riding on his or her accuracy. Of course, that does not mean that you should accept the writer's *conclusions*, especially if the writer is trying to persuade you to accept his or her particular point of view.

Exercise 6.1

Discuss which of the following statements can be objectively verified as facts and which can not.

1. In California, bicycle riders under the age of eighteen are required by law to wear a bicycle helmet.
2. If I had not eaten any sugar at the fair yesterday, I would have had a better time.
3. No loyal American would ever burn the American flag.
4. I saw a Plymouth Voyager hit a Nissan Sentra on the freeway today.
5. Former President Gerald Ford's middle name is Rudolph.
6. Betsy Ross sewed the first American flag.
7. The 1994 earthquake in Northridge, California, registered 6.6 on the Richter scale.
8. "Dear Abby" is the most widely published advice column in the world.
9. Most homeless people won't work even if you offer them jobs.
10. Cashews taste better than peanuts. ■

As you can see from the above sentences, some statements are more clearly facts than others. That the Northridge earthquake measured 6.6 on the Richter scale could easily be verified if you had to do so, but how would you verify the statement that most homeless people won't work even if they are offered jobs? You would need to find a study of all homeless people in America; they would all have to have been offered jobs, and most would have to have refused. How likely is it that you will find such a study?

For that matter, how would you verify that cashews taste better than peanuts? Such a statement would be a fact only if it were worded this way: "I like cashews better than peanuts." Do you see the difference? The second statement refers only to the speaker's personal preference, which the speaker verifies merely by making the statement. By the way, one of the ten sentences above has long been accepted as a fact by most people even though scholars know that it has never been verified and is probably not a fact at all. Which sentence is it?

Opinions

When people say something like "That's just my opinion," they usually mean that they don't want to argue about the point. In fact, "That's just my opinion" is often a way of saying that you don't have any facts to support your idea. Of course, at one time or another we all hold opinions without having examined the facts behind them. Perhaps we hold them because people we respect—our parents, friends, or teachers—hold them or because they reinforce what we already believe to be true about the world or the society in which we live.

Clear, responsible thinking, however, demands that we examine our opinions and discard those that are not well supported. Although it is true that we are all entitled to our own opinions, certainly the unexamined, unsupported opinion is not as valuable as the opinion formed after one has carefully considered the facts. When you think about opinions, consider these three distinctions.

Personal Opinion

The term *personal opinion* is often used when the speaker really means *unsupported* or *unexamined opinion*. If you hear someone say (or if you yourself say) "Well, that's just my personal opinion," be aware that such a statement probably means the opinion has not been very thoroughly examined. In addition to referring to an unexamined opinion, a personal opinion may also refer to matters of personal taste, such as "Suspense novels are more fun to read than science fiction novels."

Considered Opinion

A *considered opinion* is one reached after you have considered the relevant facts and other types of support. If, for example, you have read various articles on the pros and cons of handgun control, you can be said to have developed a considered opinion of your own. Remember, however, that any considered opinion should be open to change if new evidence or support demands it.

Expert Opinion

As you learned in Chapter 3, one type of support is *reference to authority*. For the most part, you should be able to accept an opinion held by experts in a particular field as long as their opinion is related to their field of expertise. For example, you would probably accept an orthopedic surgeon's opinion about the usefulness of a particular knee brace, but there would be no reason to accept that surgeon's opinion about a particular political issue. In addition, even an expert's opinion about an issue in his or her own field must be questioned if other experts in the same field disagree.

Exercise 6.2

Indicate which of the following opinions you would take more seriously than others. Which of these opinions are more likely to be personal opinions, considered opinions, or expert opinions?

1. Your neighbor says that the Los Angeles Lakers are more fun to watch than the New York Knicks.

2. A person at a party says that capital punishment discriminates against those who cannot afford expensive attorneys.

3. A palm reader advises you not to take that trip to Hawaii.

4. One homeless person tells another that a particular police officer will not care if he sleeps on the park bench.

5. A Marine Corps colonel says that only a coward would refuse to fight for his country.

6. A local business owner says that the state lottery takes money from the people who can least afford to spend it.

7. A state senator says that restricting handgun sales will not help to reduce crime.

8. A member of the city council says that crime will not be reduced until we start locking up criminals and throwing away the key.

9. Your girlfriend (or boyfriend, or wife, or husband) says that you are no longer as romantic as you used to be.

10. A Honda salesperson says that Hondas have better maintenance records than Buick Skylarks. ■

Generalizations versus Specific Statements

Much of your ability to evaluate what you read will depend on how well you can distinguish between a generalization and a specific statement. A specific statement will refer to specific people, places, events, or ideas, usually giving names and dates as it does, while a generalization will refer to groups of people, places, events, or ideas.

| specific statement | Yesterday, John McIntyre, a homeless man in San Diego, California, went the entire day without eating a thing. |
| generalization | Many homeless people often go an entire day without eating a thing. |

Both specific statements and generalizations can be facts or opinions, depending on what they say. For example, one of the following specific statements is clearly a fact, and one is clearly an opinion.

fact

This morning Samantha spilled a cup of coffee on Angelo.

opinion

This morning Samantha's carelessness caused her to spill a cup of coffee on Angelo.

As you can see, both of the above statements are specific, but only one can be called a fact.

Like specific statements, generalizations may be either facts or opinions. Generalizations that are based on obviously verified facts rarely require support and are usually treated as facts, while generalizations requiring further support are treated as opinions. Of the following generalizations, which should be treated as a fact and which should not?

People who smoke face a higher risk of developing lung cancer than people who don't smoke.

Students' sloppy style of dress today reflects a general "I don't care" attitude toward all of society.

As you can see, both specific statements and generalizations can express facts, so both can be used to support a writer's ideas. However, most writing instructors will ask you to provide specific statements as often as possible, primarily because specific statements are more interesting to read and are more persuasive than generalizations. It is simply more compelling to hear that someone's best friend, who smoked two packs of cigarettes a day, died two days ago after a painful battle with lung cancer than it is to hear the generalization that people who smoke die of lung cancer more often than people who don't.

Exercise 6.3

First, explain whether each of the following statements is a generalization or a specific statement. Then explain whether each statement should be considered a fact or an opinion. If it is an opinion, discuss whether or not it could be reasonably supported with facts.

1. Throughout most of civilized history, people have relied on animals or on their own feet for transportation.

2. The Honda Accord was the best-selling car in the United States in 1990 and 1991.

3. The cartoon characters Beavis and Butthead caused my sister's son to set fire to the First Interstate Bank.

4. Today's social problems are indicators of our immoral society.

5. Many people today do not discipline their children very effectively.

6. Jerry has AIDS because God is punishing him for being a homosexual.

7. Rioting swept South Central Los Angeles when the police officers accused of assault and the use of excessive force in the arrest of Rodney King were acquitted.

8. The gang problem has become a serious concern in high schools throughout the United States.

9. Uneducated people are crass and insensitive.

10. Lee Harvey Oswald was not the only person who fired shots when John F. Kennedy was assassinated. ■

Considering Your Own Knowledge and Experience

Evaluating the support in a text demands that you also think about what *you* know to be true and compare it to what you are reading. For example, if you are a single mother who is successfully raising a happy, well-adjusted child, your experience will certainly contradict an article that asserts that single mothers cannot provide a healthy home environment for their children. You must then consider whether the argument in the article is flawed or overgeneralized or if your own experience is an unusual exception. Whatever you decide, remember that your own knowledge and experience are important sources of information that you should consult before accepting the support offered by any writer.

Considering Unstated Objections

A final point to think about as you evaluate an argument is whether or not the writer has considered points that might contradict or otherwise weaken his or her position. For instance, if you are reading a newspaper editorial arguing that competition in school sports damages our children, consider what objections may not have been addressed by the writer. Do school sports benefit children in any ways that the writer has ignored? Is competition a valuable quality in any way?

Of course, a writer does not have to cover every—or any—objection to write an interesting, thought-provoking paper. If the purpose of the article is to raise issues that the reader should think about, you may not find any objections considered at all. However, the more a paper is intended to convince or persuade the reader, the more thoroughly the writer must consider and respond to major objections.

Steps in Evaluating a Text

1. Read the text actively.
   - Determine its purpose and intended audience.
   - Identify its thesis.
   - Identify its main points.

2. Determine how well the main points are supported.
   - Distinguish between facts and opinions.
   - Distinguish between specific support and generalizations.
   - Identify statistics, examples, and references to authority.
3. Test the article's points against your own knowledge and experience.
4. Consider any obvious objections that have been ignored.

Readings

Before You Read

1. What is your opinion about people who live together without being married? Upon what is your opinion based?
2. Should people who live together without marrying consider how their actions affect other members of their families?

I Wish They'd Do It Right

Jane Doe

My son and his wife are not married. They have lived together for seven   1
years without benefit of license. Though occasionally marriage has been a
subject of conjecture, it did not seem important until the day they
announced, jubilantly, that they were going to have a child. It was happy
news. I was ready and eager to become a grandmother. Now, I thought,
they will take the final step and make their relationship legal.

I was apprised of the Lamaze method of natural childbirth. I was   2
prepared by Leboyer for birth without violence. I admired the expectant
mother's discipline. She ate only organic foods, abstained from alcohol,
avoided insecticides, smog and trauma. Every precaution was taken to
insure the arrival of a healthy, happy infant. No royal birth had been prepared for more auspiciously. All that was lacking was legitimacy.

Finally, when my grandson was two weeks old, I dared to question   3
their intentions.

"We don't believe in marriage," was all that was volunteered.   4

"Not even for your son's sake?" I asked. "Maybe he will."   5

Their eyes were impenetrable, their faces stiffened to masks. "You   6
wouldn't understand," I was told.

And I don't. Surely they cannot believe they are pioneering, making   7
revolutionary changes in society. That frontier has long been tamed.
Today marriage offers all the options. Books and talk shows have
surfeited us with the freedom offered in open marriage. Lawyers,

psychologists and marriage counselors are growing rich executing marriage contracts. And divorce, should it come to that, is in most states easy and inexpensive.

On the other hand, living together out of wedlock can be economically impractical as well as socially awkward. How do I present her—as my son's roommate? his spouse? his spice, as one facetious friend suggested? Even my son flounders in these waters. Recently, I heard him refer to her as his girl friend. I cannot believe that that description will be endearing to their son when he is able to understand.   8

I have resolved that problem for myself, bypassing their omission, introducing her as she is, as my daughter-in-law. But my son, in militant support of his ideology, refutes any assumption, however casual, that they have taken vows.   9

There are economic benefits which they are denying themselves. When they applied for housing in the married-students dormitory of the university where he is seeking his doctorate, they were asked for their marriage certificate. Not having one, they were forced to find other, more expensive quarters off campus. Her medical insurance, provided by the company where she was employed, was denied him. He is not her husband. There have been and will be other inconveniences they have elected to endure.   10

Their son will not enjoy the luxury of choice about the inconveniences and scurrility to which he will be subject from those of his peers and elders who dislike and fear society's nonconformists.   11

And if in the future, his parents should decide to separate, will he not suffer greater damage than the child of divorce, who may find comfort in the knowledge that his parents once believed they could live happily ever after, and committed themselves to that idea? The child of unwed parents has no sanctuary. His mother and father have assiduously avoided a pledge of permanency, leaving him drifting and insecure.   12

I know my son is motivated by idealism and honesty in his reluctance to concede to what he considers mere ceremony. But is he wise enough to know that no one individual can fight all of society's foibles and frauds? Why does he persist in this, a battle already lost? Because though he rejects marriage, California, his residence, has declared that while couples living together in imitation of marriage are no longer under the jurisdiction of the family court, their relationship is viewed by the state as an implicit contract somewhat like a business agreement. This position was mandated when equal property rights were granted a woman who had been abandoned by the man she had lived with for a number of years.   13

Finally, the couple's adamancy has been depriving to all the rest of the family. There has been no celebration of wedding or anniversaries. There has been concealment from certain family elders who could not cope with the situation. Its irregularity has put constraint on the grandparents, who are stifled by one another's possible embarrassment or hurt.   14

I hope that one day very soon my son and his wife will acknowledge   15
their cohabitation with a license. The rest of us will not love them any
more for it. We love and support them as much as possible now. But it
will be easier and happier for us knowing that our grandson will be
spared the continued explanation and harassment, the doubts and anxieties of being a child of unmarried parents.

After You Read

Work with other students to develop responses to these questions or to compare
responses that you have already prepared.

1. State the thesis of the article in your own words. What sentences in the article, if
   any, best express the idea?
2. This article was originally published in *The New York Times*. Who would you say is
   Doe's audience? What is the purpose of her essay?
3. Divide the article into sections according to each major point that Doe makes.
4. Consider the support that Doe provides for each of her points. Does she use generalizations or specific statements? Facts or opinions? Are her opinions reasonably
   supported?
5. Consider your own experience or the experiences of people you know. Do they confirm or contradict Doe's points?
6. Do any of Doe's points seem particularly weak or particularly strong? Why?
7. Are there any objections to Doe's arguments that you should consider?

Before You Read

1. What do you consider to be the benefits and the drawbacks of competition? List as
   many benefits and drawbacks as you can think of.
2. Which list seems stronger—benefits or drawbacks?
3. Explain how your attitude toward competition might be a result of the culture in
   which you live.

Why Competition?

Alfie Kohn

W-H-I-T-E! White Team is the team for me!" The cheer is repeated, becom-   1
ing increasingly frenzied as scores of campers, bedecked in the appropriate color, try to outshout their Blue opponents. The rope stretched over

the lake is taut now, as determined tuggers give it their all. It looks as if a few will be yanked into the cold water, but a whistle pierces the air. "All right, we'll call this a draw." Sighs of disappointment follow, but children are soon scrambling off to the Marathon. Here, competitors will try to win for their side by completing such tasks as standing upside-down in a bucket of shampoo or forcing down great quantities of food in a few seconds before tagging a teammate.

As a counselor in this camp over a period of several years, I witnessed a number of Color Wars, and what constantly amazed me was the abrupt and total transformation that took place each time one began. As campers are read their assignments, children who not ten minutes before were known as "David" or "Margie" suddenly have a new identity; they have been arbitrarily designated as members of a team. The unspoken command is understood by even the youngest among them: Do everything possible to win for your side. Strain every muscle to prove how superior *we* are to the hostile Blues.

And so they will. Children who had wandered aimlessly about the camp are suddenly driven with a Purpose. Children who had tired of the regular routine are instantly provided with Adventure. Children who had trouble making friends are unexpectedly part of a new Crowd. In the dining hall, every camper sits with his or her team. Strategy is planned for the next battle; troops are taught the next cheer. There is a coldness bordering on suspicion when passing someone with a blue T-shirt—irrespective of any friendship B.C. (Before Colors). If anyone has reservations about participating in an activity, he needs only to be reminded that the other team is just a few points behind.

"Why Sport?" asks Ed Cowan (*The Humanist,* November/December 1979). When the sports are competitive ones, I cannot find a single reason to answer his rhetorical query. Mr. Cowan's discussion of the pure—almost mystical—aesthetic pleasure that is derived from athletics only directs attention away from what is, in actuality, the primary impetus of any competitive activity: winning.

I would not make such a fuss over Color War, or even complaint about the absurd spectacle of grown men shrieking and cursing on Sunday afternoons, were it not for the significance of the role played by competition in our culture. It is bad enough that Americans actually regard fighting as a sport; it is worse that the outcome of even the gentlest of competitions—baseball—can induce fans to hysteria and outright violence. But sports is only the tip of the proverbial iceberg. Our entire society is affected by—even structured upon—the need to be "better than."

My thesis is admittedly extreme; it is, simply put, that *competition by its very nature is always unhealthy.* This is true, to begin with, because competition and cooperation are mutually exclusive orientations. I say this fully aware of the famed camaraderie that is supposed to develop among players—or soldiers—on the same side. First, I have doubts, based on personal experience, concerning the depth and fullness of relationships that result from the need to become more effective against a common enemy.

Second, the "realm of the interhuman," to use Martin Buber's, phrase, is severely curtailed when those on the other side are excluded from any possible community. Worse, they are generally regarded with suspicion and contempt in any competitive enterprise. (This is not to say that we cannot remain on good terms with, say, tennis opponents, but that whatever cooperation and meaningful relationship is in evidence exists in spite of the competitiveness.) Finally, the sweaty fellowship of the locker room (or, to draw the inescapable parallel again, the trenches) simply does not compensate for the inherent evils of competition. 7

The desire to win has a not very surprising (but too rarely remarked upon) characteristic: it tends to edge out other goals and values in the context of any given competitive activity. When I was in high school, I was a very successful debater for a school that boasted one of the country's better teams. After hundreds and hundreds of rounds of competition over three years, I can assert in no uncertain terms that the purpose of debate is not to seek the truth or resolve an issue. No argument, however compelling, is ever conceded; veracity is never attributed to the other side. The only reason debaters sacrifice their free time collecting thousands of pieces of evidence, analyzing arguments, and practicing speeches, is to win. Truth thereby suffers in at least two ways. 8

In any debate, neither team is concerned with arriving at a fuller understanding of the topic. The debaters concentrate on "covering" arguments, tying logical knots, and, above all, sounding convincing. Beyond this, though, there exists a tremendous temptation to fabricate and distort evidence. Words are left out, phrases added, sources modified in order to lend credibility to the position. One extremely successful debater on my team used to invent names of magazines which ostensibly printed substantiation for crucial arguments he wanted to use. 9

With respect to this last phenomenon, it is fruitless—and a kind of self-deception, ultimately—to shake our heads and deplore this sort of thing. Similarly, we have no business condemning "overly rough" football players or the excesses of "overzealous" campaign aides or even, perhaps, violations of the Geneva Convention in time of war (which is essentially a treatise on How to Kill Human Beings Without Doing Anything *Really* Unethical). We are engaging in a massive (albeit implicit) exercise of hypocrisy to decry these activities while continuing to condone, and even encourage, the competitive orientation of which they are only the logical conclusion. 10

The cost of any kind of competition in human terms is incalculable. When my success depends on other people's failure, the prospects for a real human community are considerably diminished. This consequence 11 speaks to the profoundly antihumanistic quality of competitive activity, and it is abundantly evident in American society. Moreover, when my success depends on my being *better than,* I am caught on a treadmill, destined never to enjoy real satisfaction. Someone is always one step higher, and even the summit is a precarious position in light of the hordes waiting to occupy it in my stead. I am thus perpetually insecure and, as psychologist Rollo May points out, perpetually anxious.

> . . . individual competitive success is both the dominant goal in our culture and the most pervasive occasion for anxiety. . . . [This] anxiety arises out of the interpersonal isolation and alienation from others that inheres in a pattern in which self-validation depends on triumphing over others (*The Meaning of Anxiety,* rev. ed.) 12

I begin to see my self-worth as conditional—that is to say, my goodness or value become contingent on how much better I am than so many others in so many activities. If you believe, as I do, that unconditional self-esteem is a singularly important requirement for (and indicator of) mental health, then the destructiveness of competition will clearly outweigh any putative benefit, whether it be a greater effort at tug-of-war or a higher gross national product. 13

From the time we are quite small, the ethic of competitiveness is drummed into us. The goal in school is not to grow as a human being or even, in practice, to reach a satisfactory level of intellectual competence. We are pushed instead to become brighter than, quicker than, better achievers than our classmates, and the endless array of scores and grades lets us know at any given instant how we stand on that ladder of academic success. 14

If our schools are failing at their explicit tasks, we may rest assured of their overwhelming success regarding this hidden agenda. We are well trained to enter the marketplace and compete frantically for more money, more prestige, more of all the "good things" in life. An economy such as ours, understand, does not merely permit competition: *it demands it.* Ever greater profits becomes the watchword of private enterprise, and an inequitable distribution of wealth (a polite codeword for human suffering) follows naturally from such an arrangement. 15

Moreover, one must be constantly vigilant lest one's competitors attract more customers or conceive some innovation that gives them the edge. To become outraged at deceptive and unethical business practices is folly; it is the competitiveness of the system that promotes these phenomena. Whenever people are defined as opponents, doing everything possible to triumph must be seen not as an aberration from the structure but as its very consummation. (I recognize, of course, that I have raised a plethora of difficult issues across many disciplines that cry out for a more detailed consideration. I hope, however, to at least have opened up some provocative, and largely neglected, lines of inquiry.) 16

This orientation finds its way into our personal relationships as well. 17 We bring our yardstick along to judge potential candidates for lover, trying to determine who is most attractive, most intelligent, and . . . the best lover. At the same time, of course, we are being similarly reduced to the status of competitor. The human costs are immense.

"Why Sport?", then, is a good question to begin with. It leads us to 18 inquire, "Why Miss Universe contests?" "Why the arms race?" and—dare we say it?—"Why capitalism?" Whether a competition-free society can actually be constructed is another issue altogether, and I readily concede that this mentality has so permeated our lives that we find it difficult even to imagine alternatives in many settings. The first step, though, consists in understanding that rivalry of any kind is both psychologically disastrous and philosophically unjustifiable, that the phrase "healthy competition" is a contradiction in terms. Only then can we begin to develop saner, richer lifestyles for ourselves as individuals, and explore more humanistic possibilities for our society.

From the Jan./Feb. issue of The Humanist. *Reprinted by permission of the American Humanist Association, © 1980.*

After You Read

Work with other students to develop responses to these questions or to compare responses that you have already prepared.

1. State the thesis of the article in your own words. What sentences in the article, if any, best express the idea?

2. This article was originally published in *The Humanist*. Who would you say is Kohn's audience? What is the purpose of his essay?

3. Divide the article into sections according to each major point that Kohn makes.

4. Consider the support that Kohn provides for each of his points. Does he use generalizations or specific statements? Facts or opinions? Are his opinions reasonably supported?

5. Consider your own experience or the experiences of people you know. Do they confirm or contradict Kohn's points?

6. Are there any objections to Kohn's points that you should consider?

Before You Read

1. What do you think about the use of movies in the classroom? Do movies help students learn the subject matter?

2. Make a list of both the advantages and disadvantages of using movies in a classroom setting.

3. Which seems stronger, the advantages or the disadvantages?

History 101: Pass the Popcorn, Please

Elaine Minamide

On the face of it, the arguments make sense: 1

"Films provoke students to not only think about history, but to experience it to its fullest." 2

"Movies give educators a priceless opportunity to connect to young students bored by textbooks." 3

"Anything that gets the kids thinking and talking can only be positive." 4

It's difficult to argue with success. Opening to chapter eight in a history book rarely evokes the kind of hand-flailing, call-on-me-teacher response most educators only dream about. Switching on the VCR is a different story. From the opening credits, kids are hooked, involved, and—dare we say it?—learning. 5

That's the bottom line, isn't it? So what if *Amistad* has, as some critics have charged, "rewritten history"? Who cares if *Titanic* is merely a backdrop for a hyped-up, modern love story? Does it matter, as long as kids are thinking about the grander issues, like slavery or the tragic arrogance of man? 6

The debate over the use of contemporary films in the classroom may be stimulating, but something else is at stake that has nothing to do with blurring the line between fact and fiction. Any competent teacher can address head-on disputes over historical accuracy or propaganda. That's what education is all about, after all: guiding students into becoming discriminating, critical thinkers. 7

The greater issue has to do with declining literacy and can be traced back to the days when the letter "b" first danced across the television screen. While older siblings sweated through math problems and penmanship at school, the preschool set of the '70s sat cross-legged on their carpets, mesmerized by Bert and Ernie singing catchy jingles about the alphabet. Parents, of course, were delighted: What better way for your precocious 3-year-old to learn her ABCs than to plop her in front of the TV while you made a few phone calls? *Sesame Street* was a godsend. 8

Wouldn't you know it—most educators didn't agree. By the time those preschoolers entered kindergarten, not only did they already know their ABCs, but they sat in their little chairs, waiting for the song and dance to begin. The Entertain Me pupils were in their seats, and they're seated still. Today's high schoolers are yesterday's *Sesame Street* watchers, clamoring to be entertained. 9

Evidently, teachers are accommodating them. A recent feature article in the *San Diego Union-Tribune* focused on local teachers who frequently supplement classroom instruction with contemporary films. One eighth-grade history teacher, for example, has a must-see list of 10 flicks that she either encourages her students to see or brings to the class-room herself.

A high school social-studies teacher uses movies to introduce new 11
subjects to his students. And they're not alone. Some film companies
(notably, the producers of *Amistad*) now supply schools across the nation
with study guides to accompany their current releases.

It's been argued that since students spend so much more time watch- 12
ing TV and movies than reading books, it's best to meet them on common ground if you want them to learn. Furthermore (the argument
goes), since movies motivate students to further inquiry (researching the
sinking of the *Titanic* is currently in vogue), their use in the classroom is
not only justifiable but highly innovative.

Their arguments contradict sound educational philosophy. The 13
purpose of education is to challenge students, not cater to them. Children may prefer cookies and candy, but wise parents still serve fruits
and vegetables. The issue should be explored from a broader perspective. To what degree do the apparent short-term gains become long-term
liabilities?

As time goes by, will students' dependency upon audio-visual learn- 14
ing make it difficult, if not impossible, for them to extract meaning from
books alone? In our quest to capture the wayward attention of kids
raised on song and dance, do we handicap them instead? It doesn't take
much mental acumen to be inspired and even informed by a well-made
Hollywood movie. The question is not do movies enhance learning, but
rather, are they becoming a substitute for actual learning?

That's not to say movies shouldn't be utilized in the classroom. By 15
all means, use them, but as dessert, not the main course. Incorporate film
into the curriculum after the historical subject matter is fully grasped,
not before, and only then as part of a broader process of research and
analysis. Use films to teach critical thinking, to train students to look for
bias, propaganda, commercial exploitation, historical accuracy. Allow
students' knowledge of a subject to influence their appreciation of a
movie, rather than the reverse.

More to the point, however, require that they read. If one of the goals 16
of education is to foster literacy, it seems counter-productive to assign
movies as a supplement to learning when historical fiction may be just as
effective. Assigning books like *Les Miserables* or *Gone with the Wind* has
the added benefit of broadening students' literary background. Teachers
should be providing students with a must-read book list rather than a
must-see movie list.

Why should kids read *Les Miserables* when they can see the movie 17
instead? Answer: They probably won't. That's why acquiescing to the
"entertain me" style of learning serves little purpose other than to reinforce students' reluctance to read. Movie-watching is one more marsh-
mallow in the sugar-laden diet of popular curricula. We have no one to
blame but ourselves if all kids know about history or culture is what they

learned from their VCRs. After all, they came to us expecting a song and dance. And we haven't disappointed.

San Diego Union-Tribune. *Copyright 1998. Reprinted by permission.*

After You Read

Work with other students to develop responses to these questions or to compare responses that you have already prepared.

1. State the thesis of the article in your own words. What sentences in the article, if any, best express the idea?

2. This article was originally published in a San Diego newspaper. Who would you say is Minamide's audience? What is the purpose of her essay?

3. Divide the article into sections according to each major point that Minamide makes.

4. Consider the support that Minamide provides. Does she use generalizations or specific statements? Facts or opinions? Explain why you do or do not find her support convincing.

5. Consider your own experience or the experiences of people you know. Do they confirm or contradict Minamide's points?

6. Are there any objections to Minamide's points that you should consider?

Before You Read

1. Consider the title. What "dreamland" do you think the author has in mind?

2. Are teenagers today more or less independent than teenagers of past years?

3. Is the difference an improvement or a problem?

Teenagers in Dreamland

Robert J. Samuelson

Meet Carlos. He's a senior at American High School in Fremont, California. He's also a central character in a recent public television documentary on U.S. education. Carlos is a big fellow with a crew cut and a friendly manner. We see him driving his pickup truck, strolling with a girlfriend and playing in a football game. "I don't want to graduate," he says at one point. "It's fun. I like it." 1

If you want to worry about our economic future, worry about Carlos and all those like him. It is the problem of adolescence in America. Our teen-agers live in a dreamland. It's a curious and disorienting mixture of adult freedoms and childlike expectations. Hey, why work? Average 2 high school students do less than an hour of daily homework. Naturally, they're not acquiring the skills they will need for their well-being and the nation's.

Don't mistake me: I'm not blaming today's teen-agers. They are simply the latest heirs of an adolescent subculture—we have all been part of it—that's been evolving for decades. American children are becoming more and more independent at an earlier and earlier age. By 17, two-fifths of Americans have their own car or truck. About 60 percent have their own telephones and televisions. Adult authority wanes, and teen-age power rises. It's precisely this development that has crippled our schools.

Consider the research of sociologist James Coleman of the University of Chicago. He found that students from similar economic and social backgrounds consistently do better at Catholic high schools than at public high schools. The immediate explanation is simple: students at Catholic schools take more rigorous courses in math, English and history, and they do nearly 50 percent more homework. But why do Catholic schools make these demands when public schools don't?

The difference, Coleman concluded, lies with parents: "Parents [of public school students] do not exercise as much authority over their high-school-aged students as they one did," he recently told a conference at the Manhattan Institute. Since the 1960s, public schools have become less demanding—in discipline, required course work and homework—because they can't enforce stiffer demands. By contrast, parents of parochial school students impose more control. "The schools therefore [are] able to operate under a different set of ground rules," Coleman said.

There are obviously many good public schools and hard-working students. But the basic trends are well-established and have been altered only slightly by recent "reforms." Change comes slowly, because stricter academic standards collide with adolescent reality. In the TV documentary, Tony—a pal of Carlos—is asked why he doesn't take tougher math courses to prepare him as a computer technician, which is what he wants to be. "It's my senior year," he says, "and I think I'm going to relax."

Adolescent autonomy continues to increase. "Teens have changed so dramatically in the past decade that more advertisers . . . are targeting 'adults' as 15-plus or 13-plus rather than the typical 18-plus," notes Teen-age Research Unlimited, a market research firm. It estimates that the average 16-to-17-year-old has nearly $60 a week in spending money from jobs and allowances. By junior year, more than 40 percent of high school students have jobs.

These demanding school-time jobs are held predominantly by middle-class students. Popular wisdom asserts that early work promotes responsibility, but the actual effect may be harmful. In a powerful book (*When Teenagers Work*), psychologists Ellen Greenberger of the University of California (Irvine) and Laurence Steinberg of Temple University show that jobs hurt academic performance and do not provide needed family

3

4

5

6

7

8

income. Rather, they simply establish teen-agers as independent consumers better able to satisfy their own wants. Jobs often encourage drug use.

Our style of adolescence reflects prosperity and our values. We can 9 afford it. In the 19th century, children worked to ensure family survival; the same is true today in many developing countries. Our culture stresses freedom, individuality and choice. Everyone has "rights." Authority is to be questioned. Self-expression is encouraged. These attitudes take root early. My 4-year-old daughter recently announced her philosophy of life: "I should be able to do anything I want to do."

Parental guilt also plays a role. The American premise is that the 10 young ought to be able to enjoy their youth. Schools shouldn't spoil it, as if an hour and a half of daily homework (well above the average) would mean misery for teen-agers. Finally, more divorce and more families with two wage-earners mean that teen-agers are increasingly left to themselves. They often assume some family responsibilities—shopping or caring for younger children. Many teen-agers feel harried and confused, because the conflicts among all these roles (student, worker, child and adult) are overwhelming.

Americans, young and old, delude themselves about the results of 11 these changes. A recent study of 13-year-olds in six countries placed Americans last in mathematics and Koreans first. But when students were asked whether they were "good at mathematics," 68 percent of the Americans said yes (the highest) compared with only 23 percent of the Koreans (the lowest).

This was no quirk. Psychologist Harold Stevenson of the University 12 of Michigan, who has studied American and Asian students for years, finds the same relationship. Americans score lower in achievement but, along with their parents, are more satisfied with their performance. "If children believe they are already doing well—and their parents agree with them—what is the purpose of studying harder?" he writes.

Good question. No one should be surprised that U.S. businesses 13 complain about workers with poor skills, or that a high school diploma no longer guarantees a well-paying job. More school spending or new educational "theories" won't magically give students knowledge or skills. It takes work. Our style of adolescence is something of a national curse. Americans are growing up faster, but they may not be growing up better.

After You Read

Work with other students to develop responses to these questions or to compare responses that you have already prepared.

1. State the thesis of the article in your own words. What sentences in the article, if any, best express the idea?

2. This article was originally published in *Newsweek*. Who would you say is Samuelson's audience? What is the purpose of his essay?

3. Divide the article into sections according to each major point that Samuelson makes.

4. Consider the support that Samuelson provides. Does he use generalizations or specific statements? Facts or opinions? Explain why you do or do not find his support convincing.

5. Consider your own experience or the experiences of people you know. Do they confirm or contradict Samuelson's points?

6. Are there any objections to Samuelson's points that you should consider?

Writing Assignment

Choose one of the reading selections from this chapter or a selection assigned by your instructor. After a discussion with other members of your class, determine whether or not you find the reading selection convincing by identifying which points seem particularly weak or particularly strong. Then write a paper in which you evaluate the reading selection. Focus each body paragraph of your paper on a separate point from the article, explaining why it is or is not convincing to you.

Evaluating Sample Papers

As you read and evaluate the following essays, consider these areas.

Evaluation Essay

1. Introduction

   Does the introduction accurately and clearly state the central idea and purpose of the article? Does it smoothly and easily move the reader into the paper?

   1   2   3   4   5   6

2. Thesis

   Does the introduction end in a clear statement of evaluation of the effectiveness of the article?

   1   2   3   4   5   6

3. Unity

   Does each paragraph have a clear and specific topic sentence that accurately introduces and states an evaluation of one of the main points of the article? Is the material in each paragraph clearly related to its topic sentence?

   1   2   3   4   5   6

4. Development

   Is each topic sentence supported with clear references to the article as well as to details and examples from the writer's own knowledge and experience? Are references to ideas from the article accurately explained?

   | 1 | 2 | 3 | 4 | 5 | 6 |

5. Coherence

   Are transitions used between paragraphs? Where needed, are transitions used between sentences within each paragraph?

   | 1 | 2 | 3 | 4 | 5 | 6 |

6. References to the Text

   Are direct quotations and paraphrases correctly introduced and smoothly incorporated into the text? Do they reflect the writer's point accurately?

   | 1 | 2 | 3 | 4 | 5 | 6 |

7. Subordination and Sentence Variety

   Do the sentences combine ideas that are related, using coordination, subordination, or verbal or appositive phrases when appropriate? Are there too many brief, choppy main clauses?

   | 1 | 2 | 3 | 4 | 5 | 6 |

8. Grammar and Mechanics

   Does the paper contain fragments, comma splices, fused sentences, errors in subject-verb agreement, pronoun use, modifiers, punctuation, or spelling?

   | 1 | 2 | 3 | 4 | 5 | 6 |

9. Overall Ranking of the Essay

   | 1 | 2 | 3 | 4 | 5 | 6 |

Student Essay 1

In the article "I Wish They'd Do It Right," Jane Doe points out various reasons that her son and "his wife" should get married. Throughout the article, Doe tries to point out the social and economic reasons why her sons marriage should occur. From the announcement of her grandson, to the simple awkwardness of the "daughter-in law's" introductions to friends, to her grandson dealing with his peers at school. Doe tries to convince her readers that socially "It just isn't right." From housing at the student dormitory, to medical insurance coverage, to California state laws. Doe argues that not being married just isn't "right." I, as a reader, however, am not entirely convinced by this article.

Doe asks, "How do I present her—as my son's roommate? his spouse? his spice? my daugher-in-law?" I'll respond with, "Why don't you ask her?" In the 90's, American's will come across many varieties of "marriages," and the socially correct thing to do should be to ask the couple what they prefer.

Another of Doe's points is that her grandson will have many obstacles in his future in school because his parents are not married. Doe's grandson is growing up in a country that has a fifty percent divorce rate, so when he starts school, all he will know is that his mom and dad live in the same house and show affection for each other.

From an economic standpoint, Doe shows her readers that this couple was denied student dormitory housing and endured "other inconviences." I am somewhat convinced on this point because when I married my husband, we had to show our marriage license to apply for base housing at Camp Pendleton, and also to apply for my military identification card. Without proof of a written document, it would have been impossible to take advantage of these benefits, however, there are many situations that do not require a marriage license.

Doe goes on to say, "the couple's adamancy has been depriving to all the rest of the family. There have been no celebration of wedding or anniversaries." I have been married for three years and have not experienced a "celebration" of my anniversary with my parents or my husband's parents. I do not think Doe was very persuasive on this point.

Overall, Doe states that she "love[s] and support[s]" the couple as much as possible now. The preceding issues in her article do not convince me that Doe supports the couple and their choices. My idea of support would be to show the couple that they make their own decisions and she will wait for them to ask her opinion on raising their child. Doe says her grandson needs to be "spared the continued explanation and harrassment . . . of being a child of unmarried parents." The only "doubts and anxieties" being shown in this article are Doe's.

Student Essay 2

In his essay "Why Competition?" Alfie Kohn attacks a trait embedded in the very fabric of American society, competition. By concluding that relationships between both teammates and rivals are undesireable and illustrating the pitfalls competition holds for both individuals and American society, Kohn tries to prove that "competition by its very nature is always unhealthy." Although Kohn uses several strong personal examples to support his claims, the essay contains little substantiated support. However, since Kohn's purpose was "to at least have opened up some provocative, and largely neglected, lines of inquiry," he was successful.

I disagree in part with Kohn's first point which concerns relationships between both teammates and rivals. Kohn believes that the relationships between teammates lack depth and fullness and also observes that rivalry causes the teammates to not only exclude their rivals from "any possible community," but often to regard them with "suspicion and contempt." Kohn supports this two pronged attack with his personal experiences as a camp counselor and also compares teammates to soldiers. After attending scores of high school football games, I cannot disagree with Kohn's observations about rivals, but, as an athlete, I always played on teams with people who were my true friends and not just "comrades."

Kohn's second point is that "the desire to win . . . tends to edge out other goals and values in the context of any given competitive activity." He claims that when people are competing, winning becomes all important, and values fly out the window. His support is another personal experience which consists of his participation on a debate team. Perhaps these "debaters" are just overzealous, or they just take themselves too seriously. When I compete recreationally, whether I'm arguing a point or dribbling a basketball, I'm concerned with having fun first and winning second.

After making it clear that none among us is above behaving competitively, Kohn states his third and most convincing argument, that the cost of competition in human terms is immeasurable. With individual success, says Kohn, comes anxiety. A person's self worth starts becoming conditional. Kohn says, "my . . . values become contingent on how much better I am than so many others in so many activities." With this kind of pressure on us, Kohn continues, we can never be satisfied. Kohn doesn't rely solely on personal experiences to support this argument, but also includes a quote from a psychologist. I agree with this final argument because during my eight years of ballet school, I often felt the envy competition breeds and also found myself measuring my own accomplishments in terms of other, more experienced, dancers.

Although Kohn does bring up some interesting points, his support is mainly from personal experience. The basis of the argument is strong and, with further development, could be pretty convincing. Despite its weaknesses, this essay definitely made me rethink the term "healthy competition."

Student Essay 3

Everyone agrees that children cannot afford to be uneducated. It is simply the means of educating children that provokes a controversy. In the article "History 101: Pass the Popcorn, Please," Elaine Minamide quotes those with opposing views in saying, "Movies give educators the priceless opportunity to connect to young students bored by textbooks." However, Minamide believes that watching contemporary films in class makes students dependent on audio-visual learning instead of books. She points out that students get used to the "song-and-dance" routine from

Sesame Street. Unlike Minamide, I feel that kids need a more intriguing, interactive approach in order to learn and retain the material. I did not find Minamide's arguments very effective. Watching movies in the classroom is beneficial to the student because it is a more interesting way of presenting the material.

Minamide asks, "As time goes by, will students' dependency upon audio-visual learning make it difficult, if not impossible, for them to extract meaning from books alone?" To answer her question, I would say that's unlikely, but even if it that were the case, the students would still be learning, only in a more interesting fashion. In fact, one of the educational advantages of audio-visual learning is the interest it sparks in students. Most kids can't get an education from dry textbooks and boring lectures. Kids learn in many different ways, so the material must be presented in an interesting fashion. While I was doing an internship in a seventh-grade classroom at Diegueno Junior High School, the students were learning about Chinese dynasties. The teacher divided them into groups that would rotate through five stations. They would watch a movie about the dynasties, research it on the Internet, read from the text, listen to a lecture, and discuss it in groups. The kids ended up enjoying the movie most because it gave them a true sense about the different Chinese dynasties, and it provided a mental picture as well. Another example of audio-visual learning being successful is when my eleventh-grade history class watched *Schindler's List*. We had read about the Holocaust in the textbook, but none of us had a clear picture, and the fragments of the history we had learned were not put together. As we watched the movie, most everyone was in tears, and I must say that I've never seen quite such a reaction from reading a textbook.

Besides the benefit of providing more interesting ways to educate by using movies, the so-called song-and-dance routine, which Minamide thinks will handicap students, is really an effective way to learn. In order to learn the material, the students must enjoy themselves. Did you every wonder why kids in kindergarten have smiles on their faces while many high school students wear frowns? It's because the younger students are intrigued by the teacher's presentation, causing them to learn more. My history teacher sings songs to our class with his guitar. We listen to the lyrics and get lost in true history. As we all look pleasantly at our teacher, we find ourselves experiencing history instead of reading it. We must be involved; it is essential. As Benjamin Franklin put it, "Tell me and I forget. Teach me and I remember. Involve me and I learn."

Minamide writes, "More to the point, require that they read." Unlike the "song-and-dance" routine, reading is only beneficial if you enjoy it. Unless a student has an astounding imagination, he/she probably cannot absorb as much knowledge from textbooks as they would from historical films. When I was in fifth grade, my class was learning about the American presidents. Our class was split into two groups, the "readers" and the "watchers." Half of us reading the textbook, the other half watching a film. The next day, both groups were tested on the material, and the "watchers'" average test scores were double that of the "readers." Need I say more?

I most definitely believe that using audio-visual technology is beneficial to the students. It allows the student to learn from whatever means of education helps them the most. As Minamide quoted her critics, "Films provoke students to not only think about history, but to experience it to the fullest." Maybe students do need to be entertained, but is that such a bad thing? It's human nature to be interested in interesting things. As time goes on, we must move and advance along with it. Why keep students in the past with only reading books when they can learn from so many different methods? Children cannot afford to be uneducated. It is our job to spark their interests, which will soon grow into bright, luminous flames.

Student Essay 4

In "Teenagers in Dreamland," Robert J. Samuelson states that children live in a dreamland, curious and disorienting "mixture of adult freedoms and childlike expectations." Children are becoming more and more independent at an earlier age and adult authority is becoming less. He also explains the difference of children's attitudes if they attend private and public schools. Children are also working while they are attending school which causes problems with their schoolwork. Working while going to school makes kids think they are more independent and have more freedom. Society thinks the kids are growing up fine, but statistics show differently. I feel that Samuelson's argument about private schools educating students better than public school is weak; however, I agree with his arguments that students want more responsibility and freedom, and that students have jobs that demand more time than they have to do schoolwork.

I disagree with Samuelson's idea that private schools educate students better than public schools. He states that private schools give 50% more homework and have "rigorous courses in math, English, and history." When I was in high school, I felt that I had the same amount of homework as my friends in private schools. I also feel that they were more rebelling than I was because they had more authority watching over them. Private schools may provide better education for a small group, but Samuelson overlooks the fact that private schools have fewer students so they can focus more on their students. On the other hand, public schools can't limit their attendance so they have to focus on students with more needs. I feel that if I went to a private school, I would have turned out totally different. I think I would be more rebelling and not willing to go to college.

Samuelson states that children are growing up too soon. For example, they want to own their own cars and want to have more freedom to do what they please and do it when they want. Students move out of their parent's houses earlier than when their parents were their age. I see youths getting married really young and depending on others for support. When I was a high school student, I saw pregnancy within the high school population. Most of the girls were just about to finish high school and now they have a long road ahead of them. For example, one of my friends is 17 and pregnant. Her boyfriend is 25 and they thought they had all this freedom to what they wanted. Now he is going off to Okinawa, and she will have to depend on others to help take care of the child. This is a case of a young woman growing up too fast.

Students are running into the dilemma of going to school and having a job. They feel that the only way to get freedom is to have a job. I had a job when I was going to high school, and it took away time from my schoolwork. It was hard to budget my time so I had time for schoolwork and still be able to spend time with my friends. My job was demanding more of my time from my friends and schoolwork. I liked the money because I was able to buy what I wanted, but my grades were bad.

I feel that Samuelson has a strong point that when children work while they are going to school, it takes away from their education. I also agree that children are growing up too soon. They want to be adults while in some ways they want to be kids. However, I disagree that private schools are better than public schools because he has not concerned the size of the populations in the school.

Sentence Combining: Parallelism

You were introduced to the concept of parallelism in Chapter 2 when you used coordination to combine sentences. At that time, you learned that ideas joined with coordinating conjunctions should be worded similarly. For example, two words joined with a coordinating conjunction, such as *and*, should both be nouns, or both adjectives, or both adverbs—the point is that they should both be the same type of word.

The same is true of two phrases or clauses joined with a coordinating conjunction. You can join two prepositional phrases or two participial phrases with a coordinating conjunction, but you should not join a prepositional phrase to a participial phrase with one.

Items in a Series

When you write three or more ideas in a series, you should word them similarly, just as you do when you join two ideas with a coordinating conjunction. The key is to use similar types of words, phrases, or clauses as you write the series. *The principle of parallelism requires that you use similar grammatical constructions when you join two ideas with coordinating conjunctions or when you join several ideas in a series.*

The following sentences are drawn from the reading selections in this text. Note that each sentence uses parallel sentence structure.

Parallel Words

nouns

Our culture stresses <u>freedom</u>, <u>individuality</u>, and <u>choice</u>.

adjectives, nouns

But it will be <u>easier</u> and <u>happier</u> for us knowing that our grandson will be spared the continued <u>explanation</u> and <u>harassment</u>, the <u>doubts</u> and <u>anxieties</u> of being a child of unmarried parents.

Parallel Phrases

infinitives

To be a hero you have <u>to stand out</u>, <u>to excel</u>, <u>to take risks</u>. . . .

verb phrases

Like millions of Americans, the cabdriver was probably a decent human being who had never <u>stolen anything</u>, <u>broken any law</u> or <u>willfully injured another</u>. . . .

participial phrases

The only reason debaters sacrifice their free time <u>collecting thousands of pieces of evidence</u>, <u>analyzing arguments</u>, and <u>practicing speeches</u>, is to win.

Parallel Clauses

subordinate clauses

A fellow commits a crime <u>because he's basically insecure</u>, <u>because he hated his stepmother at nine</u>, or <u>because his sister needs an operation</u>.

main clauses

<u>Strategy is planned for the next battle</u>; <u>troops are taught the next cheer</u>.

As you can see from the above examples, you can use parallelism to join all kinds of sentence parts, as long as they are the same type of sentence part. You can join nouns to nouns, infinitives to infinitives, and subordinate clauses to subordinate clauses.

Items Joined by Correlative Conjunctions

Correlative conjunctions are pairs of words that combine related ideas. The most common correlative conjunctions are *either . . . or, neither . . . nor, not only . . . but also,* and *both . . . and.* Follow the principles of parallel sentence structure when you use these correlatives. Each word, phrase, or clause joined to another by a correlative conjunction should be worded similarly to the other. The following examples illustrate both correct and incorrect usage.

Incorrect

The timber wolf will **either** <u>adapt to its new environment</u> **or** <u>it will die a slow death</u>. (verb phrase combined with main clause)

Correct

> The timber wolf will **either** aduqt to its new environment **or** die a slow death. (verb phrase combined with verb phrase)

Correct

> **Either** the timber wolf will adapt to its new environment **or** it will die a slow death. (main clause combined with main clause)

Exercise 6.4

Use parallel sentence structure to combine each group of sentences into one sentence.

Example

> Chelsea was startled by the sudden applause. She was also confused by the bright lights. She stuttered a few words. Then she ran from the stage.
>
> Startled by the sudden applause and confused by the bright lights, Chelsea stuttered a few words and then ran from the stage.

1. The swan was waddling out of the lake. It was heading toward Leda. It had a strange look in its eye.

2. Last week's storm caused mudslides in the foothills. The storm also caused traffic jams on the freeways. Power outages throughout the city were another result.

3. The winning skier slipped. She broke her ankle. It happened after the race had ended. It was before the medal was awarded.

4. The horse was wandering down the freeway. It was stopping all the traffic. It was soon captured by the police officer.

5. Spiderman climbed out of the window. He scaled the side of the building. He fired his spiderweb at the thief.

6. Carmen could not decide if she wanted to risk the earthquakes on the West Coast. Another possibility was that she could risk the hurricanes on the East Coast.

7. The produce manager knew it. The price of the oranges was too high. The quality of the oranges was too low.

8. Senator Milkwood proposed his new legislation. He was determined to preserve the disappearing forests. He was also determined to promote the lumber industry.

9. The Sphinx looked at Oedipus and asked, "What creature goes on four feet in the morning? The same creature goes on two feet at midday. It also goes on three feet in the evening."

10. By the time the play was over, Hugo was thoroughly disgusted. The play had made him completely depressed. He decided to buy a gallon of vanilla ice cream. He planned to cover it with chocolate sauce. Then he was going to eat it all by himself. ■

Exercise 6.5

Revise the following sentences to correct any errors in parallelism.

Example

> The farmer knew that for the rest of his life he would be planting seeds, his crops needed tending, and prayers for a good harvest.

> The farmer knew that for the rest of his life he would be planting seeds, tending his crops, and praying for a good harvest.

1. In the early 1800s, John Palmer, a farmer with a long white beard, stood by his principles and refusing to be intimidated.
2. When the people in his town told him that he should be not only ashamed of his beard but also that he should cut it off, he refused.
3. Children jeered at him, stones were heaved through his windows by grown men, and women crossing to the opposite side of the street.
4. Saying that he was a vain man and with the insistence that he cut his beard, the local pastor denounced him.
5. When several men tried to grab him, hold him down, and shave him, he fought back.
6. As a result, he was arrested, a trial was held, and jailed for "unprovoked assault."
7. He was told either that he could cut his beard or stay in jail.
8. When Henry David Thoreau and Ralph Waldo Emerson heard of his plight, they persuaded people to support his cause and his release was arranged with their help.
9. John Palmer refused to leave his jail cell, saying that his jailers must admit that they were not only wrong but also must publicly state that he had a right to wear a beard. ■

Exercise 6.6

Use parallel sentence structure to combine each group of sentences into one sentence.

1. The unicorn is a legendary animal. It resembles a horse. It also is said to resemble a deer. Or it could be described as looking like a kid. It has a single horn on its forehead.
2. It has also been described as having other characteristics. It has been described as having the hind legs of an antelope. In addition, some have said it has the tail of a lion. It has also been said to have the beard of a goat.
3. The unicorn is represented in the art of Asian cultures. It is also in the art of European cultures. It is in art that is ancient. In addition, it is in medieval art.
4. In 400 B.C. a Greek physician described the unicorn. He said it has a white body. Its head is purple. It has a horn that is straight.
5. He said that the horn has a white base. The horn's middle is black. It has a red tip.

6. The unicorn was said to be a fleet animal. It was also supposed to be fierce. It was a solitary animal too. It would fight savagely when cornered. However, it was gentle at mating time.

7. Many people believed that the powdered horn of a unicorn would protect them. They thought it would give them protection from poison. It was also supposed to prevent stomach trouble. Epilepsy was supposed to be prevented by it too.

8. True powder from unicorn horns was supposed to do certain things. It was supposed to generate bubbles in water. It emitted a sweet odor when burned. Poisonous plants and animals were killed by it.

9. In medieval times the unicorn represented chastity. It also stood for purity. It could only be tamed by the touch of a virgin.

10. In some medieval paintings the unicorn is associated with the Virgin Mary. Jesus is represented by it in other medieval paintings. ■

Exercise 6.7

Combine the following sentences, using coordination, subordination, verbal phrases, appositives, and parallel sentence structure where appropriate.

1. Of the five senses, many animals possess at least one that is special.
   That one is much more highly developed than it is in other animals.
   The five senses are sight, hearing, touch, smell, and taste.

2. A buzzard will be flying hundreds of feet in the air.
   It can see a beetle on the ground.
   An owl can hear the slight rustle of a mouse.
   It can home in on the rustle.
   That sound is inaudible to the human ear.

3. Most animals that hunt have many rod cells in their eyes.
   Rod cells are sensitive to movement.
   Animals that gather stationary food have many cone cells.
   Cone cells are sensitive to colors.

4. Dogs have over 200 million olfactory cells.
   Humans have 5 million olfactory cells.
   Dogs are literally millions of times better at detecting odors than are humans.

5. A female butterfly carries only 1/10,000 of a milligram of perfume.
   She releases that perfume into the air.
   A male butterfly can detect her scent up to seven miles away.

6. The sense of hearing is spectacularly developed in bats.
   Bats emit high-frequency squeaks.
   They use the echoes to find their way in the dark.

They also use them to hunt fast-flying insects.

7. Bats often fly in groups of thousands.

   They are always able to recognize the echoes of their own squeaks.

   They never confuse them with those of another bat.

8. Scientists have tried to "jam" the bats' signals.

   They have broadcast on the same wavelength.

   They have broadcast at 2,000 times the volume of a bat's squeak.

   The bats were still able to recognize their own echoes.

9. Bees seem to have a sixth sense.

   It is a sensitivity to the earth's magnetic field.

   It enables them to navigate at great distances from their hive.

10. There are two dimples on each side of a rattlesnake's head.

    They serve as heat-sensing organs.

    They allow the snake to locate its prey.

    They also allow it to determine the size of its prey.

    And they help the snake determine the shape of its prey. ■

Chapter 7

Synthesizing Ideas from Reading Selections

The Small Society. Reprinted by permission of King Features Syndicate.

One of the goals of a college education is to learn to search out new ideas and to consider those that are different from our own. After all, we really can't claim to be educated about an issue if we know only one side of it. Many college assignments will ask you to discuss or explain the various issues involved in a particular topic. A philosophy instructor, for example, might ask you to explain the concept of love as it is developed by a number of philosophers; a health instructor might ask you to discuss different theories about the best way to prevent high cholesterol; and a political science instructor might ask you to write about the arguments involved in the debate over the balanced-budget amendment.

People who are able to consider ideas from a number of sources, to see the relationships among those ideas, and to pull those ideas together into one coherent whole possess a valuable skill. They are the people who will be able to consider all sides of an issue and then reach reasonable, considered judgments about how they should vote, where they should work, or why they should accept one idea rather than another. They are also the people who will not oversimplify a complex issue, who will recognize that sometimes there is no one "correct" answer but merely one alternative that is only slightly better than other possible alternatives.

A **synthesis** is a paper or report that pulls together related ideas. In one sense, a synthesis is similar to a summary in that both papers require careful reading and accurate reporting. However, writing a synthesis is often more difficult than writing a summary because a synthesis requires that you read a number of sources, identify the related ideas, and then explain how those ideas are related. Sometimes several sources on the same topic will discuss very different points yet reach the same conclusion, and your synthesis will need to reflect that. Sometimes related sources will discuss the same points but reach quite different conclusions. And sometimes sources will simply repeat ideas you have already read in other sources.

Preparing the Synthesis

1. The first step in writing a good synthesis is to identify the ideas discussed by each writer. On a sheet of paper, identify the thesis idea of each writer. Then make a list of the supporting ideas discussed by that writer. If any examples, statistics, or other types of support seem particularly important, make a note of them too.

2. Once you have listed the ideas that each writer discusses, you need to look for the relationships among those ideas. Sometimes the relationships are easy to see. For instance, let's say you have read several articles on gun control and have noticed that most of them referred in one way or another to the Second Amendment to the Constitution. Part of your synthesis paper, then, would report how the writers used the Second Amendment in their arguments. Unfortunately, sometimes the relationships between ideas are not easy to see. If you do not see any clear relationships among the points you have listed, consider these questions:

   a. Do one writer's ideas support another writer's ideas? If so, how?

   b. Do the writers who reach the same conclusion use the same ideas in their writing? Or do they use very different ideas to reach the same conclusion?

c. Do the writers who disagree discuss similar points, or do they discuss completely different points?

d. Are any of the ideas you have listed actually the same idea in different words?

Organizing the Synthesis

How you organize your synthesis will depend upon the sources that you have read. Let's consider the following example: Suppose you have read several articles about protecting an endangered species in America's northwestern forests. One of the articles was written by a spokesperson for the logging industry, one by a member of the Sierra Club, one by a homeowner in Seattle, Washington, and one by a biologist at Washington State University. Perhaps each article reached a different conclusion about protecting the endangered species, yet you were able to find three or four points that some of the articles had in common—even if they disagreed about those points. You could organize such a paper as follows.

Point-by-Point Organization

I. Introduction

II. One point discussed by two or more of the articles

III. Another point discussed by two or more of the articles

IV. Another point discussed by two or more of the articles

V. An optional paragraph mentioning one or more major points discussed in only one article each

VI. Conclusion

The above organization will work if you can identify similar points discussed by different sources. (Remember, the sources do not need to agree about the points.) However, sometimes you will read several articles that do not discuss any similar points, even though they are about the same topic. In such a case, you can briefly summarize what each source has to say. If each source focuses on one major issue, you can summarize the major issue in each paragraph.

Source-by-Source Organization

I. Introduction

II. Summary of one source

III. Summary of another source

IV. Summary of another source

V. Conclusion

Alternate Source-by-Source Organization

    I.   Introduction

    II.   One major point discussed by only one source

    III.   Another major point discussed by only one source

    IV.   Another major point discussed by only one source

    V.   Conclusion

Of course, as often as not, you will find some points that overlap from article to article and some that do not. In such cases, you can use an organization that is a blend of the ones shown above.

A Blended Organization

    I.   Introduction

    II.   One point discussed by two or more articles

    III.   Another point discussed by two or more articles

    IV.   One major point discussed by only one source

    V.   Another major point discussed by only one source

    VI.   Conclusion

Documenting Your Sources

Whenever you use someone else's words or ideas in your writing, you must let the reader know the source of those words or ideas. It really doesn't matter whether you have paraphrased, summarized, or quoted—in each case, you must let the reader know whose material you are using.

Up to this point, your writing assignments have focused on one reading selection at a time. In them you have used simple transitions to tell the reader when you were using material from the reading selection. (See Chapter 5 for a discussion of transitions with paraphrases, summaries, and quotations.) There are, however, more formal methods of documentation that you will need to learn to use as you write in college classes.

The two most common methods of documentation are the MLA (Modern Language Association) method, used primarily in the humanities, and the APA (American Psychological Association) method, used mostly in the social sciences. Both methods use parentheses within the paper to identify the author and page number of a particular passage that is paraphrased, summarized, or quoted. They also both use a separate page at the end of the paper to give more detailed and complete identification of the sources used. In most classes, your instructor will tell you which method to use and will suggest a documentation guide that you should purchase.

Because this text includes its own reading selections, you do not need to write a separate page that gives detailed identification about the sources you use. However, the papers you write for Chapters 7 and 8 will be clearer if you learn to use parentheses to identify the particular article you are referring to at any given time. Use these guidelines to help you:

- Each paraphrase, summary, and quotation should be identified by author and page number in parentheses. Do not use the author's first name within the parentheses.

  According to one writer, "Educational TV corrupts the very notion of education and renders its victims uneducable" (Robinson 373).

  In defense of television, another writer claims that many schoolchildren learn the alphabet from *Sesame Street* and that high school students learn about the problems that our planet faces (Henry 370).

- If the author's name is already included in the transition, it does not need to be repeated in the parentheses.

  According to Paul Robinson, "Educational TV corrupts the very notion of education and renders its victims uneducable" (373).

  In defense of television, William Henry III claims that many schoolchildren learn the alphabet from *Sesame Street* and that high school students learn about the problems that our planet faces (370).

- When your source quotes or paraphrases someone else and you want to use that material, indicate it by using "qtd. in" as is done in the following example. (Here the quotation of Daniel Anderson comes from the article by Madeline Drexler that is included in this chapter.)

  According to Daniel Anderson, a psychologist at the University of Massachusetts at Amherst, children watching TV "muse upon the meaning of what they see, its plausibility and its implications for the future—whether they've tuned in to a news report of a natural disaster or an action show" (qtd. in Drexler 377).

- No punctuation is placed between the author's last name and the page number (see above examples).

- The parenthetical citation is placed at the end of the borrowed material but before the period at the end of the sentence (see above examples).

Readings: The Toy Weapon Debate

Before You Read

1. The following articles were written by fathers who reached different conclusions about whether or not they should buy toy guns for their children. What issues would you expect to see discussed in such a debate?

2. Do you think parents should buy toy guns for their children? Why or why not?

Why I Bought My Son a Toy Gun

Michael Golden

During my college years, you could have called me a peacenik. In my pantheon of heroes, Mahatma Gandhi and Dr. Martin Luther King, Jr., rank only behind Mickey Mantle. My wife, Joan, considers it an act of violence to step on any multi-legged creature that crawls (with the possible exception of large, hairy spiders). The only guns either of us ever touch are the caulking and staple guns that I use solely under extreme duress. And after our son, Andrew, was born, we raised him on a steady diet of Dr. Seuss, *Sesame Street*, and *Reading Rainbow*.

    Now, in a world saturated with violence, I find myself in a rather ironic position: defending my decision to buy my son a toy gun. I think, however, that I can justify this apparent contradiction.

    When we bought Andrew his first toy gun, he was all of six years old—an age so advanced that most of his friends had already acquired arsenals that would be the envy of several Third World countries.

    We were in a gift shop in Disney World, having just viewed the "Pirates of the Caribbean" exhibit. Andrew was fascinated by pirates and was eagerly eyeing the authentic-looking replica of a pirate's pistol. Joan and I looked at each other, waiting.

    "Please, please, can I get this gun?" Andrew asked.

    Joan tried plea bargaining first. "You know how Mommy feels about guns, Andrew. Why, just look at this wonderful book about pirates. Or this model of a pirate ship. Wouldn't you rather have one of those?"

    Andrew wouldn't bite. He turned to me.

    "But Dad, you said I could get something in the gift shop. Can't I please get this gun?"

    Looking at my eager, questioning child, I said what I presume any father would under the circumstances:

    "You know how your mother feels about guns, Andrew."

    "But, Dad, it's only a toy. It's not like a real gun."

    Six-year-old logic won out over parental reservations.

    As I look back on this incident three years later, questions surface: Did Joan and I "give in," abandoning our parental authority? Did we, by buying him that first gun, somehow sanction what guns represent: violence, bloodshed, death, and mayhem?

    I don't think so. As parents, we have to pick and choose our battles, to know when to stand firm and when to compromise. This was just not an issue on which we were prepared to dig in our heels.

    Why? For one thing, we felt that it was not realistic to think that forbidding Andrew to play with toy guns would keep him from doing so. He would play with them anyway at his friends' houses or fashion them out of any available material, from sticks to blocks. Or he might, as boys so often do, simply use his pointing finger and some sound effects for a rousing shoot-out. And besides, we wondered, wouldn't denying him his own guns only make them that much more attractive (the "forbidden fruit" theory)?

But the practical arguments, admittedly, don't make it right to buy a toy gun; the everybody's-doing-it and forbidden fruit theories are not morally compelling. We had to consider what message we were giving Andrew by purchasing the gun. 16

The message *wasn't* that real guns are acceptable or that real violence is. Andrew had already shown us that he understood that the gun we bought him is a toy and that toys don't kill. And he knows our attitude toward guns and violence; he understands that allowing the use of a toy gun does not give him license to commit acts of destruction. 17

I also believe that it is healthy for Andrew to act out his fantasies and actively engage his imagination. I would rather see him play cops and robbers with his toy gun than see him sit in front of a mindless television program. 18

Finally, as a father, I retain some of the little boy in me, vestiges of my childhood that enable me to relate to Andrew in an intimate way. As a small boy, my heroes were often symbols of authority and order: the policeman, the soldier, the gun-toting cowboy. I emulated them by acting out bold adventures, secure in the knowledge that the sharp-shooting good guys would win. I recall lining up my "enemy" soldiers and mowing them down with my cork rifle, not from any bloodthirsty impulse but out of desire to destroy the "bad guys" that threatened my world. 19

In the end, it came down to this: If I enjoyed playing with toy guns in my youth and managed to grow up and become a reasonably responsible, nonviolent adult, how could I justify denying my son the same opportunity? 20

Now, three years later, Joan and I are convinced that the purchase of that gun did not signify a lapse in our moral judgment. We are proud of Andrew; he occasionally plays with his toy guns, but he also plays the piano and violin, and tennis and chess and baseball. He is, we feel, developing a healthy and balanced set of values. Most important, he is sensitive and caring—even, remarkably, to the five-year-old sister who loves to torment him. 21

And so Andrew has his toy guns, and Joan and I are at peace with our decision. Despite the dilemma it posed, we don't feel we had to "bite the bullet" on this one. 22

Why I Won't Buy My Sons Toy Guns

Robert Shaffer

I've often seen a child go up to another child or an adult, pull a trigger on 1
a toy gun (or a pretend trigger on a pretend gun), and exclaim "You're
dead." Just yesterday, my seven-year-old son was "attacked" by a total
stranger, a boy of eight or nine carrying a two-foot-long plastic gun. Usually, I just move on after such an incident, although living in New York
City, where death by stray bullets regularly makes headlines, I shudder
whenever I witness these make-believe murders.

I cannot shrug off, however, the mother I know who apologized for 2
her son's similar behavior by saying, "I can't understand where Steven
gets these ideas. It's not like his father and I sit around talking about
killing people, or going 'bang-bang' to everything we see." In fact,
Steven's parents did sanction his behavior by providing him with a room-
ful of toy weapons, whose only function is to attack people, and by allowing him to sit in front of television shows filled with fights, shootings, and
mutilations.

Any toy is a teacher. A toy hammer helps children act out repair or 3
construction activities they see around them. A toy typewriter helps our
sons model my work as a teacher. Bakers' caps, play food, and sample
menus put children in charge of the restaurant experience.

Toy weapons, too, develop children's skills and coping mechanisms. 4
But the lesson toy guns teach is that solving problems with violence is
acceptable. These are not skills my wife and I want to encourage in our
two sons, so we won't be buying any toy weapons for them this holiday
season, just as we haven't in past years.

Does our stance mean that we never expect our children—Alan, 5
seven, and Ross, five—to act out their emotions with pretend or real
violence? Of course not. Last night Ross was uneasy about sitting in the
car next to an adult friend of ours. He demonstrated his discomfort by
punching our friend and pretending to shoot him. A little attention and a
familiar toy to hold on to calmed his fears.

Allowing anger and aggressive play to surface is not the same as en- 6
couraging play with toy weapons, however—and buying a toy gun or
missile is encouragement. I have, of course, often seen a block, a stick, a
finger, a doll, or even a half-eaten cookie become, in the hands and minds
of my sons, a gun or a club. But the same process of imagination that
made weapons of these objects can make them into constructive and
peaceful objects. The blocks on the living room floor right now were a fort
yesterday, but over the last three days they have also been a garage, a
kitchen, and a "safe place" to put little people and animal figures. A toy
weapon, however, stays a toy weapon.

Furthermore, so many of the toy weapons for sale are hopelessly in-   7
tertwined with violent television shows which determine how children
will play with the toys. Nancy Carlsson-Paige and Diane Levin, in their
excellent recent book about war toys, *Who's Calling the Shots?* (New Society Publishers), bemoan the increasingly imitative nature of war play, as
opposed to creative and dramatic play. Aggressive play and war play,
they say, *could* have a value in allowing children to develop ideas of right
and wrong, good and bad, teamwork, and organizational skills. Increasingly, however, the toys rather than the children write the script.

In addition, Carlsson-Paige and Levin point out that the Reagan ad-   8
ministration in the 1980s deregulated commercial children's television to
allow more product tie-ins, more ads, and more violence at the same time
that military spending skyrocketed. Not surprisingly, sales of war toys
soared in the late 1980s, to become a billion-dollar-a-year industry.

Many parents I know do not like to buy war toys but do so upon in-   9
sistent and incessant demands from their children. We've found, however, that laying down certain ground rules has limited Alan's and Ross's
demands for war toys.

We discourage our children from watching commercial television,   10
avoid television news shows, and tell relatives and close friends that war
toys are not welcome as presents.

We've also checked our sons' day-care centers and schools to make   11
sure they do not allow toy weapons. Friends' houses are more difficult,
but we don't encourage play dates at other children's homes if we know
that they will mainly watch TV or play with war toys.

Can the elimination of toy weapons eliminate war? Modern wars are   12
caused by many factors more complex than the legacies of childhood war
play, but toy weapons certainly serve to make war appear more acceptable to future voters and future soldiers. In a season ostensibly devoted to
peace and good will, we certainly will not participate in purchasing toy
weapons.

After You Read

Work with other students to develop responses to these questions or to compare
responses that you have already prepared.

1. Is Robert Shaffer's idea that any toy is a teacher related to any point that Michael
   Golden makes?
2. What does each writer have to say about the role of the imagination in his
   argument?
3. What other ideas do the writers consider?

Readings: Flag Burning and Freedom of Speech

Before You Read

1. Should the burning of the American flag be prohibited by law? Why or why not?
2. Make a list of the reasons you would expect to find for outlawing the burning of the flag and for allowing the burning of it.

The American Flag: A Symbol We Should Protect

Paul Greenberg

The flag amendment is back. And well on its way to becoming the 28th Amendment to the Constitution of the United States. What's this? It was supposed to be dead a couple of years ago, remember? 1

But now the House of Representatives has voted in favor of a simple declaration that, once upon a common-sense time, would scarcely have attracted notice, let alone controversy: "The Congress and the States shall have the power to prohibit the physical desecration of the flag of the United States." The vote was 312 to 120, easily more than the two-thirds' vote (280) required to propose a constitutional amendment. The prospect for Senate approval is good, and the states are primed to ratify. 2

But didn't our intelligentsia explain to us yokels again and again that burning the flag of the United States isn't an action, but speech, and therefore a constitutionally protected right? That's what the Supreme Court decided, too, if only in one of its confused and confusing 5-to-4 splits. 3

But the people don't seem to have caught on. They still insist that burning the flag is burning the flag, not making a speech. Stubborn lot, the people. Powerful thing, public opinion, Congress certainly seems to be reflecting it. 4

It isn't the *idea* of desecrating the flag that the American people propose to ban. Any street-corner orator who takes a notion to should be able to stand on a soapbox and bad-mouth the American flag all day long— and apple pie and motherhood, too, if that's the way the speaker feels. It's a free country. 5

It's actually burning Old Glory, it's defacing the Stars and Stripes, it's the physical desecration of the flag of the United States that ought to be against the law. And the people of the United States just can't seem to be talked out of that notion—or orated out of it, or lectured out of it, or condescended and patronized out of it. 6

Maybe it's because the people can't shut their eyes to homely truths as easily as our Advanced Thinkers. How many legs does a dog have, Abraham Lincoln once asked, if you call its tail a leg? And he answered: 7

still four. Calling a tail a leg doesn't make it one. Not even a symbolic leg. The people have this stubborn notion that calling something a constitutional right doesn't make it one, despite the best our theorists and pettifoggers can do.

The people keep being told that their flag is just a symbol. 8

Just a symbol. 9

"We live by symbols," said a justice of the United States Supreme 10 Court (Felix Frankfurter) when the standards for appointees, whether liberals or conservatives or neither, were considerably higher. And if a nation lives by its symbols, it also dies with them.

To turn aside when the American flag is defaced, with all that the flag 11 means—yes, all that it *symbolizes*—is to ask too much of Americans.

There are symbols and there are Symbols. There are some so rooted 12 in history and custom, and in the heroic imagination of a nation, that they transcend the merely symbolic; they become presences.

Many of us may not have the words to express it (which is why na- 13 tions wave flags instead of computer printouts), but we know it's right to protect the flag—by law. To do nothing when that flag, that presence, is desecrated is not simply to let the violent bear it away; it is to join the mob, to aid and abet it by our silence, our permission, our unnatural law. It is to become one more accessory to the general coarsening of society, to the desensitizing of America, to the death of the symbolic.

No, this is not an argument over who loves the flag more. Patriots 14 can disagree; American ones almost have an obligation to. This Republic was not conceived as some kind of factory for manufacture of robots. And those on the other side of this issue have every right to resent it if somebody wants to turn this disagreement over law and the role of the symbolic in American life into some kind of loyalty test. No one political persuasion has a monopoly on the American flag. May it long wave over every kind of political rally.

But this also isn't a fight over who loves the Bill of Rights more. And 15 those of us who favor a simple constitutional amendment to protect the flag have every reason to resent it when others try to monopolize the Bill of Rights, or confuse it with the Supreme Court's confused reading of the First Amendment where the flag is concerned.

Burning the flag is no more speech than vandalizing a cemetery, or 16 scrawling slogans on a church or synagogue, or spray-painting a national monument—all of which are *acts* properly forbidden by the laws of a civilized country. Not to mention public decency.

Even if no flag were ever burned, or no cemetery or church ever de- 17 faced, laws against such acts would be proper, and should be constitutional. Because the law is a great teacher, and one thing it needs to teach a less-and-less-civil society is a little respect.

The great Italian—what? historian? philosopher? moralist? philoso- 18 pher of history? proto-anthropologist?—Giambattista Vico spoke of a barbarism of the intellect that confuses concept with reality (speech with action?) and so loses touch with the *sensus communis*, the common-sense values of language and custom in which nations are rooted. Today's strange arguments from our best-and-brightest against protecting the national emblem are not symptomatic of any kind of treason-of-the-intellectuals, but of a different malady: an isolating intellectualism cut off from a sense of reverence, and so from the historical memory and heroic imagination that determines the fate of any nation.

Flag Burning and The First Amendment

Charles Levendosky

1   Click on Internet's Flag Burning Page, and you can flick a virtual Bic and burn a virtual American flag. Is that desecration?

2   Members of the House of Representatives, in a stampede to show us just how super patriotic they are, overwhelmingly passed a proposed amendment to the Constitution which would allow Congress and the states "to prohibit the physical desecration of the flag of the United States."

3   As they rushed to vote, their heels stomped all over the core meaning of the First Amendment. Reason couldn't head them off. Argument couldn't. Not even the Constitution can halt a herd of congressmen when they want to prove to voters they are patriotic.

4   If the Senate doesn't stop this proposed amendment, free speech will have another exception carved out. One that impacts political speech.

5   The First Amendment is clear and decisive: "Congress shall make no law . . . abridging the freedom of speech . . ." But once again Congress is mucking about with our liberties.

6   Some say that flag burning isn't speech. Then why are these folks so upset about the flag being burned? Obviously, the act does communicate something. It expresses a profound disagreement with the policies of the federal government.

7   The "not speech" ploy is an attempt to persuade us that the proposed amendment would not limit the First Amendment.

8   Of course, there is symbolic speech.

9   And some acts are eloquent speech.

10   The U.S. Supreme Court recognized that more than 60 years ago when it ruled that raising a red flag to show support for worker unity was protected speech. And again 25 years ago, when the high court protected the right of students to wear black armbands to protest our role in Vietnam.

11   Even silent sit-ins to protest racial segregation were recognized as symbolic speech and thus protected by the court.

Burning the flag is the act of someone who has little or no political   12
power.

It is an act of someone who desperately wants to communicate a dis-   13
agreement with U.S. policy. It shocks us into paying attention to those
who could not otherwise command the interest of the media. It presents a
grandstand forum in order to express political dissent. Our dissidents are
then heard.

This is a profound First Amendment issue for the powerless.   14

It is easy for those in the power structure to ignore this side of the   15
issue. A member of Congress can call a news conference whenever he or
she wishes. The media will be there. The little guy, the working class stiff,
commands no such attention.

The flag proposal is another piece of elitism parading in the guise of   16
patriotism.

Nothing in our Constitution could be more significant than protect-   17
ing the right of the ordinary citizen to express his or her disagreement
with the government—so that the dissent will be heard. This is a profound First Amendment issue for our nation.

Political speech must have the broadest protection—even to include   18
burning the American flag—for us to be able to contend that We the
People govern ourselves.

We protect waving the flag or displaying it as a statement of political   19
assent. The First Amendment means that we must protect burning the
flag as a counter-statement, a statement of political dissent. That is the
essence of freedom of speech.

What your congressmen aren't telling you is that, if they wished—   20
even if the amendment is ratified—they could burn the American flag on
the floor of either house of Congress during congressional debate and not
be taken to court for it.

Read Article I, sec. 6 of the U.S. Constitution: they cannot be held le-   21
gally accountable for any speech while in debate on the floor of Congress.

So, We the People, who by inalienable right should have the most ex-   22
pansive reading of the First Amendment, will have a narrower one, while
our political servants have the greater. Seems backward, doesn't it?

That's because this amendment is flagrantly, deeply un-American.   23

And where will this erosion of liberty stop? Will a few ministers be-   24
gin a movement to stop people from burning the cross—after all can't the
cross be considered a more important symbol than the flag?

What does physical desecration of the flag mean? Does it mean you   25
can be arrested if you wear a bikini with a representation of the flag
on it? The U.S. Code defines the American flag as "any substance" that
shows the colors, stars and stripes, and could be considered a clear
representation.

Will the flag be desecrated if you sit down while wearing your flag   26
pants?

Will a frosting flag on a Fourth of July cake be desecrated if you eat   27
the cake?

Is burning a virtual flag in the cyberspace of Internet desecration? 28

Confused? That's because we are dealing with a symbolism. Symbolism has few boundaries in the real world. But liberty is tangible in our daily lives. 29

Our Congress seems willing to protect the symbol of our liberties—at the expense of those liberties. Our representatives have sworn to protect the Constitution, yet in this proposal they violate the very essence of it. 30

Clearly, our stampeding congressmen have charged off the edge— just to prove they are patriotic. What sad irony. 31

Reprinted by permission of the author.

May Americans Do Battle to Save Our Flag

Robert Dole

On Dec. 7, 1941, exactly 54 years ago today, more than 2,300 brave Americans lost their lives during the attack on Pearl Harbor. As a testament to their great sacrifice, some of the dead are permanently entombed in the Arizona, one of the ships sunk during the morning raid. 1

As World War II raged on, thousands of other brave American soldiers followed their country's flag into battle. The great sacrifices made by our fighting men and women during this war and in subsequent conflicts—Korea, Vietnam, the Persian Gulf, Somalia—reflect the courage, the strength of character and the resilience of the American people. 2

Our flag is a unique and beloved symbol of these qualities. It also represents our principles and ideals as a nation. There is no other symbol that so captures the American spirit and experience. The flag, representing Americans of every race, creed and social background, is the one symbol that brings to life the phrase *"e pluribus unum"*—out of many, one. 3

Indeed, one of our most enduring national images is the famous picture of the Marines raising Old Glory at the top of Iwo Jima's Mount Suribachi. Nearly 6,000 Americans gave their lives during their deadly ascent up that hill. 4

Yet, today, the act of burning the American flag is constitutionally protected. In its misguided Texas vs. Johnson decision, the Supreme Court effectively overturned 48 state statutes and a federal law proscribing flag desecration. Most of these statutes had been on the books for decades, without any threat to our freedom, but five of the nine justices of the Supreme Court somehow concluded in 1989 that flag burning should be wrapped around the First Amendment's free-speech guarantee. Although the First Amendment does not protect obscenity or "fighting words" or yelling "fire" in a crowded theater, the court concluded that the act of desecrating our nation's symbol deserved such protection. 5

Like most Americans, I strongly disagree with the Johnson decision.   6
That's why I have joined with the Citizens' Flag Alliance, the American
Legion, and 113 other civic and patriotic organizations in supporting a
constitutional amendment that would overturn this decision and restore
to the American people the power to protect our flag.

We must remember that the Framers of the Constitution intention-   7
ally made the amendment process a difficult one, requiring the assent of
two-thirds of each house of Congress and three-fourths of the state legis-
latures before an amendment's ratification. These sensible hurdles were
designed to protect the Constitution from frivolous changes. But once an
amendment has been ratified, clearing the hurdles built into the amendment process itself, the American people have spoken.

The flag, of course, belongs to all of us—not just to veterans, not just   8
to native-born Americans, but also to those whom we welcome to our
shores as immigrants.

Stephan Ross is one of these immigrants. In 1940, at the age of nine,   9
the Nazis seized Ross from his home in Krasnik, Poland. For five years,
he was held in 10 different Nazi death camps, and barely survived.

The U.S. Army eventually liberated Ross from the Dachau death   10
camp. As Ross headed to Munich for medical care, an American tank
commander jumped off his vehicle to lend his help to Ross and to the
other victims of Nazi brutality. As Ross recounts: "He gave me his own
food. He touched my withered body with his hands and heart. His love
instilled in me a will to live, and I fell at his feet and shed my first tears in
five years."

The American soldier then gave Ross what he thought was a hand-   11
kerchief, but he soon realized, "it was a small American flag, the first
I had ever seen. It became my flag of redemption and freedom."

Even today, Stephan Ross still keeps that same cherished flag: 12

"It represents the hope, freedom and life that the American soldiers   13
returned to me when they found me, nursed me to health, and restored
my faith in mankind."

Ross now works as a psychologist in Boston.   14

"Even now, 50 years later," Ross says, "I am overcome with tears and   15
gratitude whenever I see our glorious American flag, because I know
what it represents not only to me, but to millions around the world. . . .
Protest if you wish. Speak loudly, even curse our country and our flag,
but please, in the name of all those who died for our freedoms, don't
physically harm what is so sacred to me and to countless others."

Stephan Ross is right: We must protect that which is sacred to us as   16
citizens of this great country. Amid the rich diversity that is America, we
must cherish the principles and ideals that bind us together as one people, one nation, and for which thousands of Americans have given their
lives. As the unique symbol of these principles and ideals, the flag must
receive the constitutional protection it so richly deserves.

Flag-Burning Ban: Protecting What It Symbolizes or the Symbol?

Jeffrey P. Kaplan

Should we amend the Constitution to let Congress ban flag desecration? Despite its defeat Tuesday in the Senate, the proposed amendment won't go away, its supporters vow, and polls indicate that up to 80 percent of Americans find such an amendment desirable. But the better term may be "seductive." 1

The word "speech" in the First Amendment covers speech, writing, sign language, Morse code, auction gestures, etc.—any way we encode meanings in language. More importantly, the Supreme Court has applied the free speech guarantee through the years not just to language, but to conduct: picketing, sitting-in, contributing money to political candidates, displaying a red banner as a symbol of opposition to government, wearing a military uniform in a manner calculated to discredit the military, wearing a black armband to protest the Vietnam War, civil rights boycotts of merchants and displaying a U.S. flag with a peace symbol attached. 2

What unites all these forms of conduct is that they function as communication. In fact, what the First Amendment really guarantees is freedom of communication, according to Loyola law professor (and linguist) Peter Tiersma in a 1993 article in the *Wisconsin Law Review*. 3

Is flag-burning communication? What is communication? First, it involves meaning. While sometimes a communicative act naturally resembles its meaning—as in pointing and beckoning—most human communication involves symbols, to which meaning attaches "conventionally." The word "road" means road, despite the fact that the sequence of sounds represented by "r," "oa," and "d" don't resemble a road at all. 4

In the same arbitrary way, a swastika represents Nazism, a black armband symbolizes mourning the dead, and a peace symbol means opposition to war. Meaningless vocalizations like "Gleeg!" aren't communicative; and conduct that doesn't encode a meaning—sleeping, eating a doughnut—generally isn't communicative either. 5

Flag-burning is meaningful. Ceremonial book- and effigy-burnings indicate that burning can carry the meaning of harsh condemnation. This meaning arises partly naturally: Burning is an effective way to destroy something we hate. 6

The meaning is partly conventional: Burning is just one of many ways to show strong revulsion (others: averting eyes, making illegal, smashing); and burning does not always operate as a symbol for condemnation (as when we burn trash). The symbolic function of burning arises only in ritual contexts. 7

Second, communication requires an audience. Talking to oneself isn't really communicative. The flag-burning addressed by the proposed amendment is effective, from the flag burner's perspective, only when carried out before an audience.

8

Third, to be communication, an instance of language must be intended by the speaker or actor to have a meaning. The monkey at the typewriter who fortuitously produces the text of "Hamlet" does not intend the words to have meaning, though they do. There is no communication because there is no intent.

9

Intentional meaningfulness is necessary also for communicative, nonverbal conduct. Placing lights in Boston's Old North Church any night but April 18, 1775, would probably not have manifested an intent to convey meaning, but that night, placing them there did, and Paul Revere understood the intended meaning.

10

Political flag-burners intend their act to have meaning, since the point is not to reduce fabric to ashes, but to dramatically express hatred toward what the flag symbolizes.

11

Actually, for communication, the essential intent is, subtly, more than just intending that words or acts have meaning. The speaker or actor must intend the audience to recognize, in the words or action, the intention to communicate.

12

Awaiting service in a tavern, you might clear your throat in order to get noticed. That's not communication. But if you clear your throat in an exaggerated way, it is; you intend to get the bartender to recognize not only that you seek attention but also that you are making a noise in order to signal that.

13

Flag-burners similarly intend to communicate by having their audience recognize the intention embodied in their act, and they fail if no one recognizes what they are doing. Imagine their personal frustration if an observer compliments them for disposing of a soiled flag.

14

Flag-burning is communication. Because it is so striking a form of communication, with such offensive content, many Americans want to empower the state to ban it.

15

But since its content is quintessentially political, it receives First Amendment protection, even though—and partly because—it is so offensive. The proposed amendment could trump the First Amendment, but only at the cost of gutting its fundamental protection of free political expression.

16

The flag itself is a symbol. The words of the Pledge of Allegiance "with liberty and justice for all" suggest that it symbolizes, beyond the nation, ideals of liberty, including, presumably, First Amendment liberties.

17

Those who would change the Constitution to permit Congress to ban flag-burning must face two questions: Which is more important to defend, the symbol, or what it symbolizes? Is it rational to seek to shield the former at the cost of damaging the latter?

18

After You Read

Work with other students to develop responses to the following suggestions or to compare responses that you have already prepared.

1. Identify the thesis of each article. Then divide each article into major sections.

2. To clarify the arguments presented by each article, ask yourself, "What are this writer's reasons for his position?" Examine each major division and make a list of the different reasons offered.

3. Once you have developed such a list, consider ways the various writers' points can be grouped. Which points from different articles would you put together? Why?

Readings: English as the "Official" Language of the United States

Before You Read

1. Do you know whether English is the "official" language of your state?

2. What might an "official" language refer to?

3. What might be the reasons for and against establishing English as an "official" language?

English Should Be Official

Bradley S. O'Leary

No other country has been able to assimilate so many people, from so many backgrounds, for so long a time as the USA.

1

What draws immigrants to America's shores today is the same as it was in the days of Ellis Island: religious, political and economic freedom—all of which are possible because there are more ties that bind us than misunderstandings that divide us. The strongest of those ties is a common language. That language is English.

2

Many Americans are surprised to learn that English is not our official language. English is the official language of 14 other countries, yet not ours. English also is the language that 90 percent of immigrants' children speak. It is the language of 80 percent of the world's electronic databases and communications networks. Yet some politicians oppose making our common language our official language. English has been our common language for more than 200 years, but its future as our common language is threatened by those who court ethnic groups by spending tax dollars to Balkanize our language.

3

Making English official wouldn't mean: "If you can't speak the language, get out." It would mean the government encourages the learning of English, and it would stress that it's vital to speak English to reap the benefits of American life and contribute to America. 4

A common language fosters growth and understanding. We can be taught by others only if we can understand what they say. 5

With out-of-control government costs in the news, we must address the exorbitant price of multilingualism. Last year, politicians in L.A. spent $900,000 to translate voting documents into seven languages. 6

Just look north for an example of how expensive multilingualism is. Canada, with one-tenth our population, spends $6 billion a year translating into two languages. The USA, with nearly 150 ethnic languages, could see the costs of multilingualism reach many billions of dollars more. The costs of civil fragmentation defy economic calculations. 7

The USA has become the planet's oldest democracy because of its ability to absorb, rather than accommodate, immigrants. We should accept legal immigrants only if they accept the responsibility of learning our laws, our language and our way of life. 8

From USA Weekend, *Oct. 22, 1993. Reprinted by permission of the author.*

English Shouldn't Be Official

Victor Kamber

If "English-only" proponents would put half their resources into increasing opportunities for immigrants to learn English, rather than into oppressive, pointless legislation, they would solve whatever problems non-English speakers may cause society. 1

But that isn't the point. They aren't interested in solving problems. They are cynically using "English only" to whip up anti-immigrant frenzy for political gain, exploiting our ugliest instincts. 2

We don't need a law formalizing what already is a fact: English is the language in which this nation's business is conducted. English somehow has maintained this status through endless immigration. In spite of the hysteria of the "English-only" Chicken Littles, the sky hasn't fallen and the republic hasn't collapsed. 3

Any immigrant smart enough to get into this country is smart enough to realize that a good command of English is essential to success. Immigrants work hard to learn the language. But we lack the resources to accommodate the high demand. In New York City this year, 35,000 to 40,000 students were enrolled in adult English classes, but 50,000 had to be put on the waiting list. This is the real scandal. 4

Making English our official language won't help. And it would do real damage. For example: The testimony of crime victims who can't yet 5 speak English might be prohibited in court. Police officers and doctors might be left without the interpreters they rely on to protect people who don't speak English. Schools might find it more difficult to communicate with pupils' parents.

A failure to pass "English-only" laws would benefit all, because   6
multilingualism will help the USA compete in the new global economy. While we must give every immigrant access to English classes, let's not inhibit the use of other languages. In most of the rest of the world, educated people speak more than one language. The more Spanish speakers in the USA, the better we can compete in Latin America. The more speakers of Asian languages, the better we can compete in the Pacific Rim.

Immigrants are a resource for economic development, not a burden.   7
They should be cultivated, not bashed.

From USA Weekend, *Oct. 22, 1993. Reprinted by permission of the author.*

Does America Need an "Official" Language?

Rubén G. Rumbaut and Alejandro Portes

During the last 10 years, U.S. English, the Federation for American Immi-   1
gration Reform (FAIR), and similar organizations have gained national attention by denouncing the impending demise of the English language in the wake of massive Latin and Asian immigration to the United States.

In a book called *The Immigration Time Bomb,* a former Colorado gov-   2
ernor accused Hispanic immigrants of not wanting to assimilate and deplored their arrival, which, in his opinion, is leading to the "fragmenting of America."

U.S. English has not yet succeeded in dictating how people should   3
speak, but it has succeeded in defining the terms of the debate. By planting the concern that today's immigrants do not want to assimilate, it has focused the discussion on the survival of English as the nation's only language and as its cultural centerpoint.

Perhaps we're missing something. We are, after all, Latin immigrants   4
ourselves and still speak Spanish when allowed to. But we find the "problem" to be as illusory as the solutions that the nativist organizations propose. For a quarter of a century—since 1965 to be exact—the United States has received a growing number of newcomers from all over the world. But after these 25 years of accelerated immigration, 90 percent of the population speak English and most of the remainder speak English and another language.

How is this possible? A first reason is that the vast majority of the   5
population is still native-born of native parentage. A second, and more important, reason is that children of immigrants give up their language in one or two generations.

Most first-generation immigrants learn English in order to survive   6
and typically combine it with their home language. Some even forget that
language after a while. But it is among their children that the real shift
takes place. The typical second-generation adolescent makes a concerted
effort not to speak anything other than English. Despite parental en-
treaties to preserve their "heritage," these kids are far more interested in
rock, rap, clothing, and peer acceptance than in the latest news from
Thailand.

The available census figures tell the story in stark terms. Ninety-   7
three percent of native-born Americans speak only English at home.
Among immigrants with less than 10 years in the country the figure is
only 16 percent, but it reaches 75 percent among their children. This
last figure is actually an average. The lowest point is found among children of European immigrants (71 percent), the highest among Filipino-
Americans (95 percent).

By the third generation, however, virtually no one recalls how their   8
ancestors talked to each other. This process explains why the United
States has been called a "language graveyard." Literally dozens of languages spoken by the foreign-born have disappeared in the course of
50 years or less.

The threat that the self-appointed guardians of English agitate today   9
may yield juicy donations, but it is illusory. Immigration has never challenged the absolute dominance of English, nor is it doing so today.

The question, in fact, may be reversed. If every second-generation   10
child is going to speak English, does this mean that he or she should
speak English *only*? Is it really necessary that youth who could grow up
speaking English and another language be compelled to give up bilingualism as the price of full assimilation? Is knowledge of two languages
incompatible with good citizenship?

As the United States finds itself more enmeshed in global economic   11
competition, the need for pools of Americans who can speak foreign languages fluently becomes compelling. The second generation now growing up in many cities could fulfill such a need.

Unfortunately, the available evidence suggests that the combined   12
weight of peer pressures, school programs to "mainstream" children of
immigrants as soon as possible, and the generalized absence of support
for bilingualism leads to rapid English acquisition *and* the equally rapid
loss of the home language.

U.S. English, FAIR, and like-minded organizations contribute to a   13
peculiar paradox. While thousands of children of immigrants lose the
treasure of knowing another language, thousands of young Americans
enroll in high school and college courses to acquire a halting command of
Spanish, French, Chinese, etc.—the very tongues that immigrants are told
to forget. Apparently, for these nativist organizations, the only acceptable
way of speaking a foreign language is poorly and with an accent.

This enforced linguistic homogeneity is not a desirable goal in a   14
country that prides itself on being at the center of the international economy. While English undoubtedly will remain the language of the land,
the presence of pockets where other languages are spoken fluently
enriches the nation's culture and strengthens its international standing.

From the San Diego Union-Tribune, *November 10, 1991.*

Language Cements Nationhood

Ron Saunders

Why do we need to designate English as the nation's official language of   1
government? The United States has never had an official language. Why
do we need one now?

Government deals with issues as they arise. Day care, education   2
reform, and term limits are relatively new to our national agenda. Just
because we've never faced these issues before doesn't mean we don't
need to now. Language policy also has evolved into an issue of national
concern.

U.S. English is a national, multi-ethnic group of almost 500,000 Amer-   3
icans. We believe that maintaining the tie of common language is crucial
for the unity and stability of this country.

The central issue is communication. Democracy, more than any other   4
system of government, depends upon communication. Our democracy
could not function if the people could not communicate with their elected
representatives. Through our common language, we argue, debate, and
reach compromises.

That our democracy works is a tribute to our ability to communicate.   5
As a people, Americans have little in common. For more than 200 years,
we have come with every cultural heritage, religious belief, nationality,
and race to share in the riches of this country. More than 150 languages
are represented within our borders, yet we live together in peace and
freedom. Our common language unites us and promotes understanding
through communication.

Although our people are diverse, we share a common culture, heri-   6
tage and, of course, language. As a nation, Americans must strive to preserve those things that unite us because unity is more difficult than diversity to achieve and maintain. Unity must be nurtured, encouraged and
affirmed; diversity comes naturally.

U.S. English opposes the segregation of our country along language   7
lines. Our central argument is for unity—not uniformity. We believe
attempts to make our country officially multilingual are expensive and
divisive. Bills supporting official multilingualism have been introduced

in at least 12 states and passed in three. And in Congress bills have been presented that would require local education offices and private businesses to operate in Spanish—even if they don't serve Spanish-speaking communities.

Language-of-government legislation is often misrepresented and misinterpreted. Official language is language of government. Period. It says that the business of the legislative, executive, and judicial branches of government will be conducted in English. Official language does not affect the home, the community, the church, the private business. It does not affect essential government services in other languages, such as 911 calls for emergency assistance.

8

The Language of Government Act establishes a common-sense policy where today there is none. Multiple language usage is subtly expanding in government bureaucracies. We must establish a government policy that puts the focus and the money back where it belongs: on teaching our new citizens English. We need a policy that says: English is important in the United States. To benefit fully from the social, political, and economic opportunities our country offers, you should know the English language.

9

Language is at the core of nationhood. More than half the nations of the world have official languages, many of them in our own hemisphere. Venezuela, for instance, is a democracy with Spanish as its official language. Spanish is not the only language used in Venezuela, but government business is conducted in Spanish and elections are conducted in Spanish. If you travel or move to Venezuela, you would be wise to know Spanish.

10

Every viable nation fosters a common culture to survive. When we speak of "multiculturalism," we should be aware that American culture is constantly changing, like a kaleidoscope, making this country unique among nations. We could not be a truly multicultural society without a common language because we would be unable to share our diverse traditions and heritages. Instead we would be divided into enclaves separated by language and ethnic barriers—segregated and apart.

11

English is the logical choice as our nation's official language, not because it is "better" than other languages but because it is our common language. English is the only language that crosses all ethnic, racial, and religious lines in our country. With our common language, we have dissolved mistrust and fear and drawn up understandings that make our society possible.

12

Around the world—in Yugoslavia, Sri Lanka, Canada, Estonia, Cyprus—countries without a common language are in turmoil, illustrating that language can divide as well as unite. In this country there is a need for logical, well-constructed, long-term language policies that take care of legitimate needs. We must strengthen the strongest and most durable bond that we as Americans share, through passage of the Language of Government Act.

13

Reprinted by permission.

After You Read

Work with other students to develop responses to the following suggestions or to compare responses that you have already prepared.

1.   Identify the thesis of each article. Then divide each article into major sections.

2.   To clarify the arguments presented by each article, ask yourself, "What are this writer's reasons for his position?" Examine each major division and make a list of the reasons offered.

3.   Once you have developed such a list, consider ways the various writers' points can be grouped. Which points from different articles would you put together? Why?

Writing Assignments

Note   Working with several sources can be substantially more difficult than working with only one source. As you respond to one of these assignments, consider working with other students to clarify and organize your ideas.

1.   The articles about buying toy guns for children were published together in the parents' guide to a children's magazine. As a result, they cover many of the same points from differing points of view. Synthesize the issues discussed. Obviously the writers disagree, but watch for areas where they might be said to agree too. A point-by-point organization would work well here.

2.   Write a synthesis of the ideas presented in the articles involving "Flag Burning and Freedom of Speech" or "English as the 'Official Language' of the United States." In each case, notice that opposing writers often discuss the same points yet reach directly opposite conclusions. Several individual articles in each group also contain points not discussed by the others. Consider a blended organization for your essay.

3.   Write a synthesis of related articles assigned by your instructor from Part 4 or from Chapter 8.

Evaluating Sample Papers

Synthesis Essay

Use the following criteria to evaluate the student essays below.

1.   Introduction

Does the first paragraph introduce the topic and establish its complexity? Does the thesis make it clear that the point of the paper is to explain the issues discussed by a number of writers?

1   2   3   4   5   6

2. Unity

   Does each paragraph have a clear and specific topic sentence that accurately introduces an idea discussed by one or more of the articles? Is the material in each paragraph clearly related to its topic sentence?

   1   2   3   4   5   6

3. Support

   Are all of the major points discussed? Is each point accurately and fully explained?

   1   2   3   4   5   6

4. Coherence

   Are transitions used between paragraphs? Are they used within paragraphs, especially when the writer is moving from what one article says to what is said in another?

   1   2   3   4   5   6

5. References to the Text

   Are direct quotations and paraphrases correctly introduced and smoothly incorporated into the text? Do they reflect the articles' points accurately?

   1   2   3   4   5   6

6. Sentence Structure

   Do the sentences combine ideas that are related, using coordination, subordination, verbal phrases, or parallelism when appropriate? Are there too many brief, choppy main clauses?

   1   2   3   4   5   6

7. Mechanics, Grammar, and Spelling

   Does the paper contain a distracting number of errors of these kinds?

   1   2   3   4   5   6

8. Overall Ranking of the Essay

   1   2   3   4   5   6

Evaluate the following student essays. Use the criteria above to determine which essay is most effective.

Student Essay 1

When I was young, I owned a toy rifle that I used in many games of "cops and robbers" with other children in my neighborhood. I don't think that my parents gave a moment's thought to whether or not my gun was an appropriate toy. However, today children carry real guns into elementary schools, and gang members shoot innocent bystanders in drive-by shootings, so people worry more about whether they should buy toy guns for their children. Michael Golden in "Why I Bought My Son a Toy Gun" and Robert Shaffer in "Why I Won't Buy My Sons Toy Guns" examine this issue and reach different conclusions.

One area of concern is that toy guns might teach children that violence is no problem. Robert Shaffer says that "the lesson toy guns teach is that solving problems with violence is acceptable" (205). He goes on to say that the kinds of skills taught by toy weapons are not the kind he and his wife want to encourage (205).

Both writers agree that toy weapons can help children learn the difference between right and wrong. Golden says that when he owned a toy gun as a boy, he emulated his heroes who "were often symbols of authority and order . . . " (204). Shaffer says that toy weapons "*could* have a value in allowing children to develop ideas of right and wrong, good and bad . . . " (206). However, he also says that children today do not use toy weapons creatively. Instead, they imitate violent television shows, so they don't develop any worthwhile values in their play with toy weapons (206).

Clearly, it's not easy to decide whether or not to buy toy weapons for children There are many issues involved, and Shaffer and Gordon have covered only a few of them. However, parents today need to consider these issues so that they can make intelligent decisions.

Student Essay 2

Should we amend the constitution and put a ban on flag desecration? This topic has been an argument before Congress and the American people for a long time and something needs to be done about it. In the articles "May Americans Do Battle to Save Our Flag" by Robert Dole, and "The American Flag: A Symbol We Should Protect" by Paul Greenberg, they discuss the reasons for such a law. In the articles "Flag-Burning Ban: Protecting What It Symbolizes Or The Symbol?" by Jeffrey P. Kaplan and "Flag Burning and the First Amendment" by Charles Levendosky, they discuss the reasons against such a law.

One argument is that the flag is a strong symbol and should not be disrespected. Robert Dole says that the flag symbolizes our principles and ideals as a nation and that no other symbol can capture what we as Americans are and what we experience (211). According to Greenberg, the flag is not just a symbol, but a presence. If we do nothing when this presence is desecrated, we have joined this mob in killing it's symbolic meaning (208). Levendosky, on the other hand, says that symbolism has few constrictions in the world and by banning the symbolic meaning of flag burning, we are violating the very essence of our constitution (211). Kaplan explains that those in favor of changing the constitution to ban flag desecration must ask themselves if it is more important to defend the symbol or what it symbolizes (214).

Another argument is the Freedom of Speech issue. According to Greenberg, people insist that burning the flag is just that, it's not making a speech. The American people aren't against verbal bashing of the flag, but the physical desecration of the flag is what ought to be against the law (207). Dole disagrees with the Supreme Court that the desecration of the symbol of our nation should be protected in our Constitution under the First Amendment (211).

Levendosky and Kaplan agree that flag burning should be protected under Freedom of Speech. Levendosky says that flag burning is speech because it is a form of communication. The Supreme Court ruled that raising a red flag to show support for worker unity and wearing black armbands to protest our role in Vietnam were both protected speech. Neither were physically saying something as with flag burning but these acts are considered speech as should flag burning (209). Kaplan agrees that the desecration of the flag is a form of communication. First, it communicates through a meaning. Burning is an effective way to get rid of something we hate. Second, it requires an audience which flag burning is usually carried out in front of. Finally, communication should be intended by the speaker to say something. Flag burners are intending to show their hatred for what the flag symbolizes. Because of these, Kaplan believes that flag burning should be constitutionally protected (213–214).

I have found a few miscellaneous points in these articles which I believe are important in this argument. One is that we have laws forbidding the destruction of public property. These laws teach respect and even if no one ever burned a flag, an act like this should still be unconstitutional (Greenberg 208). Another is where will this law lead us? Will cross burning be the next symbol to be put under such restrictions (Levendosky 210)? A third point is that the flag belongs to all of us. It is the symbol that brings all the races in this country together and it should be beloved, not burned (Dole 211).

As you can see, there are many arguments for and against such an amendment. These four articles have covered only some of them. It is up to the individual to decide for himself if flag desecration is constitutional or not.

Student Essay 3

Have you ever been in a heated discussion over whether television is good or bad? Often people have strong opinions of whether or not tv is educational, has any values, or confuses reality and illusion. Paul Robinson's "TV Can't Educate," William Henry III's "The Meaning of TV," and Donna Woolfolk Cross's "Shadows on the Wall" are three articles which discuss these issues.

First, Robinson and Henry disagree on whether tv is or is not educational. Robinson claims that tv is not at all educational. In fact, he says "Educational TV corrupts the very notion of education and renders its victims uneducable" (373). Robinson explains that tv programs are not enough to rely on for real knowledge, and that even ignorance is better "because ignorance at least preserves a mental space that might someday be filled with real knowledge . . ." (373). Henry, on the other hand, says that tv can provide useful learning. For instance, he mentions that there are probably children who learn the alphabet from *Sesame Street,* and some older students who "through TV have grasped some basic truths about the planet" (370). Henry also points out that tv makes us aware of occurrences such as beaches being closed to bathers because of toxic wastes on shore. Furthermore, he recognizes the importance of tv as a source of news for editors and reporters during elections (370).

As for the next topic, Robinson and Henry have different ideas of whether tv is significant or valuable. According to Robinson, tv, such as soap operas like *All My Children,* attempts to be similar to the great American novel and therefore of literary value. He doesn't think tv has any literary value, but he says it does have entertainment value and is "superbly fit to amuse" (374). Henry points out that tv is strongly influential on our behavioral values, and says its deepest power is "the way its innocuous-looking entertainment reaches deep into the national mind" (370). Henry goes on to say that the characters on tv portray how the nation feels about itself and that "they teach behavior and values" (370). Henry contradicts Robinson by noting a relationship of power between tv and literature, and even sees tv as going one step further than literature's ability to be philosophical. He says, "Television simply does this more effectively, more touchingly, than any kind of art that went before" (371).

The third issue that is discussed is the tendency for tv to cause people to confuse reality and illusion. This topic includes a similar recognition from Robinson, Henry, and Cross, although all three authors have different opinions of whether this is good or bad. Robinson, as he explains that tv is entertaining, yet not educational, implies negativity when he states that tv "at the very least provides an escape from the world and from ourselves" (374). Henry says that unlike stage and movies, "the episodic TV series does not end in catharsis" (371). The characters return, and therefore tv is more representative of ordinary life, and for some, he claims, this is barely distinguishable from reality. Cross has more of an emphasis on this issue throughout her article than Robinson and Henry. She uses two reports to prove her point that people's confusion of reality and illusion caused by tv is bad. The first example is of behavior in the courtroom. She says that juries often expect real-life courtroom activities to be identical to tv's version of courtroom activities. She adds a contributor's story of watching a jury that was confused because the defendant didn't follow the expected role of a defendant (as seen on tv), and the result was a hung jury (376–377). The second example she used was a crime report that UPI filed explaining that a father was killed. His dead body was found within feet of his children who were watching tv and were clearly oblivious to the killing (376).

As you can see through these comparisons and contrasts, there are unique personal opinions of whether tv is good or bad. Robinson, Henry, and Cross have covered a few issues that they feel are significant.

Sentence Combining: Sentence Variety

Have you ever listened to someone talk who never varies the pitch or tone of his or her voice? Have you ever had to listen to a speaker (perhaps an instructor?) who drones on and on with no changes in the sound of her voice to help emphasize the important points or just to make what she is saying more interesting? If you have heard such a person, you know—as we do—how *boring* such a voice can be. Even if you aren't sleepy to begin with, you are ready to nod off within five minutes, right?

Writers have the same problems as speakers. They need to express their ideas in ways that will prevent their readers from taking a big yawn, closing their eyes, and starting to snore. **Sentence variety** is one technique that writers use to add interest to what they write. As the term implies, *sentence variety* means that the sentences in your paragraph or essay are somehow different from each other—they are *varied*—just as a good speaker's voice is frequently varied to keep the attention of the audience.

Actually, you have been practicing sentence variety throughout the sentence-combining sections of this text. When you embedded adjectives, adverbs, and prepositional phrases in Chapter 1, when you practiced using main and subordinate clauses in Chapters 2 and 3, when you used verbal phrases in Chapter 4 and appositives in Chapter 5, and when you practiced parallelism in Chapter 6—in each case, you were learning ways to vary the kinds of sentences that you write. In this section, you will work on writing sentences that are varied both in length and in structure.

Sentence Length

One of the chief causes of monotonous writing is a series of relatively brief sentences, one after the other. Take a look at the following paragraph.

> It was a warm, miserable morning last week. We went up to the Bronx Zoo. We wanted to see the moose calf. We also needed to break in a new pair of black shoes. We encountered better luck than we had bargained for. The cow moose and her young one were standing near the wall of the deer park. The wall was below the monkey house. We wanted a better view. We strolled down to the lower end of the park. We were by the brook. The path there is not much traveled. We approached the corner where the brook trickles under the wire fence. We noticed a red deer getting to her feet. Beside her was a spotted fawn. Its legs were just learning their business. The fawn was small and perfect. It was like a trinket seen through a reducing glass.

Wouldn't you agree that this writing is rather lackluster? The constant repetition of separate, short sentences makes the writing seem childlike and overly simple. However, with just a little work, many of the ideas in the excessively short sentences can be combined into longer sentences. Here is how the passage was actually written by the well-known essayist E. B. White.

On a warm, miserable morning last week we went up to the Bronx Zoo to see the moose calf and to break in a new pair of black shoes. We encountered better luck than we had bargained for. The cow moose and her young one were standing near the wall of the deer park below the monkey house, and in order to get a better view we strolled down to the lower end of the park, by the brook. The path there is not much traveled. As we approached the corner where the brook trickles under the wire fence, we noticed a red deer getting to her feet. Beside her, on legs that were just learning their business, was a spotted fawn as small and perfect as a trinket seen through a reducing glass.

—E. B. White, "Twins"

What do you think? Isn't the difference dramatic? E. B. White's paragraph is so effective not just because he is a master of descriptive detail (both paragraphs contain the same details) but because his sentences have a rhythm and flow that result from his ability to vary the lengths of his sentences.

Exercise 7.1

1. Count the number of sentences in E. B. White's paragraph and compare that to the number of sentences in the choppy paragraph.

2. Now look at the lengths of the sentences in E. B. White's paragraph and point out where the lengths vary. Try to explain the effect of the shorter and longer sentences.

3. Point out where details from the choppy paragraph are embedded in the E. B. White paragraph as prepositional phrases.

4. Point out where E. B. White's paragraph uses coordination and subordination to combine ideas that were separate sentences in the choppy paragraph. ■

Sentence Structure

Although a series of short, choppy sentences can be quite distracting, a more commonly cause of lifeless writing is a repetitive sentence structure. Perhaps the most commonly repeated sentence structure—and the easiest to vary—is the sentence that opens with the subject and verb of its main clause. Here are some examples of this common sentence pattern.

     S   *V*
Television has been blamed for a number of problems in our society.

     S   *V*
The house slid into the ravine after the rain weakened the cliffs below it.

      S   *V*
The committee voted to reduce the homeowners' fees.

As you can see, each of the above sentences opens with a main clause, and the subject and verb of each main clause are quite close to the start of the sentence. To add some variety to your writing, try opening many of your sentences with something other than the main clause. Here are some possibilities.

1. Open your sentence with a subordinate clause.

    <u>After the rain weakened the cliffs below it</u>, the house slid into the ravine.

2. Open your sentence with a prepositional phrase.

    <u>Over the past forty years</u>, television has been blamed for a number of problems in our society.

3. Open your sentence with a verbal phrase.

    <u>Responding to the complaints from a majority of the owners</u>, the committee voted to reduce the homeowners' fees. (present participial phrase)

    <u>Concerned about the rising cost of living</u>, the committee voted to reduce the homeowners' fees. (past participial phrase)

    <u>To prevent people from having to sell their homes</u>, the committee voted to reduce the homeowners' fees. (infinitive phrase)

Of course, another way to vary your sentence structures is to use subordinate clauses, prepositional phrases, verbal phrases, and appositives within as well as at the ends of sentences. The trick is to avoid using the same sentence pattern from one sentence to another to another.

Exercise 7.2

Rewrite the following paragraphs to improve their sentence variety. In both the original and revised versions, compute the average number of words in each sentence by counting all the words and dividing by the number of sentences. In each revised copy, underline any words, phrases, or subordinate clauses that open sentences before the appearance of the main clause.

1. Silly Putty was one of the most popular toy items of the '50s and '60s. It was originally developed as a possible substitute for rubber. In the 1940s, the U.S. War Production Board was looking for an inexpensive replacement for synthetic rubber. It wanted to use the replacement in jeep and airplane tires. It also wanted to use it in gas masks and other military gear. It asked General Electric to try to develop such a product. James Wright was the engineer who worked on the project. He eventually developed a rubbery goo. It stretched farther than rubber. It rebounded 25 percent more than the best rubber ball. It was impervious to molds and decay. It withstood a wide range of temperatures without decomposing. It delighted children everywhere. It was pressed against the color print of newspaper comic pages. It lifted the image right onto itself. The new product really had no special advantages over synthetic rubber. It was never used commercially.

It was not long before a man operating a toy store realized its possibilities. He began to market it inside colored plastic eggs. In its first year, Silly Putty outsold every item in the toy store. For the next two decades it was one of the most popular small toys in the country.

Average number of words per sentence: _____

Average number of words per sentence in your revision: _____

2. It was in the early years of our country. It was common for both soldiers and officers to wear long hair. They tied the hair back in a ponytail. In 1803 a Tennessee commander ordered all his officers to cut off their ponytails. Colonel Thomas Butler refused. He was a career officer with a distinguished record dating back to the Revolution. Butler was not about to cut his hair so easily. He was arrested and charged with insubordination. Friends of Butler rallied to his defense. Those friends included Andrew Jackson. They petitioned even President Jefferson to intervene on Butler's behalf. The President would not do so. On July 10, 1805, Butler was found guilty of mutinous conduct. He was sentenced to a year's suspension without pay. He died shortly after his conviction. He left a will requesting that a hole be drilled in his coffin. It requested that his ponytail be allowed to hang through it. He wanted everyone to see that, even when dead, he had not obeyed the order to cut it.

Average number of words per sentence: _____

Average number of words per sentence in your revision: _____

Chapter 8

Arguing from Several Reading Selections

What Is an Argument?

Well, an argument is probably *not* what Calvin proposes in the above cartoon ("I say, either agree with me or take a hike!"). Attitudes like Calvin's usually lead to quarrels and angry confrontations, which are, unfortunately, what many people think of when they hear the word *argument*.

The "argument" that you will write in this chapter will not be a quarrel in which you beat your reader into submission. Instead, it will be exactly the kind of writing you have been practicing all semester—a reasonable presentation of facts, statistics, examples, and other support in an attempt to convince your reader that your thesis makes sense. To a degree, you have been arguing every time you have written a paper this semester, for in each assignment you have attempted to support a thesis statement with reasonable and convincing evidence.

The difference between the earlier assignments and what is normally called an "argumentative" paper is that an argumentative thesis takes a stand on a *debatable* subject. As a result, your readers may already have opinions about your subject. Your job is to convince them that the opinion you have expressed in your thesis is reasonable and worthy of their serious consideration. That's easier said than done.

To write a convincing argument, you will need to draw upon the writing skills you have been practicing so far:

- You will need to choose an appropriate topic, one that you can support with facts, examples, statistics, and statements from authority.
- You will need to organize your support into unified paragraphs that are introduced by clear and accurate topic sentences.
- You will need to summarize, paraphrase, and quote accurately when you draw material from reading selections.
- You will need to distinguish between facts and opinions as well as between specific and general statements.

The Attitude of the Effective Arguer

When you argue a position, no matter what the situation, your *attitude* can make all the difference in the world. Obviously, if your attitude, like Calvin's, is "I'm right, period! End of discussion!" you will not have much success. But even if you present evidence to support your ideas, you probably will not have much success if you are close-minded and show no understanding of your opposition's point of view. In fact, on many debatable issues, you should not expect to write a completely convincing argument; after all, an issue is debatable precisely *because* there are convincing arguments on both sides of it. As you approach any complicated, debatable issue, keep in mind the following points.

Keep an open mind until you have looked closely at the issue. Perhaps the biggest mistake that many people make is to decide *first* what they think and *then* set out to prove that they are right. This is probably a natural thing to do—after all, nobody likes to be wrong—but will not lead to clear thinking and well-written arguments.

Whatever your beliefs are, set them aside until you have completed your study of the issue. As you read articles, talk to people, and consider your own experience, *be willing to change your mind* if the evidence suggests that you should—that willingness is one of the characteristics of a clear thinker.

Don't write as if your evidence completely resolved the issue. Debatable topics exist because the "one, true" answer is not at all clear, so don't take the attitude that your support proves your opinion is right and all others are wrong. It probably doesn't. What it *may* prove, if your support is effective enough, is that your opinion is *reasonable* and should be considered by reasonable people. Too often people approach arguments as battles in which the other side must be thoroughly destroyed and discredited. But the "other side" is usually a figment of our imagination. There may be two or three or four or more ways of approaching a debatable issue—not one right way (yours) and one wrong way (theirs).

Don't misunderstand us. You *should* support your argument as well as you can, and you *should* be willing to take a stand. But you should also be willing to recognize points that might weaken your argument and to qualify your position if you need to.

Preparing the Argument

Collecting Information

As you have already read, the first step is *not* to take a stand or write a thesis statement. Even though you may already have an opinion on your topic, remember that the sign of a good thinker is the willingness to modify, qualify, or change an opinion once the information has been collected and examined. For example, suppose you think that watching too much television can cause serious problems, especially for children, so you decide to make television viewing the subject of your essay. Your *first* step is to try your best to set aside your personal opinion, keep an open mind, and start collecting information related to *both sides* of your topic. Your goal should be to come to an understanding of the opposing arguments related to television viewing and *only then* to draw a conclusion of your own. For the most part, the information you collect will come from material you read, from people you talk to, and from your own experiences.

Listing and Evaluating Information

As you collect information, organize it into lists that reflect opposing attitudes toward the subject. For instance, a writer investigating the benefits and drawbacks of television viewing might develop the lists presented below after examining the articles in Part 4 by William Henry III, Paul Robinson, Donna Woolfolk Cross, Madeline Drexler, and James Herrick and after considering her personal experiences and the experiences of people she knows. (When you list an item, identify the source it came from so you can look back at the article for more information when you evaluate the arguments.)

Is Television Educational?

Pro

- TV can provide learning.
- Children learn alphabet from *Sesame Street*.
- High school students learn about toxic waste on beaches.

  (Henry)

- A study by psychologist Daniel Anderson says children learn to think and draw inferences as they watch TV.
- Same study—TV does not replace reading; it replaces other recreational activities.
- Same study—TV watching does not lower IQ, although people with lower IQ do tend to watch more TV.

  (Drexler)

- Personal Experience—I have used movies like *Gone with the Wind* to discuss history with my kids. A special about Bill Cosby led to questions about typical lifestyle of African-Americans.

Con

- TV cannot provide the time needed to learn.
- Learning requires time to absorb facts. It requires reading.
- A documentary about Marin County cannot really be accurate because it does not have the time to cover the complexities of life there.
- Educational TV is the worst kind— it makes people think they know something when they really don't.

  (Robinson)

- Most TV programming is vacuous, noxious, or both.
- TV shows a heavily edited view of world events. It shows shallow comedies and tragedies.
- Time would be better spent reading.

  (Herrick)

Does Television Make Us Better People?

Pro

- TV's characters embody human truths.
- They epitomize what we feel about ourselves.
- They teach behavior and values. The character of Mary Richards summed up the lives of a whole generation of women.
- Without TV we might be less violent, have more respect for institutions, be healthier, but we also might be less alert, less informed, less concerned about world matters, lonelier.

  (Henry)

Con

- Opinion of psychologist Daniel Anderson—The violence, sexism, and materialism on TV are having a major social impact on our children.

  (Drexler)

- TV robs relationships of time.
- Does not set high standard for personal conduct or ask viewers to think about what to value.
- Even when TV does accomplish a worthwhile goal, there are better paths to that end.

  (Herrick)

- Personal knowledge—I have seen news reports about children imitating violent acts on television.

Is Television Valuable as Entertainment?

Pro	Con
• TV is very good at entertaining. Jack Benny and Art Carney would not be nearly as funny in print. You need to see them and watch their timing. (Robinson)	• TV based on unexamined concept of entertainment.
• My personal experience—I use TV to relax and entertain myself.	• There are many better sources of entertainment and better ways to relax. (Herrick)
• A study by psychologist Daniel Anderson says when parents and kids watch together, kids tend to think about what they see. (Drexler)	• TV entertainment causes a confusion between reality and illusion.
• Personal Experience—My children have never confused TV with reality as far as I know, but we watch TV together and talk about what we see.	• Boys on a raft ride were disappointed because it was more fun on TV.
	• In an experiment by Jerry Kozinski, kids would not leave the TV to see something fascinating outside the room, and they watched a video of a fight rather than the real thing happening in front of them.
	• UPI reported children watching TV next to the corpse of their dead father.
	• In a Univ. of Nebraska study, over half of children chose TV over their fathers.
	• Former DA Mario Merola says a jury wants the drama of TV and is less likely to convict if it doesn't get it. (Woolfolk Cross)

As you can see, there is quite a bit of material to consider before you decide exactly where you stand, and not all of the material can be neatly divided into pro/con arguments. This writer, however, has attempted to divide the points she has found into three general groupings. The first focuses primarily on the educational value of television; the second seems to concern itself with television's impact on our behavior and values; and the third discusses both television's entertainment ability and the fear that television blurs the distinction between what is real and what is not.

At this point, you are in a position to evaluate the evidence. You have before you several major arguments about the benefits and drawbacks of television, some of which seem to directly contradict each other. Which seem more convincing? Consider which arguments use facts, examples, and expert testimony and which seem to rely more on unsupported opinions. Compare your own personal experiences to the arguments presented to see if they support or refute them.

As you evaluate the arguments, do not fall into the trap of thinking that one side must be right and the other must be wrong. Often that is just not the case. Do you see, for example, that it is possible that television has some benefits *and* some drawbacks, that the question is not necessarily a black-or-white, right-or-wrong issue? Such complexity is exactly why debatable, controversial issues *are* debatable and controversial. Both sides usually have points that need to be taken seriously. If you recognize the valid points on both sides of an issue and are willing to admit it when your opposition makes a good argument, you will have a better chance of convincing your reader that your own stand is a reasonable one that you have carefully thought out.

Taking a Stand

Perhaps the most important point to note here is that taking a stand is the *final* step in preparing an argument, not the first step. Once you have collected, listed, and evaluated the various arguments related to your topic, you need to decide exactly what your opinion is. Remember that you do not have to prove that everything your opposition says is wrong for you to hold a differing opinion. Nor do you have to pretend that the reasons you give for your opinion should convince a reasonable person that you are right. What you *will* have to do is take a stand that you can reasonably support with the evidence available and that does not require you to simply ignore evidence that refutes your opinion.

Outlining and Organizing the Argument

There are several ways to organize the material in an effective argument, but they all involve presenting points in support of your position and responding to points that seem to refute your position. *Before* you write the first draft of your paper, you should outline the points you intend to cover and the organizational pattern that will best serve your argument.

Below are some possible organizational patterns you can use. For shorter essays, each Roman numeral indicates a separate paragraph, but for longer essays, each numeral might indicate two or more paragraphs. In either case, you must remember to support each point with facts, examples, statistics, and references to authority, drawn either from your reading or from your own experiences or the experiences of people you know.

    I.   Introduction and thesis

   II.   First point in support of your thesis

  III.   Second point in support of your thesis

  IV.   Third point in support of your thesis
       (more points as needed)

   V.   Major objection to your thesis and your response to it

  VI.   Concluding paragraph

As you can see, this organization focuses primarily on presenting points that support your thesis, saving your discussion of any major objection until the end of the essay. Some topics, however, work better if the major objection is covered first, as in an organization like this:

I.   Introduction and thesis

II. Major objection to your thesis and your response to it

III. First point in support of your thesis

IV. Second point in support of your thesis

V.   Third point in support of your thesis
     (more points as needed)

VI. Concluding paragraph

Sometimes you may be taking a particularly unpopular stand, to which there are many obvious objections. In such a situation, consider this kind of organization:

I.   Introduction and thesis

II.   First objection and your response to it

III. Second objection and your response to it

IV.   Third objection and your response to it
      (more objections and responses as needed)

V.   First point in support of your thesis

VI.   Second point in support of your thesis
      (more points as needed)

VII. Concluding paragraph

Obviously, the organization and length of your argument can vary greatly, depending on how many objections you need to respond to and how many points you intend to cover. Here is an outline for a possible paper on the benefits of television.

I.   Introduction
     - Open with example of when I came home and kids were watching *The Simpsons.*
     - Tentative thesis: TV has more benefits than drawbacks.

II. One benefit: It's entertaining and relaxing.
     - Support with personal experience of how it helps me after a long day as a student, employee, and mom.
     - Use Robinson's point about importance of entertainment.

III. Another benefit: It can educate us and make us better thinkers.
     - Use examples from Henry article.
     - Use personal examples of *Gone with the Wind* and the special about Bill Cosby.

IV. Another benefit: It makes people more aware of the world they live in.
- Use personal examples of my kids asking questions about reruns of *I Love Lucy* and *Roseanne*.
- Use Drexler's article about psychologist who says children think when helped by parents.

V. Major objections: Woolfolk Cross says TV blurs reality and fantasy.
- If TV is used incorrectly, she is right.
- Refer to Drexler article again about parents guiding their children.

Another objection: TV hinders education because it replaces reading.
- Use personal experience of my kids to show this isn't so.

VI. Conclusion

Writing the Argument

If you have outlined and organized your points, writing the first draft of your paper should be no more difficult than writing the first drafts of every other paper you have written so far. Consider these points as you write:

1. Opening your paper with an interesting lead-in. See Chapter 3 for a discussion of the many possibilities available to you.

2. Write a thesis statement that takes a clear position, but do not hesitate to qualify it if you need to. Notice, for example, how the qualification before this thesis helps the writer to sound like a reasonable person: *"I know that the television can be abused and misused, but so can any good thing.* On the whole, it seems to me that television watching has far more benefits than drawbacks."

3. Write clear topic sentences that refer to the central idea expressed in your thesis.

4. Support your topic sentences with facts, examples, statistics, and references to authority drawn either from your reading or from your own experiences or the experiences of people you know.

5. Respond to major objections in a reasonable manner. If the objection is simply inaccurate, explain why, giving support of your own. If the objection is reasonable yet does not change your point of view, explain why the reader should find your overall argument more persuasive.

6. See Chapter 3 for effective ways to conclude your essay.

Paraphrasing, Quoting, and Documenting Your Sources

When you use material from the reading selections, identify the sources of all paraphrases, summaries, and quotations. Use clear transitions to introduce borrowed material. (See "Writing Paraphrases and Quotations," pages 134–137.) Use parentheses to identify the author and page number of each source. (See "Documenting Your Sources," pages 201–202.)

Readings: Should Drugs Be Legalized?

Before You Read

1. What is your initial reaction to the suggestion that drugs be legalized? Would you call your reaction a personal opinion or a considered opinion?
2. What arguments do you expect to find in favor of and opposed to legalizing drugs?
3. As you read the following articles, set aside any personal opinions you may hold. Try to keep an open mind as you collect information about the issue.

Police and Jails Have Failed

Lionel Van Deerlin

Legalize narcotics? It was deemed unthinkable as recently as five years ago. But no longer.

We're being told that America's drug laws and their enforcement are a disaster . . . that they have failed to curb our worst social problem, tending instead to make it worse . . . that the answer is to "decriminalize" drug use, or to legalize all but the most debilitating substances, like crack cocaine.

It is not the druggies or their looney friends telling us this. The talk about overhauling drug laws comes lately from a broad sweep of national leadership—from the ranks of law enforcement, from judges, from professional people and from the clergy. Try this array of advocates:

- The new attorney general, Janet Reno.
- George Shultz, who held three cabinet posts in the Nixon years and was Ronald Reagan's secretary of state.
- Milton Friedman, the dean of conservative economists, a Nobel laureate.
- Judicial figures ranging from New York's federal judges Robert W. Sweet and Whitman Knapp to Superior Judge James P. Gray of hidebound Orange County.
- William F. Buckley, the rightist columnist-commentator.
- The Rev. Robert Schuller, whose culturally conservative sermons are aired nationally from the Crystal Cathedral.
- Kurt Schmoke, the black mayor of Baltimore and one-time Rhodes scholar.

There are differences of opinion within this group on how best to deal with drug addiction—but total agreement that what we have been doing for many years is wrong-headed. All think it's time for change. Radical change.

What's bothering them? Mounting evidence that the campaign against drugs has proved no more successful than the ill-remembered Prohibition law aimed at alcohol in an earlier day. Indeed, comparisons seem ominous. As with Prohibition (which lasted only 13 years) our government's war on drugs has led to ever-widening abuse and a frightening increase in crime. 5

How is one to defend a federal enforcement program which has failed so conspicuously as this one has done, yet finds more Americans today locked up on drug-related crimes alone than were imprisoned on *all* offenses just 12 years ago? 6

This, with no visible reduction of drugs on the streets. 7

Only one other industrialized nation now keeps a higher percentage of its people behind bars. But there is a profound difference. Government intent in South Africa has aimed to check a rising tide of black resentment against apartheid. Jammed jails in this country reflect efforts to deal with an addiction which reaches from the pinnacle of society down to ghetto streets, where drug trafficking can mean instant riches for a school dropout. 8

However worthy their intent, the framers of Prohibition failed to look ahead. By making liquor illegal, they automatically scrapped all controls over its manufacture, labeling and distribution. The 1920s became a time of "rotgut" and bathtub gin. 9

The same is sadly true of banned drugs today. Beyond their addictive peril, poisoning from contamination is widespread, as are overdoses from drugs of unknown strength. 10

But Prohibition, with its Keystone Kops-style pursuit of bootleggers, left a far more serious legacy. From the rum runners and mob violence of that era came a blueprint for today's illegal drug business—for criminal syndicates and cartel management reaching into supplier countries whose deliveries we find almost impossible to interdict. 11

From her prior experience spanning four terms as a state prosecutor in drug-porous Miami, Attorney General Reno says she questions the effectiveness of massive federal spending aimed at interdiction. A study by the General Accounting Office found that Air Force patrols with sophisticated AWACS surveillance planes over a 15-month period brought a grand total of eight drug seizures. Meanwhile combined efforts of the Navy and Coast Guard, sailing 2,512 ship-days at a cost of $40 million, resulted in the seizure of only 20 drug-carrying vessels. 12

"It's time we come up with hard data (on) whether or not interdiction is efficient and effective," the attorney general concludes. 13

Drugs are easy to smuggle. The cash return on supplies getting through more than justifies the risk of being caught. The actual transporters, moreover, are not drug kingpins but well-paid hired hands eager to take their chances. 14

The sky-high prices driving this traffic rest solely on its illegality. 15
While failing to keep an illicit product off the market, the effect of our
laws is to provide a subsidy as certain as the price supports legislated for
wheat, cotton and corn.

If that is not hypocrisy enough, consider a comment by the Rev. 16
Joseph P. Kane, S. J., for 20 years the chaplain to inmates at New York's
Rikers Island. He asks: "Is there not something dishonest about drug policies in which lower-class drug users, labeled *criminals,* go to prison while
middle-class addicts, labeled *alcoholics,* go to therapy?"

National priorities seem skewed when we spend three or four times 17
as much on the chase and on punishment as we do for drug treatment and
rehabilitation. It costs more than $50,000 a year to keep someone in a fed-
eral prison.

President Clinton has named a highly regarded big-city police com- 18
missioner to be the nation's new drug "czar."

We must hope that Lee Brown, the first authentic cop to hold this job, 19
has seen enough to know that more police and more jail sentences are not
the answer.

Best Remedy: Crack Down on Users

Joseph Perkins

Joycelyn Elders is unfit to be surgeon general. A person who advocates 1
legalized sale and use of cocaine, heroin, LSD, PCP and other deadly
drugs clearly does not have the nation's best health interests at heart.

In an appearance this week at the National Press Club in Washington, 2
Elders revealed her ignorance of the nature of America's drug problem.
"I do feel that we would markedly reduce our crime rate if drugs were
legalized," she said.

What was she smoking? All she had to do was call her colleague 3
Louis Freeh, over at the FBI, and he would have told her that 75 percent of
crimes in America are committed by substance abusers—in many cases to
support their habit. Making drugs even more freely available than they
are now hardly would make America's streets safer.

Elders also wildly claimed that "some of the countries that have le- 4
galized drugs" have shown "no increase in their drug use rate." Yeah?
Which ones?

For the surgeon general's information, no country in the world has 5
actually legalized drugs. As to the handful of European nations that have
effectively decriminalized drugs, their social experiments have been anything but successful.

In Zurich, Switzerland, for instance, a public park was turned over to   6
drug users in 1989. By 1991, drug-related deaths were up 80 percent. Half
the drug-takers in the park were under age 22. A fifth were infected with
the AIDS virus.

Amsterdam has been a haven for drug users since 1976, when the   7
Netherlands liberalized its narcotics laws. In the ensuing 17 years, the
country's population of heroin addicts has more than tripled.

These are the models that Elders would have this country emulate.   8

President Clinton was right to rebuke his surgeon general for betray-   9
ing the nation's continuing war on drugs. He is the first man to sit in the
Oval Office who has ever had a family member known to be addicted to
drugs. Clinton often has noted that if drugs were more widely available—
as Elders would have it—his brother Roger probably would be dead by
now.

Clearly, there is no pathology that exacts a heavier toll on American   10
society than illegal drug use. This was well documented in a 1991 tract by
Mitchell Rosenthal, in the *UC Davis Law Review.*

"The fastest rising costs of drug abuse today are associated, not with   11
crime," wrote Rosenthal, "but with homelessness, chronic mental illness,
adolescent suicide and runaways, the spread of [AIDS], domestic violence, child abuse, and the number of new drug-impaired, addicted and
abandoned infants."

Rosenthal presented evidence showing that 60 percent of the nation's   12
homeless are drug abusers. He noted that in New York State, up to 50 percent of patients admitted to hospitals through emergency services are
mentally ill drug users.

In California, as many as 75 percent of teen-age runaways use drugs.   13
And, in general, drug-abusing youth are three times as likely to commit
suicide as kids who do not use drugs.

Largely because of drug abuse, there was a nearly 30 percent rise in   14
the number of foster care children in the United States between 1987 and
1990. In 1988, more than 10 percent of first-time mothers used drugs during their pregnancies. That means that as many as 375,000 newborn
babies experienced prenatal exposure to drugs—a 300 percent increase
from 1985.

It seems clear that legalization of drugs would neither reduce the   15
level of drug-related crime and violence nor ameliorate other drug-
related social pathologies. The only viable approach to attacking America's drug problems is to crack down on users.

The 12.5 million Americans who use an illegal narcotic once a month   16
provide a fertile market for drug merchants. A kilogram of cocaine costs
roughly $15,000 to deliver to the United States. It fetches $250,000 when
sold on the streets in one-ounce packets. With that kind of return on
investment sellers will go to almost any lengths to provide product.

So what if the occasional cache of drugs is interdicted? There's al-   17
ways more where it came from. So what if this drug lord or that one is

gunned down? There is always someone ready to take that person's place.

The only way to bring down the drug cartels is to deprive them of their customers and, thus, their tremendous profits. This hardly would be achieved by legalizing drugs (which would only provide drug merchants with an even larger market for their deadly product). The key is zero tolerance of drug use.   18

A national strategy to reduce demand for drugs should employ a carrot-and-stick approach. The government ought to provide drug treatment on demand to users who need help to overcome their habit. Meanwhile, the emphasis of drug enforcement should shift from the supply to the demand side.   19

Anyone caught buying or using drugs ought to be given mandatory jail time, if only a day or two. First-time offenders should not be excused (as the shock of spending a night behind bars would be an excellent deterrent to future use).   20

Arrests for repeated drug use should carry progressively stiffer jail sentences. As time passed, a clear message would be sent to users that if they are caught, they will face swift and sure punishment.   21

America's drug users must be made to understand that they are as responsible as drug dealers for the rise in drug-related crime and violence and pathology that afflicts our society today. By legalizing drugs, as Elders and other social nihilists suggest, drug users would be absolved of this responsibility.   22

From The San Diego Union Tribune, *December 10, 1993, B5. Reprinted by permission.*

We're Losing the Drug War Because Prohibition Never Works

Hodding Carter III

There is clearly no point in beating a dead horse, whether you are a politician or a columnist, but sometimes you have to do it just the same, if only for the record. So, for the record, here's another attempt to argue that a majority of the American people and their elected representatives can be and are wrong about the way they have chosen to wage the "war against drugs." Prohibition can't work, won't work, and has never worked, but it can and does have monumentally costly effects on the criminal justice system and on the integrity of government at every level.   1

Experience should be the best teacher, and my experience with prohibition is a little more recent than most Americans for whom the "noble experiment" ended with repeal in 1933. In my home state of Mississippi, it lasted for an additional thirty-three years, and for all those years it was a truism that the drinkers had their liquor, the preachers had their prohi-   2 bition, and the sheriffs, made the money. Al Capone would have been proud of the latitude that bootleggers were able to buy with their payoffs of constables, deputies, police chiefs, and sheriffs across the state.

But as a first-rate series in the *New York Times* made clear early last year, Mississippi's Prohibition-era corruption (and Chicago's before that) was penny ante stuff compared with what is happening in the United States today. From Brooklyn police precincts to Miami's police stations to rural Georgia courthouses, big drug money is purchasing major breakdowns in law enforcement. Sheriffs, other policemen, and now judges are being bought up by the gross. But that money, with the net profits for the drug traffickers estimated at anywhere from $40 billion to $100 billion a year, is also buying up banks, legitimate businesses and, to the south of us, entire governments. The latter becomes an increasingly likely outcome in a number of cities and states in this country as well. Cicero, Illinois, during Prohibition is an instructive case in point.

The money to be made from an illegal product that has about 23 million current users in this country also explains why its sale is so attractive on the mean streets of America's big cities. A street salesman can gross about $2,500 a day in Washington, which puts him in the pay category of a local television anchor, and this in a neighborhood of dead-end job chances.

Since the courts and jails are already swamped beyond capacity by the arrests that are routinely made (44,000 drug dealers and users over a two-year period in Washington alone, for instance), and since those arrests barely skim the top of the pond, arguing that stricter enforcement is the answer begs a larger question: Who is going to pay the billions of dollars required to build the prisons, hire the judges, train the policemen, and employ the prosecutors needed for the load already on hand, let alone the huge one yet to come if we ever get serious about arresting dealers and users?

Much is made of the costs of drug addiction, and it should be, but the current breakdown in the criminal justice system is not one of them. That breakdown is the result of prohibition, not addiction. Drug addiction, after all, does not come close to the far vaster problems of alcohol and tobacco addiction (as former Surgeon General Koop correctly noted, tobacco is at least as addictive as heroin). Hard drugs are estimated to kill 4,000 people a year directly and several tens of thousands a year indirectly. Alcohol kills at least 100,000 a year, addicts millions more and costs the marketplace billions of dollars. Tobacco kills over 300,000 a year, addicts tens of millions, and fouls the atmosphere as well. But neither alcohol nor tobacco threatens to subvert our system of law and order, because they are treated as personal and societal problems rather than as criminal ones.

Indeed, every argument that is made for prohibiting the use of currently illegal drugs can be made even more convincingly about tobacco and alcohol. The effects on the unborn? Staggeringly direct. The effects on adolescents? Alcoholism is the addiction of choice for young Americans on a ratio of about one hundred to one. Lethal effect? Tobacco's murderous results are not a matter of debate anywhere outside the Tobacco Institute.

Which leaves the lingering and legitimate fear that legalization might 8 produce a surge in use. It probably would, although not nearly as dramatic a one as opponents usually estimate. The fact is that personal use of marijuana, whatever the local laws may say, has been virtually decriminalized for some time now, but there has been a stabilization or slight decline in use, rather than an increase, for several years. Heroin addiction has held steady at about 500,000 people for some time, though the street price of heroin is far lower now than it used to be. Use of cocaine in its old form also seems to have stopped climbing and begun to drop off among young and old alike, though there is an abundantly available supply.

That leaves crack cocaine, stalker of the inner city and terror of the 9 suburbs. Instant and addictive in effect, easy to use and relatively cheap to buy, it is a personality-destroying substance that is a clear menace to its users. But it is hard to imagine it being any more accessible under legalization than it is in most cities today under prohibition, while the financial incentives for promoting its use would virtually disappear with legalization.

Proponents of legalization should not try to fuzz the issue, nonetheless. Addiction levels might increase, at least temporarily, if legal sanctions were removed. That happened after the repeal of Prohibition, or so at least some studies have suggested. But while that would be a personal disaster for the addicts and their families, and would involve larger costs to society as a whole, those costs would be minuscule compared with the costs of continued prohibition.

The young Capones of today own the inner cities, and the wholesalers behind these young retailers are rapidly buying up the larger system which is supposed to control them. Prohibition gave us the Mafia and organized crime on a scale that has been with us ever since. The new prohibition is writing a new chapter on that old text. Hell-bent on learning nothing from history, we are witnessing its repetition, predictably enough, as tragedy.

Should Drugs Be Legalized?

William J. Bennett

Since I took command of the war on drugs [as director of National Drug 1 Control Policy in Washington, D.C.], I have learned from former secretary of state George Shultz that our concept of fighting drugs is "flawed." The only thing to do, he says, is to "make it possible for addicts to buy drugs at some regulated place." Conservative commentator William F. Buckley, Jr., suggests I should be "fatalistic" about the flood of cocaine from South America and simply "let it in." Syndicated columnist Mike Royko contends it would be easier to sweep junkies out of the gutters "than to fight a hopeless war" against the narcotics that send them there. Labeling our efforts "bankrupt," federal judge Robert W. Sweet opts for legalization, saying, "If our society can learn to stop using butter, it should be able to cut down on cocaine."

2   Flawed, fatalistic, hopeless, bankrupt! I never realized surrender was so fashionable until I assumed this post.

3   Though most Americans are overwhelmingly determined to go toe-to-toe with the foreign drug lords and neighborhood pushers, a small minority believe that enforcing drug laws imposes greater costs on society than do drugs themselves. Like addicts seeking immediate euphoria, the legalizers want peace at any price, even though it means the inevitable proliferation of a practice that degrades, impoverishes, and kills.

4   I am acutely aware of the burdens drug enforcement places upon us. It consumes economic resources we would like to use elsewhere. It is sometimes frustrating, thankless, and often dangerous. But the consequences of *not* enforcing drug laws would be far more costly. Those consequences involve the intrinsically destructive nature of drugs and the toll they exact from our society in hundreds of thousands of lost and broken lives . . . human potential never realized . . . time stolen from families and jobs . . . precious spiritual and economic resources squandered.

5   That is precisely why virtually every civilized society has found it necessary to exert some form of control over mind-altering substances and why this war is so important. Americans feel up to their hips in drugs now. They would be up to their necks under legalization.

6   Even limited experiments in drug legalization have shown that when drugs are more widely available, addiction skyrockets. In 1975 Italy liberalized its drug law and now has one of the highest heroin-related death rates in Western Europe. In Alaska, where marijuana was decriminalized in 1975, the easy atmosphere has increased usage of the drug, particularly among children. Nor does it stop there. Some Alaskan schoolchildren now tout "coco puffs," marijuana cigarettes laced with cocaine.

7   Many legalizers concede that drug legalization might increase use, but they shrug off the matter. "It may well be that there would be more addicts, and I would regret that result," says Nobel laureate economist Milton Friedman. The late Harvard Medical School psychiatry professor Norman Zinberg, a longtime proponent of "responsible" drug use, admitted that "use of now-illicit drugs would certainly increase. Also casualties probably would increase."

8   In fact, Dr. Herbert D. Kleber of Yale University, my deputy in charge of demand reduction, predicts legalization might cause a "five-to-sixfold increase" in cocaine use. But legalizers regard this as a necessary price for the "benefits" of legalization. What benefits?

1. *Legalization will take the profit out of drugs.* The result supposedly 9
will be the end of criminal drug pushers and the big foreign drug wholesalers, who will turn to other enterprises because nobody will need to
make furtive and dangerous trips to his local pusher.

But what, exactly, would the brave new world of legalized drugs look 10
like? Buckley stresses that "adults get to buy the stuff at carefully regulated stores." (Would you want one in *your* neighborhood?) Others, like
Friedman, suggest we sell the drugs at "ordinary retail outlets."

Former City University of New York sociologist Georgette Bennett 11
assures us that "brand-name competition will be prohibited" and that
strict quality control and proper labeling will be overseen by the Food
and Drug Administration. In a touching egalitarian note, she adds that
"free drugs will be provided to government clinics" for addicts too poor
to buy them.

Almost all legalizers point out that the price of drugs will fall, even 12
though the drugs will be heavily taxed. Buckley, for example, argues that
somehow federal drugstores will keep the price "low enough to discourage a black market but high enough to accumulate a surplus to be used
for drug education."

Supposedly, drug sales will generate huge amounts of revenue, 13
which will then be used to tell the public not to use drugs and to treat
those who don't listen.

In reality, this tax would only allow government to share the drug 14
profits now garnered by criminals. Legalizers would have to tax drugs
heavily in order to pay for drug education and treatment programs.
Criminals could undercut the official price and still make huge profits.
What alternative would the government have? Cut the price until it was
within the lunch-money budget of the average sixth-grade student?

2. *Legalization will eliminate the black market.* Wrong. And not just be- 15
cause the regulated prices could be undercut. Many legalizers admit that
drugs such as crack or PCP are simply too dangerous to allow the shelter
of the law. Thus criminals will provide what the government will not. "As
long as drugs that people very much want remain illegal, a black market
will exist," says legalization advocate David Boaz of the libertarian Cato
Institute.

Look at crack. In powdered form, cocaine was an expensive indul- 16
gence. But street chemists found that a better and far less expensive—and
far more dangerous—high could be achieved by mixing cocaine with bak-
ing soda and heating it. Crack was born, and "cheap" coke invaded low-
income communities with furious speed.

An ounce of powdered cocaine might sell on the street for $1200. That 17
same ounce can produce 370 vials of crack at $10 each. Ten bucks seems
like a cheap hit, but crack's intense ten- to fifteen-minute high is followed
by an unbearable depression. The user wants more crack, thus starting a
rapid and costly descent into addiction.

If government drugstores do not stock crack, addicts will find it in the clandestine market or simply bake it themselves from their legally purchased cocaine. 18

Currently crack is being laced with insecticides and animal tranquilizers to heighten its effect. Emergency rooms are now warned to expect victims of "sandwiches" and "moon rocks," life-threatening smokable mixtures of heroin and crack. Unless the government is prepared to sell these deadly variations of dangerous drugs, it will perpetuate a criminal black market by default. 19

And what about children and teenagers? They would obviously be barred from drug purchases, just as they are prohibited from buying beer and liquor. But pushers will continue to cater to these young customers with the old, favorite come-ons—a couple of free fixes to get them hooked. And what good will antidrug education be when these youngsters observe their older brothers and sisters, parents, and friends lighting up and shooting up with government permission? 20

Legalization will give us the worst of both worlds: millions of *new* drug users and a thriving criminal black market. 21

3. Legalization will dramatically reduce crime. "It is the high price of drugs that leads addicts to robbery, murder, and other crimes," says Ira Glasser, executive director of the American Civil Liberties Union. A study by the Cato Institute concludes: "Most, if not all 'drug-related murders' are the result of drug prohibition." 22

But researchers tell us that many drug-related felonies are committed by people involved in crime *before* they started taking drugs. The drugs, so routinely available in criminal circles, make the criminals more violent and unpredictable. 23

Certainly there are some kill-for-a-fix crimes, but does any rational person believe that a cut-rate price for drugs at a government outlet will stop such psychopathic behavior? The fact is that under the influence of drugs, normal people do not act normally, and abnormal people behave in chilling and horrible ways. DEA agents told me about a teenage addict in Manhattan who was smoking crack when he sexually abused and caused permanent internal injuries to his one-month-old daughter. 24

Children are among the most frequent victims of violent, drug-related crimes that have nothing to do with the cost of acquiring the drugs. In Philadelphia in 1987 more than half the child-abuse fatalities involved at least one parent who was a heavy drug user. Seventy-three percent of the child-abuse deaths in New York city in 1987 involved parental drug use. 25

In my travels to the ramparts of the drug war, I have seen nothing to support the legalizers' argument that lower drug prices would reduce crime. Virtually everywhere I have gone, police and DEA agents have told me that crime rates are highest where crack is cheapest. 26

4. Drug use should be legal since users only harm themselves. Those who 27
believe this should stand beside the medical examiner as he counts the
thirty-six bullet wounds in the shattered corpse of a three-year-old who
happened to get in the way of his mother's drug-crazed boyfriend. They
should visit the babies abandoned by cocaine-addicted mothers—infants
who already carry the ravages of addiction in their own tiny bodies. They
should console the devastated relatives of the nun who worked in a
homeless shelter and was stabbed to death by a crack addict enraged that
she would not stake him to a fix.

Do drug addicts only harm themselves? Here is a former cocaine 28
addict describing the compulsion that quickly draws even the most
"responsible" user into irresponsible behavior: "Everything is about getting high, and any means necessary to get there becomes rational. If it
means stealing something from somebody close to you, lying to your
family, borrowing money from people you know you can't pay back,
writing checks you know you can't cover, you do all those things—things
that are totally against everything you have ever believed in."

Society pays for this behavior, and not just in bigger insurance pre- 29
miums, losses from accidents, and poor job performance. We pay in the
loss of a priceless social currency as families are destroyed, trust between
friends is betrayed, and promising careers are never fulfilled. I cannot
imagine sanctioning behavior that would increase that toll.

I find no merit in the legalizers' case. The simple fact is that drug use 30
is wrong. And the moral argument, in the end, is the most compelling argument. A citizen in a drug-induced haze, whether on his backyard deck
or on a mattress in a ghetto crack house, is not what the founding fathers
meant by the "pursuit of happiness." Despite the legalizers' argument that
drug use is a matter of "personal freedom," our nation's notion of liberty is
rooted in the ideal of a self-reliant citizenry. Helpless wrecks in treatment
centers, men chained by their noses to cocaine—these people are slaves.

Imagine if, in the darkest days of 1940, Winston Churchill had rallied 31
the West by saying, "This war looks hopeless, and besides, it will cost too
much. Hitler can't be *that* bad. Let's surrender and see what happens."
That is essentially what we hear from the legalizers.

This war *can* be won. I am heartened by indications that education 32
and public revulsion are having an effect on drug use. The National Institute on Drug Abuse's latest survey of current users shows a 37 percent
decrease in drug consumption since 1985. Cocaine is down 50 percent;
marijuana use among young people is at its lowest rate since 1972. In my
travels I've been encouraged by signs that Americans are fighting back.

I am under no illusion that such developments, however hopeful, 33
mean the war is over. We need to involve more citizens in the fight,
increase pressure on drug criminals, and build on antidrug programs that
have proved to work. This will not be easy. But the moral and social costs
of surrender are simply too great to contemplate.

Reprinted by permission from the Reader's Digest, *March 1990. © 1990 by The Reader's Digest Association, Inc.*

After You Read

Work with other students to develop responses to these questions or to compare responses that you have already prepared.

1. As in most debates, you should be able to find reasonable arguments on both sides of the issue. Make a list of the arguments for and against the legalization of drugs.

2. As you evaluate the arguments and take a stand, consider also your own experiences or the experiences of people you know. How would the arguments you have read in these articles affect them?

Readings: School, Teenagers, and Part-Time Jobs

Before You Read

1. Consider whether or not you think it is a good idea for teenagers to work part-time while they are going to school. What are the advantages and/or disadvantages involved?

2. Did you work as a teenager? If you did, explain in what ways your experience benefited you. Did your experience have any negative results?

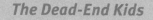

The Dead-End Kids

Michele Manges

If just showing up accounts for 90 percent of success in life, as Woody Allen claims, then today's teenagers ought to make great recruits for tomorrow's permanent work force.   1

Well over half of them are already showing up in the part-time work force doing after-school and summer jobs. In times past, this kind of youthful zeal was universally applauded; the kids, we thought, were getting invaluable preliminary training for the world of work. But now a lot of people are *worried* about the surge in youth employment. Why?   2

Because a lot of today's eight million working teens—55 percent of all 16- to 19-year-olds—aren't learning anything much more useful than just showing up.   3

Taste of Adulthood

Not that long ago many youngsters could get part-time or summer jobs that taught them the rudiments of a trade they could pursue later. If this wasn't the case, they at least got a taste of the adult world, working closely with adults and being supervised by them. Also, in whatever they did they usually had to apply in a practical way at least some of the skills they'd learned in school, thus reinforcing them.   4

Today, however, a growing majority of working youngsters hustle at monotonous, dead-end jobs that prepare them for nothing. They certainly make up one of the largest groups of underemployed people in the country.

Many work in adolescent ghettos overseen by "supervisors" barely older than they are, and they don't need to apply much of anything they've learned in school, not even the simplest math; technology has turned them into near-automatons. Checkout scanners and sophisticated cash registers tot up bills and figure the change for them. At fast-food joints, automatic cooking timers remove the last possibility that a teen might pick up a smidgen of culinary skill.

Laurence Steinberg, a Temple University professor and co-author of a book on teenage employment, estimates that at least three out of every four working teenagers are in jobs that don't give them any meaningful training. "Why we think that wrapping burgers all day prepares kids for the future is beyond me," he says.

In a study of 550 teens, Prof. Steinberg and his colleagues found that those working long hours at unchallenging jobs tended to grow cynical about work in general. They did only their own defined tasks and weren't inclined to help out others, their sense of self-respect declined, and they began to feel that companies don't care about their employees. In effect, they were burning out before they even joined the permanent work force.

A lot of teenaged workers are just bone-tired, too. Shelley Wurst, a cook at an Ohio franchise steakhouse, got so worn out she stopped working on school nights. "I kept sleeping through my first-period class," she says. "If it wasn't for the crew I'm working with, I wouldn't want to work there at all."

This sort of thing is all too common. "Some kids are working past 2 A.M. and have trouble waking up for morning classes," says Larry Morrison, principal of Sylvania (Ohio) Northview High School. Educators like him are beginning to wonder whether teenage work today is not only irrelevant to future careers but even damaging to them; the schoolwork of students who pour so much time and energy into dead-end jobs often suffers—thus dimming their eventual prospects in a permanent job market that now stresses education.

As for the teens themselves, a great number would much rather be working elsewhere, in more challenging or relevant jobs. Some, like Tanya Paris, have sacrificed to do so.

A senior at Saratoga (Calif.) High School, she works six hours a week with a scientist at the National Aeronautics and Space Administration, studying marine algae, for no pay and no school credit. The future biologist hopes that her NASA work will help her decide which area of biology to pursue.

But most others either are lured by the money they can make or can't find what they're looking for. Jay Jackson, a senior at Northview High, says he'd take a pay cut from his $3.40-an-hour job as a stock boy if he could find something allied to psychology, his prospective career field.

He hasn't been able to. Schoolmate Bridget Ellenwood, a junior, yearned for a job that had something to do with dentistry but had to settle for slicing up chickens at a local Chick-fil-A franchise—a job, she says, "where you don't learn much at all."

And More to Come

Expect more teen jobs where you don't learn much at all. The sweeping change in the economy from making things to service, together with the growth of computerized service-industry technology that leaves almost nothing to individual skill and initiative, is expected to accelerate.   14

So the mindless and irrelevant part-time jobs open to teens in the near future will probably increase, while the better jobs continue to decline. On top of that, a growing labor shortage, which would drive up pay, figures to draw more kids into those jobs—against their interests. "Teen-agers would be much better off doing a clerical-type job or studying," says Prof. John Bishop of Cornell University's Industrial and Labor Relations Center.   15

Efforts have been under way to cut back the number of hours teens can work, but the worsening labor shortage is undercutting them. Many educators are instead urging the states to start or expand more high-school cooperative education programs. These plans tie school and outside work to future career goals and provide more structure and adult supervision than ordinary outside work.   16

Employers also prefer students with this kind of experience. A recent study by the Cooperative Work Experience Education Association found that 136 of 141 businesses in Arkansas would hire a young applicant who had been in such a program over one who had worked independently. "The goal is not to get kids to stop working," says Prof. Bishop of Cornell. "It's to get them to learn more."   17

Part-Time Work Ethic: Should Teens Go for It?

Dennis McLellan

John Fovos landed his first part-time job—as a box boy at Alpha Beta on West Olympic—the summer after his sophomore year at Fairfax High School in Los Angeles. "I wanted to be independent," he said, "and I felt it was time for me to see what the world was really like."   1

Now an 18-year-old senior, Fovos works the late shift at the supermarket stocking shelves four nights a week. He saves about $50 a week, but most of his paycheck goes to his car payment and membership at a health spa. "The rest is for food—what I don't eat at home—and clothes."   2

Shelley Staats went to work part-time as a secretary for a Century 21   3
office when she was 15. Since then, she has worked as a cashier for a
marine products company, scooped ice cream at a Baskin-Robbins,
cashiered at a Video Depot and worked as a "floater" at May Co.

The Newport Harbor High School senior currently works about 25   4
hours a week in the lingerie department at the new Broadway in Costa
Mesa. Although she saves about $200 a month for college, she said she
works "to support myself: my car and clothes and just stuff I do, like
going out."

Working also has helped her to learn to manage both her time and   5
money, Staats said, and her work in the department store is providing
experience for a future career in fashion merchandising.

But, she acknowledged, there are times when working while going to   6
school has taken its toll.

"Last year I was sleeping in my first-period class half the time," ad-   7
mitted Staats, who occasionally has forgone football games and school
dances because of work. "After a while, it just wears you out."

Nathan Keethe, a Newport Harbor High School senior who works   8
more than 20 hours a week for an exterminating service, admits to sometimes feeling like the odd man out when he sees that fellow students "are
out having a good time after school and I'm working. But then I think
there's a lot of other kids out there working, too, and it doesn't seem so
unusual."

Indeed, what clearly was the exception 40 years ago is now the rule.   9

Fovos, Staats and Keethe are riding the crest of a wave of part-time   10
student employees that began building at the end of World War II and has
steadily increased to the present. In 1981, according to a study by the
National Center for Education Statistics, 80% of high school students
have held part-time jobs by the time they graduate.

Part-time work during the school years traditionally has been viewed   11
as an invaluable experience for adolescents, one that builds character,
teaches responsibility and prepares them for entering the adult world.

But the authors of a provocative new book challenge conventional   12
wisdom, contending that an over-commitment to work during the school
years "may make teenagers economically wealthy but psychologically
poor. . . ."

The book, *When Teenagers Work: The Psychological and Social Costs of*   13
Adolescent Employment, is by Ellen Greenberger, a developmental psychologist and professor of social ecology at the University of California,
Irvine, and Laurence Steinberg, a professor of child and family studies at
the University of Wisconsin.

Based on national research data and on the authors' own study of   14
more than 500 working and non-working students at four Orange County
[California] high schools, the book reports that:

- Extensive part-time employment during the school year may   15
  undermine youngsters' education. Students who work long hours

are more likely to cut back on courses at school, taking easier classes and avoiding tougher ones. And, say the authors, long hours of work begun early in the school years increase the likelihood of dropping out.

- Working leads less often to the accumulation of savings or financial contributions to the family than to a higher level of spending on cars, clothes, stereos, concerts and other luxury items. 16

- Working appears to promote, rather than deter, some forms of delinquent behavior. About 30% of the youngsters in their first part-time job have given away goods or services; 18% have taken things other than money from work; 5½% have taken money from work; and 17% have worked under the influence of drugs or alcohol, according to the Orange County study. 17

- Working long hours under stressful conditions leads to increased alcohol and marijuana use. 18

- Teen-age employment—typically in dull or monotonous jobs for which the sole motivation is the paycheck—often leads to increased cynicism about working. 19

Moreover, the authors contend that adolescents who work long hours may develop the superficial social skills of an adult, but by devoting too much time to a job they severely curtail the time needed for reflection, introspection and identity experimentation that is required to develop true maturity. 20

Such findings lead Greenberger and Steinberg to conclude "that the benefits of working to the development of adolescents have been overestimated, while the costs have been underestimated." 21

"We don't want to be read as saying that kids shouldn't work during the school year," Greenberger said in an interview. "Our argument is with over-commitment to work: That working long hours may interfere with other very important goals of the growing years." 22

The authors place the blame partly on the types of jobs available to young people today. By working in unchallenging, monotonous jobs in fast-food restaurants or retail shops, they contend, teen-agers learn few new skills, have little opportunity for meaningful contact with adults and seldom gain work experience that will lead to future careers. 23

"Parents and schools," Greenberger said, "should wake up from the dream that having a kid who works 30 hours a week is promoting his or her transition to adulthood." 24

Greenberger and Steinberg's findings, not surprisingly, do not sit well with the fast-food industry. 25

"The fast-food industry is probably the largest employer of young people in the United States," said Paul Mitchell, spokesperson for Carl Karcher Enterprises, which employs thousands of teen-agers in its Carl's Jr. restaurants. 26

"For most of those young people," Mitchell said, "it's their first job, 27 the first time they are told that you make a product a certain way, the first time they work with money, the first time they are made aware to be there on time and do it right . . . and it's just a tremendous working experience."

Terry Capatosto, a spokeswoman for McDonald's, calls Greenberger 28 and Steinberg's findings "absurd, to say the least."

"Working at McDonald's contributes tremendously to [young peo- 29 ple's] personal development and work ethic," said Capatosto, noting that countless McDonald's alumnae have gone on to professional careers and that about half of the people at all levels of McDonald's management, including the company's president and chairman of the board, started out as crew people.

"The whole idea of getting students out in the community during 30 the time they're also a student is a very productive thing to do," said Jackie Oakes, college and career guidance specialist at Santa Ana High School.

Although she feels most students work "for the extras kids want," 31 Oakes said they worked for a variety of reasons, including earning money to go on a trip with the school band and saving for college.

As for work taking time away from studying, Oakes said, "I think if 32 a kid isn't interested in studying, having a job doesn't impact that."

Newport Harbor High School's Nathan Keethe, who usually earns 33 Bs, doesn't think he'd devote more time to schoolwork if he weren't working. "Not really, because even when I wasn't working I wasn't too devoted to school," he said, adding that "for somebody who is, I wouldn't recommend working too much. I do think it would interfere."

Fairfax High's John Fovos, who works about 27 hours a week, how- 34 ever, said his grade-point average actually has risen since he began work-ing part time. The motivation? "My parents told me if my job hindered my grades, they'd ask me to quit," he said.

Although she acknowledges that some teen-age workers may experi- 35 ence growth in such areas as self-reliance and improved work habits, Greenberger said, "It's not evident that those things couldn't be realized in other settings as well. There's no evidence that you have to be a teen-age drone in order to grow in those areas."

As for the notion that "it would be great to get kids out into the work- 36 place because they'll learn," Greenberger said that "the news is not so good. On the one hand we find that relatively little time on the job is spent using anything resembling higher-order cognitive skills," she said. "Computation nowadays is often done automatically by the cash register; so much for practicing arithmetic. Kids do extremely little writing and reading [on the job]. There's also very little job training. In fact, most of the youngsters in our survey reported their job could be done by some-body with a grade-school education or less."

© 1986, The Los Angeles Times. *Reprinted by permission.*

Balancing Act: High School Students Making the Grade at Part-Time Jobs

Maureen Brown

First jobs have a way of permanently etching themselves in our memories. Often, more than a paycheck was gained from that initial working experience. 1

Many of today's teens, like teens a generation ago, cut their working teeth at fast-food restaurants. I always find it of interest to learn that a successful executive, attorney, physician or teacher was once a member of this business sector—and in a position well below management. 2

A teen-ager's first job is one of many rites of passage children and parents must go through. A dialogue of limits is appropriate when the subject of taking a job arises. 3

It's important to determine what are acceptable hours of employment and how many hours a week are permitted so that the student can maintain studies and other school-related activities. What about transportation? Job safety? How will the earnings be spent? 4

For some families, the discussion of employment is frequently not initiated by the child but rather by the parent. "I think it's time we discuss the possibility of a job," has been uttered in numerous households after a weekend of distributing funds to teen-agers for entertainment and clothing. 5

While not feigning to have the answers to the question of employment and teen-agers, a recent discussion with a group of Mira Mesa teen-agers proved that more than money is gained from a job. 6

Charlotte Iradjpanah, 17, a senior at Mira Mesa High, has been working 10 to 20 hours a week at a Mira Mesa Burger King since September. 7

"The job is close to my house and I needed the money for senior activities," says Charlotte. "I'm also saving for college and working keeps me out of trouble. A job is an opportunity to know what it's like to hold responsibility. Sometimes I have to face the fact that I have to go to work today and put aside my personal preferences." 8

Working at Burger King does not exclude Charlotte from participating in extracurricular activities at school. She is a member of the speech and debate team and president of the photography club. 9

"The job has actually strengthened my GPA since I've taken on additional responsibilities," said Charlotte. 10

Jenni Hada, 18, a senior at Mira Mesa Summit High has been at Burger King for 3 months. "I owe my parents some money and want to buy a car, but working actually gives me something constructive to do with my free time," she says. 11

Mike Vo, 17, a junior at Mira Mesa High, who has been at Burger King for the past month, has held a part-time job since he turned 16. "I didn't like living off of my parents," he says. 12

Mike's parents were skeptical when their son first brought up the subject of having a part-time job in addition to school. "Once they saw that I could still bring home good grades and have a job, they felt differently," says Mike. 13

As well as school and a part-time job, Mike is a participant in the junior tennis circuit. 14

Charlotte, Jenni and Mike work with a manager who perceives the commitment and organization it demands to have a part-time job while in high school. Manager Wade Palmer, 28, started work at Burger King at age 17 while in high school and senses the importance of allowing for flexibility in scheduling. 15

"We can work around your schedule," Palmer assures the students. 16

Palmer views "listening to these teen-agers" as an important facet of his role as a manager. Believing that "there are many valuable qualities one can develop on the job," Palmer delights in seeing former student-workers from his decade of work in North County who have gone on into other fields. 17

"One is a banker in Mira Mesa, another is a paralegal, and another is an assistant manager with Dixieline," proudly claims Palmer. 18

Before In-N-Out Burger in Mira Mesa opened its doors in August last year, the company sent out employment flyers and solicited workers in the local high schools and colleges. 19

"We had over 800 applications for employment," says Bill Mayes, 31 the manager of the store on Mira Mesa Boulevard. "Of those 800 applicants, we selected 50." 20

Like Wade Palmer, Mayes started working with In-N-Out Burger at age 17 while still in high school. He continued part-time in college, and eventually went into management. 21

"I think students, with their great amount of energy, work out very well in our restaurant," Mayes says. "At In-N-Out, we're looking for bright, friendly, outgoing people to meet our customers." 22

Ba Hog, 17, a Mira Mesa High student, is one of the 50 applicants who met Mayes' criteria. 23

"At first, my parents doubted I could get a job here—lots of people were applying," recalls Ba. "After I passed the first interview, they cautioned me to not get my hopes up. When I passed the second interview, I could not wait to go home and tell them!" 24

"Since I've had this job, my parents have been giving me a little more freedom—like staying out later," says Ba, who is trilingual—speaking Chinese, Vietnamese and English. "Now they feel I can better decide between what is right and wrong. Plus, my grades have not been affected since I started this job." 25

One other advantage of working, according to Ba, is that he has been able to delegate some of his previous home responsibilities to his older 26 brother, Nghia, 18, who now carries out the trash and rakes leaves for the employed Ba.

Michelle Gust, 17, a senior at Mt. Carmel High, has been working 10 to 15 hours a week at In-N-Out since its opening. Balancing school and a part-time job with senior class council, peer counseling groups, cross-country running and the Girl Scouts, which recently awarded her the "Silver Award," has made Michelle aware of meticulous time scheduling. In addition to these activities, Michelle also spent her fall learning about deadlines as she filled out college applications.   27

"Working has taught me the importance of communicating with people," says Michelle. "The management wants you to communicate well with them and the customer. I've learned to be flexible."   28

When the lead part of Corie in the school play "Barefoot in the Park" was won by Kimberley Belnap, 17, of Mt. Carmel High, her work schedule at In-N-Out required adjustment.   29

"My mom also talked to Bill, the manager, and we were able to work out a schedule where I could still continue to work, be in the play and maintain my grades," she said.   30

"I've learned to budget my time. I'm the type of person who, when I have more to do, I find more time," she said.   31

In addition to organizing her schedule, Kimberley notes that since starting work at In-N-Out, she is painfully conscious of the service she receives in other restaurants. "I take a critical look at how others serve the public."   32

© 1992, The Los Angeles Times. *Reprinted by permission of the author.*

After You Read

Work with other students to develop responses to these questions or to compare responses that you have already prepared.

1. As you can see, there are conflicting ideas about whether or not part-time work benefits teenagers who are attending school. To come to terms with the issues involved, list the advantages or disadvantages that are discussed in each article.

2. Look for different ways in which these writers say part-time work affects school performance. Do they discuss positive as well as negative points?

3. Not all of the ideas in these articles are related to school performance. Make a list of the ideas that are not necessarily related to school but that are important to the thesis of each article.

Writing Assignments

Note Working with several sources can be substantially more difficult than working with only one source. As you respond to one of these assignments, consider working with other students to clarify and organize your ideas.

1. Write an essay in which you argue for or against the legalization of drugs. To support your thesis, use arguments and evidence from the articles you have read and from whatever relevant experiences you or people you know may have had.

2. What is your position regarding the benefits or drawbacks of high school students working while attending school? Write an essay in which you argue for or against such a practice. To support your thesis, use arguments and evidence from the articles you have read and from whatever relevant experiences you or people you know may have had.

3. Develop an argument based on reading selections in Chapter 7 or those in Part 4. Use arguments and evidence from those articles as well as from your own experiences or observations to support your position.

Evaluating Sample Papers

Argument Essay

Use the following criteria to evaluate the student essays below.

1. Introduction

   Does the first paragraph employ an effective lead-in to introduce the topic? Does the thesis take a definite stand and make it clear that the author intends to support a debatable point?

   1   2   3   4   5   6

2. Unity

   Does each paragraph have a clear and specific topic sentence that introduces an argument in support of the thesis? Does the material in each paragraph clearly relate to its topic sentence?

   1   2   3   4   5   6

3. Support

   Is the argument within each paragraph supported with facts, examples, statistics, and/or references to authority?

   1   2   3   4   5   6

4. Coherence

   Are transitions used between paragraphs? Are they used within paragraphs, especially when the writer is moving from one type of support to another?

   1   2   3   4   5   6

5. References to the Text

Are direct quotations and paraphrases correctly introduced and smoothly incorporated into the text? Do they reflect the articles' points accurately?

1   2   3   4   5   6

6. Tone and Attitude

Has the writer recognized that other responses to this topic are possible? Has he or she raised and responded to obvious objections?

1   2   3   4   5   6

7. Sentence Structure

Do the sentences combine ideas that are related, using coordination, sub-ordination, verbal phrases, or parallelism when appropriate? Are there too many brief, choppy main clauses?

1   2   3   4   5   6

8. Mechanics, Grammar, and Spelling

Does the paper contain a distracting number of errors of these kinds?

1   2   3   4   5   6

9. Overall Ranking of the Essay

1   2   3   4   5   6

Student Essay 1

Drugs, alcohol, and tobacco are all substances that can manipulate the body and mind. Out of those three substances, most people feel that one out of the three substances should be illegal even though they all have similar effects to the body. That one substance is drugs. Drugs today are seen as a big threat to society, even though it only kills 4,000 people per year compared to alcohol's 100,000 per year and tobacco's 300,000 per year rate. Knowing the death rates of all three substances, which one do you feel should be illegal? I feel that drugs should be legalized because the war on drugs will never be won, it will destroy the black market, and the value of drugs will decrease.

By legalizing drugs, we would be able to control the quality of drugs. William J. Bennett states that if the government does not stock crack in government drugstores, the crack junkies would go elsewhere to get it (246). Where else would they go? None other than the dealers that sell crack cocaine that has been "laced with insecticides and animal tran-quilizers to heighten its effect" (Bennett 247). Would you be able to sleep at night knowing that if we do not legalize drugs to control its quality, we will allow these types of drugs to infest our cities, suburbs, and homes. If we legalize drugs, we can control its quality and produce drugs that are weaker. By making weaker drugs, we would help drug addicts gradually kick the habit.

In order to destroy the black market of drug sales, we need to legalize drugs. In "Should Drugs Be Legalized?" William J. Bennett states that if we legalize drugs, the black market will remain (246). The black market remaining may be true, but the value of drugs will decrease causing the profits that the drug cartels make to be not worth selling through the black market. For example, back in the prohibition days of the late 1920's, alcohol was the moneymaker for the Mafia and other organized crime groups. For years the Mafia profited off of alcohol which most Americans felt was illegal and immoral during that time period. But as soon as prohibition was repealed in 1933, the black market of alcohol was destroyed. Hodding Carter III states in "We're Losing the Drug War Because Prohibition Never Works," "Prohibition can't work, won't work, and never worked" (242). Today these words still hold some truth. The prohibition of drugs is only resulting in a rapidly growing black market. Unless we finally come to realize that prohibition is not the answer, the black market will remain.

Finally, the war on drugs is a complete waste of time. Why fight a war that will never be won? In fact, Van Deerlin states in "Police and Jails Have Failed" that "Mounting evidence that the campaign against drugs has proved no more successful than the ill-remembered Prohibition law aimed at alcohol in an earlier day" (239). For example, waiting in their car from a distance, two undercover police officers tape a drug sale that is about to go down between a junkie and a dealer. The junkie approaches the dealer, checks the merchandise, pays the dealer, and in an instant wrestles the dealer to the ground. While this is happening, the two police officers taping the sale, rush to the junkie's side, who is also another undercover police officer. They handcuff the dealer, book him, and lock him up. Twenty-four hours later, the dealer is released because the court system is booked for the next year or so. Within hours, the dealer restocks his supply and goes back to the same corner to sell the same drugs. This is the type of war that our justice department has been fighting for years. So how can we win the war? In "Best Remedy: Crack Down on User," Joseph Perkins states that the only way to bring down the drug cartels is to deprive them of their customers and, thus, their tremendous profits" (242). Do you really want to pay more taxes to build more jails, train more police officers, and train more judges? Statistics have shown that housing an inmate for one-year can cost as much as $50,000. I feel that the only way to win this war, is to stop treating users as criminals by giving them jail time, and start treating them as addicts by giving them therapy, a more effective and cheaper treatment.

A lot of time and money has been put into war on drugs and the education on how to say no to the use of them. But neither has been proven successful. We are wasting time trying to eliminate drugs from our world; therefore, we should open our eyes and legalize them.

Student Essay 2

Is it really meaningful for a person to work while attending school? Many students have a part time job while going to high school or college. Some enjoy the experience while others completely hate it. The pros and cons of working while going to school were discussed in Michele Manges' "The Dead End Kids," Dennis McLellan's "Part-Time Work Ethic: Should Teens Go For It?" and Maureen Brown's "Balancing Act: High School Students Making the Grade at Part-Time Jobs." After reading all three articles I came to the conclusion that working while going to school is not just okay, but better than not having a job.

Although I feel working is a plus while going to school, I do feel there are some disadvantages. One point against working is that while working nights one may not get home until late and he may still have homework to complete. Michele Manges says, "A lot of teenage workers are just bone-tired" (250), and one of the teenage workers that she interviewed explained that to do her job so late at night "I kept sleeping through my first period class" (250). Another negative effect that working may have on students is the stress that both the job and school bring to the student. Based on national research data and her own study of more than 500 students in Orange County, Ellen Greenberger found that working appears to promote forms of delinquent behavior and has also led students to increased alcohol and marijuana use (McLellan 253). All of these effects are being blamed on the jobs students are working while attending school. However, I feel there are many more positive effects from working than these few negative results.

One of the positive results from working a part-time job is the fact that a person learns how to manage their time and money. Shelley Staats, a senior at Newport Harbor High School, said that working has helped her to manage both her time and money, while her work in the department store is providing experience for a future career in fashion merchandising. Not only does she learn new responsibilities, she is gaining important information by working in the department store that will help her to decide what she likes and dislikes about her future careers (McLellan 252). Personally, I have run into a similar situation as Shelley's. As for my job, working at Eastview Community Center, I get to see all of the financial documents go through the office. Because I want to be an accountant after graduating from college, I enjoy seeing and observing the financial statements and balance sheets every month. After observing all the paperwork I have become aware of a few of the things my future job holds for me.

Not only do I not believe working causes a students grades to suffer, but I believe that in many instances getting a job has resulted in the student receiving better grades. John Fovos, a student at Fairfax High School, said as a result of getting a job his grade point average has actually risen due to the fact his parents told him if his grades dropped he would have to quit his job (McLellan 254). Following the same pattern, Charlotte Iradjpanah works 10 to 20 hours a week at a Mira Mesa Burger

King. She states, "The job has actually strengthened my GPA since I have taken on additional responsibilities" (Brown 255). I believe in these situations the students were aware that if their grades slipped the parents would place the blame on their new jobs. This fear of losing their jobs caused the students to work harder than they had before.

The biggest plus to working is that it puts one out into the real world. Michelle Gust, a senior at Mt. Carmel High, explained "Working has taught me the importance of communicating with people. The management wants you to communicate with them and the customer. I have learned to be flexible" (Brown 257). I believe these are very important skills young people need to learn and a job for many young people is usually the first experience they receive in the real world. Personally, I have also gained many essential traits while working. One of these experiences also came across the lines of communication. My job consists of enforcing the rules throughout the community center. One day about a month ago I let some teenage kids onto the tennis courts even though they were not wearing the appropriate shoes. As a result, I ended up cleaning all of their black marks off of the court as well as getting docked some points on my evaluation.

Don't get me wrong, for when it comes to school, I believe that school should come first. However, having a job while going to school brings many plus's along with the job. A young person learns how to manage his money as well as managing his time between school, homework, and work. Many times the job will also result in the student bringing home better grades for he wants his parents to let him keep his job. Most importantly, receiving a job while still young lets one know and understand how the real world operates.

Student Essay 3

> . . . a burglar . . . broke into a home and killed the father of three children, aged nine, eleven, and twelve. The crime went unnoticed until ten hours later, when police entered the apartment after being called by neighbors and found the three children watching television just a few feet away from the bloody corpse of their father. (Cross 376)

Doesn't this scene read like an unbelievable script for a bad movie? Unfortunately, according to Donna Woolfolk Cross in "Shadows on the Wall," it is a real-life situation, reported by United Press International. It illustrates the powerful hold that television has over young minds, and it points out how television can draw attention away from the real world, replacing reality with its own distorted fantasy world. I have to admit that I am one of the 1980's generation that grew up glued to the television, but I still think that in many ways the TV is one of the most dangerous devices invented in the last century.

One reason it's so dangerous is that it does exactly what the above quotation suggests—it replaces reality with illusion. Ms. Cross gives several studies to prove this point. One of them involved a group of children in a room where two people started to yell at each other and fight. The fight was projected on video screens, and rather than reacting to what was happening, the kids all sat and watched the screens. It was as if the video were more important than the people themselves (376). I've seen other situations that make me believe that television causes children to confuse reality and illusion. For instance, when I started high school, shows like *Beverly Hills 90210* had me thinking that all the kids there would look cool and be going to bed with each other. I was so worried that I would never fit in that for the first month I didn't even talk to anybody. Luckily, I finally figured out that real life was different from what I'd seen on TV, but I sure went through a lot of misery for nothing.

I think that TV is also dangerous because it pretends to be educational when it's really not. According to Paul Robinson in "TV Can't Educate," television cannot provide the time that is needed for a person to really think about an issue. Instead, all it can do is present bits and pieces of facts that ignore all sorts of more involved questions (373). I think this is really true. I remember watching *Sesame Street* as I grew up, and I can't remember ever really learning anything from it. I just liked Big Bird and Cookie Monster. I thought they were funny, but mostly I ignored or already knew all the things they did with the alphabet and numbers. Also, I practically never watch the news or shows like *Nightline* because I like to relax when I watch television, so for the most part the television is not really very educational for me.

The worst part about television is the violence and sex that are becoming so common, even during early evening hours. It seems to me that there is no way children can avoid being affected by all of the negative things they see every day and evening on television. Even the writers who argue in favor of TV admit how damaging this part of it can be. In "Don't Touch That Dial," Madeline Drexler refers to the "violence of primetime shows . . . the sexism of MTV . . . [and] the materialism of commercials" (378). Also, in "The Meaning of TV," William Henry III admits that without TV we might have a less violent society and a more restrained world where "premarital pregnancy and divorce were still treated with distaste rather than with sympathy" (371).

Some people think that TV doesn't cause as many problems as I have listed, but I don't see how they can really think that. Television is entertaining, and I have to admit that I watch it for that reason, but it's not educational, and it really does cause people to make bad judgments about what reality is like. When I have children, I don't think I'll want them to sit and stare at the TV all day, but I will let them watch shows that are entertaining and amusing.

Sentence-Combining Review

In the first seven chapters of this text, you have practiced using a variety of techniques to combine related ideas. In the paragraphs that follow, combine the related sentences using whichever techniques seem most appropriate. Here is a brief summary of the sentence-combining ideas you have studied.

Chapter 1: Embed adjectives, adverbs, and prepositional phrases in related sentences.

Chapter 2: Use coordination to combine sentences or parts of sentences that are grammatically alike.

Chapter 3: Use subordinate clauses to indicate the relative importance of related ideas.

Chapter 4: Use present participial phrases, past participial phrases, and infinitive phrases to combine related ideas.

Chapter 5: Use appositives when nouns or pronouns are used to rename other nouns and pronouns.

Chapter 6: Use parallel sentence structure to join items in a series or with correlative conjunctions.

Chapter 7: Vary the length and structure of your sentences to achieve sentence variety.

Exercise 8.1

1 Roger Williams was the great seventeenth-century religious emancipator. **2** He died in 1683. **3** He was buried in a poorly marked grave in the backyard of his home in Providence, Rhode Island. **4** Fifty-six years later, in 1739, a workman was excavating a nearby grave. **5** He accidentally broke into the coffin and exposed the bones. **6** Years after that, in 1860, a descendant of Williams ordered workmen to exhume the remains. **7** He wanted to transfer them to a more suitable tomb. **8** When the coffin was opened, no bones were found. **9** Instead, the coffin contained the root of a nearby apple tree. **10** It was exactly where the body should have been. **11** It was in the exact shape of Williams's body, from head to toe. **12** Apparently the root had entered the coffin when it was broken open in 1739. **13** It encountered Williams's skull. **14** Then it followed the path of least resistance. **15** It inched down the side of his head, backbone, hips, and legs. **16** It molded itself closely to the contours of his body. **17** The corpse itself was gone. **18** It had been absorbed into the tree through the roots. **19** The human-shaped root was removed for safekeeping. **20** Today it is on display at the Rhode Island Historical Society in Providence.

1 Many actors and actresses are superstitious people. **2** They rely not only on their talent, looks, and charm. **3** They also rely on rabbits' feet and a whole host of other superstitions. **4** Some stage superstitions are purely personal. **5** Others have been picked up from tradition. **6** They are treasured by those who have no idea how or why the superstitions originated. **7** For example, real flowers are welcome after a performance. **8** They are unlucky for stage decorations. **9** Of course, real flowers would fade and have to be replaced regularly. **10** The superstition probably derives from a very practical concern. **11** An artist might slip and fall if he stepped on a petal or leaf that had fallen from a vase. **12** There are other common stage superstitions. **13** A fall on stage is the sign of a long run. **14** Wishing an actor good luck will bring bad luck. **15** Performing or even quoting from Macbeth is unlucky. **16** Tradition also has it that something going wrong during dress rehearsal means the opening night's performance will be a success. **17** In fact, many actors have a firm belief. **18** A bad dress rehearsal heralds a smash opening night. **19** The list of superstitions goes on and on. **20** Flowers should be handed over the footlights instead of delivered backstage. **21** One should never mention the exact number of lines he has in a show. **22** Congratulatory telegrams should not be read during a run. **23** One should not write on the dressing room mirror. **24** If someone whistles in the dressing room, one should go outside. **25** Then one should turn around three times and spit before re-entering.

1 Ever since 1966, a scientific controversy has raged. **2** The controversy is about whether apes actually exhibit signs of human intelligence. **3** In 1966, a chimpanzee named Washoe first began to use American Sign Language, or AMESLAN. **4** Apes that have been taught sign language have developed significantly large vocabularies. **5** They recognize nouns, like "fruit," "candy,'" and "banana." **6** They also recognize verbs, such as "give," "hug," and "take." **7** Sometimes they combine these words in creative ways. **8** One chimp did not know the term for citrus fruit. **9** It called them "smell fruit." **10** Others called watermelons "candy drink" and cucumbers "banana which is green." **11** Apes apparently recognize the meaning of certain words. **12** They seem able to string together some words into meaningful sentences. **13** Critics of ape research assert that supposed ape "language ability" is due solely to drill, imitation, or mere conditioned response. **14** These critics claim that ape trainers misinterpret ape "language." **15** They say that the trainers are too eager to believe that apes are truly displaying human-type intelligence. **16** In addition to language ability, researchers have discovered evidence that apes also possess self-awareness. **17** Self-awareness has long been considered an exclusive trait of the human race. **18** For example, apes can learn to recognize themselves in mirrors. **19** No primate other than humans seems able to do that. **20** It is suspected that other species with large brains, such as whales, porpoises, and elephants, may also be self-aware.

Part 3

Editing Skills

Effective writing requires care and precision, much more so than speaking does. When speaking, we always have the opportunity to stop and explain ourselves further. When we write in college, business, and the professions, we make hundreds, even thousands, of separate choices, even in relatively brief pieces of writing. Some of the choices are large, such as those concerning the overall organization of our writing, and some of the choices are small, such as those concerning the placement of an apostrophe or comma. Other choices involve sentence patterns, words, and punctuation.

Skillful editing can enhance the quality of your writing and allow you to express yourself in the way that you desire. Not only does it allow you to write effectively, but it also gains you the confidence of your readers. Poor grammar and usage can cause your readers to feel that you have not thought carefully about either the form or the content of your writing. In this section, we will present the basic editing skills of a good writer. We begin with a few important definitions.

Chapter 9

Some Basic Editing Terms

Clause

A **clause** is a group of words that contains at least one subject and one verb. Here are some clauses:

   S   *V*

Harvey cares about Beatrice.

    S   *V*

The train was late.

      S *V*

Almost all cats hate dogs.

Here are some groups of words that are not clauses:

To find out the cause of the problem.

Trying out for the team.

To find out the cause of the problem is not a clause because it does not contain a subject and a verb. It does contain a form known as an infinitive ("to find"), but the infinitive is a **verbal,** and verbals cannot be used as the verb of a sentence.

Trying out for the team also lacks a subject and verb. This phrase contains another verbal—the "-ing" form of the verb. However, the "-ing" form cannot be used as the verb of a clause unless it is accompanied by a helping verb, as in the following clause:

  S V

I <u>was trying</u> out for the team.

Clauses come in two types—main and subordinate.

Main Clause

A **main clause** expresses a complete idea. Here are some main clauses:

Cromwell was a serious man.

Have some red beans and rice. (Here, the understood subject is *you*.)

What have I done wrong?

Subordinate Clause

A **subordinate clause** begins with a word that prevents it from expressing a complete idea. Here are some subordinate clauses.

$\overset{S}{\underline{When}}$ $\overset{V}{I}$ arrive at the airport. . .

. . . $\overset{S}{\underline{which}}$ $\overset{V}{Joe}$ kept for himself.

$\overset{S}{\underline{After}}$ $\overset{V}{you}$ inspect the kitchen. . .

The words that begin the above subordinate clauses are called subordinators. They come in two types—**subordinating conjunctions** and **relative pronouns.**

Subordinating Conjunctions		Relative Pronouns	
after	so that	that	who(ever)
although	than	which	whom(ever)
as	though	(and sometimes *when* or *where*)	
as if	unless		
as long as	until		
because	when		
before	whenever		
even though	where		
if	wherever		
since	while		

Subordinate clauses may appear at the start, at the end, or in the middle of a sentence.

<u>After he had passed the bar exam</u>, Eduardo was ready to join a law firm.

Sarah was angry at her coach <u>because he refused to listen to her excuses.</u>

The movie <u>that I rented last night</u> was really boring.

(See pages 93–94 for a further discussion of subordinate clauses.)

Sentence

A **sentence** is a group of words that contains at least **one main clause.**

not a sentence	Just staring into the sky.
not a sentence	Because he was so angry.
sentence	He just stared into the sky.
sentence	Because he was so angry, he just stared into the sky.

Exercise 9.1

Indicate whether the following are main clauses (MC), subordinate clauses (SC), or neither (N).

1. Gordon forgot his sunscreen. _____
2. Shifting into warp speed. _____
3. Griffins are scary creatures. _____
4. If you say that one more time. _____
5. Why don't you understand? _____
6. To point his pistol at the intruder. _____
7. Charles and Ann are proud of the magazine. _____
8. Because Suzanne likes to ride horses. _____
9. Having already made up his mind. _____
10. He ordered a Spam-and-okra pizza. _____
11. Because Sam Lucas gave him such good advice. _____
12. Even though Jack had to use a cane. _____
13. He never missed one meeting. _____
14. Play it again, Sam. _____
15. When Brent fakes out the point guard. _____
16. To watch Charles and Louis comparing hatchets. _____
17. When Steve and Marste are chatting. _____
18. They do not want to be interrupted. _____
19. And I want an answer immediately. _____
20. It is a double pleasure to deceive the deceiver. ■ _____

Coordinating Conjunction

The **coordinating conjunctions** are *and, but, or, nor, for, so* and *yet*. An easy way to learn the coordinating conjunctions is to remember that their first letters can spell

BOYSFAN (*But Or Yet So For And Nor*). These words join parts of a sentence that are grammatically equal. For example, they may join two subjects, two verbs, or two adjectives. They may also join two similar phrases, two subordinate clauses, or two main clauses.

two subjects	Fred **and** Ethel own this building.
two verbs	Lucy stared at the wallpaper **and** started to cry.
two adjectives	Alicia felt awkward **and** uncomfortable in the dentist's office.
two similar phrases	Jaime wanted to win the marathon **or** to place in the top three finishers.
two subordinate clauses	After they ate the dessert **but** before they washed the dishes, Dan and Roseanne yelled at the kids.
two main clauses	I have mockingbirds in my backyard, **and** they mimic the sounds of the neighborhood's car alarms.

(See pages 59–61 for a further discussion of coordinating conjunctions.)

Conjunctive Adverb

A **conjunctive adverb** is a word or phrase that serves as a transition, usually between two main clauses. When a conjunctive adverb joins two main clauses, it is preceded by a semicolon and followed by a comma.

> Percival enjoyed artichoke hearts; **however,** Consuela could not stand them.

Here is a list of the most common conjunctive adverbs:

accordingly	however	next
as a result	indeed	otherwise
consequently	in fact	second
first	instead	still
for example	likewise	therefore
for instance	meanwhile	thus
furthermore	moreover	unfortunately
hence	nevertheless	

Do not use a semicolon before a conjunctive adverb that does not begin a main clause. For example, in the following sentences, the conjunctive adverbs are not immediately preceded by semicolons.

> The man on the left, **meanwhile,** studied his bus schedule.
> The cat yowled all night long; none of the neighbors, **however,** seemed to mind.

(See pages 63–64 for a further discussion of conjunctive adverbs.)

Exercise 9.2

In the following sentences, identify all main clauses by underlining them once and all subordinate clauses by underlining them twice. Identify all coordinating conjunctions by labeling them CC, all subordinating conjunctions by labeling them SC, all relative pronouns by labeling them RP, and all conjunctive adverbs by labeling them CA.

1. While Wally worked on his bicycle, Beaver watched television.
2. The CDs that I had bought were stolen from my car.
3. The pelicans skimmed the water as the sun came up.
4. The group of men kept shouting loudly; consequently, we moved to another part of the stadium.
5. The *Reader* comes out every Thursday, and it has a great deal of handy information.
6. Duke Ellington wrote many beautiful pieces, but my favorite is "Concerto for Cootie."
7. Cootie Williams played trumpet for the Duke Ellington orchestra; next, he formed his own band.
8. Some great blue herons have nested in some trees near our house, so we often see them flying majestically overhead.
9. Walter Benjamin occupied Brent's mind much of the time when he was pondering the meaning of the life that spooled out endlessly before him.
10. At other times, he worked on his jump shot, or he prepared burritos and broccoli for Kyle.
11. My friend named his German shepherd Beethoven because he admired the composer so much.
12. If Ludwig were alive, he might be insulted.
13. The soldiers that fought for the South during the Civil War did not wear gray; in fact, they wore butternut.
14. Joseph Campbell taught us much about myth, but Louis Armstrong taught us to swing.
15. Leda had a phobia about swans; therefore, she refused to ride the swan boats in Boston.
16. Although red beans and rice is my favorite dish, I would not mind some hushpuppies right now.
17. Sometimes Hamlet could not stop talking; consequently, he hardly got any work done.
18. Homer is a heroic eater because he eats sushi; moreover, he eats snails.
19. Jazz may be the United States' only original art form although, according to some people, the short story was also developed here.
20. The manual for my VCR is unreadable, so I have never recorded a program. ■

Chapter 10

Sentence Fragments

The easiest way to identify a **sentence fragment** is to remember that *every sentence must contain a main clause*. If you do not have a main clause, you do *not* have a sentence. You can define a fragment, then, as follows: A **sentence fragment** occurs when a group of words that lacks a main clause is punctuated as a sentence.

Using this definition, you can identify almost any sentence fragment. However, you will find it easier to locate fragments in your own writing if you know that fragments can be divided into three basic types.

The Three Types of Sentence Fragments

1. **Some fragments contain no clause at all.** This type of fragment is simple to spot. It usually does not even sound like a sentence because it lacks a subject or a verb or both.

    The child in the park.

2. **Some fragments contain a verbal but still no clause.** This fragment is a bit less obvious because a verbal can be mistaken for a verb. But remember, neither a participle nor an infinitive is a verb. (See Chapter 9 if you need to review this point.)

    participle   The child <u>playing</u> in the park.

    infinitive   <u>To play</u> on the swings in the park.

3. **Some fragments contain a subordinate clause but no main clause.** This type of fragment is perhaps the most common because it does contain a subject and a verb. But remember, *a group of words without a main clause is not a sentence.*

    As the child played in the park.

    Because the swings in the park were wet.

Repairing Sentence Fragments

Once you have identified a fragment, you can repair it in one of two ways:

1. **Add words to give it a main clause.**

fragment	The child in the park.
sentence	The child <u>played</u> in the park.
sentence	The child in the park <u>looked worried</u>.
fragment	The child playing in the park.
sentence	The child <u>was</u> playing in the park.
sentence	The child playing in the park <u>ran toward the swings</u>.
fragment	Because the swings in the park were wet.
sentence	<u>The child played on the slide</u> because the swings in the park were wet.

2. **Join the fragment to a main clause written before or after it.**

incorrect	I saw a ball rolling down the walk. And a child playing on the swings.
correct	I saw a ball rolling down the walk and a child playing on the swings.
incorrect	A dog chased a cat into the bushes. As a child played on the swings.
correct	A dog chased a cat into the bushes as a child played on the swings.

Of the two possible ways to correct fragments shown above, try to use the second method of joining fragments to nearby main clauses as often as possible. Doing so will help you to avoid writing a string of short, choppy sentences, and it will help to clarify the relationship between the ideas you are joining.

One final point might help you identify and correct sentence fragments. Remember that we all speak in fragments every day. (If a friend asks you how you are, you might respond with the fragment "Fine.") Because we speak in fragments, you may find that your writing seems acceptable to you even though it contains fragments. When you work on the exercises in this chapter, do not rely on your "ear" alone. Look at the sentences. **If they do not contain main clauses, they are fragments, no matter how correct they may sound.**

Exercise 10.1

Underline any fragment you find. Then correct it either by adding new words to give it a main clause or by joining it to a main clause next to it.

1. Sarah stared at the cotton candy. Wondering if she could eat the whole thing.
2. The dog that had been barking all night long.
3. After visiting the dentist. Zelda stopped at the ice cream store. Where she ate two hot fudge sundaes and a banana split.
4. Sit in the chair by the door. Until your number is called.

5. While visiting his cousins in France, where he had spent all of his childhood and most of his teenage years.

6. The word *mutant* might be considered redundant in the name *Teenage Mutant Ninja Turtles.*

7. Because Fabio had kissed her hand. Andrea did not wash it for three weeks.

8. Disgusted with the performance of his new Corvette. Which he had just purchased for $30,000. Heathcliff threw his car keys into the lake.

9. To prevent Lois from discovering his true identity. Clark told her that he was afraid of heights.

10. A mouse scampered across the floor. Stopped to stare at the cat in the chair. And then disappeared into a crack in the wall.

11. From where she stood, Myna was able to hear every word. She kept repeating whatever the speaker said.

12. The recent earthquake caused all the dishes to fall out of the cupboard. And the microwave oven to crash to the floor.

13. Some skiers like to take unnecessary risks. Jumping from high ledges above steep slopes. They seem to enjoy the danger.

14. Turning restlessly from side to side. Henry dreamed about Walden Pond. Which he knew would soon freeze over.

15. Even though Huck had never painted a fence before. Tom assured him that he could do a good job.

16. Dorothy stared at the Munchkins and then looked at the dead witch. She knew that she wasn't in Kansas anymore.

17. Tomorrow we will experience a full solar eclipse. For the last time in this decade. It should be rather exciting.

18. Whenever Sam and Ella visit a restaurant. All of the patrons scream and run away.

19. My neighbor down the street, who needs to make more money to support his family but who has never held a steady job, even though several have been offered to him.

20. The deep blue skies. The rich green grass. The gentle afternoon breezes. The smell of the ocean. Karen missed them all. ■

Chapter 11

Fused Sentences and Comma Splices

The **fused sentence** and the **comma splice** are serious writing errors that you can correct with little effort. Either error can occur when you write a sentence that contains two or more main clauses.

Fused Sentences

The **fused sentence** occurs when two or more main clauses are joined without a coordinating conjunction and without punctuation.

fused   Chelsea jumped into the pool she waved at her father.

As you can see, the two main clauses in the above fused sentence (*Chelsea jumped into the pool* and *she waved at her father*) have been joined without a coordinating conjunction and without punctuation of any kind.

Comma Splices

The **comma splice** is a similar error. The comma splice occurs when two or more main clauses are joined with a comma but without a coordinating conjunction.

comma splice   The rain soaked all of the campers, they wondered when it would finally stop.

In this comma splice, the two main clauses (*The rain soaked all of the campers* and *they wondered when it would finally stop*) are joined by a comma, but a comma alone is not enough to join main clauses.

One of the most frequent comma splices occurs when a writer joins two main clauses with a comma and a conjunctive adverb rather than with a semicolon and a conjunctive adverb.

comma splice   I saved enough money to take a trip to Hawaii, however, at the last minute I had to change my plans.

Repairing Fused Sentences and Comma Splices

Because both fused sentences and comma splices occur when two main clauses are joined incorrectly, you can correct either error using one of five methods. Consider these two errors:

fused   Leroy won the lottery he decided to buy a car.

comma splice   Leroy won the lottery, he decided to buy a car.

Both of these errors can be corrected in one of five ways:

1. **Use a comma and a coordinating conjunction.** (See page 60 for a list of coordinating conjunctions.)

   Leroy won the lottery, **so** he decided to buy a car.

2. **Use a semicolon.**

   Leroy won the lottery; he decided to buy a car.

3. **Use a semicolon and a conjunctive adverb.** (See page 63 for a list of conjunctive adverbs)

   Leroy won the lottery; **therefore,** he decided to buy a car.

Do not use a semicolon before a conjunctive adverb that does not join two main clauses. For example, in the following sentence, *however* does not need a semicolon.

   The person in the blue raincoat, **however,** has not seen this movie.

4. **Change one of the clauses to a subordinate clause by beginning it with a subordinating conjunction or relative pronoun.** (See page 94 for a list of subordinating conjunctions and relative pronouns.)

   When Leroy won the lottery, he decided to buy a car.

5. **Punctuate the clauses as two separate sentences.**

   Leroy won the lottery. He decided to buy a car.

Sometimes the two main clauses in a fused sentence or comma splice are interrupted by a subordinate clause. When this sentence pattern occurs, the two main clauses must still be connected in one of the five ways.

fused   Roberta sold her house even though she had thought she would always live there she could not afford the payments.

comma splice   Roberta sold her house even though she had thought she would always live there, she could not afford the payments.

possible correction Roberta sold her house even though she had thought she would always live there; unfortunately, she could not afford the payments.

Exercise 11.1

Identify the following sentences as fused (F), comma splice (CS), or correct (C). Then correct each incorrect sentence using one of the five methods just discussed.

_____ 1. Samantha turned sadly away from the window it had started to rain.

_____ 2. The pilot said that he was not superstitious, nevertheless, he always avoided the Bermuda Triangle.

_____ 3. Two alley cats climbed over the fence then they began to yowl.

_____ 4. Halfway through the first act, the prima donna's voice began to waver and crack.

_____ 5. Mickey told Pluto to fetch the stick, Pluto told Mickey to forget it.

_____ 6. Suddenly a message appeared on the computer screen, it said that the hard drive had crashed.

_____ 7. Don Quixote stared at the windmill he raised his lance and attacked it.

_____ 8. The miner threw his helmet into the air and gave a victorious shout because he had finally found the Lost Dutchman's Mine.

_____ 9. Mother Abigail stared toward Las Vegas she knew she would win all of the money that she needed.

_____ 10. All of the wiring had been installed correctly, however, the lights still would not turn on.

_____ 11. After visiting Earth, the extraterrestrials headed for home, disappointed by their failure to discover any intelligent life.

_____ 12. Michael refuses to drink diet soft drinks also he hates coffee.

_____ 13. Ahmed knew it was time to leave even though he was not ready he picked up his bags and boarded the plane.

_____ 14. The German shepherd down the street, however, is quite gentle.

_____ 15. Although it was nearly 2:00 A.M., the party was still going strong, then one of the neighbors called the police.

_____ 16. Clive has some rather unusual eating habits, for instance, yesterday morning he ate Frosted Flakes and mayonnaise for breakfast.

_____ 17. A deranged-looking man claimed giant ants were living in the sewers of Los Angeles nobody believed him.

_____ 18. Leonardo's knock-knock jokes were rather dumb, consequently, all Mona Lisa would do was smile politely.

_____ 19. The sun had reached its zenith Doc Holliday and the Earp brothers entered the O.K. Corral.

_____ 20. After fifteen years of hard labor, Jackson wondered if he would ever again see his home and family, but little did he know that his brother, Seymour, had decided to rescue him and was about to make his move. ■

Chapter 12

Consistency in Verb Tense and Verb Voice

Shifts in Verb Tense

Like almost all English speakers and writers, you use verb tenses quite unconsciously. If you are discussing something that happened in the past, you use the past tense without giving it a second thought (*I ate that entire turkey!*). If you are writing about future events, you very naturally shift to future tense (*I **will eat** that entire turkey!*). Sometimes, however, writers accidentally shift from one tense to another when there is no reason to do so. Such unnecessary shifts occur most commonly between the past and present tenses:

> *past*   *present*
> When Joel <u>saw</u> the lion at the circus yesterday, he <u>sits</u> right in front of its cage
>
>   *present*
> and <u>starts</u> to tease it.

Would you agree that there is no reason for the writer to shift to the present tense in the above example? All three actions occurred in the past, so all three should be written in the past tense. Of course, you *should* shift tenses if the meaning requires such a shift, as in the following example:

> *present*   *future*   *past*
> Alex <u>hopes</u> that he <u>will win</u> tonight's lottery because last weekend he <u>lost</u>
> all of his rent money in Las Vegas.

Past-Tense Verbs Ending in -*d* and -*ed*

Sometimes you might mistakenly write a past-tense verb in its present-tense form by leaving off a -*d* or -*ed* ending. This problem is particularly common for students who do not pronounce those endings when they speak. If such is the case in your writing, you need to look closely at each of your verbs as you proofread your papers. If you are discussing an event that occurred in the past, add -*d* or -*ed* where such endings are needed.

Incorrect

> After the party last night, Mark <u>thank</u> Fiona for giving him a ride home.

Correct

> After the party last night, Mark <u>thanked</u> Fiona for giving him a ride home.

Supposed to, Used to

Two verbs that are often incorrectly written without the *-d* ending are *suppose* and *use* when they are followed by the word *to*. Don't leave the *-d* off the ending just because you don't hear it. (It tends to be combined with the *t* in *to*.)

Incorrect

> Calvin is <u>suppose to</u> be on a diet, but he can't get <u>use to</u> skipping his usual dessert of chocolate chip ice cream.

Correct

> Calvin is <u>supposed to</u> be on a diet, but he can't get <u>used to</u> skipping his usual dessert of chocolate chip ice cream.

Verb Tense When Discussing Someone Else's Writing

Throughout this text, you are asked to respond to what other writers have written. You should use the present tense when you write about someone else's writing—whether it be nonfiction, fiction, or poetry—or when you write about film. Be careful not to inadvertently shift to the past tense.

Incorrect

> In "Why I Won't Buy My Sons Toy Guns," Robert Shaffer <u>claims</u> toys are teachers. He <u>said</u> that toy guns will teach children to solve problems with violence.

Correct

> In "Why I Won't Buy My Sons Toy Guns," Robert Shaffer <u>claims</u> toys are teachers. He <u>says</u> that toy guns will teach children to solve problems with violence.

Exercise 12.1

Revise the following paragraphs to correct any unnecessary shifts in verb tense.

> **1** In "The Thin Grey Line," Marya Mannes says that the difference between right and wrong is becoming blurred. **2** She wrote that today's society was losing its moral fiber. **3** I agreed with many of the points that Mannes makes.
> **4** One point I agree with was that the parents of today's children cross the "thin grey line" many times a day. **5** When I was a child, my

parents use to hide my brother and me on the floor of our Pinto so they would not have to pay for us when we go to drive-in movies. **6** And when I am too old for a Kids' Meal at McDonald's, they would lie and get me one anyway. **7** As I grew older, these things do not seem wrong to me. **8** I thought that as long as I didn't get caught there is nothing wrong.

9 Mannes also wrote, "Your son's friend admitted cheating at exams because 'everybody does it.'" **10** I have to admit that I also have cheat on an exam or two and that many people I know have done the same. **11** In the eleventh grade a student I know manage to get a copy of the exam we were suppose to take the next day. **12** He then proceeds to distribute it to his friends, and no one ever was caught. **13** Did we all learn a lesson? **14** We sure did. **15** We learn how easy it is to cheat.

16 All in all, the morality of the nation was headed in the wrong direction. **17** And if this generation is bad, what will the next generation be like? **18** Mannes's solution was a good one. **19** We use to be a moral nation, and we can be one again if we educate people. **20** We should start with the children before they became corrupt in their thinking. ■

Shifts in Verb Voice

Verb voice refers to the relationship between the subject and the verb of a sentence. If the subject is *performing* ("doing") the action of the verb, the sentence is in the **active** voice. If the subject is *receiving* the action of the verb, the sentence is in the **passive** voice. Note that the subject is the "doer" in the following active-voice sentence:

active voice

$$S \qquad V$$

A red-tailed hawk seized the unsuspecting rabbit.

(The subject—the hawk—*performs* the action.)

Now compare the above active-voice sentence with its passive-voice counterpart:

passive voice

$$S \qquad V$$

The unsuspecting rabbit was seized by a red-tailed hawk.

(The subject—the rabbit—*receives* the action.)

Identifying Verb Voice

To distinguish between active and passive voice, first identify the verb itself, and then ask the following questions:

1. Does the subject perform the action of the verb, or does it receive the action? If the subject performs the action, the sentence is in the active voice; if the subject receives the action, the sentence is in the passive voice.

2. Does the verb consist of a form of *to be* and a past participle? The forms of *to be* are *am, are, is, was, were, be, being,* and *been. Any* verb consisting of one of these verb forms *and* a past participle is in the passive voice. All of the following verbs, therefore, are automatically passive: *has been eaten, is passed, was purchased, might be seen, were stolen.*

Choosing the Active Voice

Most writers prefer the active voice, so they try not to shift to the passive voice unless there is a good reason to do so. One reason writers prefer the active voice is that it requires fewer words than the passive. In the above examples about the hawk and the rabbit, for instance, the active voice requires only seven words while the passive voice requires nine. Two extra words don't seem excessive, do they? But over the course of an entire essay, those needless words begin to add up, creating a sense of looseness and wordiness that can detract from the effectiveness of your writing.

Another reason writers choose active voice is that passive-voice verbs, as the word *passive* implies, lack the forcefulness of active-voice verbs. Because the subject in the passive voice *receives* the action rather than *performs* it, there is a sense that the sentence is not moving forward. In fact, too many passive-voice verbs can make your writing dull and lifeless.

Finally, the passive voice often obscures the real performer of the action, either by placing that performer in a prepositional phrase following the verb or by omitting the performer altogether. Who, for example, is the person who denies the building permit in the following sentence?

> After serious consideration, your request for a building permit has been denied.

Not all verbs must be either active or passive. For example, when a form of *to be* (*am, are, is, was, were, be, being, been*) is the main verb of a sentence, no action is shown at all, so the verb is neither active nor passive. Verbs of this type are called linking verbs. Although these verbs are not passive, you can often improve your writing by replacing them with active-voice verbs.

linking verb

                          S   *V*
Mrs. Mallard's driving <u>is</u> quite reckless.

active voice

                 S   *V*
Mrs. Mallard <u>drives</u> quite recklessly.

Choosing the Passive Voice

If the above discussion has left you with the impression that you should write in the active voice, it has achieved its purpose. But don't be misled—the passive voice does have a place in good writing, particularly in the following situations:

1. Use the passive voice when the performer of an action is unimportant or when the receiver of the action needs to be emphasized.

S
V
<u>All</u> of the buildings <u>had been inspected</u> by noon yesterday.
(Who did the inspecting is not important.)

2. Use passive voice when the performer of the action is unknown.

S V
Last night my <u>car</u> <u>was stolen</u> from the Wal-Mart parking lot.
(Who stole the car is not known.)

3. Use passive voice when the receiver of the action needs to be emphasized.

S V
During the Holocaust, <u>Jewish people</u> <u>were executed</u> by the hundreds of thousands.
(The receiver of the action—Jewish people—is being emphasized.)

Changing the Passive Voice to the Active Voice

Some people write too many sentences in the passive voice merely because they cannot figure out how to change them to the active voice. Use these suggestions to help you revise your passive sentences to active ones:

1. If the performer of the action is an object (usually following the verb), reverse the subject and the object.

S   *O*

passive voice   The CD-ROM drive was purchased by John for $200.

S   *O*

active voice   John purchased the CD-ROM drive for $200.

2. If the performer of the action has been left out of the sentence, write it in as the subject.

S   *V*

passive voice   Every official transcript was destroyed last night.

S   *V*

active voice   Last night's fire destroyed every official transcript.

3. Change the verb.

V

passive voice   Stephen Spielberg was given an Academy Award for directing *Schindler's List*.

V

active voice   Stephen Spielberg received an Academy Award for directing *Schindler's List*.

Exercise 12.2

Rewrite the following sentences so that they use the active voice. When necessary, supply the missing performer of the action. Some of the sentences may already use the active voice.

1. Alice was invited to play croquet by the Queen of Hearts.

2. Several trees were uprooted during the recent storm.

3. Mario had been training for the marathon for six months.

4. Janet was not allowed to watch the movie because her homework was not yet completed.

5. Hundreds of oil workers were flown to Kuwait to help put out oil fires.

6. Airline passengers are routinely checked by security guards to make sure no weapons are being carried on board.

7. Many scenes of American life in the 1950s were painted by Norman Rockwell.

8. Fireworks are considered dangerous by many people and have been outlawed by many cities.

9. The check from her employer had been mailed to Ms. McCormick on Friday.

10. The algebra rules were read over and over until they were finally memorized.

11. The strong wind bent the newly planted birch tree to the ground.

12. Blue skies and warm weather are hoped for by everyone who has been invited to the picnic.

13. Darnell is studying to be a doctor even though he does not know how his tuition will be paid.

14. Herman started to worry when he was told that wasps had been seen flying into his bedroom.

15. A llama and an aardvark were chased from one end of the park to the other by six worried zookeepers. ■

Chapter 13

Subject-Verb Agreement

Subject-verb agreement refers to the need for the form of the verb you have used in a sentence to match the form of its subject. If the subject of your sentence is singular, your verb must be singular. If the subject is plural, your verb must be plural.

You need to pay special attention to subject-verb agreement when you use present-tense verbs. **Most present-tense verbs that have singular subjects end in _s_. Most present-tense verbs that have plural subjects do not end in _s_.** Here are some examples:

Singular	**Plural**
The bird flies.	The birds fly.
He sings.	They sing.
It is.	They are.
The child has.	The children have.
She does.	They do.

Notice that in each case the verb ends in _s_ when the subject is singular. This rule can be confusing because an _s_ at the end of a _noun_ almost always means that the noun is plural, but an _s_ **at the end of a _verb_ almost always means it is singular.**

Problem Areas

Almost all subject-verb agreement errors occur for one of two reasons: Either the writer has identified the wrong word as the subject of the verb or the writer has mistaken a singular subject for a plural one (or vice versa). The following points address these two problems.

1. **Subjects are never part of a prepositional phrase.** Prepositional phrases often occur between the subject and the verb. Do not confuse the object of the prepositional phrase with the subject of the verb.

   S   V

   <u>One</u> of our neighbor's dogs <u>barks</u> every night.

   The subject is _One,_ not _dogs,_ because _dogs_ is part of the prepositional phrase _of our neighbor's dogs._

Here is a list of common prepositions to help you identify prepositional phrases:

about	because of	except	of	toward
across	behind	from	onto	until
after	below	in	over	up
among	beside	in spite of	past	upon
around	between	into	through	with
as	by	like	till	without
at	during	near	to	

2. **The order of the subject and verb is reversed in sentences that begin with** *there* **or** *here* **and in questions.**

       V   *S*
There were several people in the park this morning.

      V   *S*
Here is the person with the keys.

V   *S*
Is the plane on time?

  V   *S*
Was the photo album in the box in the attic?

3. **Only the subject affects the form of the verb.**

     S   *V*
Our least concern is the people next door.

The singular verb form is correct here because the subject is the singular noun *concern*. The plural noun *people* does not affect the form of the verb.

4. **Two subjects joined by** *and* **are plural.**

   S   *S*   *V*
The puppet and the grasshopper were an unusual pair.

 S   *S*   *V*
Steak and eggs sound good to me.

5. **If a subject is modified by** *each* **or** *every,* **it is singular.**

    S   *S*   *V*
Every can and bottle on the beach was picked up.

    S   *S*   *V*
Each driver and bicyclist is eligible to enter the contest.

6. **Indefinite pronouns are usually singular.** See pages 291–292 for a list of indefinite pronouns.

S   V
Each of the contestants is on the stage.

S   V
Everyone in the stadium has a white flag.

7. **A few nouns and indefinite pronouns, such as** *none, some, all, most, more, part,* **and** *half* **(and other fractions), may sometimes be considered plural and sometimes singular, depending on the prepositional phrase that follows them.**

singular

S   V
Some of the food is missing.

plural

S   V
Some of the cars were stolen.

8. **When the subjects are joined by** *either/or, neither/nor, not only/but also,* **or just** *or,* **the verb agrees with the subject closer to it.**

S   S V
Neither Maria **nor** her sisters want to leave the house.

Of course, if you reverse the order of the subjects above, you must change the verb form.

S   S V
Neither her sisters **nor** Maria wants to leave the house.
This rule also applies to questions.

V S S V
Does Maria **or** her sisters want to leave the house?

V S S V
Do her sisters **or** Maria want to leave the house?

Note When you have helping verbs in a sentence, as in the example above, the helping verb—not the main verb—changes form.

9. **Collective nouns usually take the singular form of the verb.** Collective nouns represent groups of people or things, but they are considered singular. Some common collective nouns are *audience, band, class, committee, crowd, family, flock, group, herd, jury, society,* and *team.*

S V
The jury was told to reach its verdict quickly as possible.

S V
My family goes to Yellowstone National Park every summer.

10. **The relative pronouns *that*, *which*, and *who* may be either singular or plural.** When one of these pronouns is the subject of a verb, you will need to know which word it refers to before you decide whether it is singular or plural.

singular

$$\overset{S \quad V}{}$$
I bought the peach that was ripe.

plural

$$\overset{S \quad V}{}$$
I bought the peaches that were ripe.

plural

$$\overset{S \quad V}{}$$
Colleen is one of the students who are taking flying lessons.

singular

$$\overset{S \quad V}{}$$
Colleen is the only one of the students who is taking flying lessons.

11. **A few nouns end in *s* but are considered singular; they take the singular form of the verb.** These nouns include *economics, gymnastics, mathematics, measles, mumps, physics,* and *politics.*

$$\overset{S \quad V}{}$$
International politics is not my favorite field of study.

$$\overset{S \qquad V}{}$$
Mathematics has been difficult for me.

12. **When units of measurement for distance, time, volume, height, weight, money, and so on are used as subjects, they usually take the singular verb form.**

$$\overset{S \qquad\qquad V}{}$$
Two teaspoons of sugar was all that the cake recipe called for.

$$\overset{S \quad V}{}$$
Five dollars is too much to pay for a hot dog.

Exercise 13.1

Circle the subjects and underline the correct verb form (in parentheses) for each one.

1. Someone with too many children (has)(have) been turned away from the theater.
2. (Do)(Does) the guard at the gate or the people waiting in line know whether or not the concert is canceled?
3. His dream of success and his fear of failure always (keep)(keeps) Joe feeling frustrated.
4. The audience attending last night's premiere (was)(were) disgusted by the performance.
5. Even though many people do not think so, measles (is)(are) a serious illness.
6. A sofa with two matching chairs (cost)(costs) $1,000 at Jerome's Furniture.

7. Five hundred miles (is)(are) a long way from home.

8. Here (is)(are) the lawn food and snail bait that you ordered.

9. Every man, woman, and child attending the recent Padres baseball games (has)(have) wondered if things can get much worse.

10. Neither his sisters nor his wife (visit)(visits) Mr. Parker in the rest home very often.

11. One of the children who (live)(lives) on our street has green hair.

12. Politics (seem)(seems) to be all that Mr. Washington ever wants to discuss.

13. A group of anti-lepidopterists (has)(have) recently started to demand equal rights for butterflies.

14. Anyone from the nearby apartment houses along with any relatives (is)(are) allowed to use the recreation room.

15. There (was)(were), according to every report that Salvatore had ever read, only one reason to reduce the tuna fishing fleet. ■

Exercise 13.2

Correct any subject-verb agreement errors in the following sentences. If a sentence is correct, do nothing to it. To check your answers, circle the subjects.

1. Either the telephone book or the encyclopedia have enough weight to press that flower.

2. After last night's concert, everyone who had attended were praising the quality of the orchestra.

3. Every book and magazine in the library has been attacked by bookworms.

4. No matter how hard he studied, mathematics were Albert's worst subject.

5. In the past two weeks, there has been a fistfight and a mugging in the walkway near the cafeteria.

6. Marge, along with her friend Leona, send letters to the editor every week.

7. A herd of buffalo cross the stream behind my house every evening.

8. Does the Del Mar Fair or the Pomona County Fair make the most money?

9. Mr. Gadget is one of the people who applies for a new patent nearly every year.

10. On the roof of the business across the street stands a large wooden chicken and a gigantic ax.

11. Each of the fifteen applicants from the three different cities were presented with a bowl of fruit.

12. My family, together with the people next door, help to clean up the street every month.

13. Elmer's main concern was the flies and bugs that kept invading his house.

14. Everyone who knows the Delgados think that they should have been asked to lead the parade.

15. Fifteen minutes have passed since we received our last telephone solicitation. ■

Chapter 14

Pronoun Agreement and Reference

Pronoun-Antecedent Agreement

Because pronouns stand for or take the place of nouns, it is important that you make clear in your writing which pronouns stand for which nouns. The noun that the pronoun takes the place of is called the **antecedent**. The term **pronoun-antecedent agreement** refers to the idea that a pronoun must match, or "agree with," the noun that it stands for in **person** and **number**.

Person

Person, in describing pronouns, refers to the relationship of the speaker (or writer) to the pronoun. There are three persons: **first person, second person,** and **third person.**

1. **First-person** pronouns refer to the person speaking or writing:

Singular	Plural
I	we
me	us
my, mine	our, ours

2. **Second-person** pronouns refer to the person spoken or written to:

Singular	Plural
you	you
you	you
your, yours	your, yours

3. **Third-person** pronouns refer to the person or thing spoken or written about:

Singular	Plural
he, she, it	they
him, her, it	them
his, her, hers, its	their, theirs

Because nouns are almost always in the third person, pronouns that refer to nouns should also be in the third person. Usually this rule poses no problem, but sometimes writers mistakenly shift from third to second person when they are referring to a noun.

> When <u>a person</u> first enters the Department of Motor Vehicles, <u>you</u> might feel overwhelmed by the crowd of people.

In this sentence, *you* has mistakenly been used to refer to *person*. The mistake occurs because the noun *person* is in the third person, but the pronoun *you* is in the second person. There are two ways to correct the sentence:

1. You can change the second-person pronoun *you* to a third-person pronoun.

    > When <u>a person</u> first enters the Department of Motor Vehicles, <u>he or she</u> might feel overwhelmed by the crowd of people.

2. You can change the noun *person* to the second-person pronoun *you*.

    > When <u>you</u> first enter the Department of Motor Vehicles, <u>you</u> might feel overwhelmed by the crowd of people.

Here is another incorrect sentence.

> Most <u>visitors</u> to the Wild Animal Park will have a good time if <u>you</u> follow the signs and do not stray off the marked path.

One way to correct this sentence is to change *you* to *they* so that it agrees with *visitors*.

> Most <u>visitors</u> to the Wild Animal Park will have a good time if <u>they</u> follow the signs and do not stray off the marked path.

Number

Errors in number are the most common pronoun-antecedent errors. To make pronouns agree with their antecedents in **number,** use singular pronouns to refer to singular nouns and plural pronouns to refer to plural nouns. The following guidelines will help you avoid errors in number.

1. **When you use a pronoun to refer to words joined by *and*, you should use a plural pronoun unless the words are modified by *each* or *every*.**

    <u>Benjamin Franklin</u> and <u>Thomas Edison</u> were both known for <u>their</u> work with electricity.

    Every <u>dog</u> and <u>cat</u> in the kennel had lost <u>its</u> appetite.

2. **Because the following indefinite pronouns are singular, you should use singular pronouns to refer to them.**

anybody	either	neither	one
anyone	everybody	nobody	somebody

| anything | everyone | no one | someone |
| each | everything | nothing | something |

<u>Everything</u> that he said seemed to have <u>its</u> own secret meaning.

<u>Neither</u> of the contestants wanted to trade <u>her</u> prize for an unmarked door.

<u>One</u> of the children was staring sadly at <u>his</u> broken toy.

Note   In spoken English, the plural pronouns *they, them,* and *their* are often used to refer to the antecedents *everyone* or *everybody*. However, in written English the singular pronoun is still more commonly used.

<u>Everybody</u> on the men's hockey team determined to do <u>his</u> best.

3. **You should use singular pronouns to refer to collective nouns.** Some common collective nouns are *audience, band, class, committee, crowd, family, flock, group, herd, jury, society,* and *team*.

The <u>class</u> decided to skip <u>its</u> scheduled break in order to review for the test.

The <u>family</u> next door spent <u>its</u> summer in the Grand Canyon last year.

4. **When antecedents are joined by the following words, you should use a pronoun that agrees with the closer antecedent.**

| either/or | neither/nor | nor |
| or | not only/but also | |

Neither <u>Mr. Snead</u> nor the <u>golfers</u> remembered to bring <u>their</u> golf shoes.

The plural pronoun *their* agrees with the plural noun *golfers* because *golfers* is the closer noun.

Sexist Language

In the past it has been traditional to use masculine pronouns when referring to singular nouns whose gender could be either masculine or feminine. A good example is the sentence *A **driver** should slow down whenever **he** approaches a blind intersection.* Although the noun *driver* could be either masculine or feminine, traditionally only masculine pronouns like *he* or *his* have been used in a case like this one.

Because females make up over 50 percent of the English-speaking population, many of them have been justifiably dissatisfied with this tradition. The problem is that the English language does not contain a singular personal pronoun that can refer to either sex at the same time in the way that the forms of *they* can.

The solutions to this problem can prove awkward. One of the solutions is to use feminine pronouns as freely as masculine ones to refer to singular nouns whose gender could be masculine or feminine. Either of the following sentences using this solution is acceptable.

A driver should slow down whenever <u>she</u> approaches a blind intersection.

A driver should slow down whenever <u>he</u> approaches a blind intersection.

Another solution is to change the *he* to *he or she.* Then the sentence would look like this:

A <u>driver</u> should slow down whenever <u>he or she</u> approaches a blind intersection.

As you can see, this solution does not result in a very graceful sentence. Still another alternative is to use *she/he,* but the result would be about the same as the one above. Sometimes a better solution is to change a singular antecedent to a plural one and use the forms of *they,* which can refer to either gender. Doing so would result in a sentence like this:

<u>Drivers</u> should slow down whenever <u>they</u> approach a blind intersection.

This sentence is less awkward and just as fair. Finally, in some situations, the masculine pronoun alone will be appropriate, and in others the feminine pronoun alone will be. Here are two such sentences:

<u>Each</u> of the football players threw <u>his</u> helmet into the air after the victory.

(The football team is all male.)

One member of the Arabian swim team passed <u>her</u> opponent ten yards before the finish line.

(The swim team is all female.)

Whatever your solutions to this problem, it is important that you be logical and correct in your pronoun-antecedent agreement in addition to being fair.

Exercise 14.1

Choose the pronoun (in parentheses) that agrees with the antecedent. When you choose a pronoun, you may also need to change the verb.

1. If a motorcyclist rides without a helmet in California, (you)(he or she)(they) will be given a ticket.
2. Everybody who attended the Fourth of July party brought (their)(his or her) own food.
3. When a person is first learning to work with a computer, (you)(they)(he or she) might feel a little intimidated.
4. While the jury delivered (their)(its) verdict, the defendant stood and stared at the floor.
5. Neither Oliver nor Stanley visited (his)(their) mother on Mother's Day.
6. The zookeeper was stunned when he realized that not only an orangutan but also three monkeys had managed to escape from (its)(their) enclosure.

7. Last year the most successful company in the county refused to give (its)(their) employees a raise.

8. Although Esther likes to visit Lake Arrowhead, the drive up to the lake tends to make (you)(her) nervous.

9. Someone keeps calling me on the phone, but (she)(they) won't tell me (her)(their) name.

10. A noisy patron of that library will sometimes be asked to lower (their)(his or her) voice.

11. Each of the members of Footwear Anonymous vowed to throw all of (their)(his or her) shoes into the garbage.

12. After the humiliating defeat, the team boarded (their)(its) bus and headed for home.

13. Skinner could tell that either the pigeon or the mouse would soon learn to signal for (its)(their) food.

14. Leona grabbed her scuba gear and headed for the beach even though she knew that (you)(she) shouldn't dive without a partner.

15. Andrea, who moved here from Vermont, and Charlie, who used to live in Australia, were distressed when (they)(he or she) first saw all the smog. ■

Unclear Pronoun Reference

Sometimes, even though a pronoun appears to agree with an antecedent, it is not clear exactly which noun in the sentence is the antecedent. And sometimes a writer will use a pronoun that does not clearly refer to any antecedent at all. The following two points will help you to use pronouns correctly.

1. **A pronoun should refer to a specific antecedent.**

   After <u>James</u> gave his brother the present, <u>he</u> began to cry.

In this sentence, *he* could refer to James or his brother. To correct this problem, you can eliminate the unclear pronoun.

   After <u>James</u> gave <u>his brother</u> the present, <u>his brother</u> began to cry.

Or you can revise the sentence so the pronoun refers to one specific antecedent.

   <u>James</u> began to cry after <u>he</u> gave his brother the present.

2. **Pronouns should not refer to implied or unstated antecedents. Be especially careful with the pronouns *this*, *that*, *which*, and *it*.**

   The game was canceled even though we had driven five hundred miles to see it; <u>this</u> was unfair.

   In Paul Goodman's "A Proposal to Abolish Grading," <u>it</u> says that grades do more harm than good.

In the first example, there is no antecedent to which *this* can refer. In the second example, *it* seems to refer to something inside the article, but there is no antecedent given. The following sentences clarify the pronoun references.

> The game was canceled even though we had driven five hundred miles to see it; <u>canceling the game after we had driven so far</u> was unfair.

> In "A Proposal to Abolish Grading," <u>Paul Goodman says</u> that grades do more harm than good.

Sometimes a pronoun refers to a noun that is only implied in the first part of the sentence.

> Mr. Brouillard is a fisherman, <u>which</u> he does every weekend.

In this sentence, the *which* apparently refers to *fishing,* which is implied in the noun *fisherman;* however, there is no specific noun for the pronoun *which* to refer to. The faulty pronoun reference can be cleared up in several ways.

> Mr. Brouillard is a fisherman, <u>and he goes fishing</u> every weekend.

> Mr. Brouillard is a fisherman <u>who fishes</u> every weekend.

Exercise 14.2

Correct all errors in pronoun-antecedent agreement as well as in pronoun reference in the following sentences. If a sentence is correct, do nothing to it.

1. Juan had planned to visit his uncle last weekend, but he was not feeling well.
2. Mr. Baurmeister missed his bus three days in a row, which frustrated him.
3. When someone is blindfolded and turned in a circle, you can easily lose your sense of direction.
4. That flock of homing pigeons seems to have lost their sense of direction.
5. Anybody who responds to this questionnaire will receive a free trip to the country of her choice.
6. Rats were recently found in a local restaurant, so the health department closed it down. This worried many people.
7. The rock group at last night's concert must know that their performance was absolutely terrible.
8. If a person is rude to retail clerks, you shouldn't be surprised if they are rude back.
9. In George Will's "Printed Noise," it says that cute restaurant names have been replaced with cute names for menu items.
10. Just as the police officer was about to write my mother a ticket for speeding, she fainted.
11. Whenever one of Jethro's sisters tastes his homemade beer, they shudder from head to toe.

12. Will you please take either the grapes on the counter or the watermelon in the refrigerator and put it into the picnic basket?

13. On the news it said that last night's fire was started by an arsonist.

14. Whenever a driver hears a siren, you should pull to the side of the road until the emergency vehicle has passed.

15. Estella knew that she had to get out of the freezing snow, which was making her feet turn numb. ■

Chapter 15

Pronoun Case

Pronouns, like verbs, can appear in a variety of forms, depending on how they function in a sentence. For example, the pronoun that refers to the speaker in a sentence may be written as *I, me, my,* or *mine.* These different spellings are the result of what is called **pronoun case.**

The three pronoun cases for English are the **subjective,** the **objective,** and the **possessive.**

Subjective Case

Singular	*Plural*
I	we
you	you
he, she, it	they
who	who

Objective Case

Singular	*Plural*
me	us
you	you
him, her, it	them
whom	whom

Possessive Case

Singular	*Plural*
my, mine	our, ours
your, yours	your, yours
his, her, hers, its	their, theirs
whose	whose

Subjective Pronouns

The subjective pronouns are *I, we, you, he, she, it, they,* and *who.* They are used in two situations:

1. **Subjective pronouns are used as subjects of sentences.**

   S
   I will take the test next week.

     S
   They have stolen my car.

2. **Subjective pronouns are used when they follow linking verbs.** Because the linking verb *identifies* the pronoun with the subject, the pronoun must be in the same case as the subject.

   S
   It was he who found the missing link.

   (The subjective pronoun *he* is identified with the subject *it* by the linking verb was.)

     S
   That was I you heard speaking on the phone.

   S
   It was they who won the final game of the series.

Objective Pronouns

The **objective pronouns** are *me, us, you, him, her, it, them,* and *whom.* They are used in three situations:

1. **Objective pronouns are used as objects of prepositions.**

   Oliver stared at the birthday card that Stanley had given to him.

   The disagreement between Shayla and me was not really very serious.

2. **Objective pronouns are used as direct objects of action verbs.** The noun or pronoun that receives the action of the action verb is called the **direct object.** For example, in the sentence *Tuan visited Serena yesterday,* the verb is *visited,* an action verb. The direct object of *visited* is *Serena* because *Serena* receives the action of the verb *visited.* If you substitute a pronoun for *Serena,* it must be the objective pronoun *her: Tuan visited **her** yesterday.*

   Tyrone insulted her at the party last night.

   After we ate dinner, Juanita took me to the mall.

   Mr. Kong picked up all of the banana peels and threw them out the window.

3. **Objective pronouns are used as indirect objects.** The **indirect object** indicates **to whom or for whom (or to what or for what) an action is directed,** but the prepositions *to* and *for* are left out.

prepositional phrase	He gave the flowers <u>to her</u>.
indirect object	He gave <u>her</u> the flowers.

In the first sentence, *her* is the object of the preposition *to*. In the second sentence, the *to* is omitted and the pronoun is moved, making *her* the indirect object. In both sentences, the direct object is *flowers*. Here are other examples:

She had already told <u>him</u> the secret password.

My sister showed <u>them</u> a baseball that had been autographed by Babe Ruth.

Possessive Pronouns

The **possessive pronouns** are *my, mine, our, ours, your, yours, his, her, hers, its, their, theirs,* and *whose*. They are used in two situations:

1. **Possessive pronouns are used as adjectives to indicate possession.**

   Mrs. Cleaver could not believe what <u>her</u> ears had just heard.

   Lumpy and Eddie looked sheepishly at <u>their</u> feet.

   Wally looked at the car and wondered who had stolen <u>its</u> tires.

   Note The contraction *it's* means "it is." The word *its* is the only possessive form for *it*. (In fact, you do not use apostrophes with any of the possessive pronouns.)

2. **Some possessive pronouns indicate possession without being used as adjectives.** In this case, they may be used as subjects or objects.

   I used my father's watch because <u>mine</u> was broken.
   (Here the possessive pronoun *mine* is the subject of its clause.)

   Maria's room is neat, but <u>yours</u> is a mess.
   (In this example, *yours* is the subject of its clause.)

   Arlo rented a car because he had sold <u>his</u>.
   (Here the possessive pronoun *his* is a direct object.)

Common Sources of Errors in Pronoun Case

Compound Constructions

Compound subjects and objects often cause problems when they include pronouns. If your sentence includes a compound construction, be sure you use the correct pronoun case.

compound subject	<u>Melissa and she</u> own a fifty-acre ranch.
compound after linking verb	That was <u>Leslie and I</u> whom you spoke to last night.
compound object of a preposition	After the fire, the police took statements from <u>my brother and me</u>.
compound direct object	Julio saw <u>Mark and him</u> at the racetrack.
compound indirect object	She gave <u>him and me</u> a reward when we found her lost dog.

In most cases, you can use a simple test to check whether you have chosen the right pronoun case when you have a compound construction. Simply remove one of the subjects or objects so that only one pronoun is left. For example, is this sentence correct? *Our host gave **Erin and I** a drink.* Test it by dropping **Erin and**. *Our host gave **I** a drink.* Now you can see that the *I* should be *me* because it is an object (an indirect object). The correct sentence should read: *Our host gave **Erin and me** a drink.*

Who and Whom

When to use *who* or *whom* is a mystery to many writers, but you should have no problem with these pronouns if you remember two simple rules:

1. Use the subjective pronoun *who* or *whoever* if it is used as the subject of a verb.

2. Use the objective pronoun *whom* or *whomever* if it is not used as the subject of a verb.

    While standing in line at the bus depot, I saw someone <u>who</u> looked like my long-lost brother.

    (*Who* is the subject of *looked*.)

    The position will be given to the person <u>whom</u> the committee finds most qualified.

    (*Whom* is not the subject of a verb.)

    This wallet should be returned to <u>whoever</u> lost it.

    (*Whoever* is the subject of *lost*.)

Comparisons

When a pronoun is used in a comparison, you often need to supply the implied words in order to know what pronoun case to use. For example, in the sentence *My brother cannot skate as well as I*, the implied words are the verb *can skate*: *My brother cannot skate as well as I [can skate.]*

When we visited the petting zoo, the animals seemed to like my brother more than <u>me</u>.

You can tell that *me* is the correct case in this sentence when you supply the implied words:

When we visited the petting zoo, the animals seemed to like my brother more than [they liked] <u>me</u>.

Appositives

An appositive is a word group containing a noun or pronoun that renames another noun or pronoun. When the appositive contains a **pronoun** that does the renaming, be sure that the pronoun is in the same case as the word it renames. (For more discussion of appositives, see pages 160–164.)

Three employees—Miguel, Pierre, and <u>I</u>—were fired for insubordination.

Here *I* is in the subjective case because the appositive *Miguel, Pierre, and I* renames the word *employees*, the subject of the sentence.

This report is the responsibility of only two people, Mark and <u>her</u>.

Here *her* is in the objective case because the appositive *Mark and her* renames *people*, the object of the preposition *of*.

Exercise 15.1

In each sentence, underline the correct pronoun form (in parentheses).

1. Just between you and (I)(me), do you really think we should eat this entire gallon of ice cream?
2. A small striped kitten is drinking (its)(it's) milk from a green bowl.
3. The tram took Bill and (he)(him) on a ride through Universal Studios.
4. It was (she)(her) (who)(whom) your cousin met at the party last night.
5. The Leonards next door bought many more fireworks for the Fourth of July than (we)(us).
6. Ask Amy and (she)(her) to water our lawn while we are on vacation.
7. The hunters (who)(whom) had exceeded their limit drove slowly down the dark road.
8. Do Tiffany and (her)(she) have any extra money with them?
9. Two skiers, Alberto and (he)(him), have a chance to win the gold medal.
10. Was it (they)(them) (who)(whom) we saw coming out of the House of Mirrors?
11. The prize goes to (whoever)(whomever) can eat this 5-gallon jar of pickles in the least amount of time.

12. Sam wondered why his parents would not buy a new jet ski for his sister and (he)(him).

13. The instructor knew that three students—Marcia, Fred, and (I)(me)—had not studied for the test.

14. Horace complained that the judges gave the other participants more attention than (he)(him).

15. (It's)(Its) loud, grinding sound frightened Steve and (she)(her). ■

Exercise 15.2

Correct any errors in pronoun case in the following sentences. Some sentences may not contain errors.

1. Mr. Livingston loves to visit Africa, but his sister is much less fond of that country than him.

2. Where have Orville and he put the parachute?

3. Henrietta was sure that it was George who she saw on the Ferris wheel.

4. On the camping trip, our guide told Armando and I a terrifying story.

5. Karen was irritated when the guard gave passes to only two people, Jodi and she.

6. Its too bad that your dog hurt it's neck when its chain became caught in the tractor.

7. The giraffe stared at Yolie and I as we crept into its enclosure.

8. Until he insulted our daughter, Oscar and we have always been good friends.

9. Yvonne and Eunice, whom were passengers on the *Titanic*, feel uncomfortable whenever they take a bath.

10. Although Frank and Joe spoke to all of the neighbors, the Bobbsey twins still sold more tickets than them.

11. Between Ramona and he stood a huge marble column covered with mysterious inscriptions.

12. Show the guest of honor and them to the table.

13. Both Mary and Jorge were seriously ill, but the doctor gave Mary more medication than him.

14. The flight attendant who Salvatore kept harassing finally dumped a cup of coffee on his lap.

15. To the winners of the marathon, Hal and him, the judges gave blister ointment and bandages. ■

Chapter 16

Misplaced and Dangling Modifiers

Misplaced Modifiers

Misplaced modifiers are exactly what their name says they are—modifiers that have been "misplaced" within a sentence. But how is a modifier "misplaced"? The answer is simple. If you remember that a modifier is nearly always placed just before or just after the word it modifies, then a misplaced modifier must be one that has been mistakenly placed so that it causes a reader to be confused about what it modifies. Consider the following sentence, for example:

A police officer told us <u>slowly</u> to raise our hands.

Does the modifier *slowly* state how the officer told us, or does it state how we were supposed to raise our hands? Changing the placement of the modifier will clarify the meaning.

A police officer <u>slowly</u> told us to raise our hands.

(Here the word modifies the verb *told*.)

A police officer told us to raise our hands <u>slowly</u>.

(Here the word modifies the infinitive *to raise*.)

Misplaced Words

Any modifier can be misplaced, but one particular group of modifiers causes quite a bit of trouble for many people. These words are *only, almost, just, merely,* and *nearly.* Consider, for example, the following sentences:

By buying her new waterbed on sale, Maureen <u>almost</u> saved $100.

By buying her new waterbed on sale, Maureen saved <u>almost</u> $100.

As you can see, these sentences actually make two different statements. In the first sentence, *almost* modifies *saved.* If you *almost* saved something, you did *not* save it. In the second sentence, *almost* modifies *$100.* If you saved *almost* $100, you saved $85, $90, $95, or some other amount close to $100.

Which statement does the writer want to make—that Maureen did *not* save any money or that she *did* save an amount close to $100? Because the point was that she bought her waterbed on sale, the second sentence makes more sense.

To avoid confusion, be sure that you place all of your modifiers carefully.

Incorrect

Her coach told her <u>often</u> to work out with weights.

Correct

Her coach <u>often</u> told her to work out with weights.

Incorrect

Kara <u>nearly</u> ate a gallon of ice cream yesterday.

Correct

Kara ate <u>nearly</u> a gallon of ice cream yesterday.

Misplaced Phrases and Clauses

Phrases and clauses are as easily misplaced as individual words. Generally, phrases and clauses should appear immediately before or after the words they modify. Notice how misplaced phrases and clauses confuse the meaning of the following sentences.

A bird flew over the house <u>with blue wings</u>.

The irritated secretary slapped at the fly <u>typing the report</u>.

They gave the food to the dog <u>left over from dinner</u>.

Lucia smashed the car into a telephone pole <u>that she had borrowed from her sister.</u>

Obviously, misplaced phrases and clauses can cause rather confusing (and sometimes even humorous) situations. However, when such clauses are placed close to the words they modify, their meaning is clear.

A bird <u>with blue wings</u> flew over the house.

The irritated secretary <u>typing the report</u> slapped at the fly.

<u>Typing the report</u>, the irritated secretary slapped at the fly.

They gave the food <u>left over from dinner</u> to the dog.

Lucia smashed the car <u>that she had borrowed from her sister</u> into a telephone pole.

Whether the modifier appears before or after the word it modifies, the point is that you should place a modifier so that it clearly refers to a specific word in the sentence.

Dangling Modifiers

A **dangling modifier** is usually an introductory phrase (usually a verbal phrase) that lacks an appropriate subject to modify. Since these modifiers usually represent some sort of action, they need a **doer** or **agent** of the action represented.

For example, in the following sentence, the introductory phrase "dangles" because it is not followed by a subject that could be the "doer" of the action represented by the phrase.

> Singing at the top of his voice, the song was irritating everybody at the party.

The phrase *Singing at the top of his voice* should be followed by a subject that could logically perform the action of the phrase. Instead, it is followed by the subject *song*. Was the song *singing*? Probably not. Therefore, the modifying phrase "dangles" because it has no subject to which it can logically refer. Here are some more sentences with dangling modifiers.

> Completely satisfied, the painting was admired.
>
> (Was the *painting* satisfied?)

> After reviewing all of the facts, a decision was reached.
>
> (Did the *decision* review the facts?)

> To impress the judges, Cecil's mustache was waxed.
>
> (Did the *mustache* want to impress the judges?)

As you can see, you should check for dangling modifiers when you use introductory phrases.

Correcting Dangling Modifiers

You can correct a dangling modifier in one of two ways:

1. **Rewrite the sentence so that its subject can be logically modified by the introductory modifier.**

   > Completely satisfied, Vincent admired the painting.
   >
   > (*Vincent* was completely satisfied.)

   > After reviewing all of the facts, I reached a decision.
   >
   > (*I* reviewed all of the facts.)

   > To impress the judges, Cecil waxed his mustache.
   >
   > (*Cecil* wanted to impress the judges.)

2. **Change the introductory phrase to a clause.**

   > When Vincent was completely satisfied, he admired the painting.
   >
   > After I reviewed all of the facts, I reached a decision.
   >
   > Because Cecil wanted to impress the judges, he waxed his mustache.

Note Do not correct a dangling modifier by moving it to the end of the sentence. In either case, it will still "dangle" because it lacks a "**doer,**" or **agent,** that could perform the action of the modifier.

Incorrect

> After missing three meetings, the request was denied.
> (There is no "doer" for *missing*.)

Still Incorrect

> The request was denied after missing three meetings.
> (There is no "doer" for *missing*.)

Still Incorrect

> After missing three meetings, Alfredo's request was denied.
> (Adding the possessive form Alfredo's does not add a "doer" of the action.)

Correct

> After Alfredo had missed three meetings, his request was denied.
> (Here the "doer" of the action is clear.)

Correct

> After missing three meetings, Alfredo was told that his request was denied.
> (Here *Alfredo* is clearly the person who missed the meetings.)

Exercise 16.1

Identify and correct any misplaced or dangling modifiers in the following sentences. Some of the sentences may be correct.

1. Waiting impatiently in the car, the party had already started.
2. The painting was found in a pawnshop that had been stolen from the museum.
3. Amber only decided to study after she had received poor grades on her first two tests.
4. Whistling under her breath, Julissa walked her dogs down the street and into the park.
5. Disappointed by his poor performance, Eli's eyes stared at the ground.
6. The dog groomer put the collie on the table with the shaggy tail and began to clip its fur.
7. After almost eating three strawberry pies, Oscar felt a bit woozy.
8. Slowly sinking toward the horizon, Bonnie and Clyde held hands and admired the sunset.
9. Butch Cassidy pulled out his pistol and shot at a coyote riding his favorite horse.
10. After robbing dozens of trains, Jesse James's luck finally ran out.
11. Sara Lee finally decided to serve the dessert to her guests that she had been keeping in the refrigerator.

12. The doctor performing the autopsy carefully recorded her findings.
13. Stepping into the living room, the television blared at me.
14. Herman will only eat vegetables if they are covered in cheese sauce.
15. While camping in the desert, a snake crawled next to my sister with a triangular head. ■

Chapter 17

Comma Usage

The comma is probably more troublesome to writers than any other punctuation mark. Long ago commas were used to tell readers where to put in a slight pause. Although the placement of the comma does affect the rhythm of a sentence, today it also conveys many more messages than when to pause. Comma use can be broken down into four general rules:

1. **Use commas before coordinating conjunctions that join main clauses.**
2. **Use commas between elements in a series.**
3. **Use commas after introductory elements.**
4. **Use commas before and after interrupting elements.**

Commas Before Coordinating Conjunctions That Join Main Clauses

1. **Place a comma before a coordinating conjunction that joins two main clauses.**

   Richard Pryor is a hilarious comedian, **and** Robin Williams is also great in his own unique way.

   Hercules had to shovel a huge amount of horse manure, **or** he would never complete his task.

2. **Do not put a comma before a conjunction that joins other parts of a sentence, such as two words, two phrases, or two subordinate clauses.**

   Every morning Charlie shaves with his favorite cleaver **and** then goes down to breakfast with his family.

   No comma is needed before *and* because it does not join two main clauses. It joins the verbs *shaves* and *goes*.

   You can find good coffee **and** conversation at Kafana Coffee House **or** at Spill the Beans.

   No comma is required before *and* because it joins the nouns *coffee* and *conversation*.
   No comma is required before *or* because it just joins the names of the coffee shops.

Commas with Elements in a Series

1. **Separate with commas three or more elements (words, phrases, clauses) listed in a series.** When the last two elements are joined by a coordinating conjunction, a comma before the conjunction is optional.

Words

The film *The Piano* was **intriguing, puzzling, and controversial.**

Phrases

Omar enjoyed **cooking okra and Spam for his friends, competing in the Spam cooking contest at the fair, and betting on horses with strange names at the racetrack.**

Clauses

While shopping at the mall, **Quinlan bought pants that were much too big, his brother bought him a hat that he could wear backwards, and his girlfriend bought some Doc Marten black boots.**

2. **Separate with commas two or more adjectives used to modify the same noun if you can put *and* between the adjectives without changing the meaning or if you can easily reverse the order of the adjectives.**

The bear waded into the **shallow, swift** river after the salmon.

The **witty, gregarious** comedian kept us laughing for hours with her stories.

Note that you could use *and* between the adjectives. (The river is *shallow* and *swift;* the comedian is *witty* and *gregarious*.) You could also reverse the adjectives (the *swift, shallow* river or the *gregarious, witty* comedian).

3. **On the other hand, no commas are necessary if the adjectives cannot be joined by *and* or are not easily reversed.**

The computer technician wore **white cotton** gloves as she worked.

Notice how awkward the sentence would sound if you placed *and* between the adjectives (the *white and cotton* gloves) or if you reversed them (the *cotton white* gloves).

Commas with Introductory Elements

1. **Use a comma after introductory words and phrases.**

Introductory Words

next	third	similarly	indeed
first	nevertheless	moreover	yes
second	therefore	however	no

Introductory Phrases

on the other hand	for example	in addition
in a similar manner	for instance	as a result
in other words	in fact	

Next, Persephone made the mistake of eating a pomegranate.

In addition, Charles purchased a remote electronic noise device to embarrass his colleagues.

2. **Use a comma after introductory prepositional phrases of five words or more.** However, you may need to use a comma after a shorter introductory prepositional phrase if not doing so would cause confusion.

   Before the famous main attraction, a very good harmonica band entertained the audience.

   In the film, actors kept changing into androids.

   Without the comma, this sentence might be read as *in the film actors.*

3. **Use a comma after all introductory infinitive and participial phrases.**

infinitive phrase

To eat a hot dog, Ambrose had to forget his diet.

present participial phrase

Running in the marathon, Sam finally achieved his goal.

past participial phrase

Congregated in the student union, the students planned their protest.

   (See pages 121–123 for a further discussion of infinitive and participial phrases.)

4. **Use a comma after a subordinate clause that precedes a main clause.**

   Because Ulysses was bored, he wanted to go fishing again.

   Although I am an English major, I sometimes say "Ain't."

   (See page 95 for a further discussion of punctuating subordinate clauses.)

Commas with Interrupting Elements

Sometimes certain words, phrases, or clauses will interrupt the flow of thought in a sentence to add emphasis or additional information. These **interrupting elements** are enclosed by commas.

1. **Use commas to set off parenthetical expressions.** Common parenthetical expressions are *however, indeed, consequently, as a result, moreover, of course, for example, for instance, that is, in fact, after all, I think,* and *therefore.*

   A new baseball glove was, **after all,** a luxury.

   Her old one, **therefore,** would have to do for another season.

Note Whenever a parenthetical expression introduces a second main clause after a semicolon, the semicolon takes the place of the comma in front of it.

Colin was looking forward to his vacation; **moreover,** he was eager to visit his family in England.

2. **Use commas to set off nonrestrictive elements.** **Nonrestrictive** elements are modifying words, phrases, or clauses that are *not* necessary to identify the words they modify. On the other hand, **restrictive** elements are those that *are* necessary to identify the words they modify. Restrictive elements are not set off with commas. Adjective subordinate clauses, participial phrases, and appositives require that you decide whether they are nonrestrictive or restrictive.

Adjective subordinate clauses begin with one of the relative pronouns: *who, whom, whose, which, that,* and sometimes *when* or *where.* They follow the nouns or pronouns that they modify. An adjective clause is **nonrestrictive** when it *is not necessary to identify the word it modifies.* It is enclosed in commas.

nonrestrictive

Dizzy Gillespie, **who helped to develop the form of jazz known as bebop,** played an unusual trumpet.

Because Dizzy Gillespie is named, the adjective clause *who helped to develop the form of jazz known as bebop* is nonrestrictive. It is not needed to identify Dizzy Gillespie.

restrictive

One of the people **who helped to develop the form of jazz known as bebop** was Dizzy Gillespie.

Because *who helped to develop the form of jazz* is needed to identify the "people" you are referring to, it is restrictive and is not set off with commas.

Here is another example of a nonrestrictive clause:

nonrestrictive

My youngest sister, **who is a paleontologist,** showed me her collection of skulls.

Because a person can have only one youngest sister, the adjective clause *is not needed to identify her,* making it nonrestrictive.

(See page 95 for a further discussion of punctuating adjective clauses.)

Participial phrases that *do not contain information necessary to identify the word they modify* are nonrestrictive and are therefore set off by commas. Restrictive participial phrases do not require commas.

nonrestrictive

Van Gogh, **seeking something to paint,** looked up into the night sky.

Because Van Gogh is named, the participial phrase *seeking something to paint* is nonrestrictive. It is not needed to identify Van Gogh.

restrictive

The man **painting in the middle of the night** called the work *Starry Night.*

Because the man is not named, the participial phrase *painting in the middle of the night* is restrictive.

(See pages 121–123 for a further discussion of participial phrases.)

An **appositive** is a noun or pronoun, along with any modifiers, that **renames** another noun or pronoun. The appositive almost always follows the word it refers to, and it is usually set off by commas.

> The computer, **an extremely useful tool,** has advanced a long way in just a few years.
>
> (The noun *tool* renames the noun *computer.*)

> On the street, the Yugo, **the one with the rusty doors,** is an eyesore.
>
> (The pronoun *one* renames the noun *Yugo.*)

(See pages 160–163 for a further discussion of appositives.)

3. **Use commas to set off words of direct address.** If a writer addresses someone directly in a sentence, the words that stand for that person or persons are set off by commas. If the words in direct address begin a sentence, they are followed by a comma. If they end a sentence, they are preceded by a comma.

> What if, **Charlie,** you were to hurt someone with one of your weapons?
>
> **Brent,** you are hogging the ball.
>
> I am sorry if I hurt your feelings, **Aaron.**

4. **Use commas to set off dates and addresses.** If your sentence contains two or more elements of a date or address, use commas to set off these elements. The following sentences contain two or more elements:

> We went to Magic Mountain on **Thursday, November 18, 1993,** because children were admitted free that day.
>
> Concepcion had lived at **4590 Portello Street, San Francisco, California,** for twelve years.
>
> In 1992 she moved to **1754 Pacific Court, Vista, California 92083,** to be near her mother.

Note   The state is not separated from the zip code by a comma.

Exercise 17.1

Add commas to the following sentences where necessary.

1. Even though she had such a hard time she is greatly admired as a person and artist.
2. I have always enjoyed driving up the coast of California so we will leave for Big Sur on Saturday.
3. Alberto opened his first restaurant in San Diego in 1987 with only $300.

4. Chico in fact had never even heard of okra.

5. Tomorrow Oedipus intends to go to the foot doctor talk to the Sphinx eat lunch with his wife and ponder his fate.

6. The salesperson's considerate kind attention impressed Mr. Gutierrez.

7. The melodious soothing sound of the flute helped Favio to relax.

8. Homer liked the collard greens yet avoided the beets.

9. Craig's mother who doubted he could swim very well asked him to be careful.

10. Sunday June 4 1994 was an important day in Jose's life.

11. Billie Holiday who is one of the greatest jazz singers lived a hard life.

12. King Lear a stupid old man finally saw the errors that he had committed.

13. Suzanne called Brent packed her belongings said her goodbyes and moved to her new place.

14. The man who corrupted Hadleyburg just disappeared.

15. Carlos did not want to go to Disneyland nor did he want to go fishing.

16. Send the feathers and wax to 8965 Maze Way Minotaur Ohio 09999 and make it quick Otto.

17. Crying for help the people in the first raft went over the falls.

18. To force the owners of factories to listen to their demands they threw shoes into the machinery.

19. Friar Laurence did you say that Juliet was just sleeping?

20. Beginning on July 1 1863 the Civil War battle that took place at Gettysburg Pennsylvania was probably the most decisive battle of the war. ■

Exercise 17.2

Add commas to the following sentences where necessary.

1. Yes Icarus flew like a bird but he lived to regret it.

2. Remember Carlos to bring a flashlight a compass a sleeping bag and some matches.

3. Ken's bicycle had a flat near Taos New Mexico so he camped there overnight.

4. Because it had been almost a year Bruce had to perform one of his most feared tasks a trip to the dentist.

5. On July 9 1898 Torvald refused to do the dishes or change the baby's diapers.

6. Nora enraged by his behavior told him how she felt; moreover she packed her bags and left.

7. Torvald a notoriously insensitive man did not understand her feelings.

8. The rugged dependable DC-3 passenger plane served in World War II and it is still in service all over the world.

9. Putting her finger to her lips Olga pointed to their mother who was placing presents under the tree.

10. In the middle of a serious speech on poverty the senator suddenly recited a taste-less poem a bawdy limerick.

11. Of course Scylla liked eating at Greek restaurants but she liked attacking the various ships that came by more.

12. Grabbing his wallet and sword Achilles headed for Troy New York to join his friends.

13. When he arrived they had already started building a large wooden horse.

14. Joy feeling quite contented just sat and watched all of the birds at her bird feeders.

15. New Orleans for instance is my favorite city because of the music the food the coffee and the wide variety of people who like to have fun.

16. June 24 1981 was a special day for Michelle for on that day she saw sunshine clouds and sky for the first time.

17. Soaked by the rain the cat ran under the small green table outside the resort hotel in Naples Italy and curled up.

18. Josefina completely exasperated by her car's performance painted the word lemon all over it in bright yellow paint.

19. Dr. Nguyen teaches her psychology class in unique ways; for instance she has her students act out parts of the plays *Hamlet* and *Oedipus Rex* to illustrate the Oedipus complex and manic depression.

20. In fact Katie included most of the characters from *Alice in Wonderland* in her "Alice" paintings which are now being shown at the Museum of Modern Art. ■

Chapter 18

Semicolons and Colons

The Semicolon

1. **A semicolon is used to join two main clauses that are not joined by a comma and a coordinating conjunction.** Sometimes a conjunctive adverb follows the semicolon. (See page 63 for a list of conjunctive adverbs.)

   The generals checked Hitler's horoscope; it told them when to attack.

   Nancy wanted to check her horoscope; however, Ron advised against it.

2. **A semicolon can be used to join elements in a series when the elements require further internal punctuation.**

   By the time Guillermo reached home, he had worked for eighteen hours, which tired him out; he had had a car accident, which depressed him; he had drunk too much coffee, which made him jittery; and he had yelled at his partner, which made him remorseful.

3. **Do not use a semicolon to separate two phrases or two subordinate clauses.**

   Incorrect

   Sonia is going to Little Vietnam because she likes the spring rolls; and because she likes the atmosphere.

   Correct

   Sonia is going to Little Vietnam because she likes the spring rolls and because she likes the atmosphere.

   (See pages 63–64 for further discussion of semicolon usage.)

The Colon

1. **A colon is used to join two main clauses when the second clause is an example, an illustration, or a restatement of the first clause.**

   The party had been a great success: everyone had had fun and had gotten safely home.

This incident is the same as all of the others: Wolfgang never agrees with any of our ideas.

2. **A colon is used when a complete sentence introduces an example, a quotation, a series, or a list.**

The magazine covered a number of subjects related to biking: racing bicycles, touring bicycles, mountain bicycles, and safety equipment.

In "The Cautious and Obedient Life," Susan Walton made the following statement: "Some people are born to follow instructions."

The list on the refrigerator included the following requests: clean the kitchen, wash the car, make reservations at Jake's, and take a shower.

3. **A colon is generally not used after a verb.**

Incorrect

My favorite foods are: red beans and rice, catfish, and pasta carbonara.

Correct

My favorite foods are red beans and rice, catfish, and pasta carbonara.

Exercise 18.1

Add semicolons or colons where necessary. (Some commas may need to be replaced with semicolons or colons.)

1. Form a line then walk to the cafeteria.
2. Describe one of the following characters Hamlet, Captain Ahab, Emma, Roseanne, Joan of Arc, Holden Caulfield, or Iago.
3. The elves enjoyed the shade of the mushroom, however, they lamented the lack of dew.
4. Here is the equipment that I will need a laptop computer, a printer, paper, envelopes and stamps.
5. Raul was unable to solve the puzzle therefore, he sent for a book of hints.
6. You take the high road, I will take the low road.
7. Mabel desperately wanted to visit her favorite aunt, who lived in Denver, Colorado, to spend some days gambling in Deadwood, South Dakota, and to tour Graceland, where Elvis had lived.
8. The ingredients are pink beans, ham hocks, hominy, and okra.
9. The dog whined because of the scratch on his nose meanwhile, the cat sauntered away.
10. In "Why I Won't Buy My Sons Toy Guns," Robert Shaffer makes an interesting point "Any toy is a teacher."
11. The man from Laredo, on the other hand, was not wearing a cowboy hat.

12. Bill could not believe his good fortune he had actually found a signed first edition of *The Scarlet Letter.*

13. We had spent a long day at the Del Mar Fair it was time to go home.

14. Mark Twain once said, "The lack of money is the root of all evil."

15. Last summer we visited my cousin Alice, who lives in Monroe, South Dakota, my brother John, who lives in San Luis Obispo, California, and my best friend, Jim, who lives in Atlanta, Georgia. ▪

Chapter 19

The Apostrophe

1. **Apostrophes are used to form contractions.** The apostrophe replaces the omitted letter or letters.

it is	it's	cannot	can't
I am	I'm	were not	weren't
they are	they're	is not	isn't
would have	would've	does not	doesn't

2. **Apostrophes are used to form the possessives of nouns and indefinite pronouns.**

   - Add 's to form the possessive of all singular nouns and indefinite pronouns.

   singular nouns
   The <u>boy's</u> bicycle was new.
   <u>Louis's</u> courage was never questioned.

   indefinite pronouns
   <u>Someone's</u> horn was honking.

   compound words
   My <u>father-in-law's</u> car had a flat.

   joint possession
   <u>Julio and Maria's</u> mountain cabin is for rent.

   - Add only an apostrophe to form the possessive of plural nouns that end in s. However, add 's to form the possessive of plural nouns that do not end in s.

   plural nouns that end in s
   Both <u>teams'</u> shoes were lined up on the field.
   The <u>Smiths'</u> house was on fire.

   plural nouns that do not end in s
   The <u>women's</u> cars were parked in front of the house.

   - Expressions referring to time or money often require an apostrophe.

   Sheila asked for a <u>dollar's</u> worth of candy.

   The player was given three <u>days'</u> suspension.

3. **Do not use apostrophes with the possessive forms of personal pronouns.**

Incorrect	**Correct**
her's	hers
our's	ours
their's	theirs

Note *It's* means "it is." The possessive form of *it* is *its*.

Exercise 19.1

Add apostrophes (or 's) to the following sentences where necessary.

1. That is Barrys baseball glove; he wont mind if you use it.
2. Do you think Charles tie goes well with his socks?
3. Mel Gibsons portrayal of Hamlet was lively, but Ive seen better.
4. In two hours time the mechanic had the clutch fixed.
5. People thought that Bridgets monologue on roadkill wasnt in good taste.
6. Its customary for the female black widow spider to kill its mate.
7. Were all going for coffee after the meeting, and youre invited.
8. The childrens bicycles shouldnt have been left out in the rain.
9. I dont want to hear anyones excuses after the game.
10. My mother-in-laws visits to her five relatives homes were a pleasant surprise.
11. The dog could not find shelter, and its puppies cries were beginning to grow louder.
12. Hasnt the McDonalds house been painted yet?
13. Arlos savings account consisted of one hundred dollars worth of empty Coke cans.
14. The womens department in Sears wasnt open yesterday.
15. A weeks vacation in the Bahamas had nearly erased the worry lines from my brothers face. ■

Chapter 20

Quotation Marks

1. **Quotation marks are used to enclose direct quotations and dialogue.**

   As Oscar Wilde once said, "Fashion is a form of ugliness so intolerable that we have to alter it every six months."

   Will Rogers said, "Liberty doesn't work as well in practice as it does in speeches."

2. **Quotation marks are not used with indirect quotations.**

   direct quotation   Tony said, "I'll play trumpet in the band."

   indirect quotation   Tony said that he would play trumpet in the band.

3. **Place periods and commas inside quotation marks.**

   Eudora Welty wrote the short story "A Worn Path."

   "I am a man more sinned against than sinning," cried Lear.

4. **Place colons and semicolons outside quotation marks.**

   The class did not like the poem "Thoughts on Capital Punishment": it was silly, sentimental, and insipid, and the rhythm was awkward and inappropriate.

   The local newspaper ran a story entitled "Mayor Caught Nude on the Beach"; it was just a joke for April Fools' Day.

5. **Place the question mark inside the quotation marks if the quotation is a question. Place the question mark outside the quotation marks if the quotation is not a question but the whole sentence is.**

   Homer asked, "What is for dinner, my dear Hortense?"

   Did Hortense really reply, "Hominy, okra, and barbecued Spam"?

6. **Place the exclamation point inside the quotation marks if the quotation is an exclamation. Place it outside the quotation marks if the quotation is not an exclamation but the whole sentence is.**

   "I have a dream!" yelled Martin Luther King, Jr.

   I insist that you stop calling me "dude"!

(See pages 135–137 for a further discussion of quotation marks.)

Exercise 20.1

Add quotation marks to the following sentences where necessary.

1. Hal said, Squid tentacles are my favorite snacks.
2. Will you get the tickets for the concert? asked Georgette.
3. Oscar said that he would clean up his house.
4. Paul Greenberg opens his article with the following statement: The flag amendment is back.
5. Did Bob Dylan really sing Moon River?
6. Dive, dive! yelled the captain of the submarine.
7. Mark Twain once muttered that a classic was a book that everyone praised, but no one read.
8. I wish you would leave me alone, said Henry, but I know that you won't.
9. Did the Cyclops actually believe him when he said, My name is No Man?
10. According to Charles Levendosky, Burning the flag is the act of someone who has little or no political power.
11. Camilla said, I am going to write a short story about an aardvark in Ireland; afterwards, she changed her mind.
12. Are we there yet? asked the children over and over.
13. *Star Trek* fans used to say, Beam me up, Scotty.
14. Willy told his boys that they needed to be well liked.
15. Send in the clowns, sang the frustrated coach. ■

Chapter 21

Titles, Capitalization, and Numbers

Titles

1. **Underline or place in italics the titles of longer works, such as books, periodicals, plays, CDs, and television programs.**

   - Books: *Moby Dick, Bartlett's Familiar Quotations*
   - Plays: *The Glass Menagerie, A Doll House*
   - Pamphlets: *Grooming Your Labrador, Charleston's Ten Best Restaurants*
   - Long musical works: Mozart's *String Quartet in C Major,* Miles Davis's *Sketches of Spain*
   - Long poems: *Howl, The Faerie Queene*
   - Periodicals: *The Washington Post, Time*
   - Films: *Shakespeare in Love, Saving Private Ryan*
   - Television and radio programs: *60 Minutes, Masterpiece Theater*
   - Works of art: El Greco's *Saint Matthew, Nike of Samothrace*

2. **Use quotation marks to enclose the titles of all shorter works, such as songs, poems, and short stories, as well as parts of larger works, such as articles in magazines and chapters in books.**

   - Songs: "The Sweetest Days," "Friends"
   - Poems: "My Last Duchess," "Dover Beach"
   - Articles in periodicals: "Three-Headed Snake Born As Two-Headed Brother Looks On," "The Last Stand"
   - Short stories: "A Jury of Her Peers," "Resurrection"
   - Essays: "Male Fixations," "A Custody Fight for an Egg"
   - Episodes of radio and television shows: "What's in a Name?"
   - Subdivisions of books: "The Cassock" (Chapter 29 of Moby Dick)

Capitalization

1. Capitalize the personal pronoun *I*.
2. Capitalize the first letter of every sentence.
3. Capitalize the first letter of each word in a title except for *a*, *an*, and *the*, coordinating conjunctions, and prepositions.

Note   The first letter of the first or last word of a title is always capitalized.

Dictionary of Philosophy and Religion

"A Good Man Is Hard to Find"

4. Capitalize the first letter of all proper nouns and adjectives derived from proper nouns.

- Names and titles of people: President Clinton, William Shakespeare, Uncle Christopher, Ms. Hohman
- Names of specific places: Chicago, Smoky Mountains, Tennessee, The Armenian Cafe, Saturn, the South

Note   Do not capitalize the first letter of words that refer to a direction (such as *north, south, east,* or *west*). Do capitalize such words when they refer to a specific region.

Alabama and Mississippi are among the states in the <u>South</u>.

Turn <u>south</u> on Hill Street and go four blocks to the end of the street.

- Names of ethnic, national, or racial groups: Native American, British, French, Canadian, Hispanic, Russian
- Names of groups or organizations: National Organization for Women, Girl Scouts of America, Methodists
- Names of companies: General Motors, Nordstrom, Pepsi-Cola Bottling Company, R. J. Reynolds
- Names of the days of the week and the months of the year but not the seasons: Saturday, April, winter, spring
- Names of holidays and historical events: the Gulf War, Christmas, the Battle of Concord
- Names of *specific* gods and religious writings: God, Zeus, Buddha, Koran, Yahweh, Bible

The names of academic subjects are not capitalized unless they refer to an ethnic or national origin or are the names of specific courses. Examples include *mathematics, history, Spanish, and Physics 100.*

Numbers

The following rules about numbers apply to general writing rather than to technical or scientific writing.

1. **Spell out numbers that require no more than two words. Use numerals for numbers that require more than two words.**

   <u>Ninety-three</u> people attended the dean's retirement party.

   We have now gone <u>125</u> days without rain.

2. **Spell out numbers at the beginning of sentences.**

   <u>Two hundred thirty-five</u> miles is a long distance to rollerblade.

3. **Use numerals in the following situations:**
   - Dates: June 24, 1981; 55 B.C.
   - Sections of books or plays: Chapter 26, page 390; Act 5, scene 2, lines 78–90
   - Addresses: 3245 Sisyphus Street
                 Stonewall, Nebraska 90345
   - Decimals, percentages, and fractions: 7.5; 75%, 75 percent; 1/8
   - Exact amounts of money: $10.86; $6,723,001
   - Scores and statistics: Padres 10, Reds 0; a ratio of 4 to 1
   - Time of day: 5:23; 12:45

Note   Round amounts of money that can be expressed in a few words can be written out: *thirty cents, twelve dollars, three hundred dollars.* Also when the word o'clock is used with the time of day, the time of day should be written out: eight o'clock.

4. **When numbers are compared, are joined by conjunctions, or occur in a series, either consistently use numerals or consistently spell them out.**

   For the birthday party we needed <u>one hundred fifteen</u> paper hats, <u>two hundred twenty</u> napkins, <u>one hundred fifteen</u> paper plates and forks, <u>eight</u> gallons of ice cream, <u>three</u> cakes, <u>forty</u> candles, and <u>eight</u> cases of soda.

   or

   For the birthday party we needed <u>115</u> paper hats, <u>220</u> napkins, <u>115</u> paper plates and forks, <u>8</u> gallons of ice cream, <u>3</u> cakes, <u>40</u> candles, and <u>8</u> cases of soda.

Exercise 21.1

The following sentences contain errors in the use of titles, capitalization, and numbers. Correct any errors you find.

1. Holly Hunter won an academy award for the film the piano even though she spoke only in the last scene.

2. The character of edgar in the play king lear and the character of iago in the play othello are two of shakespeare's worst Villains.

3. 375 cats were believed to have been killed in the city of pompeii when mount vesuvius erupted in seventy-nine A.D.

4. The Principal of imperial valley high school canceled classes when the Temperature reached 100 degrees.

5. Yesterday, the houston rockets beat the new york knicks eighty-six to 84.

6. When the japanese fishing boat was attacked by a Whale, 7 sailors were seriously injured.

7. My fine was three dollars and seventy-five cents when i returned the book the hero with a thousand faces to the Library.

8. Before he closed up, amador ordered 2 new computers, one hundred fifty reams of paper, 90 gallons of ink, and two hundred boxes of staples and paper clips for his copy shop.

9. Brent likes to listen to the radio program fresh air on national public radio.

10. One of my favorite Essays, entitled smoking ads: a matter of life, is written by ellen goodman, a syndicated columnist whose work appears in many Newspapers, including the kansas city star.

11. On their album kiko, the band los lobos included a song called arizona skies.

12. The works of many great mystery writers, including p. d. james, appear on the television show mystery.

13. A psychologist, dr. john gavion, claims that as many as fifty percent of the homeless people are vietnam veterans.

14. Andre took notes as professor guerra talked about south american art in his hispanic studies 120 class.

15. All 30 of the students were able to recognize the painting madonna and child by fra lippo lippi. ▪

Chapter 22

Clear and Concise Sentences

If you are like most writers, your first drafts will have their share of confusing, murky sentences. Sometimes the point of a sentence can be completely lost in a maze of words that seems to lead nowhere. One sure way to improve such sentences is to learn to cut and rewrite and then to cut and rewrite again. Here are some areas to consider as you work toward clear, concise sentences.

Redundancies

Redundant wording consists of saying the same thing twice (or more than twice), using different words each time. Cut and rewrite redundancies.

redundant	We left for Los Angeles at 10:00 **p.m. at night.**
concise	We left for Los Angeles at 10:00 p.m.
redundant	My **brother is a man** who always pays his bills.
concise	My brother always pays his bills.
redundant	Good baseball players know the **basic fundamentals** of the game.
concise	Good baseball players know the fundamentals of the game.

Needless Repetition

Repeating a word or phrase can weaken a sentence unless you are intentionally trying to emphasize the idea. Cut and rewrite needless repetition.

repetitive	My favorite **picture** is the **picture** of our house in Newport Beach.
concise	My favorite picture is the one of our house in Newport Beach.
repetitive	When my sister called me on the **telephone** at **two o'clock this morning,** I told her that **two o'clock in the morning** was too early **in the morning** for her to call on **the telephone.**
concise	When my sister phoned me at two o'clock this morning, I told her that she should not be calling so early.

Roundabout Phrases

Replace phrases that say in four or five words what can be said in one or two.

Roundabout	Concise
at all times	always
at the present time	now
at this point in time	now
on many occasions	often
in this modern day and age	today
because of the fact that	because
due to the fact that	because
for the purpose of	for
until such time as	until
in spite of the fact that	although, even though
make reference to	refer to
be of the opinion that	think, believe
in the event that	if

Exercise 22.1

Revise the following sentences to eliminate redundancies, needless repetition, and roundabout phrases,

1. My sister was chosen for jury duty in spite of the fact that she is in opposition to capital punishment.

2. In this modern day and age, no one should ever be homeless or not have a place to live.

3. The car that hit the pedestrian was the car weaving in and out of traffic a few seconds before it hit the pedestrian.

4. Please remain seated in your chairs until such time as the plane comes to a complete stop.

5. Whenever it rains, we always stay indoors.

6. Randy's new teak desk was very expensive in price, but he needed to buy it for the purpose of his growing business.

7. The death penalty is an unfair penalty because it is applied more often to poor people because poor people do not have the money to hire expensive attorneys to fight the death penalty.

8. The light from his flashlight nearly blinded me when he shined the light directly into my eyes.

9. At this point in time you know only the basic fundamentals of the game, so don't become overconfident.

10. In my memory I remember what my hometown, where I was born, looked like. ∎

Weak Subjects and Verbs

You can improve most writing by treating each sentence as if it told a story. Find the action of the story and make it the verb. Find the actor or "doer" of the action and make it the subject. Watch for the following situations in particular.

Needless *to be* Verbs

Replace *to be* verbs (*am, are, is, was, were, been, being, be*) with verbs that express an action.

weak	She **is** the one who **is** responsible for your damaged car.
improved	She **damaged** your car.
weak	His behavior **was** a demonstration of my point
improved	His behavior **demonstrated** my point.
weak	Sergio and Rene **were** the winners of the $10,000 raffle.
improved	Sergio and Rene **won** the $10,000 raffle.

Nominalizations

Nominalizations are nouns formed from verbs. From *realize* we have *realization*. From *argue* we have *argument*. From *criticize* we have *criticism*. Nominalizations can hide both the action of the sentence as well as the performer of the action. When possible, change nominalizations to verb forms to clarify the actor and the action of the sentence.

weak	Mario's **realization** of his **betrayal** by his business partner occurred when he saw the bank statement.
improved	Mario **realized** that his business partner **had betrayed** him when he saw the bank statement.
weak	Shelley's **request** was that we conduct an **examination** of the finances of the city council members.
improved	Shelley **requested** that we **examine** the finances of the city council members.

Unnecessary Initial *it* and *there*

Sentences beginning with *it* and *there* often contain needless extra words. When possible, revise such sentences to focus on the actor and the action of the sentence.

wordy	There is a belief held by many people that we should lower taxes.
improved	Many people believe that we should lower taxes.
wordy	It is imperative that we leave in five minutes if we want to arrive on time.
improved	We must leave in five minutes if we want to arrive on time.

Unnecessary Passive Voice

See Chapter 12 for a discussion of active and passive voice. In general, use active voice verbs to emphasize the actor and the action of your sentences.

passive | The car **was driven** two hundred miles by Mr. Ogilvey before he **was found** by the police

active | Mr. Oglivey **drove** the car two hundred miles before the police **found** him.

Exercise 22.2

Revise the following sentences to strengthen weak subjects and verbs.

1. The promise of freedom in America has been a great attraction for many immigrants.
2. There are several factors involved when coming to this conclusion.
3. Sometimes lying is necessary in order to provide protection for innocent people.
4. The hope on the part of the taxi driver and her impatient passenger was an early arrival at the airport.
5. It is my father's encouragement that he gives to me whenever something new is tried.
6. The ability for a woman to have choice and the tolerance of others' choices in their intimate partners has lessened in support.
7. The reason behind it is better than the knowledge of nothing at all behind it.
8. Music is used by many people as an experience in meditation and relaxation.
9. It is with great regret that we have reached the decision that it is necessary to terminate your employment.
10. Aside from Faulkner's story being an examination of family conflict, there are also considerations of racial conflict added to it. ■

Part 4

Additional Readings for Writing

The reading selections on the following pages present ideas and opinions on a range of topics. The articles in the section entitled "Changing Times" discuss consumerism, sexism, family life, and the legal drinking age. Those in "Culture and Country" present the perspectives of writers from a variety of ethnic and racial backgrounds. The selections in "Behavior" examine some contemporary attitudes and behaviors that worry many people. The topics in "Education" discuss the problems of cheating, grading, student and teacher respect (or the lack of it), and the evaluation of instructors. The final three sections—"Physician-Assisted Suicide," "The Effects of Television," and "Animal Experimentation"—present related articles that can be used as multiple sources for synthesis or argumentative papers.

As you read these selections, consider the "Steps in Evaluating a Text" from Chapter 6:

1. *Read the text actively.*
   a. *Determine its intended audience and purpose.*
   b. *Identify its thesis.*
   c. *Identify its main points.*
2. *Determine how well the main points are supported.*
   a. *Distinguish between facts and opinions.*
   b. *Distinguish between specific support and generalizations.*
   c. *Identify statistics, examples, and references to authority.*
3. *Test the article's points against your own knowledge and experience.*
4. *Consider any obvious objections that have been ignored.*

Kids in the Mall: Growing Up Controlled

William Severini Kowinski

Butch heaved himself up and loomed over the group. "Like it was different for me," he piped. "My folks used to drop me off at the shopping mall every morning and leave me all day. It was like a big free baby-sitter, you know? One night they never came back for me. Maybe they moved away. Maybe there's some kind of a Bureau of Missing Parents I could check with."

> Richard Peck, Secrets of the Shopping Mall *(a novel for teenagers)*

From his sister at Swarthmore, I'd heard about a kid in Florida whose mother picked him up after school every day, drove him straight to the mall, and left him there until it closed—all at his insistence. I'd heard about a boy in Washington who, when his family moved from one suburb to another, pedaled his bicycle five miles every day to get back to his old mall, where he once belonged. [1]

These stories aren't unusual. The mall is a common experience for the majority of American youth; they have probably been going there all their lives. Some ran within their first large open space, saw their first fountain, bought their first toy, and read their first book in a mall. They may have smoked their first cigarette or first joint, or turned them down, had their first kiss or lost their virginity in the mall parking lot. Teenagers in America now spend more time in the mall than anywhere else but home and school. Mostly it is their choice, but some of that mall time is put in as the result of two-paycheck and single-parent households, and the lack of other viable alternatives. But are these kids being harmed by the mall? [2]

I wondered first of all what difference it makes for adolescents to experience so many important moments in the mall. They are, after all, at play in the fields of its little world and they learn its ways; they adapt to it and make it adapt to them. It's here that these kids get their street sense, only it's mall sense. They are learning the ways of a large-scale, artificial environment; its subtleties and flexibilities, its particular pleasures and resonances, and the attitudes it fosters. [3]

The presence of so many teenagers for so much time was not something mall developers planned on. In fact, it came as a big surprise. But kids became a fact of mall life very easily, and the International Council of Shopping Centers found it necessary to commission a study, which they published along with a guide to mall managers on how to handle the teenage incursion. [4]

The study found that "teenagers in suburban centers are bored and come to the shopping centers mainly as a place to go. Teenagers in suburban centers spent more time fighting, drinking, littering and walking than [5] did their urban counterparts, but presented fewer overall problems." The report observed that "adolescents congregated in groups of two to four and predominantly at locations selected by them rather than management." This probably had something to do with the decision to install game arcades, which allow management to channel these restless adolescents into naturally contained areas away from major traffic points of adult shoppers.

The guide concluded that mall management should tolerate and even 6 encourage the teenage presence because, in the words of the report, "The vast majority support the same set of values as does shopping center management." *The same set of values* means simply that mall kids are already preprogrammed to be consumers and that the mall can put the finishing touches to them as hard-core, lifelong shoppers just like everybody else. That, after all, is what the mall is about. So it shouldn't be surprising that in spending a lot of time there, adolescents find little that challenges the assumption that the goal of life is to make money and buy products, or that just about everything else in life is to be used to serve those ends.

Growing up in a high-consumption society already adds inestimable 7 pressure to kids' lives. Clothes consciousness has invaded the grade schools, and popularity is linked with having the best, newest clothes in the currently acceptable styles. Even what they read has been affected. "Miss [Nancy] Drew wasn't obsessed with her wardrobe," noted the *Wall Street Journal.* "But today the mystery in teen fiction for girls is what outfit the heroine will wear next." Shopping has become a survival skill and there is certainly no better place to learn it than the mall, where its importance is powerfully reinforced and certainly never questioned.

The mall as a university of suburban materialism, where Valley Girls 8 and boys from coast to coast are educated in consumption, has its other lessons in this era of change in family life and sexual mores and their economic and social ramifications. The plethora of products in the mall, plus the pressure on teens to buy them, may contribute to the phenomenon that psychologist David Elkind calls "the hurried child": kids who are exposed to too much of the adult world too quickly and must respond with a sophistication that belies their still-tender emotional development. Certainly the adult products marketed for children—form-fitting designer jeans, sexy tops for preteen girls—add to the social pressure to look like an adult, along with the home-grown need to understand adult finances (why mothers must work) and adult emotions (when parents divorce).

Kids spend so much time at the mall partly because their parents allow it and even encourage it. The mall is safe, doesn't seem to harbor any unsavory activities, and there is adult supervision; it is, after all, a controlled environment. So the temptation, especially for working parents, is to let the mall be their baby-sitter. At least the kids aren't watching TV. But the mall's role as a surrogate mother may be more extensive and more profound.

Karen Lansky, a writer living in Los Angeles, has looked into the 10 subject, and she told me some of her conclusions about the effects on its teenaged denizens of the mall's controlled and controlling environment. "Structure is the dominant idea, since true 'mall rats' lack just that in their home lives," she said, "and adolescents about to make the big leap into growing up crave more structure than our modern society cares to acknowledge." Karen pointed out some of the elements malls supply that kids used to get from their families, like warmth (Strawberry Shortcake dolls and similar cute and cuddly merchandise), old-fashioned mothering ("We do it all for you," the fast-food slogan), and even home cooking (the "homemade" treats at the food court).

The problem in all this, as Karen Lansky sees it, is that while families nurture children by encouraging growth through the assumption of responsibility and then by letting them rest in the bosom of the family from the rigors of growing up, the mall as a structural mother encourages passivity and consumption, as long as the kid doesn't make trouble. Therefore all they learn about becoming adults is how to act and how to consume.

Kids are in the mall not only in the passive role of shoppers—they also work there, especially as fast-food outlets infiltrate the mall's enclosure. There they learn how to hold a job and take responsibility, but still within the same value context. When *CBS Reports* went to Oak Park Mall in suburban Kansas City, Kansas, to tape part of their hour-long consideration of malls, "After the Dream Comes True," they interviewed a teenaged girl who worked in a fast-food outlet there. In a sequence that didn't make the final program, she described the major goal of her present life, which was to perfect the curl on top of the ice-cream cones that were her store's specialty. If she could do that, she would be moved from the lowly soft-drink dispenser to the more prestigious ice-cream division, the curl on top of the status ladder at her restaurant. These are the achievements that are important at the mall.

Other benefits of such jobs may also be overrated, according to Laurence D. Steinberg of the University of California at Irvine's social ecology department, who did a study on teenage employment. Their jobs, he found, are generally simple, mindlessly repetitive and boring. They don't really learn anything, and the jobs don't lead anywhere. Teenagers also work primarily with other teenagers; even their supervisors are often just a little older than they are. "Kids need to spend time with adults," Steinberg told me. "Although they get benefits from peer relationships, without parents and other adults it's one-sided socialization. They hang out with each other, have age-segregated jobs, and watch TV."

Perhaps much of this is not so terrible or even so terribly different. Now that they have so much more to contend with in their lives, adolescents probably need more time to spend with other adolescents without adult impositions, just to sort things out. Though it is more concentrated in the mall (and therefore perhaps a clearer target), the value system there is really the dominant one of the whole society. Attitudes about curiosity, initiative, self-expression, empathy, and disinterested learning aren't necessarily made in the mall; they are mirrored there, perhaps a bit more intensely—as through a glass brightly.

Besides, the mall is not without its educational opportunities. There are bookstores, where there is at least a short shelf of classics at great prices, and other books from which it is possible to learn more than how to do sit-ups. There are tools, from hammers to VCRs, and products, from clothes to records, that can help the young find and express themselves. There are older people with stories, and places to be alone or to talk one-on-one with a kindred spirit. And there is always the passing show. 15

The mall itself may very well be an education about the future. I was struck with the realization, as early as my first forays into Greengate, that the mall is only one of a number of enclosed and controlled environments that are part of the lives of today's young. The mall is just an extension, say, of those large suburban schools—only there's Karmelkorn instead of chem lab, the ice rink instead of the gym: It's high school without the impertinence of classes. 16

Growing up, moving from home to school to the mall—from enclosure to enclosure, transported in cars—is a curiously continuous process, without much in the way of contrast or contact with unenclosed reality. Places must tend to blur into one another. But whatever differences and dangers there are in this, the skills these adolescents are learning may turn out to be useful in their later lives. For we seem to be moving inexorably into an age of preplanned and regulated environments, and this is the world they will inherit. 17

Still, it might be better if they had more of a choice. One teenaged girl confessed to *CBS Reports* that she sometimes felt she was missing something by hanging out at the mall so much. "But I'm here," she said, "and this is what I have." 18

Bikini Team: Sexism for the Many

Ronald K. L. Collins

When a single voice badgers or degrades women in the workplace because of their gender, we call it sexual harassment. When that voice is amplified for millions of people by millions of dollars, we call it advertising. The former is a legal wrong, the latter a legal right. Yet, both acts exploit women, injure them and attempt to impose male power over them. Why then do we tolerate a dichotomy that makes the larger harm the lesser evil? 1

Five women in St. Paul, Minn., turned to a court of law to get an answer to this question. To borrow a thought from noted feminist Catharine MacKinnon, these women are asking the law to "adjust a bit to accommodate the realities of sexual harassment." The everyday reality is that 2 women's sexuality is used to sell things, their commodified bodies are plastered on advertising to stimulate men to buy things. Their very identity as autonomous persons is electronically transformed into media images of marketable chattel.

What the company voice says outside of the office carries into it as well. That's part of what the St. Paul women were saying when they filed a lawsuit against their employer, Stroh Brewing Co. In Stroh's "It Does Not Get Better" television ad, bikini-clad young Swedish women parachute into a male campsite bearing six-packs of beer. (Tellingly, the "Swedish bikini team" will be featured on the cover of the January issue of *Playboy* magazine.) Buxom women convey the same message in the company's promotional posters. The advertising fantasy is that men can have both the beer and the "broads."   3

A spokesman for Stroh says that the company has a "very definite and strong policy" against sexual harassment and other forms of sex discrimination. It "simply won't tolerate it." But the very thing that it purports not to tolerate in the workplace, it promotes in the marketplace.   4

Men get mixed messages. The law tells the men at Stroh not to treat women as sex objects, while company ads tell them to revel in the thought. The law says that they must be sexually civil, while Madison Avenue says that they must be sexually uncivil. The five women of St. Paul have turned to the courts to reaffirm a single message—sexual oppression in all of its forms is an affront to civilized society.   5

If Stroh's management displayed its girlie posters at its work sites and if it broadcast its Swedish fantasy ads on company monitors, few would deny that such messages create an environment conducive to sexual harassment. But Stroh's "very definite and strong policy" does not pertain to its openly sexist ads. The five women in the lawsuit claim that it should. When, in an overt way, men verbally and physically confront women in the workplace, as is alleged in this case, their behavior only actualizes the fantasies in mass advertising that feature women as sex objects. In this sense, sexist advertising compounds the injury against women.   6

Culturally speaking, the key point is not whether any particular ad or ads directly caused Stroh's workmen to act in ways allegedly degrading and injurious to women. What is important is the infrastructure of sexism, the systematic and unjust exercise of male power over women. In this system of commercial exploitation, Stroh is one of many players. Its voice is part of a chorus of commercial forces using women to sell everything from booze to batteries. In a larger sense, what is really being sold and bought is a sexual image of subservient women. Such ad-porn shapes men's conception of women, and to that extent influences their behavior at work.   7

If not in the St. Paul case, then in the next, those who champion the commercial exploitation of women in advertising will wrap themselves in the First Amendment's flag. Any government action on this issue (like the Ontario, Canada, campaigns to outlaw sexist liquor ads) is incompatible,   8 they claim with our system of freedom of expression. Here, again, we confront a paradox. The constitutional guarantee does not categorically protect the worker's sexist voice in the workplace, but the same guarantee is said categorically to protect the company's sexist voice when it is amplified for the marketplace.

In a more noble First Amendment tradition, the women of St. Paul   9
summon us to begin a dialogue about an ideal of gender equality free of the shackles of commercial exploitation. It is high time that we amplify their voices and their message.

From the Los Angeles Times, *Nov. 20, 1991, B7. Reprinted by permission of the author.*

Are Families Dangerous?

Barbara Ehrenreich

A disturbing subtext runs through our recent media fixations. Parents   1
abuse sons—allegedly at least, in the Menendez case—who in turn rise up and kill them. A husband torments a wife, who retaliates with a kitchen knife. Love turns into obsession, between the Simpsons anyway, and then perhaps into murderous rage: the family, in other words, becomes personal hell.

This accounts for at least part of our fascination with the Bobbitts   2
and the Simpsons and the rest of them. We live in a culture that fetishes the family as the ideal unit of human community, the perfect container for our lusts and loves. Politicians of both parties are aggressively "pro-family," even abortion-rights bumper stickers proudly link "pro-family" and "pro-choice." Only with the occasional celebrity crime do we allow ourselves to think the nearly unthinkable: that the family may not be the ideal and perfect living arrangement after all—that it can be a nest of pathology and a cradle of gruesome violence.

It's a scary thought, because the family is at the same time our   3
"haven in a heartless world." Theoretically, and sometimes actually, the family nurtures warm, loving feelings, uncontaminated by greed or power hunger. Within the family, and often only within the family, individuals are loved "for themselves," whether or not they are infirm, incontinent, infantile or eccentric. The strong (adults and especially males) lie down peaceably with the small and weak.

But consider the matter of wife battery. We managed to dodge it   4
in the Bobbitt case and downplay it as a force in Tonya Harding's life. Thanks to O. J., though, we're caught up now in a mass consciousness-raising session, grimly absorbing the fact that in some areas domestic violence sends as many women to emergency rooms as any other form of illness, injury or assault.

Still, we shrink from the obvious inference: for a woman, home is, statistically speaking, the most dangerous place to be. Her worst enemies and potential killers are not strangers but lovers, husbands and those who claimed to love her once. Similarly, for every child like Polly Klaas who is killed by a deranged criminal on parole, dozens are abused and murdered by their own relatives. Home is all too often where the small and weak fear to lie down and shut their eyes.   5

At some deep, queasy, Freudian level, we all know this. Even in the ostensibly "functional," nonviolent family, where no one is killed or maimed, feelings are routinely bruised and often twisted out of shape. There is the slap or put-down that violates a child's shaky sense of self, the cold, distracted stare that drives a spouse to tears, the little digs and rivalries. At best, the family teaches the finest things human beings can learn from one another—generosity and love. But it is also, all too often, where we learn nasty things like hate and rage and shame.   6

Americans act out their ambivalence about the family without ever owning up to it. Millions adhere to creeds that are militantly "pro-family." But at the same time millions flock to therapy groups that offer to heal the "inner child" from damage inflicted by family life. Legions of women band together to revive the self-esteem they lost in supposedly loving relationships and to learn to love a little less. We are all, it is often said, "in recovery." And from what? Our families, in most cases.   7

There is a long and honorable tradition of "anti-family" thought. The French philosopher Charles Fourier taught that the family was a barrier to human progress; early feminists saw a degrading parallel between marriage and prostitution. More recently, the renowned British anthropologist Edmund Leach stated that "far from being the basis of the good society, the family, with its narrow privacy and tawdry secrets, is the source of all discontents."   8

Communes proved harder to sustain than plain old couples, and the conservatism of the 80s crushed the last vestiges of life-style experimentation. Today even gays and lesbians are eager to get married and take up family life. Feminists have learned to couch their concerns as "family issues," and public figures would sooner advocate free cocaine on demand than criticize the family. Hence our unseemly interest in O. J. and Erik, Lyle and Lorena: they allow us, however gingerly, to break the silence on the hellish side of family life.   9

But the discussion needs to become a lot more open and forthright. We may be struck with the family—at least until someone invents a sustainable alternative—but the family, with its deep, impacted tensions and longings, can hardly be expected to be the moral foundation of everything else. In fact, many families could use a lot more outside interference in the form of counseling and policing, and some are so dangerously dysfunctional that they ought to be encouraged to disband right away. Even healthy families need outside sources of moral guidance to keep the internal tensions from imploding—and this means, at the very least, a public philosophy of gender equality and concern for child wel-   10 fare. When, instead, the larger culture aggrandizes wife beaters, degrades women or nods approvingly at child slappers, the family gets a little more dangerous for everyone, and so, inevitably, does the larger world.

© 1994 Time, Inc. Reprinted by permission.

The Perils of Prohibition

Elizabeth M. Whelan

My colleagues at the Harvard School of Public Health, where I studied preventive medicine, deserve high praise for their recent study on teenage drinking. What they found in their survey of college students was that they drink "early and . . . often," frequently to the point of getting ill.

As a public-health scientist with a daughter, Christine, heading to college this fall, I have professional and personal concerns about teen binge drinking. It is imperative that we explore *why* so many young people abuse alcohol. From my own study of the effects of alcohol restrictions and my observations of Christine and her friends' predicament about drinking, I believe that today's laws are unrealistic. Prohibiting the sale of liquor to responsible young adults creates an atmosphere where binge drinking and alcohol abuse have become a problem. American teens, unlike their European peers, don't learn how to drink gradually, safely and in moderation.

Alcohol is widely accepted and enjoyed in our culture. Studies show that moderate drinking can be good for you. But we legally proscribe alcohol until the age of 21 (why not 30 or 45?). Christine and her classmates can drive cars, fly planes, marry, vote, pay taxes, take out loans and risk their lives as members of the U.S. armed forces. But laws in all 50 states say that no alcoholic beverages may be sold to anyone until that magic 21st birthday. We didn't always have a national "21" rule. When I was in college, in the mid-'60s, the drinking age varied from state to state. This posed its own risks, with underage students crossing state lines to get a legal drink.

In parts of the Western world, moderate drinking by teenagers and even children under their parents' supervision is a given. Though the per capita consumption of alcohol in France, Spain and Portugal is higher than in the United States, the rate of alcoholism and alcohol abuse is lower. A glass of wine at dinner is normal practice. Kids learn to regard moderate drinking as an enjoyable family activity rather than as something they have to sneak away to do. Banning drinking by young people makes it a badge of adulthood—a tantalizing forbidden fruit.

Christine and her teenage friends like to go out with a group to a club, comedy show or sports bar to watch the game. But teens today have to go on the sly with fake IDs and the fear of getting caught. Otherwise, they're denied admittance to most places and left to hang out on the street. That's hardly a safer alternative. Christine and her classmates now find themselves in a legal no man's land. At 18, they're considered adults. Yet when they want to enjoy a drink like other adults, they are, as they put it, "disenfranchised."

Comparing my daughter's dilemma with my own as an "underage" college student, I see a difference—and one that I think has exacerbated the current dilemma. Today's teens are far more sophisticated than we were. They're treated less like children and have more responsibilities than we did. This makes the 21 restriction seem anachronistic.   6

For the past few years, my husband and I have been preparing Christine for college life and the inevitable partying—read keg of beer—that goes with it. Last year, a young friend with no drinking experience was violently ill for days after he was introduced to "clear liquids in small glasses" during freshman orientation. We want our daughter to learn how to drink sensibly and avoid this pitfall. Starting at the age of 14, we invited her to join us for a glass of champagne with dinner. She'd tried it once before, thought it was "yucky" and declined. A year later, she enjoyed sampling wine at family meals.   7

When, at 16, she asked for a Mudslide (a bottled chocolate-milk-and-rum concoction), we used the opportunity to discuss it with her. We explained the alcohol content, told her the alcohol level is lower when the drink is blended with ice and compared it with a glass of wine. Since the drink of choice on campus is beer, we contrasted its potency with wine and hard liquor and stressed the importance of not drinking on an empty stomach.   8

Our purpose was to encourage her to know the alcohol content of what she is served. We want her to experience the effects of liquor in her own home, not on the highway and not for the first time during a college orientation week with free-flowing suds. Although Christine doesn't drive yet, we regularly reinforce the concept of choosing a designated driver. Happily, that already seems a widely accepted practice among our daughter's friends who drink.   9

We recently visited the Ivy League school Christine will attend in the fall. While we were there, we read a story in the college paper about a student who was nearly electrocuted when, in a drunken state, he climbed on top of a moving train at a railroad station near the campus. The student survived, but three of his limbs were later amputated. This incident reminded me of a tragic death on another campus. An intoxicated student maneuvered himself into a chimney. He was found three days later when frat brothers tried to light a fire in the fireplace. By then he was dead.   10

These tragedies are just two examples of our failure to teach young people how to use alcohol prudently. If 18-year-olds don't have legal access to even a beer at a public place, they have no experience handling liquor on their own. They feel "liberated" when they arrive on campus. With no parents to stop them, they have a "let's make up for lost time"   11 attitude. The result: binge drinking.

We should make access to alcohol legal at 18. At the same time, we 12
should come down much harder on alcohol abusers and drunk drivers of
all ages. We should intensify our efforts at alcohol education for adolescents. We want them to understand that it is perfectly OK not to drink.
But if they do, alcohol should be consumed in moderation.

After all, we choose to teach our children about safe sex, including 13
the benefits of teen abstinence. Why, then, can't we—schools and parents
alike—teach them about safe drinking?

Culture and Country

The Middle-Class Black's Burden

Leanita McClain

I am a member of the black middle class who has had it with being pat- 1
ted on the head by white hands and slapped in the face by black hands
for my success.

Here's a discovery that too many people still find startling: when 2
given equal opportunities at white-collar pencil pushing, blacks want the
same things from life that everyone else wants. These include the proverbial dream house, two cars, an above-average school, and a vacation for
the kids at Disneyland. We may, in fact, want these things more than
other Americans because most of us have been denied them so long.

Meanwhile, a considerable number of the folks we left behind in 3
the "old country," commonly called the ghetto, and the militants we left
behind in their antiquated ideology can't berate middle-class blacks
enough for "forgetting where we came from." We have forsaken the
revolution, we are told, we have sold out. We are Oreos, they say, black
on the outside, white within.

The truth is, we have not forgotten; we would not dare. We are sim- 4
ply fighting on different fronts and are no less war weary, and possibly
more heartbroken, for we know the black and white worlds can meld,
that there can be a better world.

It is impossible for me to forget where I came from as long as I am 5
prey to the jive hustler who does not hesitate to exploit my childhood
friendship. I am reminded, too, when I go back to the old neighborhood
in fear—and have my purse snatched—and when I sit down to a business lunch and have an old classmate wait on my table. I recall the girl
I played dolls with who now rears five children on welfare, the boy from

church who is in prison for murder, the pal found dead of a drug overdose in the alley where we once played tag.

My life abounds in incongruities. Fresh from a vacation in Paris, 6
I may, a week later, be on the milk-run Trailways bus in Deep South backcountry attending the funeral of an ancient uncle whose world stretched only 50 miles and who never learned to read. Sometimes when I wait at the bus stop with my attaché case, I meet my aunt getting off the bus with other cleaning ladies on their way to do my neighbors' floors.

But I am not ashamed. Black progress has surpassed our greatest 7
expectations; we never even saw much hope for it, and the achievement has taken us by surprise.

In my heart, however, there is no safe distance from the wretched 8
past of my ancestors or the purposeless present of some of my contemporaries; I fear such a fate can reclaim me. I am not comfortably middle class; I am uncomfortably middle class.

I have made it, but where? Racism still dogs my people. There are 9
still communities in which crosses are burned on the lawns of black families who have the money and grit to move in.

What a hollow victory we have won when my sister, dressed in her 10
designer everything, is driven to the rear door of the luxury high rise in which she lives because the cab driver, noting only her skin color, assumes she is the maid, or nanny, or the cook, but certainly not the lady of any house at this address.

I have heard the immigrants' bootstrap tales, the simplistic reproach 11
of "why can't you people be like us." I have fulfilled the entry requirements of the American middle class, yet I am left, at times, feeling unwelcome and stereotyped. I have overcome the problems of food, clothing and shelter, but I have not overcome my old nemesis, prejudice. Life is easier, being black is not.

I am burdened daily with showing whites that blacks are people. 12
I am, in the old vernacular, a credit to my race. I am my brothers' keeper, and my sisters', though many of them have abandoned me because they think that I have abandoned them.

I run a gauntlet between two worlds, and I am cursed and blessed 13
by both. I travel, observe, and take part in both; I can also be used by both. I am a rope in a tug of war. If I am a token in my downtown office, so am I at my cousin's church tea. I assuage white guilt. I disprove black inadequacy and prove to my parents' generation that their patience was indeed a virtue.

I have a foot in each world, but I cannot fool myself about either. 14
I can see the transparent deceptions of some whites and the bitter hopelessness of some blacks. I know how tenuous my grip on one way of life is, and how strangling the grip of the other way of life can be.

Many whites have lulled themselves into thinking that race relations 15
are just grand because they were the first on their block to discuss crab grass with the new black family. Yet too few blacks and whites in this country send their children to school together, entertain each other, or

call each other friend. Blacks and whites dining out together draw stares. Many of my coworkers see no black faces from the time the train pulls out Friday evening until they meet me at the coffee machine Monday morning. I remain a novelty.

Some of my "liberal" white acquaintances pat me on the head, hint-   16
ing that I am a freak, that my success is less a matter of talent than of luck and affirmative action. I may live among them, but it is difficult to live with them. How can they be sincere about respecting me, yet hold my fellows in contempt? And if I am silent when they attempt to sever me from my own, how can I live with myself?

Whites won't believe I remain culturally different; blacks won't   17
believe I remain culturally the same.

I need only look in a mirror to know my true allegiance, and I am   18
painfully aware that, even with my off-white trappings, I am prejudged by my color.

As for the envy of my own people, am I to give up my career, my   19
standard of living, to pacify them and set my conscience at ease? No.
I have worked for these amenities and deserve them, though I can never enjoy them without feeling guilty.

These comforts do not make me less black, nor oblivious to the woe   20
in which many of my people are drowning. As long as we are denigrated as a group, no one of us has made it. Inasmuch as we all suffer for every one left behind, we all gain for every one who conquers the hurdle.

It's Time to Stop Playing Indians

Arlene B. Hirschfelder

It is predictable. At Halloween, thousands of children trick-or-treat in   1
Indian costumes. At Thanksgiving, thousands of children parade in school pageants wearing plastic headdresses and pseudo-buckskin clothing. Thousands of card shops stock Thanksgiving greeting cards with images of cartoon animals wearing feathered headbands. Thousands of teachers and librarians trim bulletin boards with Anglo-featured, feath-ered Indian boys and girls. Thousands of gift shops load their shelves with Indian figurines and jewelry.

Fall and winter are also the seasons when hundreds of thousands of   2
sports fans root for professional, college and public school teams with names that summon up Indians—"Braves," "Redskins," "Chiefs." (In New York State, one out of eight junior and senior high school teams call themselves "Indians," "Tomahawks" and the like.) War-whooping team

mascots are imprinted on school uniforms, postcards, notebooks, tote bags and car floor mats.

All of this seems innocuous; why make a fuss about it? Because these trappings and holiday symbols offend tens of thousands of other Americans—the native American people. Because these invented images prevent millions of us from understanding the authentic Indian America, both long ago and today. Because this image-making prevents Indians from being a relevant part of the nation's social fabric. 3

Halloween costumes mask the reality of high mortality rates, high diabetes rates, high unemployment rates. They hide low average life spans, low per capita incomes and low educational levels. Plastic war bonnets and ersatz buckskin deprive people from knowing the complexity of Native American heritage—that Indians belong to hundreds of nations that have intricate social organizations, governments, languages, religions and sacred rituals, ancient stories, unique arts and music forms. 4

Thanksgiving school units and plays mask history. They do not tell how Europeans mistreated Wampanoags and other East Coast Indian peoples during the 17th century. Social studies units don't mention that, to many Indians, Thanksgiving is a day of mourning, the beginning of broken promises, land theft, near extinction of their religions and languages at the hands of invading Europeans. 5

Athletic team nicknames and mascots disguise real people. War-painted, buckskin-clad, feathered characters keep the fictitious Indian circulating on decals, pennants and team clothing. Toy companies mask Indian identity and trivialize sacred beliefs by manufacturing Indian costumes and headdresses, peace pipes and trick-arrow-through-the-head gags that equate Indianness with playtime. Indian figures equipped with arrows, guns and tomahawks give youngsters the harmful message that Indians favor mayhem. Many Indian people can tell about children screaming in fear after being introduced to them. 6

It is time to consider how these images impede the efforts of Indian parents and communities to raise their children with positive information about their heritage. It is time to get rid of stereotypes that, whether deliberately or inadvertently, denigrate Indian cultures and people. 7

It is time to bury the Halloween costumes, trick arrows, bulletin-board pin-ups, headdresses and mascots. It is has been done before. In the 1970s, after student protests, Marquette University dropped its "Willie Wampum," Stanford University retired its mascot, "Prince Lightfoot," and Eastern Michigan University and Florida State modified their savage-looking mascots to reduce criticism. 8

It is time to stop playing Indians. It is time to abolish Indian images that sell merchandise. It is time to stop offending Indian people whose lives are all too often filled with economic deprivation, powerlessness, discrimination and gross injustice. This time next year, let's find more appropriate symbols for the holiday and sports seasons. 9

Reprinted by permission of the author.

The Future / *El Futuro*

Richard Rodriguez

Californians are afraid of the future and cannot imagine themselves in the great world. To prove it, Gov. Pete Wilson last week published an open letter to President Bill Clinton, urging a constitutional amendment to deny citizenship to the children of illegal immigrants as well as the repeal of federal mandates requiring health and education services for illegal immigrants.

1

On the same day that the governor published his letter ("on behalf of the people of California"), I was at a chic Los Angeles hotel. All day, I saw Mexicans busily working to maintain California's legendary "quality of life." The common complaint of Californians is that the immigrants, whether legally or illegally here, are destroying our quality of life. But there the Mexicans were—hosing down the tiles by the hotel swimming pool, gardening, everywhere gardening. The woman who could barely speak English was making beds; at the Yuppie restaurant, Mexican men impersonated Italian chefs.

2

Who could accuse Wilson of xenophobia? The governor was, after all, only concerned with those immigrants illegally here. His presumption was that the illegal immigrants are here only for the umbrella of welfare services. Remove those benefits and they will go back to Mexico, the governor reasoned. Here was a presumption in Wilson's letter that betrayed naiveté about the desperation of the Third World poor and their wild ambition for work.

3

"God, do they work," a friend confides over martinis in Bel-Air. "I've never seen people work like those Mexicans."

4

What troubles us about Mexican immigrants is that they work too hard. The myth California has advertised to the world is that here is a place of leisure—the myth of blond beaches and palm trees.

5

It is embarrassing to watch the Mexican work, like watching a peasant eat. The Mexican, perhaps most especially the illegal immigrant, reminds us how hard life is; he reminds us that in much of this world, one must work or die.

6

Work becomes life. The feel of work, the assurance of a handle to hold, a hope. The peach is torn from the branch, the knife slits open the fish; the stake is plunged into the earth faster and faster. Work or die. The Mexican works.

7

Not only Mexicans are working, of course. There are also Vietnamese, Koreans, Guatemalans, Salvadorans, Chinese. Wilson's letter to the president was only concerned with Mexicans and with Mexico, but many Californians probably are made more uneasy with the Asian migration. If, as the governor believes, Mexicans are a burden because they are poor, Asians are a threat because they are poised to take over the

8

city. In San Francisco, people say it all the time: The Chinese are taking over the city.

During the Gold Rush, in the mid-19th century, Chinese miners were chased off the fields by other prospectors. Mexicans (many of whom arrived from northern Mexico, bringing with them mining skills) were also chased away. But many generations later, now, the parent in Walnut Creek, a father of three, tells me that Asians are unfair. (His daughter has not been admitted to Berkeley.) "Asians are unfair because they work so hard." 9

Californians should be thinking of ways to join with Mexico if we are as modern, as advanced, as we like to tell our fellow Americans we are. We would be imagining a global state. Instead, environmentalists are using the North American Free Trade Agreement as a way of keeping Mexico at bay, under our control. And Gov. Wilson urges the president to tie NAFTA to Mexico's policing of its northern border. Clean yourself, we tell Mexico, clean yourself and then we will embrace you. 10

Sen. Dianne Feinstein wonders if we shouldn't charge a toll for entering California from Mexico. And her fellow liberal in the Senate, Barbara Boxer, wants to enlist the National Guard to protect our border. But, of course, millions of middle-class Californians assume that they can use Mexico whenever and however they want. They go to Mexico for a tan. They go to Mexico to adopt a baby. They retire to Mexico—get a condo in Cabo. They reach into Mexico for an inexpensive gardener or nanny. 11

Despite ourselves and because of the immigrants, California is becoming a world society—an extraordinary meeting place of Asia and Latin America with white and black America. 12

Poor New York, thousands of miles away, senses that something is going on in California but hasn't a clue. All summer, New York has been taken by the notion that the California dream is tarnished. *The New Yorker* dispatched Joan Didion from her upper East Side apartment. Regis Philbin confided to his viewers: "It's so sad—all those poor people going to L.A." 13

CBS News sent several correspondents to Los Angeles a few weeks ago to view the apocalypse. Except for an eccentric Latino who predicted a Latino takeover of the Southland, the entire hour of *48 Hours* was given to white and black opinions. Lots of blond people said they were fed up with California—"it's not what we had in mind." 14

No correspondent bothered to ask the Guatemalan teen-ager or the Chinese short-order cook why they had come to California. 15

Dear Regis Philbin: California does not have an immigrant problem. California has a native-born problem. 16

Gov. Wilson, I think, would have done better addressing a letter to his fellow Californians—rich, middle-class, poor. The governor might well have asked if, as Californians, we assume too much about our right to leisure and the government's obligation to our well-being. 17

Ross Perot may have it half right. Americans are going to have to be harder on themselves. The government is running out of money for 18 savings-and-loan fat cats, Social Security grandmas and welfare mothers. But Perot is wrong in thinking that we can close ourselves from the world.

Neighbors should not live oblivious to one another. Any coyote in Tijuana can tell you that illegal immigration is inevitable as long as distinctions between rich countries and poor, developed countries and the Third World, are not ameliorated. If we want fewer illegal Mexican immigrants, we must work with Mexico, as Mexico must work with Guatemala.   19

In time, though, California will turn the Mexican and Chinese teenagers into rock stars and surfers. But I think the immigrants also will change California—their gift to us—reminding us of what our German and Italian ancestors knew when they came, hopeful, to the brick tenement blocks of the East Coast.   20

Life is work.   21

Reprinted by permission of Gorges Borchardt, Inc.

The Good Daughter

Caroline Hwang

The moment I walked into the dry-cleaning store, I knew the woman behind the counter was from Korea, like my parents. To show her that we shared a heritage, and possibly get a fellow countryman's discount, I tilted my head forward, in shy imitation of a traditional bow.   1

"Name?" she asked, not noticing my attempted obeisance.   2

"Hwang," I answered.   3

"Hwang? Are you Chinese?"   4

Her question caught me off-guard. I was used to hearing such queries from non-Asians who think Asians all look alike, but never from one of my own people. Of course, the only Koreans I knew were my parents and their friends, people who've never asked me where I came from, since they knew better than I.   5

I ransacked my mind for the Korean words that would tell her who I was. It's always struck me as funny (in a mirthless sort of way) that I can more readily say "I am Korean" in Spanish, German and even Latin than I can in the language of my ancestry. In the end, I told her in English.   6

The dry-cleaning woman squinted as though trying to see past the glare of my strangeness, repeating my surname under her breath. "Oh, *Fxuang*," she said, doubling over with laughter. "You don't know how to speak your name."   7

I flinched. Perhaps I was particularly sensitive at the time, having just dropped out of graduate school. I had torn up my map for the future,   8

the one that said not only where I was going but who I was. My sense of
identity was already disintegrating.

When I got home, I called my parents to ask why they had never   9
bothered to correct me. "Big deal," my mother said, sounding more flip-
pant than I knew she intended. (Like many people who learn English in
a classroom, she uses idioms that don't always fit the occasion.) "So what
if you can't pronounce your name? You are American," she said.

Though I didn't challenge her explanation, it left me unsatisfied. The   10
fact is, my cultural identify is hardly that clear-cut.

My parents immigrated to this country 30 years ago, two years   11
before I was born. They told me often, while I was growing up, that, if
I wanted to, I could be president someday, that here my grasp would be
as long as my reach.

To ensure that I reaped all the advantages of this country, my parents   12
saw to it that I became fully assimilated. So, like any American of my
generation, I whiled away my youth strolling malls and talking on the
phone, rhapsodizing over Andrew McCarthy's blue eyes or analyzing
the meaning of a certain upper-classman's offer of a ride to the Homecoming football game.

To my parents, I am all American, and the sacrifices they made in   13
leaving Korea—including my mispronounced name—pale in comparison to the opportunities those sacrifices gave me. They do not see that
I straddle two cultures, nor that I feel displaced in the only country I
know. I identify with Americans, but Americans do not identify with me.
I've never known what it's like to belong to a community—neither one
at large, nor of an extended family. I know more about Europe than the
continent my ancestors unmistakably come from. I sometimes wonder,
as I did that day in the dry cleaner's, if I would be a happier person had
my parents stayed in Korea.

I first began to consider this thought around the time I decided to   14
go to graduate school. It had been a compromise: my parents wanted me
to go to law school; I wanted to skip the starched-collar track and be a
writer—the hungrier the better. But after 20-some years of following
their wishes and meeting all of their expectations, I couldn't bring myself
to disobey or disappoint. A writing career is riskier than law, I remember
thinking. If I'm a failure and my life is a washout, then what does that
make my parents' lives?

I know that many of my friends had to choose between pleasing   15
their parents and being true to themselves. But for the children of immigrants, the choice seems more complicated, a happy outcome impossible.
By making the biggest move of their lives for me, my parents indentured
me to the largest debt imaginable—I owe them the fulfillment of their
hopes for me.

It tore me up inside to suppress my dream, but I went to school for a   16
Ph.D. in English literature, thinking I had found the perfect compromise.
I would be able to write at least about books while pursuing a graduate
degree. Predictably, it didn't work out. How could I labor for five years
in a program I had no passion for? When I finally left school, my parents

were disappointed, but since it wasn't what they wanted me to do, they weren't devastated. I, on the other hand, felt I was staring at the bottom of the abyss. I had seen the flaw in my life of halfwayness, in my planned life of compromises.

I hadn't thought about my love life, but I had a vague plan to make concessions there, too. Though they raised me as an American, my parents expect me to marry someone Korean and give them grandchildren who look like them. This didn't seem like such a huge request when I was 14, but now I don't know what I'm going to do. I've never been in love with someone I dated, or dated someone I loved. (Since I can't bring myself even to entertain the thought of marrying the non-Korean men I'm attracted to, I've been dating only those I know I can stay clear-headed about.) And as I near that age when the question of marriage stalks every relationship, I can't help but wonder if my parents' expectations are responsible for the lack of passion in my life.   17

My parents didn't want their daughter to be Korean, but they didn't want her fully American, either. Children of immigrants are living paradoxes. We are the first generation and the last. We are in this country for its opportunities, yet filial duty binds us. When my parents boarded the plane, they knew they were embarking on a rough trip. I don't think they imagined the rocks in the path of their daughter who can't even pronounce her own name.   18

Behavior

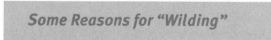

Some Reasons for "Wilding"

Susan Baker and Tipper Gore

"Wilding." It's a new word in the vocabulary of teenage violence. The crime that made it the stuff of headlines is so heinous, the details so lurid as to make them almost beyond the understanding of any sane human being.   1

When it was over, a 28-year-old woman, an investment banker out for a jog, was left brutally beaten, knifed and raped by teenagers. She was found near an isolated road in New York's Central Park, covered with mud, almost dead from brain damage, loss of blood and exposure.   2

"It was fun," one of her suspected teenage attackers, all between 14 and 17 years old, told the Manhattan district attorney's office. In the lockup, they were nonchalantly whistling at a policewoman and singing a high-on-the-charts rap song about casual sex: "Wild Thing."   3

Maybe it's the savagery, the remorseless brutality that brought the national attention to this crime. We all heard about this one, either di-   4 rectly or from a friend or family member who would end the story with an "I can't believe it."

Believe it. Because it's happening elsewhere too.   5

In 1987, in Brooklyn, N.Y., three teenagers methodically set fire to a   6
homeless couple. When at first rubbing alcohol wouldn't ignite the couple, they went to a local service station for gasoline. It worked.

In 1988, in rural Missouri, three teenagers killed a friend—partly out   7
of curiosity! They just wanted to know what it would feel like to kill
someone. One of the teenagers claimed the fascination with death began
with heavy-metal music. When the victim asked "Why?" over and over as
his friends brutally attacked with baseball bats, the answer was "Because
it's fun."

In 1988 a record 406 people died in the county of Los Angeles alone   8
in teen-gang-related attacks. One victim who survived was a pregnant
woman who was shot, allegedly by a 16-year-old as a gang initiation rite.

This is truly a "generation at risk." Indeed, the statistics reflect its   9
pain and confusion:

- The three leading causes of death among adolescents are drug- and   10
  alcohol-related accidents, suicide and homicide.

- Every year 1 million teenagers run away from home.

- Every year 1 million teenagers get pregnant.

- Every year over half a million—600,000 teenagers—attempt suicide;
  5,000 succeed.

- Alcohol and drug abuse are so prevalent among the young that a
  Weekly Reader survey recently reported that 10-year-olds often feel
  pressure to try alcohol and crack.

- According to the Department of Education, 81 percent of the victims
  of violent crime are preteens and teenagers, 19 or younger. For the
  first time, teenagers have topped adults in the percentages of serious
  crimes committed per capita.

There are many complex reasons for this sad litany. Divorce and   11
working parents strain the family's ability to cope. Latchkey kids are the
rule more than the exception. Our schools and neighborhoods have
become open-air drug markets. But it is not enough to excuse these children as products of a bad environment.

As a society, we must take full responsibility. Our music, movies and   12
television are filled with images of sexual violence and killing. The message to our kids is: it's OK to enjoy brutality and suffering: "It's fun."

The American Academy of Pediatrics released a national policy state-   13
ment on the impact of rock lyrics and music videos on adolescents last
November. In it, they noted that some lyrics communicate potentially
harmful health messages in a culture beset with drug abuse, teenage
pregnancy, AIDS and other sexually transmitted diseases.

The No. 2 album in the country this week is "GN'R Lies" from the   14
very popular group Guns N'Roses. This band is a favorite of sixth

through 12th graders. It contains the following lyrics: "I used to love her but I had to kill her, I had to put her six feet under, and I can still hear her complain."

Teen "slasher" films, featuring scenes of graphic, sadistic violence against women are so popular that characters like Jason from *Friday the 13th* and Freddie from *Nightmare on Elm Street* are considered cult heroes, and now there are spinoff television shows.

As parents, it is our responsibility to teach our children to make wise decisions. This responsibility is not only to feed and clothe their bodies, but also to feed and nurture their spirits, their minds, their values. The moral crisis facing our nation's youth requires that we *all* share the responsibility, parents and the entertainment industry.

Too often, those who produce this violence evade any discussion of their own responsibility by pretending the entire debate begins and ends with the First Amendment. We are strong advocates of its protections of free speech and free expression. We do not and have not advocated or supported restrictions on those rights: we have never proposed government action. What we are advocating, and what we have worked hard to encourage, is responsibility.

For example, producers and songwriters don't consider putting out songs, movies or videos that would portray racism in a positive way. They could. The First Amendment provides that freedom. But they don't. In part, perhaps it's because they think those products wouldn't sell. But in part, they recognize it would be irresponsible. Why is there no similar reticence when the issue is glorifying violence, generally against women?

The same sense of responsibility should be brought to a marketplace so saturated with violence that it legitimizes it for our children. It's time to stop the spilling of blood both as "entertainment" and in real life.

From Newsweek, *May 29, 1989. Reprinted by permission of Susan Baker.*

How We Have Evolved into a Culture of Rudeness

Martin J. Smith

The scene: a popular souvenir shop. The topic: the decline of civility.

"I keep wanting to do a 'remember when' book," says customer Cecilia de Baca, 41. "Remember when someone sneezed and everyone would say, 'God bless you'? Remember when people would see an older person and offer them their seat?"

She is speaking to the manager, behind whom hangs a sign: "Shoplifters will be beaten to death." A key-ring display on the counter shrieks slogans full of hostility and attitude, including "Chill me, thrill me, fulfill me, then leave me the hell alone." The T-shirt rack behind her bristles with messages—"It's not a beer belly. It's a fuel tank for a sex machine"—that suggest crudeness these days can be a profitable commodity.

"There really are a lot of nice people that come in," says Jeff Balaam, 4
34, manager of the Seal Beach, Calif., souvenir shop, "but there also are a
lot of jerks. I like the ones that come in, go straight to the back and use the
restroom, then just walk out. They don't even pretend to look around.
And they don't say thank you."

Highbrow prudes? Hardly. They are, after all, in a beachside souvenir 5
shop.

But lamentations about the decline of common courtesy and civility 6
transcend economic, social and racial lines like the ratings of a particularly juicy *Geraldo* show.

"It has nothing to do with money or social class," insists Letitia 7
Baldrige, an authority on manners who has written 13 books on the subject. "It has everything to do with character and the way Mama and Papa
brought you up, and that doesn't cost money. Some of the lowest economic classes have the best brought-up children, and some of the highest
economic classes have the least civility."

So how did we go from a ma'am-ing and sir-ing society where polite- 8
ness really counted to a society where even a corporate giant such as Del
Taco feels safe distributing children's prizes imprinted with the slogan
"Shut up and eat your beans"?

What social pathology explains the reluctance of so many people to 9
pull over for passing funeral processions, to make small talk with fellow
bus passengers, to exchange the pleasantries that for generations helped
lubricate social discourse?

What impulse moved an antique-store owner to tape a photocopied 10
cartoon in the store's front window showing two vault-type safes, apparently copulating, above the caption "Safe sex"?

Does the world really need to see unauthorized and explicit honey- 11
moon video outtakes of Tonya Harding and Jeff Gillooly, as presented in
the new *Penthouse* magazine, or the full video available, reportedly, on
pay-per-view TV this fall?

Experts agree on the symptoms but aren't sure how to explain the de- 12
cline of civility and the rise of crudeness. They cite everything from the
anti-Establishment movement of the 1960s to the unraveling of close-knit
neighborhoods to the rise of feminism. "One reason is the legitimization
of protest movements in North America and the West in general," said
Alexander Moore, a professor of anthropology at the University of Southern California.

"That legitimized bad behavior, especially among youth, and has in- 13
fluenced the problem. Protests have gone from the gentle nonviolence of
Martin Luther King to the antics of ACT-UP and Queer Nation and others
that use rudeness as a way of gaining attention."

Psychology Professor Jerald Jellison blames the phenomenon on "a 14
40-year shift away from a social life guided by social customs and personal character."

"We used to have informal rule systems which governed life," says 15
Jellison, author of "I'm Sorry I Didn't Mean To & Other Lies We Love to
Tell."

Now, Jellison says, that informal mandate for public behavior has   16
been replaced by more formal rules and government-based laws. The
question "Is it proper?" has been replaced by the question "Is it legal?"

"If it's not illegal, then a lot of people will go ahead and do it," he   17
says. "They don't worry about upsetting people. It may be offensive, but
they think, 'There's no law against it. And even if there is a law, then I
probably won't get caught. And even if I get caught, I'll get a good attorney and get out of it.' That's a large change in our society, and there are
problems associated with it."

Moore, the JSC anthropologist, says the issue of civility seemed espe-   18
cially relevant during the recent World Cup, during which competing
players frequently helped up one another from the ground and winners
often consoled losers. The behavior was very different than the in-your-
face style of more traditional U.S. sports.

Baldrige says recent events "reminded people of a different era when   18
people behaved nicely to one another"—the death of Jacqueline Kennedy
Onassis, the pomp and ceremony surrounding the death of former President Richard Nixon, the patriotic fervor of the D-Day celebrations. "In the
space of a few months," she says wistfully, "there were a lot of tragic but
very dignified events that harkened back to a time of graciousness and
kindness and caring."

The Thin Grey Line

Marya Mannes

"Aw, they all do it," growled the cabdriver. He was talking about cops   1
who took payoffs for winking at double parking, but his cynicism could
as well have been directed any of a dozen other instances of corruption,
big-time and small-time. Moreover, the disgust in his voice was overlaid
by an unspoken "So what?": the implication that since this was the way
things were, there was nothing anybody could do.

Like millions of his fellow Americans, the cabdriver was probably a   2
decent human being who had never stolen anything, broken any law or
willfully injured another; somewhere, a knowledge of what was probably
right had kept him from committing what was clearly wrong. But that
knowledge had not kept a thin grey line that separates the two conditions
from being daily greyer and thinner—to the point that it was hardly
noticeable.

On the one side of this line are They: the bribers, the cheaters, the   3
chiselers, the swindlers, the extortioners. On the other side are We—both
partners and victims. They and We are now so perilously close that the
only mark distinguishing us is that They get caught and We don't.

The same citizen who voices outrage at police corruption will slip the   4
traffic cop on his block a handsome Christmas present in the belief that
his car, nestled under a "No Parking" sign, will not be ticketed. The son
of that nice woman next door has a habit of stealing cash from her purse
because his allowance is smaller than his buddies'. Your son's friend
admitted cheating at exams because "everybody does it."

Bit by bit, the resistance to and immunity against wrong that a   5
healthy social body builds up by law and ethics and the dictation of conscience have broken down. And instead of the fighting indignation of a
people outraged by those who prey on them, we have the admission of
impotence: "They all do it."

Now, failure to uphold the law is no less corrupt than violation of the   6
law. And the continuing shame of this country now is the growing number of Americans who fail to uphold and assist enforcement of the law,
simply—and ignominiously—out of fear. Fear of "involvement," fear of
reprisal, fear of "trouble." A man is beaten by hoodlums in plain daylight
and in view of bystanders. These people not only fail to help the victim,
but, like the hoodlums, flee before the police can question them. A city
official knows of a colleague's bribe but does not report it. A pedestrian
watches a car hit a woman but leaves the scene, to avoid giving testimony.
It happens every day. And if the police get cynical at this irresponsibility,
they are hardly to blame. Morale is a matter of giving support and having
faith in one another; where both are lacking, "law" has become a worthless word.

How did we get this way? What started this blurring of what was   7
once a thick black line between the lawful and the lawless? What makes a
"regular guy," a decent fellow, accept a bribe? What makes a nice kid
from a middle-class family take money for doing something he must
know is not only illegal but wrong?

When you look into the background of an erring "kid" you will often   8
find a comfortable home and a mother who will tell you, with tears in her
eyes, that she "gave him everything." She probably did, to his everlasting
damage. Fearing her son's disapproval, the indulgent mother denies him
nothing except responsibility. Instead of growing up, he grows to believe
that the world owes him everything.

The nice kid's father crosses the thin grey line himself in a dozen   9
ways, day in and day out. He pads his expenses on his income-tax returns
as a matter of course. As a landlord, he pays the local inspectors of the
city housing authority to overlook violations in the houses he rents. When
his son flunked his driving test, he gave him ten dollars to slip the inspec-
tor on his second test. "They all do it," he said.

The nice kid is brought up with boys and girls who have no heroes   10
except people not much older than themselves who have made the Big
Time, usually in show business or in sports. Publicity and money are the
halos of their stars, who range from pop singers who can't sing to ball-
players who can't read; from teen-age starlets who can't act to television
performers who can't think. They may be excited by the exploits of space-
men, but the work's too tough and dangerous.

The nice kids have no heroes because they don't believe in heroes. Heroes are suckers and squares. To be a hero you have to stand out, to excel, to take risks, and above all, not only choose between right and wrong, but defend the right and fight the wrong. This means responsibility—and who needs it?   11

Today, no one has to take any responsibility. The psychiatrists, the sociologists, the novelists, the playwrights have gone a long way to help promote irresponsibility. Nobody really is to blame for what he does. It's Society. It's Environment. It's a Broken Home. It's an Underprivileged Area. But it's hardly ever You.   12

Now we find a truckload of excuses to absolve the individual from responsibility for his actions. A fellow commits a crime because he's basically insecure, because he hated his stepmother at nine, or because his sister needs an operation. A policeman loots a store because his salary is too low. A city official accepts a payoff because it's offered to him. Members of minority groups, racial or otherwise, commit crimes because they can't get a job, or are unacceptable to the people living around them. The words "right" and "wrong" are foreign to these people.   13

But honesty is the best policy. Says who? Anyone willing to get laughed at. But the laugh is no laughing matter. It concerns the health and future of a nation. It involves the two-dollar illegal bettor as well as the corporation price-fixer, the college-examination cheater and the payroll-padding congressman, the expense-account chiseler, the seller of pornography and his schoolboy reader, the bribed judge and the stealing delinquent. All these people may represent a minority. But when, as it appears now, the majority excuse themselves from responsibility by accepting corruption as natural to society ("They all do it"), this society is bordering on total confusion. If the line between right and wrong is finally erased, there is no defense against the power of evil.   14

Before this happens—and it is by no means far away—it might be well for the schools of the nation to substitute for the much-argued issue of prayer a daily lesson in ethics, law, and responsibility to society that would strengthen the conscience as exercise strengthens muscles. And it would be even better if parents were forced to attend it. For corruption is not something you read about in the papers and leave to courts. We are all involved.   15

As appeared in McCall's *magazine, Jan. 1964.*

Deliberate Living, Not Spontaneity, Is the Heart of Freedom

Richard Kirk

Thoreau went into the woods, he said in *Walden,* to "live deliberately," to live, in other words, with careful premeditation, methodically weighing actions in his mind's eye in order to get, as he put it, to life's "marrow."   1

Almost a century and a half later the most touted goal of American pop culture is to live spontaneously, to act, in other words, on one's instincts, impressions or feelings—to "be oneself," in the jargon of the day. This somewhat oxymoronic ideal, "achieving spontaneity," essentially amounts to the annihilation of deliberation. 2

Why, one might ask, would anyone want to do away with the characteristic Thoreau so prized? Answer: because it is considered an impediment to "freedom"—the term denoting in this case the indulgence of feeling. 3

A young man rises late in the morning and does not feel like making the bed upon which he slept. The voice of modernity intones, "No matter, let it slide. What's the big deal? You're free to do as you please." The same late riser has chores to perform but again isn't feeling up to the tasks. "So what," the internal voice again whispers, "if you aren't really motivated"—meaning if you're not enthusiastically anticipating these activities—"the work can wait." 4

Our young friend receives word that a neighbor is in need of help. He is able to provide assistance but isn't that excited about the prospect. "Oh, well"—so goes the rationalization provided by his unseen Zeitgeist—"it doesn't really do any good to help if your heart isn't in it, does it?" 5

These are examples, small and large, of the way the doctrine of spontaneity, of following one's feelings, plays out in specific cases. An implicit assumption of this ideology is that I am most "me" when I follow the urges that immediately present themselves in any situation—as if these initial passions, appetites or desires are quintessentially "me." The voices of restraint, deliberation and discipline, on the other hand, which are regularly drowned out by the aforementioned rush of emotions, are viewed skeptically as representatives of "society" or "parental authority" and thus not authentically "me." 6

"Do what you *feel* is right"—not "do what you think is right"—and "go with your feelings" are creedal affirmations of the ego-equals-id mentality. The paradoxical result of following this gospel is that one becomes a slave to his own emotions, bound like Ixion to the flaming wheel of desire, tossed at one moment whimsically this way and the next in the contrary direction. No pilot guides this ship, no rudder keeps it on course since its direction is dictated by the unpredictable winds of emotion. 7

These affective elements—name your poison, but do not forget the seven deadly sins—turn out to be less benign than advertised and belatedly reveal themselves as distinct from the "me" perched on the verge of annihilation. I find myself addicted, enslaved to . . . myself? 8

Thoreau is wiser. He does not ask which of the feelings seeking expression through my body is "me." He rather latches on to a capacity that he possesses—deliberation—and exercises it. This intention-laden capacity allows a human being to gain some leverage over bodily instincts. 9

It is superfluous in 1995 to assert that the body has its virtues. For us, the body has become the very essence of virtue. Rarely, however, does one hear it proposed that gaining "leverage" over bodily instincts is nec- 10 essary or that simply identifying the "self" with bodily passions puts one at a subhuman level.

Civilization is not the result of exterminating passions, but it is the product of directing and asserting control over them. Puritans, Victorians and the medieval church are depicted by modern proponents of spontaneity as repressive party-poopers who disparage the body. A fairer, more accurate assessment is that they were yeomen laborers facilitating the emergence of a distinctive human spirit from the bondage of bodily passion. The "ego" that psychologists pamper and often claim to enhance by indulging bodily desires is today vanishing into the vortex of passion out of which it, with heroic effort, emerged. 11

Michelangelo's "Boboli Captive" is constructed of stone. Yet it is by cutting away and molding this stone that the image itself emerges. No cutting, no molding, no sculpture. Only thus does the character imprisoned within the stone emerge. The same can be said, *mutatis mutandis*, of the"I" ("the spirit") in its relation to the body. Am I my body? Yes and no. 12

"I" exist only to the extent that I am distinguished from the body and its passions to which I am joined. "I" am "free" only to the extent that I can exercise control over "my" passions, can shape and direct them. "I" exist in the discipline of setting goals, as opposed to the passive enactment of imperatives originating in the spleen. 13

"I," in reality, means character, and character is achieved, not given. It is a product of regimen, discipline and intention. 14

"Spontaneity" and "freedom" are the deceptive ideological labels modernity has given to the ascendancy of the id, to the rule of Plato's hydra-headed monsters that animate the spirit but can give it no integrity. "True freedom" comes, paradoxically, not from indulging the whims of desire but from "living deliberately." 15

Reprinted by permission of the author.

Education

Why Most Students Cheat: It's Not What You Think

Michael Moore

Three-quarters of all college students have cheated at least once. And that may be a conservative estimate. A 1990 survey, conducted at the University of Miami, Ohio, found that 9 of 10 students there cheated by methods ranging from copying a classmate's answers during an exam to plagiarizing term papers. 1

Every day, we hear and read that America is losing its competitive edge. One explanation is that American students are graduating without 2 getting an education. Anyone who has spent some time in a college classroom can hardly disagree. But this is not entirely the fault of the undergraduate.

Many people find it hard to sympathize with students who cheat. If undergraduates, or their parents, are financing a college education, they have a responsibility to attend class, learn the subjects and complete assignments. But our institutions of higher learning also have a responsibility: to provide the kind of education that is not only interesting but stimulating. They have largely failed in this mission by choosing to become diploma mills.

The dynamics of the "system" are to blame. A majority of students don't cheat because they are lazy, or hung over. They mostly cheat in classes they are forced to take. They mostly cheat in classes that are boring. Instead of using stimulating techniques to present their subjects, professors simply teach at students. An unmotivated professor sends a distressing signal to students—it's easier for them to cheat, since they can blame their lack of intellectual interest on an uninspiring professor. Why should a student be any more interested in learning than a professor is in teaching?

Professors are the primary reason that cheating continues. If students are getting away with cheating, it's usually the result of a lack of vigilance on the part of the professor. Ask any administrator. A lot of professors refuse to enforce academic integrity codes, thereby signaling students that they have little to lose by cheating. Indeed, if more professors looked forward to class day as much as they do to payday, the incidence of cheating would dramatically diminish. They should wake up.

Still, the American college professor must contend with administrators and college boards of trustees who have traditionally placed great pressure on them to produce research, attract federal, state and private grants, and get published. These pressures ultimately shortchange the student. The "publish-or-perish" mentality relegates educating to a secondary status. And these factors, combined with traditional professional laziness (read: tenure), have distorted priorities.

So where is the student in all of this? Students will continue to cheat until "the system" is reformed. One reason I wrote *Cheating 101* was to let outsiders in on college's dirty little secret. Cheating in itself isn't that bad, when compared with a system that tolerates—even encourages—cheating. Higher education clearly needs reforming.

One reform would be to promote greater interest in learning. Cheating is a paradox. Students cheat when they are not interested in a course or there is no mutual respect between student and professor.

Honor codes can discourage cheating. At the University of Virginia, which has the nation's oldest code, student cheating is rare and does not go unpunished. The value of honor codes is that they encourage a student to be responsible. Statistics prove this approach works.

A related reform is to provide incentives for professors to be more vigilant in the classroom. Instead of simply acknowledging that cheating exists, they should push for honor codes where they don't exist, and enforce them where they do. And administrators need to be prepared to back up their professors, rather than running scared from the mere threat of lawsuits. A University of Pittsburgh professor, for example, brought charges against a student after he found evidence that the student had copied exams, quizzes and lab reports. When the student's father, a lawyer, threatened to sue, the case went nowhere. 10

No wonder cheating in college is hard to combat. 11

A Proposal to Abolish Grading

Paul Goodman

Let half a dozen of the prestigious universities—Chicago, Stanford, the Ivy League—abolish grading, and use testing only and entirely for pedagogic purposes as teachers see fit. 1

Anyone who knows the frantic temper of the present schools will understand the transvaluation of values that would be effected by this modest innovation. For most of the students, the competitive grade has come to be the essence. The naïve teacher points to the beauty of the subject and the ingenuity of the research; the shrewd student asks if he is responsible for that on the final exam. 2

Let me at once dispose of an objection whose unanimity is quite fascinating. I think that the great majority of professors agree that grading hinders teaching and creates a bad spirit, going as far as cheating and plagiarizing. I have before me the collection of essays *Examining in Harvard College,* and this is the consensus. It is uniformly asserted, however, that the grading is inevitable; for how else will the graduate schools, the foundations, the corporations *know* whom to accept, reward, hire? How will the talent scouts know whom to tap? 3

By testing the applicants, of course, according to the specific task requirements of the inducting institution, just as applicants for the Civil Service or for licenses in medicine, law, and architecture are tested. Why should Harvard professors do the testing *for* corporations and graduate schools? 4

The objection is ludicrous. Dean Whitla, of the Harvard Office of Tests, points out that the scholastic aptitude and achievement tests used for *admission* to Harvard are a super-excellent index for all-around Harvard performance, better than high-school grades or particular Harvard course grades. Presumably, these college entrance tests are tailored for what Harvard and similar institutions want. By the same logic, would not 5 an employer do far better to apply his own job aptitude test rather than to rely on the vagaries of Harvard section men? Indeed, I doubt that many employers bother to look at such grades; they are more likely to be interested merely in the fact of a Harvard diploma, whatever that connotes to them. The grades have most of their weight with the graduate schools—here, as elsewhere, the system runs mainly for its own sake.

It is really necessary to remind our academics of the ancient history   6
of examination. In the medieval university, the whole point of the grueling trial of the candidate was whether or not to accept him as a peer. His disputation and lecture for the Master's was just that, a master-piece to enter the guild. It was not to make comparative evaluations. It was not to weed out and select for an extramural licensor or employer. It was certainly not to pit one young fellow against another in an ugly competition. My philosophic impression is that the medievals thought they knew what a good job of work was and that we are competitive because we do not know. But the more status is achieved by largely irrelevant competitive evaluation, the less will we ever know.

(Of course, our American examinations never did have this purely   7
guild orientation, just as our faculties have rarely had absolute autonomy; the examining was to satisfy Overseers, Elders, distant Regents—and they as paternal superiors have always doted on giving grades, rather than accepting peers. But I submit that this setup itself makes it impossible for the student to *become* a master, to *have* grown up, and to commence on his own. He will always be making A or B for some overseer. And in the present atmosphere, he will always be climbing on his friend's neck.)

Perhaps the chief objectors to abolishing grading would be the stu-   8
dents and their parents. The parents should be simply disregarded; their anxiety has done enough damage already. For the students, it seems to me that a primary duty of the university is to deprive them of their props, their dependence on extrinsic valuation and motivation, and to force them to confront the difficult enterprise itself and finally lose themselves in it.

A miserable effect of grading is to nullify the various uses of testing.   9
Testing, for both student and teacher, is a means of structuring, and also of finding out what is blank or wrong and what has been assimilated and can be taken for granted. Review—including high-pressure review—is a means of bringing together the fragments, so that there are flashes of synoptic insight.

There are several good reasons for testing, and kinds of test. But if   10
the aim is to discover weakness, what is the point of downgrading and punishing it, and thereby inviting the student to conceal his weakness, by faking and bulling, if not cheating? The natural conclusion of synthesis is the insight itself, not a grade for having had it. For the important purpose of placement, if one can establish in the student the belief that one is testing *not* to grade and make invidious comparisons but for his own advantage, the student should normally seek his own level, where he is challenged and yet capable, rather than trying to get by. If the stu-

dent dares to accept himself as he is, a teacher's grade is a crude instrument compared with a student's self-awareness. But it is rare in our universities that students are encouraged to notice objectively their vast confusion. Unlike Socrates, our teachers rely on power drives rather than shame and ingenuous idealism.

Many students are lazy, so teachers try to goad or threaten them by grading. In the long run this must do more harm than good. Laziness is a character defense. It may be a way of avoiding learning, in order to protect the conceit that one is already perfect (deeper, the despair that one *never* can be). It may be a way of avoiding just the risk of failing and being downgraded. Sometimes it is a way of politely saying, "I won't." But since it is the authoritarian grown-up demands that have created such attitudes in the first place, why repeat the trauma? There comes a time when we must treat people as adult, laziness and all. It is one thing courageously to fire a do-nothing out of your class; it is quite another thing to evaluate him with a lordly F.

Most important of all, it is often obvious that balking in doing the work, especially among bright young people who get to great universities, means exactly what it says: The work does not suit me, not this subject, or not at this time, or not in this school, or not in school altogether. The student might not be bookish; he might be school-tired; perhaps his development ought now to take another direction. Yet unfortunately, if such a student is intelligent and is not sure of himself, he *can* be bullied into passing, and this obscures everything. My hunch is that I am describing a common situation. What a grim waste of young life and teacherly effort! Such a student will retain nothing of what he has "passed" in. Sometimes he must get mononucleosis to tell his story and be believed.

And ironically, the converse is also probably commonly true. A student flunks, and is mechanically weeded out, who is really ready and eager to learn in a scholastic setting, but has not quite caught on. A good teacher can recognize the situation, but the computer wreaks its will.

A Matter of Respect—Or Lack of It

Richard Morin

Teenagers and their teachers agree: There's a fourth R that needs to be taught in America's schools. Respect. In big ways and small, students say that they don't respect each other. They don't respect their teachers. And the particularly don't respect an educational system they say doesn't challenge them to do their best and rewards them for mediocre work, according to surveys sponsored by the Public Agenda Foundation.

"You can lie to them [teachers] to get the grades you want," says one   2
Sunnyvale, Calif., teenager who participated in a focus group convened
by Public Agenda in connection with the polling project. "You just tell
them you didn't get it in, and they believe you. It's real easy."

Too easy, America's teens admit. Half of all teenagers interviewed   3
in the national poll of more than 1,300 randomly selected high school
students said their schools failed to challenge them to do their best. Two
thirds said they could easily do "much better" if they tried harder, and
eight in 10 said they would learn more if they were challenged, if they
were forced to complete homework and turn it in on time—something
they said their teachers currently didn't demand.

"You can just glide through," says a teenager in a Seattle focus   4
group. "You can copy somebody's homework at the beginning of the
period. I mean you can do whatever you want. . . . They practically hand
you a diploma."

How can America's schools win the respect of their students? Set   5
tough standards—and then enforce them, these teenagers say. According
to the poll, 76 percent of the teenagers interviewed said students should
not be allowed to graduate unless they demonstrate a good command of
the English language, and 74 percent said schools should only pass students to the next grade when they have learned what's expected of them.

Tough talk. But researchers say these teens stood firm in their views   6
when challenged on them by emphasizing the consequence of tougher
standards. "The survey presented the teen with this choice: Should a
youngster be promoted only when he has learned the required material
or should a youngster who has tried hard and attended class regularly be
permitted to pass?" the analysts wrote.

These teenagers' answers: 61 percent said the standard should be   7
enforced, even if some well-meaning students are left behind. (Adults
interviewed in a companion national survey were even firmer in this
belief: 81 percent said students should only be passed to a higher grade if
they've learned the required material.)

In conversations with teenagers and with teachers, other issues of   8
respect surfaced. Both groups complain that schools no longer are safe
havens from the mean world outside the school house doors. Nor are
schools immune from what some social critics claim is the disappearance
of civility in our national life.

"Conversations with teachers and students indicate that both   9
sense a general coarsening of the atmosphere," Public Agenda analysts
wrote—a view that echoes the sometimes brutal assessments of teenagers in the focus groups. "People at my school, they don't have respect
for anybody," a Seattle teenage girl says. "They have their own little
groups, and you can't be in that group unless you're just like them.
They're just disrespectful to you and your . . . property and stuff."

Seven in 10 teenagers surveyed say disruptive students are a serious   10
problem at their schools, a view shared by equal proportions of black,
white and Latino students. And more than half—53 percent—say that
constant troublemakers should be kicked out of class "so teachers can

concentrate on the kids who want to learn."

Sometimes these behaviors go far beyond simple disrespect. 11

"I come in and I see guys pulling up their shirts showing me guns," 12
a teenage boy in Alabama says. "And then I go to the movies and there's
someone on the corner selling weed, and I try to stay away from that
stuff."

All of which leads one Westchester County, N.Y., teenager to con- 13
clude: "I definitely think we're worse than we used to be. I mean, if I was
an adult, I would be, you know, against teenagers too—with what I
know of what teenagers are like and how rude they are. That's me, too,
because I'm rude to them, and I'm horrible to people sometimes."

Teachers also need to learn respect, the surveys' authors wrote. 14
"The issue cuts both ways, with students in focus groups often turning
the tables and complaining that teachers were disrespectful of them."
In fact, only four in 10 students say most of their teachers treat them with
respect—a view that transcends race, with equal proportions of black
and white students saying their teachers are respectful of them.

The inevitable result is an increase in hostility between teachers 15
and students. "Short fuses and routine classes create a downward spiral:
Students believe that many teachers resent or dislike them, and teachers
think that too many students don't care," the analysts wrote.

So what do America's teens want from their teachers and their 16
schools? The survey suggests two simple answers: "More challenge and
structure—for someone to take them seriously enough to demand that
they do their best."

Yet the Public Agenda researchers acknowledge that the solution 17
isn't quite so simple. Today's kids are growing up in a "teenage culture
that the youngsters themselves fear: the cliques, the clothes, the teasing,
the cheating, the lure of dangerous drugs and weapons just a block
away—even in the best of neighborhoods. . . . Schools, teachers, parents—
and anyone else concerned about these students' futures—face a long and
difficult struggle for these youngster's minds—one that may require
more than raising academic standards and administering new tests."

Can Students Evaluate Professors?

Patrick Groff

The 1998 murder of three San Diego State University engineering pro- 1
fessors, apparently by a disgruntled student, may be graphic evidence of
the extent that discontent among today's students may be manifested.

Their perceptions that professors address them in disrespectful ways 2
is by no means a unique phenomenon. Literature through the ages is

replete with stories of professors whom students believed were exceedingly offensive. In that regard, almost every university graduate harbors a deeply felt, personal recollection.

Nonetheless, until their violence-prone rebellion in the 1960s and '70s, students generally suffered in relative silence what they discerned was abuse from professors. These young insurrectionists intimidated universities into prescribing anonymous evaluations by students of their professors' personalities, knowledge of subject matter and abilities to teach. From then on, bad ratings meant the end to an untenured professor's career.

At present, about 90 percent of universities conduct such evaluations. By 1988, there were more than 1,300 scholarly publications on various ramifications of this practice. The number per year has grown steadily since then. The topic indeed is an academic growth industry.

It is abundantly clear, however, that students' ratings of their professors at SDSU did not prevent the tragic event it just experienced. There are many other questions about the usefulness and validity of students' ratings of professors that the mountain of data gathered on this subject does not answer satisfactorily.

The first of these queries is whether assessments of professors by today's relatively unknowledgeable, marginally literate students, who are accustomed to lowered scholastic expectations, grade inflation and enhancement of their self-esteem in high school, can be accepted as authoritative and unappealable. Are students with obviously rudimentary skills and understandings (as exhibited by about 50 percent who must take remedial courses in our state universities) capable of evaluating, for example, whether professors have sufficient knowledge of their subject matter and organize it well enough when teaching it?

A second major criticism of student evaluations of professors is whether these ratings actually have any practical usefulness. There is no evidence that they lead to improvement of professors' classroom practices. There appears to be no case of a tenured professor being fired solely for low ratings from students. The ratings certainly have not led to the end of many professors' overly generous grading practices.

On the other hand, ratings from students have some unintended, but nevertheless unfortunate, consequences and features. University deans report that they result in grade inflation. Even Harvard has so succumbed. Since evaluations by students were instituted there, the number of "A's" awarded increased 370 percent. A significant correlation also is discovered between the grade a student expects and how high he or she rates a professor. There is no doubt but that a lowering of academic requirements and grade inflation has accompanied evaluations of professors by students.

Complicating the issue are the findings that humanities professors award much higher grades than do those in science, math, and engineering. (This is predictable because the latter courses are more desirable since they lead directly to jobs.) It is not surprising, then, that humanities

3

4

5

6

7

8

9

professors get higher student ratings. As do female professors from female students, professors who do not teach required courses and those who teach at the graduate level. Professors who are assertive and forceful get lower ratings than ones who are soft-spoken and compassionate.

A third objection to evaluation of professors by students is that it merely is a comparatively cheap and too-accessible public relations gimmick. The finding that universities do not require tenured professors who score low on student evaluations to submit to training on how to teach suggests as much. That no demands are made for change in such professors' course contents, instructional materials, exam questions, type of assignments given, etc., is further evidence in this respect.   10

Authentic efforts to upgrade professors' teaching would use pre- and post-tests of how much students learn in different sections of common courses. A comprehensive exam for seniors would be set up. Professors with teaching problems would be required to conduct seminars for their peers, who would judge their competencies and knowledge. Student evaluations of professors actually drive out such assessments because they are less costly, easier to administer and, above all, provide a convenient number tag for each professor's competency.   11

So far, the best that can be said for student evaluations is that they remind professors that teaching proficiency is important.   12

But such commonplace advice unfortunately does not tell professors how to improve.   13

Physician-Assisted Suicide

In Defense of Voluntary Euthanasia

Sidney Hook

A few short years ago, I lay at the point of death. A congestive heart failure was treated for diagnostic purposes by an angiogram that triggered a stroke. Violent and painful hiccups, uninterrupted for several days and nights, prevented the ingestion of food. My left side and one of my vocal cords became paralyzed. Some form of pleurisy set in, and I felt I was drowning in a sea of slime. At one point, my heart stopped beating; just as I lost consciousness, it was thumped back into action again. In one of my lucid intervals during those days of agony, I asked my physician to discontinue all life-supporting services or show me how to do it. He refused and told me that someday I would appreciate the unwisdom of my request.   1

A month later, I was discharged from the hospital. In six months, 2
I regained the use of my limbs, and although my voice still lacks its old
resonance and carrying power I no longer croak like a frog. There remain
some minor disabilities and I am restricted to a rigorous, low sodium
diet. I have resumed my writing and research.

My experience can be and has been cited as an argument against 3
honoring requests of stricken patients to be gently eased out of their pain
and life. I cannot agree. There are two main reasons. As an octogenarian,
there is a reasonable likelihood that I may suffer another "cardiovascular
accident" or worse. I may not even be in a position to ask for the surcease
of pain. It seems to me that I have already paid my dues to death—indeed, although time has softened my memories, they are vivid enough to
justify my saying that I suffered enough to warrant dying several times
over. Why run the risk of more?

Secondly, I dread imposing on my family and friends another grim 4
round of misery similar to the one my first attack occasioned.

My wife and children endured enough for one lifetime. I know that 5
for them the long days and nights of waiting, the disruption of their professional duties and their own familial responsibilities counted for nothing in their anxiety for me. In their joy at my recovery they have been
forgotten. Nonetheless, to visit another prolonged spell of helpless suffering on them as my life ebbs away, or even worse, if I linger on into a
comatose senility, seems altogether gratuitous.

But what, it may be asked, of the joy and satisfaction of living, of 6
basking in the sunlight, listening to music, watching one's grandchildren
growing into adolescence, following the news about the fate of freedom
in a troubled world, playing with ideas, writing one's testament of wisdom and folly for posterity? Is not all that one endured, together with the
risk of its recurrence, an acceptable price for the multiple satisfactions
that are still open even to a person of advanced years?

Apparently those who cling to life, no matter what, think so. I do not. 7

The zest and intensity of these experiences are no longer what they 8
used to be. I am not vain enough to delude myself that I can in the few
remaining years make an important discovery useful for mankind or can
lead a social movement or do anything that will be historically eventful,
no less event-making. My autobiography, which describes a record of
intellectual and political experiences of some historical value, already
much too long, could be posthumously published. I have had my fill of
joys and sorrows and am not greedy for more life. I have always thought
that a test of whether one had found happiness in one's life is whether
one would be willing to relive it—whether, if it were possible, one would
accept the opportunity to be born again.

Having lived a full and relatively happy life, I would cheerfully 9
accept the chance to be reborn, but certainly not to be reborn again as an
infirm octogenarian. To some extent, my views reflect what I have seen
happen to the aged and stricken who have been so unfortunate as to survive crippling paralysis. They suffer, and impose suffering on others,

unable even to make a request that their torment be ended.

I am mindful too of the burdens placed upon the community, with 10
its rapidly diminishing resources, to provide the adequate and costly services necessary to sustain the lives of those whose days and nights are
spent on mattress graves of pain. A better use could be made of these
resources to increase the opportunities and qualities of life for the young.
I am not denying the moral obligation the community has to look after its
disabled and aged. There are times, however, when an individual may
find it pointless to insist on the fulfillment of a legal and moral right.

What is required is no great revolution in morals but an enlargement 11
of imagination and an intelligent evaluation of alternative uses of community resources.

Long ago, Seneca observed that "the wise man will live as long as 12
he ought, not as long as he can." One can envisage hypothetical circumstances in which one has a duty to prolong one's life despite its costs for
the sake of others, but such circumstances are far removed from the ordinary prospects we are considering. If wisdom is rooted in the knowledge
of the alternatives of choice, it must be reliably informed of the state one
is in and its likely outcome. Scientific medicine is not infallible, but it is
the best we have. Should a rational person be willing to endure acute suffering merely on the chance that a miraculous cure might presently be at
hand? Each one should be permitted to make his own choice—especially
when no one else is harmed by it.

The responsibility for the decision, whether deemed wise or foolish, 13
must be with the chooser.

Promoting a Culture of Abandonment

Teresa R. Wagner

The death toll in Oregon will really begin to rise now. Attorney General 1
Janet Reno has decided that a federal law regulating drug usage (the
Controlled Substances Act) somehow does not apply to the use of lethal
drugs in Oregon, the only state in the country to legalize assisted suicide.
The evidence will begin pouring in on how deadly assisted suicide can
be, not just for the individuals subject to it, of course, but for the culture
that countenances it.

There are frightening and compelling policy reasons to oppose 2
assisted suicide. Foremost is the risk of abuse. Proponents of assisted
suicide always insist that the practice will be carefully limited: It will be
available, they claim, only for those who request it and only for those
who are dying anyway (the terminally ill).

Such limitations are virtually impossible. People will inevitably be killed without knowing or consenting to it. Several state courts have already ruled as a matter of state constitutional law that any rights given to competent patients (those who can request death) must also be given to incompetent ones (those who cannot). Third parties make treatment decisions for this latter group. Now legal, assisted suicide will be just another treatment option for surrogate decision makers to select, even if the patient has made no indication of wanting to die.

What's more, the cost crunch in medicine virtually guarantees that hospitals and doctors will eventually pressure, and then coerce, patients to avail themselves of this easy and cheap alternative.

Similarly, the confinement of this right to the terminally ill is impossible. As many groups opposing assisted suicide have noted, the term itself is hardly clear. The Oregon law defines terminal disease as that which will produce death within six months. Is that with or without medical treatment? Many individuals will die in much less than six months without very simple medical treatment (insulin injections, for example). They could be deemed terminal under this law and qualify for this new right to death.

More importantly, the rationale for providing this new right almost demands its extension beyond limits. After all, if we are trying to relieve pain and suffering, the non-terminal patient, who faces years of discomfort, has a more compelling claim to relief than the terminal patient, whose hardship is supposed to be short-lived. Courts will quickly recognize this and dispense with any terminal requirement.

So much for limits.

The tragedy, of course, is that we have the ability right now to relieve the suffering of those in even the most excruciating pain. Anesthesiologists and others in pain centers around the country claim that we can provide adequate palliation 99 percent of the time.

Unfortunately, certain obstacles prevent patients from getting the pain relief they need: Many in medicine fear, mistakenly, that patients will become addicted to analgesic medications; overzealous regulatory agencies penalize doctors who prescribe the large doses needed (or they penalize the pharmacies that stock them); and medical professionals generally are not trained adequately in pain and symptom management.

The more important reasons to oppose assisted suicide, however, are moral: We must decide what type of people we are and how we will care for the weak and sick among us, for it is only to these dependents, not to all individuals, that we are offering this new right. Is this because we respect their autonomy (allegedly the basis of the right to die) more than our own? Or do we unconsciously (or consciously) believe their lives are of less worth and therefore less entitled to make demands of care (not to mention money) on us?

Make no mistake: Despite incessant clamor about rights, ours is actually a culture of abandonment. The acceptance of assisted suicide and euthanasia in this culture is almost inevitable. Abortion, of course, was the foundation. It taught (and still teaches) society to abandon mothers, and mothers to abandon their children. Divorce (husbands and wives leaving or abandoning each other) sends the same message. The commitment to care for others, both those who have been given to us and those we have selected, no longer exists. We simply do not tolerate those we do not want.

What to do about the advance of this culture? Replace it with a culture of care, a culture of commitment. 12

This is obviously no easy task, for it is neither easy to administer care 13 nor easy to receive it. (Indeed, the elderly cite the fear of dependence most often when indicating why they might support assisted suicide.) But it is precisely within this context of care, of giving and receiving, that we enjoy the dignity particular to human beings. Otherwise we would simply shoot the terminal patient as we do the dying horse.

The assisted suicide question is really the battle between these two 14 cultures. We can follow the way of Jack Kevorkian or of Mother Teresa. The life of Mother Teresa was a witness to nothing if not to commitment and care. She was simply there to care for the sick and the old, to assure them of their worth. Jack Kevorkian and our culture of abandonment, epitomized by assisted suicide and all the abuses to follow, surely will not.

San Diego Union-Tribune. *June 25, 1998. Copyright 1998 by Teresa R. Wagner, Family Research Council.*

The Effects of Television

The Meaning of TV

William Henry III

We tend to talk about television as though it has always been there, as 1 though it provides the same experience for everyone, as though it were a single, living organism. In conversation almost everyone speaks of "television" doing this or that, intending this or that. A moment's thought is enough to recall that "television" is made up of a score and more broadcast and cable networks, some 1,300 local stations and countless production companies. The medium is collaborative; there are few if any *auteurs*. Yet TV is so potent a presence that it seems to have a mind, and personality, of its own.

If TV has changed over time, we take it mostly as a reflection of how 2 we who view it have changed, and in a sense that is right. While TV may not sense our moods and respond to them like a friend or family member, the people who administer, advertise on and program television all devote themselves to research that tracks each zig and zag of national mood. Their goal is to keep television exactly in step with mainstream taste, so that in most homes it will resemble a family member or a congenial neighbor. If television really were a personality, it would qualify as almost everyone's closest friend.

The average American watches TV about four hours a day; the average household has the set on for seven hours in all. Even people who say they "don't watch much television" turn out to be forgetting to count news, or sports, or Mister Rogers with the toddlers, or old movies, or vintage reruns, or something or other that they somehow consider to be not mere TV. Just why do people in all walks of life feel such guilt about watching TV, or assert such superiority in pretending that they do not? Because, despite their affection for TV, they think watching it is too passive, an inert substitute for exercise or reading, or conversation—or study.

The reality is that TV can provide plenty of learning, and not merely on *Sunrise Semester*. For every schoolchild whose reading problems might be blamed on an excess of TV, there is probably another who learned the alphabet from *Sesame Street* and began see-and-say reading with the on-screen words of commercials. High school students may have trouble spotting South America on a map, but through TV they have grasped some basic truths about the planet. Wherever they live, they were shaken last summer by images of beaches closed to bathers because the sands were strewn with toxic hospital waste. Among television's diehard critics, the print journalists, it is an open secret that the most important source of news flow during any election night or political crisis is the television set, around which editors and reporters cluster to stay abreast and to test their news judgment. And the same scholars and opinion-makers who profess to view television with disdain are nearly always avid to appear on it—fully expecting that their friends will see them. Most of the nation's elite seem to live by at least the latter half of Gore Vidal's reported dictum, "There are two things in life one must never refuse. One is sex, and the other is television."

Perhaps TV's deepest power is not the change it works on sports or commerce or any other branch of reality, but the way its innocuous-looking entertainment reaches deep into the national mind. TV has the ability to generate, or regenerate, national mythology. The great characters of television embody human truths as profound as the great characters in Moliere or Ibsen, and for vastly bigger audiences. The viewership for even one modestly successful airing of a prime-time series would fill every theater on Broadway, eight performances a week, for a couple of years. These characters linger in memory because they epitomize what the nation feels about itself. They teach behavior and values. They enter the language. Say the name Falstaff, and some minority of the population will know that you mean a vainglorious coward; say Ralph Kramden, and everyone will know what you mean. The Mary Richards character created by Mary Tyler Moore summed up their own lives for a whole generation of thirtysomething single women who could have any careers they wanted, but often at the expense of satisfaction at home. This is not new with television. The great civilizing effect of all literature is that it takes people's vision beyond the immediate, the clan and the tribe. It enables them to make the philosophical leap that Jean-Paul Sartre described as "seeing the other as another self." Television simply does this more effectively, more touchingly, than any kind of art that went before. Unlike the stage and movies, the episodic TV series does not end in catharsis. The characters come back week after week, evolving at the slow pace of ordinary life, exposing themselves more fully than most relatives or friends. Other literature provides occasional experiences. Television becomes an ongoing part of life and for some susceptible people is only barely distinguishable from real life itself.

It is hard to imagine a world without television, harder still to imagine what the world of the last half century would have been without those first flickering images from NBC and all that followed. We might have fewer terrorists, because there would be no worldwide pulpit for their propaganda. We might have a less violent society, because the typical child would not have been exposed to tens of thousands of actual and simulated violent crimes on news and entertainment by the time he or she reached adulthood. We might have a society in which people still felt respect for established institutions and their leaders, instead of one in which TV-bred skepticism had lowered the approval rating for Congress, business executives and even judges to between 20 and 40 percent. We might have a healthier society, one in which children played outside instead of watching the box hour after hour, one in which meals cooked from scratch at home had not been outdistanced by snacks and fast food loaded with sugar, salt and fat, all enticingly advertised. We might have a more restrained, less libertine world, one in which virginity and marriage were still revered while premarital pregnancy and divorce were still treated with distaste rather than sympathy. All of these effects have been attributed, sometimes convincingly, to TV. But we might also have a less alert world, one in which citizens were not so widely informed about the economy, about medical matters, about foreign military adventures that run the risk of war. We might have a less concerned world, one in which starvation in Ethiopia could never inspire Live Aid, one in which the homeless of Manhattan or Chicago might remain unseen by the rest of the nation. We might have a lonelier, more isolated world in which the old lived without much entertainment, without much company, without the sense of involvement in life that can be conferred even by watching Donahue.

Only one thing can be said for certain. Whatever world we would have, it would be different in many and unimaginable ways from this

6

7

one. Like fire and the wheel and the alphabet, television has changed the world that humans live in. And more, perhaps, than any invention or discovery before it, television has changed the definition of what it means to be human.

From William Henry III in Life *magazine. Reprinted with permission of Time, Inc.*

TV Can't Educate

Paul Robinson

On July 20 [1978] NBC aired a documentary on life in Marin County, a bedroom community just across the Golden Gate Bridge from San Francisco. The program was called "I Want It All Now" and its single theme was the predominance of narcissism in Marin. The program's host, Edwin Newman, introduced viewers, in his studied casual manner, to a variety of "consciousness-raising" groups ensconced in Marin and insinuated that this new narcissistic manner was leading to a breakdown not only of the family (a divorce rate of 75 percent was mentioned three times) but also of traditional civic virtue. The following day the *San Francisco Chronicle* carried a long front-page article on the outraged reaction of Marin's respectable citizenry to what it considered a grossly distorted portrait of itself. Several residents argued, persuasively, that Marin was in fact a highly political suburb—that it had been a hot spot of the anti-Vietnam war movement, and that only last year it had responded dramatically to the water crisis in California, cutting back on water use much more than was required by law. Television journalism appeared to be up to its old tricks: producers saw what they wanted to see, and they were not about to pass up the chance to show a woman being massaged by two nude men and chirping about how delightful it was to "receive" without having to "give."

I was reminded, however, improbably, of an experience in Berlin, where I had spent the previous six months teaching. The Germans are all exercised over a recent movie about Adolf Hitler (*Hitler: Eine Karriere*), which is based on a biography by the journalist Joachim Fest. The charge leveled against the film is that it glorifies Hitler (though it uses nothing but documentary footage; there are no actors), and it has been linked with a supposed resurgence of Nazism in Germany, particularly among the young. I saw only parts of the film and therefore can't speak to the justice of the charge. What I wish to report on—and what the Marin program brought to mind—is a lecture I attended by a young German historian from the Free University of Berlin, in which he took issue with the film because it had failed to treat Hitler's relations with the German industrialists, who were crucial in supporting the Nazi Party before it came to power and apparently benefited from its success.

The critics of the Newman program and my young scholar friend in   3
Berlin were guilty of the same error. They both bought the assumption that television and movies can be a source of knowledge, that one can "learn" from them. By knowledge and learning I obviously don't mean an assortment of facts. Rather I have in mind the analytic process that locates pieces of information within a larger context of argument and meaning. Movies and TV are structurally unsuited to that process.

There is no great mystery here. It's a simple matter of time. Learning   4
requires one kind of time, visual media are bound to another. In learning one must be able to freeze the absorption of fact or proposition at any moment in order to make mental comparisons, to test the fact or proposition against known facts and propositions, to measure it against the formal rules of logic and evidence—in short, to carry on a mental debate. Television is a matter of seconds, minutes and hours, it moves inexorably forward, and thus even with the best will in the world (a utopian assumption), it can never teach. In the last analysis there is only one way to learn: by reading. That's how you'll find out about Hitler's relations with the German industrialists, if you can find out about them at all. Such a complex, many-layered phenomenon simply cannot be reduced to a scene (which would presumably meet my scholar-friend's objection) in which Hitler has dinner with Baron Krupp. Similarly, you will not find out about life in Marin county from an hour-long TV program or, for that matter, from a 24-hour-long one. What are the control populations? What statistical methods are being used? Is there more consciousness raising going on in Marin than in Cambridge? What is the correlation between narcissism and income level, educational background, employment, religious affiliation, marital status, sexual inclination and so forth? If these questions have answers, they are to be found in the books and articles of sociologists, not on TV.

I am prepared, indeed eager, to follow my argument to its logical con-   5
clusion: the worst thing on TV is educational TV (and not just on educational stations). By comparison, the gratuitous violence of most commercial shows is a mere peccadillo. Educational TV corrupts the very notion of education and renders its victims uneducable. I hear grown-ups launching conversations with, "Mike Wallace says that . . ." as if Mike Wallace actually knew something. Viewers hold forth authoritatively about South Africa, or DNA, or black holes, or whatever because they have watched a segment about them on *60 Minutes* or some such program. Complete ignorance really would be preferable, because ignorance at least preserves a mental space that might someday be filled with real knowledge, or some approximation of it.

There is a new form of slumming popular among intellectuals: watch-   6
ing "bad" (i.e. commercial) TV and even writing books about it (as Dan Wakefield has about the afternoon soap opera *All My Children*). I would

like to think that the motive behind this development is revulsion against the intellectual pretensions of "good" TV. But, as often happens with academics, the reaction has been dressed up in phony theoretical garb. *All My Children,* we're supposed to believe, is the great American novel, heir to the tradition of Dickens and Trollope. Of course it's nothing of the sort. But it is very good entertainment. And that is precisely what TV is prepared to do: to entertain, to divert, above all to amuse. It is superbly amusing, ironically, for the same reason that it can't educate: it is tied to the clock, which has enormous comic potential. It is not accidental that one speaks of a comedian's "timing." Jack Benny would not be funny in print. He must wait just the right length of time after the robber threatens, "Your money or your life," before responding. (Imagine the situation in a novel: "The robber said, 'Your money or your life.' Jack took ten seconds trying to make up his mind.") Nor can you do a double-take in print, only on the screen. The brilliant manipulation of time made *The Honeymooners* so funny: Art Carney squandered it while Jackie Gleason, whose clock ran at double-time, burned. Audrey Meadows stood immobile, producing a magnificently sustained and silent obbligato to Gleason's frantic buffo patter.

Television, then, is superbly fit to amuse. And amusement is not to be despised. At the very least it provides an escape from the world and from ourselves. It is pleasurable (by definition, one might say), and it gives us a sense of union with humanity, if only in its foibles. Herbert Marcuse might even contend that it keeps alive the image of an unrepressed existence. Television can provide all this. But it can't educate.   7

Movies are faced with the same dilemma. The desire to educate accounts, I believe, for the increasingly deliberate pace of movies. It is as if the director were trying to provide room within his time-bound narrative for the kind of reflection associated with analysis. This was brought home to me recently when, during the same week, I saw the movie *Julia* in the theater and *Jezebel* on TV. The latter, made in 1938, portrays the tragedy of a strong-willed southern girl who refuses to conform to the rules of antebellum New Orleans society. The most striking difference between the two movies is their pace. *Jezebel* moves along swiftly (there is probably more dialogue in the first 15 minutes than in all of *Julia)*, treats its theme with appropriate superficiality and entertains effortlessly. *Julia,* on the other hand, is lugubrious and obviously beyond its depth. It succeeds only with the character of Julia herself, who, like Jezebel, is powerful, beautiful, virtuous and unburdened by intellectual or psychological complexity. By way of contrast, the narrative figure, Lilli, tries vainly to deal with issues that movies can't manage: the difficulty of writing, a relationship with an older man who is at once lover, mentor, and patient-to-be, the tension between literary success and political commitment. All of these are wonderfully captured in Lillian Hellman's memoir, but not even two fine actors like Jane Fonda and Jason Robards can bring such uncinematic matters to life on the screen. The "issue" of the memoir—despite all those meaningful silences—inevitably eluded the movie.   8

Let us, then, not ask more of movies and TV than they can deliver. In fact, let us discourage them from trying to "educate" us. 9

Shadows on the Wall

Donna Woolfolk Cross

I see no virtue in having a public that cannot distinguish fact from fantasy. When you start thinking fantasy is reality you have a serious problem. People can be stampeded into all kinds of fanaticism, folly and warfare.
    —Isaac Asimov

Why, sometimes I've believed as many as six impossible things before breakfast.
    —*Queen to Alice in Lewis Carroll's* Through the Looking Glass

In Book Four of *The Republic,* Plato tells a story about four prisoners who 1
since birth have been chained inside a cave, totally isolated from the world outside. They face a wall on which shadows flicker, cast by the light of the fire. The flickering shadows are the only reality they know. Finally, one of the prisoners is released and permitted to leave the cave. Once outside, he realizes that the shadows he has watched for so long are only pale, distorted reflections of a much brighter, better world. He returns to tell the others about the world outside the cave. They listen in disbelief, then in anger, for what he says contradicts all they have known. Unable to accept the truth, they cast him out as a heretic.

Today, our picture of the world is formed in great part from televi- 2
sion's flickering shadows. Sometimes that picture is a fairly accurate reflection of the real world; sometimes it is not. But either way, we accept it as real and we act upon it as if it were reality itself. "And that's the way it is," Walter Cronkite assured us every evening for over nineteen years, and most of us did not doubt it.

A generation of Americans has grown up so dependent on television 3
that its images appear as real to them as life itself. On a recent trip to a widely advertised amusement park, my husband, daughter, and I rode a "white-water" raft through manufactured "rapids." As we spun and screamed and got thoroughly soaked, I noticed that the two young boys who shared our raft appeared rather glum. When the ride ended, I heard one remark to the other, "It's more fun on television."

As an experiment, Jerzy Kosinski gathered a group of children, aged 4
seven to ten years, into a room to show them some televised film. Before the show began, he announced, "Those who want to stay inside and watch the films are free to remain in the classroom, but there's something fascinating happening in the corridor, and those who want to see it are free to leave the room." Kosinski describes what happened next:

No more than 10 percent of the children left. I repeated, "You know, what's outside is really fantastic. You have never seen it before. Why don't you just step out and take a look?" 5

And they always said, "No, no, no, we prefer to stay here and watch the film." I'd say, "But you don't know what's outside." "Well, what is it?" they'd ask. "You have to go find out." And they'd say, "Why don't we just sit here and see the film first?" . . . They were already too corrupted to take a chance on the outside. 6

In another experiment, Kosinski brought a group of children into a room with two giant video screens mounted on the side walls. He stood in the front of the room and began to tell them a story. Suddenly, as part of a prearranged plan, a man entered and pretended to attack Kosinski, yelling at him and hitting him. The entire episode was shown on the two video screens as it happened. The children did not respond, but merely watched the episode unfold on the video screens. They rarely glanced at the two men struggling in the front of the room. Later, in an interview with Kosinski, they explained that the video screens captured the event much more satisfactorily, providing close-ups of the participants, their expressions, and such details as the attacker's hand on Kosinski's face. 7

Some children can become so preoccupied with television that they are oblivious to the real world around them. UPI filed a report on a burglar who broke into a home and killed the father of three children, aged nine, eleven, and twelve. The crime went unnoticed until ten hours later, when police entered the apartment after being called by neighbors and found the three children watching television just a few feet away from the bloody corpse of their father. 8

Shortly after this report was released, the University of Nebraska conducted a national survey in which children were asked which they would keep if they had to choose—their fathers or their television sets. *Over half* chose the television sets! 9

Evidence of this confusion between reality and illusion grows daily. Trial lawyers, for example, complain that juries have become conditioned to the formulas of televised courtroom dramas. 10

Former Bronx District Attorney Mario Merola says, "All they want is drama, suspense—a confession. Never in all my years as a prosecutor have I seen someone cry from the witness stand, 'I did it! I did it—I confess!' But that's what happens on prime-time TV—and that's what the jurors think the court system is all about." He adds, "Such misconceptions make the work of a district attorney's office much harder than it needs to be." Robert Daley describes one actual courtroom scene in which the defendant was subjected to harsh and unrelenting cross-examination: "I watched the jury," he says. "It seemed to me that I had seen this scene before, and indeed I had dozens of times—on television. On television the murderer always cracks eventually and says something like 'I can't take it any more.' He suddenly breaks down blubbering and admits his guilt. But this defendant did not break down, he did not admit his guilt. He did 11 not blubber. It seemed to me I could see the jury conclude before my eyes: ergo, he cannot be guilty—and indeed the trial ended in a hung jury. . . . Later I lay in bed in the dark and brooded about the trial. . . . If [television courtroom dramas] had never existed, would the jury have found the defendant guilty even though he did not crack?". . .

Reprinted by permission of The Putnam Publishing Group from Donna Woolfolk Cross, Media-Speak: How Television Makes Up Your Mind. © 1983 *by Donna Woolfolk Cross.*

Don't Touch That Dial

Madeline Drexler

Television acts as a narcotic on children—mesmerizing them, stunting their ability to think, and displacing such wholesome activities as book reading and family discussions. Right?   1

Wrong, says researcher Daniel Anderson, a psychologist at the University of Massachusetts at Amherst. Anderson doesn't have any particular affection for *Garfield and Friends,* MTV clips, or *Gilligan's Island* reruns. But he does believe it's important to distinguish television's impact on children from influences of the family and the wider culture. We tend to blame TV, he says, for problems it doesn't really cause. In the process, we overlook our own roles in shaping children's minds.   2

One conventional belief about television is that it impairs a child's ability to think and to interpret the world. But Anderson's own research and reviews of the scientific literature discredit this assumption. While watching TV, children do not merely absorb words and images. Instead, they muse upon the meaning of what they see, its plausibility, and its implications for the future—whether they've tuned in to a news report of a natural disaster or an action show. Because television relies on such cinematic techniques as montage and crosscutting, children learn early how to draw inferences about the passage of time, character psychology, and implied events. Even preschoolers comprehend more than just the information supplied on the tube.   3

Another contention about television is that it displaces reading as a form of entertainment. But according to Anderson, the amount of time spent watching television is not related to reading ability. For one thing, TV doesn't take the place of reading for most children; it takes the place of similar sorts of recreation, such as going to the movies, reading comic books, listening to the radio, and playing sports. Variables such as socioeconomic status and parents' educational background exert a far stronger influence on a child's reading. "Far and away," Anderson says, "the best predictor of reading ability, and of how much a child reads, is how much a parent reads."   4

Conventional wisdom has it that heavy television-watching lowers   5
IQ scores and hinders school performance. Since the 1960s, SAT scores
have dropped, along with state and national assessments of educational
achievement. But here, too, Anderson notes that no studies have linked
prolonged television exposure in childhood to lower IQ later on. In fact,
research suggests that it's the other way around. Early IQ predicts how
much TV an older child will watch. "If you're smart young, you'll watch
less TV when you're older," Anderson says. Conversely, in the same
self-selecting process, people of lower IQ tend to be lifelong television
devotees.

When parents watch TV with their young children, explaining new   6
words and ideas to them, the children comprehend far more than they
would if they were watching alone. This is due partly to the fact that
when kids expect that TV will require thought, they spend more time
thinking. What's ironic is that most parents use an educational program
as an opportunity to park their kids in front of the set and do something
in another room. "Even for parents who are generally wary of television,"
Anderson says, "*Sesame Street* is considered a show where it's perfectly
okay to leave a child alone." The program was actually intended to be
viewed by parents and children together, he says.

Because our attitudes inform TV viewing, Anderson applauds the   7
nascent trend of offering high school courses that teach students how to
"decode" television. In these classes, students learn to analyze the persuasive techniques of commercials, compare the reality of crime to its
dramatic portrayal, inquire into the economics of broadcasting, and
understand the mechanics of TV production. Such courses, Anderson
contends, teach the kind of critical thinking central to the purpose of education. "Kids can be taught as much about television as about text or computers," he says.

If anything, Anderson's views underscore the fact that television can-   8
not be disparaged in isolation from larger forces. For years researchers
have attempted to show that television is inherently dangerous to children, hypnotizing them with its movement and color, cutting their attention span with its fast-paced, disconnected images, curbing intellectual
development, and taking the place of loftier pastimes.

By showing that television promotes none of these effects, Anderson   9
intends to shift the discussion to the real issue: content. That, of course, is
a thornier discussion. How should our society judge the violence of
primetime shows? The sexism of MTV? The materialism of commercials?
"I feel television is almost surely having a major social impact on the kids,
as opposed to a cognitive impact," Anderson says.

In this context, he offers some advice to parents: First, "Parents   10
should think of their kids as actively absorbing everything on television.
They are not just passively mesmerized—in one eye and out the other.
Some things on TV are probably good for children to watch, like educational TV, and some things are bad."

Second, "If you think your kid is spending lots of time watching tele- 11
vision, think about what alternatives there are, from the child's point of
view." Does a youngster have too much free time? Are there books, toys,
games, or playmates around? "A lot of the time, kids watch TV as a
default activity: There's nothing else to do."

Finally, "If a child persists in watching too much television, the ques- 12
tion is why. It's rare that TV shows arc themselves so entertaining." More
often than not, the motive is escapism. A teen-ager may be uncomfortable
with his or her peers; a child may want to retreat from a home torn by
marital strife; there may be problems at school.

For children, as for adults, television can be a source of enlighten- 13
ment or a descent into mindlessness—depending mostly on the choices of
lucre-driven executives. But as viewers, we can't ignore what we ourselves bring to the medium.

From The Boston Globe, *July 28, 1991. Reprinted by permission of the author.*

Animal Experimentation

Animals and Sickness

The Wall Street Journal

If it's spring, the "animal-rights movement" can't be far behind. It will 1
be on display today at the National Institutes of Health in Washington,
demonstrating on behalf of World Laboratory Animal Liberation Week.
On Wednesday, two of this country's most renowned doctors will travel
to Washington to try to counteract the demonstration with a news conference. Dr. Michael DeBakey of Baylor is the well-known pioneer in
heart surgery. Dr. Thomas Starzl of the University of Pittsburgh has
become famous in recent years for his work in providing liver trans-
plants for children. Both consider the animal-rights movement to be one
of the greatest threats to continued medical research in the United States.

Polio, drug addiction, cystic fibroids, most vaccines and antibiotics, 2
pacemakers, cancer, Alzheimer's, surgical technique—it's hard to identify many breakthroughs in medical progress that don't depend on
research using higher animal forms. For most of the past decade, the
animal-rights movements hasn't merely opposed animal research; it has
tried to destroy it.

On April 2, in an Animal Liberation Front break-in at the University 3
of Arizona, two buildings were set on fire (causing $100,000 damage)
and 1,000 animals including mice infected with a human parasite, were
stolen. The list of such incidents in the United States is long:

The director of Stanford's animal facility got a bomb threat in December. Intruders stole dogs and records of heart-transplant research at Loma Linda University in August. Indeed, dating back to 1982 there have been break-ins and thefts of animals at medical-research laboratories at Berkeley; Johns Hopkins (rats in Alzheimer's research); the head-injury lab and the veterinary school at Penn (arthritis research, sudden infant death syndrome); University of California, Davis (an arson attack); New York State Psychiatric Institute (Parkinson's research); University of Oregon; and University of California, Irvine (lung research). Currently, a trial is imminent for a woman who allegedly tried to murder the president of U.S. Surgical Corporation in Connecticut with a remote-control bomb.

The animal-rights movement is a textbook example of how many activist groups press their agendas into today's political system. It hardly matters, for instance, that an American Medical Association poll found that 77 percent of adults think that using animals in medical research is necessary. Those people answered the phone and went back to their daily lives, working at real jobs and raising families. Meanwhile the professional activists—animal-rights, antinukers, fringe environmentalists, Hollywood actresses—descend on the people who create "issues" in America.

They elicit sympathetic, free publicity from newspapers and magazines. They do Donahue and Oprah. And they beat on the politicians and bureaucrats. They create a kind of nonstop Twilight Zone of "issues" and "concerns" that most American voters are barely aware of. They do this because it has succeeded so many times.

As an outgrowth of congressional legislation, the U.S. Agriculture Department recently proposed animal-research regulations that would engulf medial scientists in reporting requirements, animal committees, "whistleblower" procedures, and directives to redesign laboratories ("the method of feeding nonhuman primates must be varied daily in order to promote their psychological well-being"). The cost of compliance, in an era of declining funding support for much research, is estimated to be $1.5 billion, and of course this will not satisfy the "movement."

If the United States is forced to work under the constant burden of all these varieties of public-issue nonsense, it can never hope to realize continued gains in either human welfare or its international competitiveness. Happily, evidence is emerging that the scientific community has decided it's time to fight back against all these activist movements.

In what should be the beginning of a countermovement against the animal-rights groups, NIH Director James Wyngaarden, HHS Secretary Louis Sullivan, and drug czar Bill Bennett all issued statements last Friday supporting medical researchers who must work with animals. Dr. David Hubel, of Harvard Medical School and 1981 winner of the Nobel Prize in medicine, has just sent a letter signed by twenty-nine other Nobel laureates, urging U.S. Surgeon General C. Everett Koop to speak out against these groups. Led by a multiple sclerosis victim, there is now a countergroup called Incurably Ill for Animal Research.

And of course, scientists rallied against the National Resources Defense Council's recent assault on the chemicals used to kill insects that prey on the U.S. food supply. The spectacle of schools protecting students from apples was too much even for the gullible. Now perhaps it's time to see through "animal rights," a clear and present danger to the health of us all.

10

Letters in Response to "Animals and Sickness"

Stephen Zawistowski, Suzanne E. Roy, Stephen Kaufman, and Marjorie Cramer

Your April 24 editorial "Animals and Sickness" perpetuates the false impression that recognition of animal rights will result in catastrophic levels of sickness and disease. Most people who seek protection of animals from abusive treatment would accept a good-faith effort by the biomedical establishment to improve conditions for research animals and increase efforts to develop nonanimal alternatives.

1

Asking the simplistic question, "Your child's health or a rat's life," is an insult to the many intelligent scientists, doctors, and citizens concerned about the medical-research practices. The real question is whether that rat (or mouse or dog or monkey) should be given a larger cage, better food and postoperative medication to alleviate pain; or whether the same information could have been collected using fewer animals, or none at all.

2

Biomedical researchers typically argue that research animals get adequate care as mandated by federal regulations, and that publicized examples of abuse are exceptions. It is difficult to verify such statements when access to animal-care facilities generally is denied to those interested in the well-being of the animals.

3

— Stephen Zawistowski
Science Advisor, ASPCA

Brutal head-trauma experiments at two universities—in which the skulls of thousands of cats and primates were crushed—have been halted. Funding for drug-addiction experiments that subjected cats to the horrors of chemical withdrawal was returned by a researcher. In each case physicians and scientists joined animal advocates in criticizing the studies for their scientific irrelevance and cruelty. A military research project at another university involved hundreds of cats who are shot in the head continues, but it has been condemned by neurosurgeons and trauma experts, and as a result, the U.S. General Accounting Office is investigating.

4

In the worst cases, animal studies do not just hurt animals and waste   5
money, they harm people too. The drugs thalidomide, Zomex, and DES
were tested on animals, but had devastating consequences when humans
used them. Just this week, the Food and Drug Administration warned
doctors against the use of two heart drugs, Tambocor and Enkaid, which
were thought to control irregular heartbeats but were found to actually
kill human patients.

— Suzanne E. Roy
Member, In Defense of Animals

You grossly exaggerate the value of animal research. Contrary to   6
scientists' self-serving interpretation of medical history, historian Bran-
don Reines has found that nearly every important advance in areas such
as heart disease and cancer has come from human clinical investigation.
While animal experiments had some value in the management of infec-
tious diseases at the turn of the century, they have made little contribution since.

The development of modern research techniques, such as CAT scans,   7
PET scans, needle biopsies, and tissue cultures, permit safe, ethical study
of disease with human patients and tissues. This has rendered many uses
of animals obsolete.

—Stephen Kaufman, M.D.
Medical Research Modernization Committee

Where, may I ask, are the "breakthroughs" in drug addiction, cancer,   8
and Alzheimer's disease that you attribute to animal research? They
have not been presented in medical journals nor in the press. Billions are
spent each year on medical and scientific "research," most of which is
worthless. Many of the real breakthroughs have been a result of clinical
work: observations in human patients.

The animal-rights movement is here to stay and has very wide grass-   9
roots support. The vast majority of the people involved are also working
at "real jobs and raising their families" and are not professional activists
as you imply.

While a few animal-rights activists have participated in terrorist   10
attacks, the vast majority are opposed to such tactics.

—Marjorie Cramer, M.D.

The Trials of Animals

Cleveland Amory

Ask an experimenter about the animals in his laboratory. Nine times out   1
of ten he will tell you that they are well cared for and that he abides by
the Animal Welfare Act passed by Congress in 1966.

What he will not say is that both he and his colleagues fought the act 2
and the amendments to it every step of the way; that, under the act, his
laboratory is inspected at most (if at all) once a year; that when his animals are under experimentation, the act doesn't apply. Nor will he say
that many laboratories ignore the act's most important amendment,
passed in 1986, which mandates that at least one member of the public
vote on the laboratory's animal-care committee.

Your experimenter is not a scofflaw. Having been for so long sole 3
judge and jury of what he does, he believes that he is above the law. A
prime example is that of the monkeys in Silver Spring, Maryland.

The monkeys were used in experiments in which, first, nerves in 4
their limbs were removed and then stimuli—including electrical shocks
and flames—were applied to see if they could still use their appendages.

Dr. Edward Taub, who ran the laboratory, was eventually tried and 5
found guilty, not of cruelty to animals but of maintaining a filthy lab.
Maryland is one of many states that exempts federally funded experiments from cruelty charges.

Dr. Taub is today a free man. His monkeys, however, are not. They 6
are still in a laboratory under the jurisdiction of the National Institutes of
Health, which first funded these cruel experiments. Three hundred
members of Congress have asked the NIH to release the monkeys; the
NIH says it does not want them; two animal sanctuaries have offered to
take them. Why can't they live what remains of their lives receiving the
first evidence of human kindness they have ever known?

In the overcrowded field of cat experimentation, researchers at 7
Louisiana State University, under an eight-year, $2 million Department
of Defense contract, put cats in vises, remove part of their skulls, and
then shoot them in the head.

More than two hundred doctors and Senator Daniel Inouye, chair- 8
man of the Defense Appropriations Subcommittee, have protested this
cruelty. The experimenters say that their purpose is to find a way to
return brain-wounded solders to active duty.

"Basic training for an Army infantryman costs $9,000," one experi- 9
menter argues. "If our research allows only 170 additional men to return
to active duty . . . it will have paid for itself." But Dr. Donald Doll of
Truman Veterans Hospital in Columbia, Missouri, said of these experiments: "I can find nothing which supports applying any of this data to
humans."

At the University of Oregon, under a seventeen-year, $1.5 million 10
grant, psychologists surgically rotated the eyes of kittens, implanting
electrodes in their brains, and forced them to jump onto a block in a pan
of water to test their equilibrium. These experiments resulted in a
famous laboratory break-in in 1986, and the subsequent trial and conviction of one of the animals' liberators.

During the trial, experimenters were unable to cite a single case in 11
which their research had benefited humans. Additional testimony
revealed instances of cats being inadequately anesthetized while having
their eye muscles cut, untrained and unlicensed personnel performing

the surgery, and mother cats suffering such stress that they ate their babies.

The trial judge, Edwin Allen, stated that the testimony was "disturbing to me as a citizen of this state and as a graduate of the University of Oregon. It would be highly appropriate to have these facilities opened to the public." 12

It would, indeed—and a judge is just what is needed. A judge first, then a jury. The experimenters have been both long enough. 13

A Scientist: I Am the Enemy

Ron Kline

I am the enemy! One of those vilified, inhumane physician-scientists involved in animal research. How strange, for I have never thought of myself as an evil person. I became a pediatrician because of my love for children and my desire to keep them healthy. During medical school and residency, however, I saw many children die of leukemia, prematurity and traumatic injury—circumstances against which medicine has made tremendous progress, but still has far to go. More important, I also saw children, alive and healthy, thanks to advances in medical science such as infant respirators, potent antibiotics, new surgical techniques and the entire field of organ transplantation. My desire to tip the scales in favor of the healthy, happy children drew me to medical research. 1

My accusers claim that I inflict torture on animals for the sole purpose of career advancement. My experiments supposedly have no relevance to medicine and are easily replaced by computer simulation. Meanwhile, an apathetic public barely watches, convinced that the issue has no significance, and publicity-conscious politicians increasingly give way to the demands of the activists. 2

We in medical research have also been unconscionably apathetic. We have allowed the most extreme animal-rights protesters to seize the initiate and frame the issue as one of "animal fraud." We have been complacent in our belief that a knowledgeable public would sense the importance of animal research to the public health. Perhaps we have been mistaken in not responding to the emotional tone of the argument created by those sad posters of animals by waving equally sad posters of children dying of leukemia or cystic fibrosis. 3

Much is made of the pain inflicted on these animals in the name of medical science. The animal-rights activists contend that this is evidence of our malevolent and sadistic nature. A more reasonable argument, however, can be advanced in our defense. Life is often cruel, both to ani- 4 mals and human beings. Teenagers get thrown from the back of a pickup truck and suffer severe head injuries. Toddlers, barely able to walk, find themselves at the bottom of a swimming pool while a parent checks the mail. Physicians hoping to alleviate the pain and suffering these tragedies cause have but three choices: create an animal model of the injury or disease and use that model to understand the process and test new therapies; experiment on human beings—some experiments will succeed, most will fail—or finally, leave medical knowledge static, hoping that accidental discoveries will lead us to the advances.

Some animal-rights activists would suggest a fourth choice, claiming 5
that computer models can simulate animal experiments, thus making the actual experiments unnecessary. Computers can simulate, reasonably well, the effects of well-understood principles on complex systems, as in the application of the laws of physics to airplane and automobile design. However, when the principles themselves are in question, as is the case with the complex biological systems under study, computer modeling alone is of little value.

One of the terrifying effects of the effort to restrict the use of animals 6
in medical research is that the impact will not be felt for years and decades: drugs that might have been discovered will not be; surgical techniques that might have been developed will not be, and fundamental biological processes that might have been understood will remain mysteries. There is the danger that politically expedient solutions will be found to placate a vocal minority, while the consequences of those decisions will not be apparent until long after the decisions are made and the decision making forgotten.

Fortunately, most of us enjoy good health, and the trauma of watch- 7
ing one's child die has become a rare experience. Yet our good fortune should not make us unappreciative of the health we enjoy or the advances that make it possible. Vaccines, antibiotics, insulin and drugs to treat heart disease, hypertension and stroke are all based on animal research. Most complex surgical procedures, such as coronary-artery bypass and organ transplantation, are initially developed in animals. Presently undergoing animal studies are techniques to insert genes in humans in order to replace the defective ones found to be the cause of so much disease. These studies will effectively end if animal research is severely restricted.

In America today, death has become an event isolated from our daily 8
existence—out of the sight and thoughts of most of us. As a doctor who has watched many children die, and their parents grieve, I am particularly angered by people capable of so much compassion for a dog or a cat, but with seemingly so little for a dying human being. These people seem so insulated from the reality of human life and death and what it means.

Make no mistake, however: I am not advocating the needlessly cruel 9
treatment of animals. To the extent that the animal-rights movement has made us more aware of the needs of these animals, and made us search

harder for suitable alternatives, they have made a significant contribution. But if the more radical members of this movement are successful in limiting further research, their efforts will bring about a tragedy that will cost many lives. The real question is whether an apathetic majority can be aroused to protect its future against a vocal, but misdirected, minority.

Subject Index

Active reading, 44–45
Active voice
    changing passive to, 283
    choosing, 282
    defined, 281
Addresses, 312
Adjective clauses
    changing to appositives, 162–163
    enclosing in commas, 311
Adjectives
    capitalization of, 323
    embedding, 31–32
    function of, 31–32
Adverbs
    conjunctive, 63, 271
    embedding, 31–32
Agreement
    with collective nouns, 287
    of present–tense verbs with subject,
        285
    pronoun–antecedent, 290–293
    of relative pronouns with verb, 288
    of subject and verbs using
        conjunctions, 286
    with units of measurement, 288
    See also Subject–verb agreement
American Psychological Association
        (APA) documentation method,
        201
Anecdotes, 77–78
Annotating text, 45
Antecedent
    agreement of pronouns and, 290–293
    unclear reference between pronoun
        and, 294–295
Apostrophes, 318–319

Appositives
    changing adjective clauses to,
        162–163
    characteristics of, 160–161
    enclosing in commas, 312
    pronoun case and, 301
    punctuating, 161
    when to use, 161–162
Arguments
    attitude and effectiveness of,
        231–232
    defined, 231
    documenting sources in, 237
    openness in preparing, 231–232
    outlining and organizing, 235–237
    preparing, 232–235
    taking a stand in, 235
    writing, 236
Audience
    defined, 167
    evaluating writer's, 168–171
Authors
    citing in writing, 202
    paraphrasing, 134–135
    quoting, 135–137

BOYSFAN acronym, 60–61, 271
Brainstorming, 4–5

Capitalization, 323
Central idea
    clarifying, 3–6, 12–13
    explaining significance of support
        for, 75–76
    finding the topic of paper, 12
    improving coherence with, 101–103

Source-by-source organization, 200, 201
Spatial order for outlines, 17
Spelling out numbers, 324
Statistics, 73
Subjective pronouns, 297–298
Subjects, 298
Subject–verb agreement, 285–289
  of collective nouns, 287
  with conjunctions, 286
  for present–tense verbs, 285
  with relative pronouns, 288
Subordinate clauses
  adjective, 311
  beginning with relative pronouns,
    269
  combining ideas with, 93–94
  defined, 269
  opening sentences with, 228
  punctuating, 95
  sentence fragments containing, 273
Subordinating conjunctions, 93–94, 269
Summaries
  characteristics of successful, 131
  paraphrasing the author, 134–135
  quoting, 135–137
  writing extended, 137–138
  writing summary–response essay,
    139–141
Summary–response essay, 139–141
Supportive ideas
  combining types of, 74–75
  considering own knowledge and
    experience, 173
  considering unstated objections, 173
  evaluating audience and purpose
    with, 168–169
  expert opinion or testimony as,
    73–74, 170–171
  explaining significance of for central
    idea, 75–76
  extended examples as, 71–72
  generalizations vs. specific
    statements, 171–172
  statistics as, 73
Suppose/supposed, 280
Synthesis essay
  defined, 199
  organizing, 200–201
  preparing, 199–200

Tense, verb, 279–281, 285
There, 286, 328
Thesis statements
  choosing, 12–14
  defined, 12
  improving unity and coherence with,
    105–106
  placing in introductory paragraph,
    16
  refining, 20
Third person pronouns, 290–291
Titles, 322
Topic sentences
  choosing, 12–14
  defined, 12
  forming, 13–14
  implied, 38–39
  improving unity and coherence with,
    105–106
  placing in paragraph, 15
  refining, 20
  stating central idea in, 37–38
  supporting with examples, 69–70
Transitions
  common words and phrases serving
    as, 102
  writing, 102–103

Underlining
  text, 44
  titles, 322
Units of measurement, 288
Unity
  defined, 99
  in thesis statements and topic
    sentences, 105–106
Use/used, 280

Varying sentence length, 226–227
Verbal clauses, opening sentences with,
  228
Verbal phrases
  dangling modifiers as, 304
  defined, 121
  using, 122–123
Verbals
  defined, 121
  sentence fragments with, 273
  unacceptable as verb of sentence, 268

Author/Title Index